THE ISLAMIC TRILOGY

VOLUME 3

A SIMPLE KORAN

READABLE AND UNDERSTANDABLE

THE ISLAMIC TRILOGY SERIES

VOLUME 1

MOHAMMED AND THE UNBELIEVERS

A POLITICAL LIFE

VOLUME 2

THE POLITICAL TRADITIONS OF MOHAMMED

THE HADITH FOR THE UNBELIEVERS

VOLUME 3

A SIMPLE KORAN

READABLE AND UNDERSTANDABLE

VOLUME 4

AN ABRIDGED KORAN

READABLE AND UNDERSTANDABLE

VOLUME 5

MOHAMMED, ALLAH AND THE JEWS

THE FOUNDATIONAL DOCTRINE

VOLUME 6

MOHAMMED, ALLAH, AND THE CHRISTIANS

THE FOUNDATIONAL DOCTRINE

VOLUME 7

MOHAMMED, ALLAH, AND HINDUISM

THE FOUNDATIONAL DOCTRINE

VOLUME 8

MOHAMMED, ALLAH, AND THE INTELLECTUALS

THE FOUNDATIONAL DOCTRINE

THE ISLAMIC TRILOGY

VOLUME 3

A SIMPLE KORAN

READABLE AND UNDERSTANDABLE

CENTER FOR THE STUDY
OF POLITICAL ISLAM

CSPI PUBLISHING

THE ISLAMIC TRILOGY
VOLUME 3

A SIMPLE KORAN

READABLE AND UNDERSTANDABLE

ISBN 0-9785528-8-1
ISBN13 978-0-9785528-8-6

V 5.23.06

PUBLISHED BY CSPI, LLC
WWW.CSPIPUBLISHING.COM

PRINTED IN THE USA

TABLE OF CONTENTS

THE CSPI MAXIM

Islam is a political system, a culture, and a religion based upon the Koran, Sira, and Hadith. To understand Islam, know the Trilogy.

PURPOSE

The Center for the Study of Political Islam is dedicated to:

- *Making the political doctrine of the Koran, Sira, and Hadith (the Trilogy) available to the world.*
- *Establishing authoritative/verifiable fact-based knowledge—statements that can be confirmed by the use of reference numbers.*
- *Integrating knowledge—using primary sources to give the complete picture of Islam's political doctrine.*

OVERVIEW

RELIGIOUS AND POLITICAL ISLAM

Islam is a political system, a culture, and a religion. The religion of Islam is what a Muslim does to go to Paradise and avoid Hell. Political Islam determines the treatment of unbelievers and the governance of Muslims. The internal politics of Islam are not of interest here.

The chief features of the religion are charity to other Muslims, prayer to Allah, fasting during the month of Ramadan, pilgrimage to Mecca, and declaring that Mohammed is the prophet of the only god, Allah. The religion of Islam is important to Muslims, but the politics affect every non-Muslim.

Islam has a complete legal code, the Sharia. The foundation of Islam's legal and political system is clearly laid out in three texts—the Koran, the Sira, and the Hadith—the Islamic Trilogy. Every book of the Trilogy is both religious and political. More than half of the Koran focuses on the unbelievers. About three-quarters of the Sira (life of Mohammed) is political. The Hadith is filled with political statements and examples. Islam is a fully developed political system and the oldest form of politics active today.

The fundamental principle of Islam is that its politics are sacred, perfect, eternal, and universal. All other political systems are man-made and must be replaced by Islamic law.

Islam's success comes primarily from its politics. In thirteen years as a spiritual leader, Mohammed converted 150 people to his religion. When he became a political leader and warrior, Islam exploded, and Mohammed became king of Arabia in ten years.

THE ISLAMIC TRILOGY

The doctrine of Islam is found in the words of Allah (the Koran) and the words and actions of Mohammed (the Sunna). The words of Allah are found in the Koran, which is divided into two parts, the early part written in Mecca and the later part written in Medina.

The words and actions of Mohammed are contained in two collections of texts—the Sira and the Hadith. His words and actions are considered to be Allah's divine pattern for all humanity.

The Sira is Mohammed's biography; the two most widely known are by Ibn Ishaq and Al Tabari. Approximately three-quarters of the Sira relates to politics and war.

A hadith, which means ***tradition***, is a short story about what Mohammed did or said. A collection of hadiths is called a Hadith. There are many collections of hadiths, but the most authoritative are those by Bukhari and Abu Muslim.

So the Trilogy is:

The Koran
The Sira, or biographies, by Ishaq and Al Tabari
The Hadith, or Traditions, by Bukhari and Muslim

The Trilogy is the foundation and totality of Islam. Every one of the hundreds of biographies of Mohammed is based upon the Sira and Hadith. All of Islamic law, the sharia, is based upon the Trilogy. Every statement and action of political and religious Islam comes from the Trilogy. 9/11, for example, was a political action based upon it. If you know the Trilogy, you can talk with an Islamic religious and political leader or critique an article written in a scholarly journal such as ***Foreign Affairs.*** If you know the Trilogy, you will see every news report about Islam with new eyes.

THE KORAN

Islam believes that the Koran is the perfect, eternal, universal, final word of the only god, Allah. The Koran does not have the slightest error. It was brought to men by Mohammed who is the ideal pattern for all behavior of all peoples for all times, now and forever.

The Koran is written in classical Arabic. Many Muslims say that the Koran cannot be translated. But since very few Muslims can read classical Arabic, it has been translated many times.

According to Islam the present day Koran was produced under the Islamic ruler, Uthman, the fourth caliph (Islamic political and religious leader), many years after Mohammed's death. Up to that time the Koran was memorized and recorded in scattered and partial copies that did not fully agree. After Uthman's manuscript (recension) was produced, all of the source documents were burned.

The Koran is divided into suras or chapters. But unlike chapters a sura has many different subjects that seem unrelated. So as you read, the subject matter jumps from one topic to the next.

The chapters are arranged in order of length, not in the order they were written. Imagine that you took a mystery novel and cut off the spine. Then you rebound the book starting with the longest chapter and so on down to the shortest chapter. As you read it you would jump back and forth in time and be completely confused. The story would be lost. Likewise, when you turn a page of the Koran, it could move forward or backward in time, and the reader is completely lost.

Not only does the Koran jump from topic to topic, but it also repeats itself. For instance, there are over thirty versions of the story of Moses and the Pharaoh.

Many of the stories from the Old Testament (Torah) are in the Koran, but they are not precisely the same stories and make different points.

The Koran is filled with unfamiliar words and pronouns that have vague antecedents. There is the matter of two or three Arabic letters, such as ALIF LAM MIM, that start twenty-nine of the suras. No one knows what they mean.

There is little context, so verses seem to come up out of nowhere. For instance, a verse abruptly talks about "cut down some palm trees." Since the reader has no idea of what is going on at the time, the result is confusion.

And there is the difficulty of many apparent contradictions.

WHY YOU WILL BE ABLE TO UNDERSTAND A SIMPLE KORAN

The language of *A Simple Koran* is easy to understand. Every unfamiliar word is explained in an editorial comment in square brackets. Pronouns are given an antecedent where there is confusion.

The text has been rearranged in the order it unfolded over the twenty-three years of its composition. The Koran is an historic text, so when you turn the page of *A Simple Koran*, you go forward in time. There is nothing mysterious about this historic order as Islamic scholars have long used this information.

Mohammed's life has been integrated into the text. The primary and definitive source for the life of Mohammed is the ***Sirat Rasul Allah*** by Ibn Ishaq. This gives the Koran the context of Mohammed's life. Think of the Koran as a box of beads and Mohammed's life as a thread. When you string the beads onto the thread, you have a necklace. When you string the verses of the Koran onto Mohammed's life, you have a story. Then when you read the Koranic verse that says to "cut down some palm trees" you will know what historic event is occurring in Mohammed's life and the verse will make sense in context.

The jump from topic to topic and the repetition have been made easier for the reader by collecting all similar topics into categories.

A Simple Koran is easy to understand because it has restored the original story to the Koran. The story of the Koran is an epic drama with soaring poetry, politics, battles, stories, sub-plots, losses and victories.

Every single verse of the Koran is included without any abridgement. Not one word has been omitted.

READING THE KORAN

The Koran may not be understood on its own. The key to its understanding is the life of Mohammed. If you read the Sira and Hadith first, then you will find the Koran can be comprehended. Resist the temptation to jump into the mystery of the Koran without reading ***Mohammed and the Unbelievers*** and ***The Political Traditions of Mohammed.***

The Koran is a difficult book when it is viewed as a religious text. But when it is viewed as a historical and political text as well as a religious text, it is a straight forward story. To understand the language, you need some background. Islam holds that the Koran is the perfect record of what the angel Gabriel (also called a spirit) told Mohammed. When the words I, We, Us, and Me are used, they refer to Allah. I and We can occur in the same verse.

The term "Say:" is used frequently and means that Gabriel is telling Mohammed to say this to the people.

Another common term is "signs." Signs can be manifestations of nature, ***e.g.*** rain after a drought, or signs can be verses of the Koran. Each verse is considered a miracle by Islam.

With this background, read one of the epic stories of history. When you finish it, you will be able to pick up any translation of the Koran and read it with understanding.

WHY THE KORAN IS NOT THE BASIS OF ISLAM

Most non-Muslims think Islam is based entirely upon the Koran. That is not true. There is not enough information in the Koran to form the religious and political system of Islam. For instance, there are apparent contradictions in the Koran that can be resolved only by knowing what was happening at that time, and that is known only by reading the Sira and Hadith. For that matter, a Muslim cannot even pray based upon the information in the Koran.

The Koran insists that it is the word of Allah, the only god. And it insists equally that Allah is pleased when the world imitates Mohammed in every aspect of his life, including religion. The Koran says more than seventy times that Mohammed is to be followed in every detail in every matter. And where is the only place that the ideal example of Mohammed can be found? Not in the Koran but in the Sira and the Hadith. The daily actions of a Muslim are governed far more by the Hadith than the Koran.

Therefore, the Islamic belief system is based upon and defined by the Sira, the Hadith, and the Koran.

No one text of the Trilogy can stand by itself; it is impossible to understand any one of the texts without the other supporting texts. The Koran, Sira, and Hadith are a seamless whole and speak with one voice. In order to understand the Koran, one must first understand the Sira and Hadith.

HOW THE VERSES ARE GROUPED

The classical arrangement of the Koran is by chapters (suras) and verses. The verses are not a useful in understanding since a verse is usually a sentence. So the first step for easy understanding is to group the verses into paragraphs. As an example:

> 93:4 ***Certainly the future will be better than the past.***
> 93:5 ***In the end your Lord will be generous to you, and you will be satisfied.***
> 93:6 ***Did He not find you living like an orphan and give you a home?***
> 93:7 ***Did He not find you lost and give you guidance?***
> 93:8 ***Did He not find you poor, and did He not give you enough?***

These verses has been grouped into a paragraph:

> 93:4 ***Certainly the future will be better than the past, and in the end your Lord will be generous to you, and you will be satisfied. Did He not find you living like an orphan and give you a home? Did He not find you lost and give you guidance? Did He not find you poor, and did He not give you enough?***

But even after making verses into paragraphs, another problem remains. Each chapter contains many different subjects and topics. This means that as you read a chapter the topic will suddenly change and be confusing. Since the same topic will be discussed in many different chapters it also helps in understanding to group the all the paragraphs about the same topic together.

To show the break in the classical order there is blank line placed at the break in topics. Example:

56:92 ***But those who mistakenly treat the prophets as deceivers, their entertainment will be scalding water, and the broiling of Hellfire. Surely this is a certain truth. Therefore, praise the name of your Lord, the Great.***

70:36 ***But what has happened to the unbelievers that causes them to rush madly around you, on the right and left-hand, in droves? Does every one of them hope to enter the Garden of Delight? Certainly not! We have created them, and they know from what.***

MAXIM

Islam is a political ideology. No action or statement by Islam can be understood without understanding its origins in the Trilogy. Any analysis, statement, or opinion about Islam is incomplete without a reference to the Trilogy. The Trilogy is the source and basis of all Islamic politics, diplomacy, history, philosophy, religion, and culture.

REFERENCE NUMBERS

The information in this book can be traced back to the source by use of the reference numbers:

I234 is a reference to Ibn Ishaq's ***Sirat Rasul Allah***, translated by A. Guillaume as ***The Life of Muhammad***. This is a reference to margin note 234.

T123 is a reference to ***The History of al-Tabari*** by the State University of New York. The number refers to the margin note 123.

M234 is a reference to ***The Life of Mohammed*** by Sir William Muir, AMS Press, New York, NY, 1975. The number is page 234.

B2,3,45 is a reference to Bukhari's Hadith. The three example numbers are volume 2, book 3, and number 45, a standard reference system.

M2,345 is a reference to Muslim's Hadith. The example would be book 2, number 345.

12:45 is Koran chapter (sura) 12, verse 45.

It is the present state of knowledge of the West about Islam that there is no standardized spelling of proper Arabic nouns. Examples: Muslim/Moslem, Mohammed/Muhammad.

IN THE BEGINNING

CHAPTER 1

33:21 You have an excellent example in Allah's Messenger for those of you who put your hope in Allah and the Last Day and who praise Allah continually.

Fourteen hundred years ago in Arabia, there was an orphan who became the first king of Arabia. Mohammed's name would become the most common name in the world. He was to create an empire that would dwarf the Roman Empire, and he was to become the ideal pattern for all men and make the god of the Arabs the god of all. The smallest aspect of his behavior would be recorded in great detail and would set the pattern of life for billions of people over the millennia.

Mohammed's father was called Abdullah, meaning slave of Allah. Allah was a high god of the many gods worshiped in the town of Mecca. His father died while his mother was pregnant. When he was five years old, his mother died and his grandfather took over his upbringing. Then Mohammed was orphaned for the third time when his grandfather died and his raising was assumed by his uncle, Abu Talib. All were of the Quraysh tribe. These brief facts are the history known about his early childhood.

MOHAMMED'S TRIBE—THE QURAYSH

When Mohammed was born, there was no nation of Arabia, no Arabian king, no political unity. The society was tribal in nature and had the usual tribal aspects. A person was not an individual as much as he was a part of a tribe. Blood relations were everything, and when someone met someone outside the tribe, the first question was what is your tribe and your lineage? Your name gave a portion of your lineage. Without your tribe you were fair game and very weak. Squabbling and fighting amongst clans were common and were ruled by blood laws.

The Quraysh came to Mecca five generations before Mohammed under the leadership of Qusayy. Under Qusayy the rituals of worship at the Kabah [a stone temple] were established. The Quraysh became the priestly tribe of Mecca. They were the nobility of the town and held the ceremonial offices.

In addition to being religious leaders, the Quraysh were traders and business men. Religion and business came together in the form of the different religious pilgrimages and the accompanying business transactions.

Mohammed's clan was the Hashim clan of the Quraysh tribe. The Hashimite clan is active in politics today.

MECCA AS A RELIGIOUS CENTER

In Mecca there was a stone building in the shape of a cube called the Kabah. The Kabah was a religious site that contained many images of several tribal gods. We know of at least six other square stone houses called Kabahs that were in other towns in Arabia. However, Islam holds that the Kabah in Mecca was built by Abraham, the patriarch of the Jews.

The Kabah was the focus of religious rituals and a community center. Rituals established by Qusayy included prostrations, ritual prayers, and circling the Kabah while praying and drinking from the well called Zam Zam. Other rituals included throwing stones at pillars which symbolized the devil. Islam's rituals come from the aboriginal Arabic religions.

Stones played an important part of the religions of Arabia. The Kabah was made of stone and had an important stone, the Black Stone, built into the corner of the Kabah. It was probably a meteorite and was a composite of several stones. It is small in size, roughly seven inches in diameter. This stone was touched only with the right hand and kissed by pilgrims. All of these native rituals were incorporated into Islam.

The god, Allah, seems to have been a male god of the moon and was probably the god of the Quraysh. Each tribe had it gods. There was not much organization of gods, unlike the Greeks or Romans. Mohammed's father was named after Allah, but his other brothers were named after other Arabic gods.

MAP OF
ARABIA
600 A.D.
MEDITER-
RANEAN
SEA
SYRIA
MESOPOTAMIA
(IRAQ)
Muta
Tabuk
Fadak
Khaybar
ARABIA
Medina
Badr
RED SEA
Mecca
Hudabiya
Hunain
EGYPT
YEMEN
N
ABYSSINIA
(ETHIOPIA)

EARLY LIFE

CHAPTER 2

3:131 Obey Allah and His messenger so that you may receive mercy.

CHILDHOOD

I115 When Mohammed was eight years old, his grandfather died. He was then taken in by Abu Talib, his uncle. His uncle took him on a trading trip to Syria, which was a very different place from Mecca. Syria was a sophisticated country that was Christian and very much a part of the cosmopolitan culture of the Mediterranean. It was Syrian Christians who gave the Arabs their alphabet. When Mohammed was a child there had never been a book written in Arabic, and only poems and business correspondence were written in Arabic.

MARRIAGE

I120 Mohammed was grown when he was hired by the wealthy widow and a distant cousin Khadija to act as her agent in trading with Syria. Mohammed had a reputation of good character and good business sense. Trading from Mecca to Syria was risky business because it took skill to manage a caravan and then to make the best deal in Syria. He managed Khadija's affairs well, and she returned a good profit on the trading.

I120 Khadija was a widow and well known among the Quraysh tribe. Sometime after hiring Mohammed as her business agent, she proposed marriage to him. They married and had six children. Their two sons died in childhood, and the four daughters lived to adulthood.

MONOTHEISM IN ARABIA

I144 The Arabs referred to monotheism as Hanifiya and to those who were monotheists as Hanifs. By far the strongest strain of monotheism was represented by the Jews. After the destruction of Jerusalem by the Romans due to the Zealot's rebellion, Jews dispersed throughout the Middle East, so there was a strong presence of Jews in Arabia. There were a few Christians who were local Arabs, in fact, Mohammed's wife had a cousin who was a Christian. But the type of Christianity in the area of Mecca was unorthodox with a Trinity of God, Jesus and Mary.

I144 Jews and Christians were called the People of the Book. Since there was no book yet published in Arabic, this distinction was a strong one. The sources of the Arabic religions were found in oral tradition and custom. The Meccans were aware of the Jewish Abrahamic myths, and though Mecca was a long way from Syria where Abraham dwelt, the Meccans claimed that Abraham and Ishmael had built the Kabah in ancient times.

I144 Even though there was a pull towards monotheism, it mixed with ancient Arabic tribal religions in a society that had a tolerance for different religious beliefs. In one clan, families would differ in the deities they included in their worship. These included deities that were brought into the home through marriage outside of the clan and a belief of spirits, or jinns, that could influence lives in good or bad ways.

I144-149 One monotheist, Zayd, abandoned all religion and created his own monotheistic religion, making his own prayers and rituals. They were a fusion of Judaism theology and tribal rituals, including use of the Kabah for a prayer focus and prostrations. He said that Abraham prayed facing in a sacred direction and condemned and publicly attacked his tribal members for their religion. The one god was to be feared, heaven was a garden, and infidels would burn in Hell. He condemned any form of worship of a god except the one god, and people submitted to the un-named one god. Much of his poetry used the same language as the Koran did. He referenced his worship to the Jewish patriarchs as they were pure in their worship. Mohammed recognized him as a precursor.

THE KORAN OF MECCA

BEGINNING TEACHINGS

CHAPTER 3

4:13 These are the limits set up by Allah. Those who obey Allah and His Messenger will be led into the Gardens watered by flowing rivers to live forever. This is the ultimate reward!

I150 Mohammed would take month long retreats to be alone and do the Quraysh religious practices. After the retreat he would go and circumambulate (circle and pray) the Kabah.

I152 At the age of forty Mohammed began to have visions and hear voices. His visions were first shown to him as bright as daybreak during his sleep in the month of Ramadan. Mohammed said that the angel, Gabriel, came to him with a brocade with writing on it and commanded him to read. "What shall I read?" The angel pressed him and said, "Read." Mohammed said again, "What shall I read?" The angel pressed him again tightly and again commanded, "Read!" Again the reply, "What shall I read?"

The angel said:

> 96:1 ***Recite: In the name of your Lord, Who created man from clots of blood.***
> 96:3 ***Recite: Your Lord is the most generous, Who taught the use of the pen and taught man what he did not know.***

T1150 Mohammed awoke from his sleep. Now Mohammed hated ecstatic poets and the insane. His thoughts were that he was now either a poet or insane, that which he hated. He thought to kill himself by jumping off a cliff. And off he went to do just that. Half way up the hill, he heard, "Mohammed, You are the apostle of Allah and I am Gabriel." He gazed at the angel and no matter which way he turned his head the vision followed his eyes. Mohammed stood there for a long time.

Then Mohammed began to receive what he called revelations such as:

> 74:1 ***You [Mohammed], wrapped up in your robe, get up and sound the alarm.***
> 74:3 ***Magnify your Lord. Purify your garment. Run from abomination. Do not give favors with the thought of reward. Wait patiently for your Lord. When the trumpet sounds, it will be a terrible day, a day without rest for the unbeliever.***

97:1 *Surely, We have revealed it [the Koran] on the night of power. And who will explain to you what the night of power is? The night of power is better than a thousand months. On that night the angels and the spirit descended with their Lord's permission, to do their every duty and all is peace until the break of day.*

53:57 *The one who warns you, also warned the people of old. The inevitable day is drawing near and only Allah can reveal the time. Do you marvel at these announcements? And that you laugh and do not cry while you amuse yourself with vanities?*
53:62 *Bow down before Allah and worship.*

55:1 *Merciful Allah has taught the Koran, has created man, and has taught him to speak. The sun and the moon follow their exact courses, and the plants and the trees bow down in adoration. He has uplifted the sky and set the balance of justice so that you may not exceed the right measure. Measure fairly, and do not cheat the balance.*
55:10 *He has prepared the earth for his creatures. On it there are fruits and palms with sheathed clusters and husked grains and fragrant plants. Which of your Lord's blessings would you deny?*
55:14 *He has created man from clay like a potter, and He created the jinn [invisible beings] from smokeless fire. Which of your Lord's blessings would you deny?*
55:17 *He is the Lord of the east. He is the Lord of the west. Which of your Lord's blessings would you deny?*
55:19 *He has freed the two seas [fresh water and salt water] so that they meet, but separated them with a barrier that they can not breach. Which of your Lord's blessings would you deny?*
55:22 *From the seas come pearls and coral. Which of your Lord's blessings would you deny?*
55:24 *His ships sail the seas, towering like mountains. Which of your Lord's blessings would you deny?*
55:26 *Everything on the earth will perish, but the majestic and glorious face of your Lord will endure forever. Which of your Lord's blessings would you deny?*
55:29 *Everything in the heavens and the earth look to Him. Every day He exercises absolute power. Which of your Lord's blessings would you deny?*
55:31 *Soon We will settle the affairs of men and jinn [invisible beings]. Which of your Lord's blessings would you deny?*

THE FIRST CONVERT

I156 Mohammed's wife, Khadija, was the first convert. From the first she had encouraged him, believed him. She knew him to be of good character and did not think him to be deceived or crazy.

Soon he stopped hearing voices or seeing visions and became depressed and felt abandoned. Then his visions started again and said:

> 93:1 *By the brightness of the noonday sun and by the night at its darkest, your Lord has not forgotten you, and He does not hate you.*
> 93:4 *Certainly the future will be better than the past, and in the end your Lord will be generous to you, and you will be satisfied. Did He not find you living like an orphan and give you a home? Did He not find you lost and give you guidance? Did He not find you poor, and did He not give you enough?*
> 93:9 *Therefore, do not oppress the orphan, and do not scold the beggar. Instead, announce the bounty of your Lord.*

Then Mohammed began to tell others who were close to him of words in his visions.

> 1:1 *In the Name of Allah, the Compassionate, the Merciful.*
> 1:2 *Praise be to Allah, Lord of the worlds. The Compassionate, the Merciful. King of the Judgment Day.*
> 1:5 *Only You do we worship, and to You alone do we ask for help. Keep us on the straight and narrow path. The path of those that You favor; not the path of those who anger You [the Jews] nor the path of those who go astray [the Christians].*

> 106:1 *For the protection of the Quraysh [the leading tribe of Mecca, Mohammed was of the Quraysh tribe] during their winter and summer caravans. Let them worship the Lord of this house [the Kabah], Who has provided them with food against hunger, and secured them from fear.*

> 107:1 *What do you think of him who treats Our religion as a lie, who trusts that others will raise the orphan, and does not urge others to feed the poor? Woe to those who pray, but whose prayers are careless and to those who make a show of devotion, but refuse to help the needy.*

> 100:1 *By the snorting war steeds! And those whose hooves strike sparks of Fire! And those who press home the dawn attack! And raise clouds of dust, and slice through the enemy!*
> 100:6 *Truly, man is ungrateful to this Lord. He proves this with his actions. His love of wealth is passionate. Does he not know that when the graves are emptied and the secrets confined in men's hearts are revealed, that on that day their Lord will be perfectly informed about them?*

Except with Their Wives or Slave-Girls

70:22 *Not the devout, who pray constantly and whose wealth has a fixed portion set aside for beggars and the destitute, and those who believe in the Judgment Day, and those who fear their Lord's punishment—because no one is safe from their Lord's punishment—and who control their sexual desires (except with their wives or slave-girls, with them there is no blame; but whoever indulges their lust beyond this are transgressors), and who keep their trusts and promises, and who tell the truth, and who are attentive to their prayers. These will live with honors in Gardens.*

113:1 *Say: I seek protection with the Lord of the daybreak: from the mischief of His creation, from the mischief of the night when it falls, from the mischief of witches and magicians, and from the mischief of the envious.*

102:1 *The desire for increased wealth preoccupies you, from the cradle to your grave. No, but in the end you will know. No, once again, in the end you will know your foolishness.*
102:5 *No, if only you knew it with certain knowledge! Certainly you will see Hellfire. You will surely see it with certainty; on that day you will be questioned concerning your pleasures.*

We Will Make the Path to Misery Easy

92:5 *He who gives alms and fears Allah and accepts the good, to him We will make the path to happiness easy. But he who is greedy and does not think he needs Allah's help and calls the good a lie, to him We will make the path to misery easy. And what good will his wealth do him when he dies?*
92:12 *Certainly it is up to Us to guide man and certainly the future and the past belong to Us. Therefore I warn you of the blazing Fire. Only the most wretched will be thrown into it, those who call the truth a lie and turn their backs.*
92:17 *Those who fear Allah will escape it and so will those who give away their wealth so that they may be purified; and who give freely without hope of reward, except seeking the pleasure of his Lord, the most high, certainly in the end they will be content.*

95:1 *I swear by the fig and the olive, by Mount Sinai, and by this inviolate land [Mecca]! We have created man in a noble image then reduced him to the lowest of the low, except those who believe and do the right things, because their reward will never fail.*
95:7 *Then, who can convince you that the judgment is a lie? Is Allah not the best of judges?*

> 86:5 *Let man consider from what he is created. He was created from a gushing fluid that comes from between the loins and ribs. Certainly Allah is able to return him to life.*
> 86:9 *On the day when all secrets are revealed, he will have no strength or helper.*

PRAYER

I157 Mohammed began to do his prayers with his new understanding. At first he did two prostrations with each prayer. Later he understood that he should use four prostrations per prayer and use two prostrations when he was traveling.

I158 Then when he was on a mountain he saw a vision in which Gabriel showed him how to do ritual ablutions as a purification ritual before prayer. He went home and showed his wife, Khadija, how he now understood the prayer rituals to be done and she copied him.

T1162 Mohammed, his wife and nephew, Ali, started praying at the Kabah with their new rituals of ablutions and prayer with prostrations. A visitor asked about this new ritual and was told that it was a new religion and that Mohammed said that he would receive the treasures of Rome and Persia.

> 73:1 *You [Mohammed] wrapped up in your robe, awake half the night, more or less, to pray and recite the Koran in a measured rhythm, because We will send down to you a weighty message. Certainly nightfall is a time when impressions are stronger and speech is more certain. Obviously, the day is filled with constant work.*
> 73:8 *Remember the name of your Lord, and devote yourself to Him with complete devotion. Lord of the east and the west; there is no god except Allah. Take Him for your protector.*
> 73:20 *Your Lord knows that you spend nearly two-thirds, or half, or a third of the night praying, just as some others do. Allah measures the day and the night. He knows that you cannot count the time accurately, and He looks at you with mercy. Therefore, recite as much of the Koran as is easy for you. He knows that sometimes people are sick, or traveling, or fighting in his cause. Recite, therefore, as much as is easy for you. Observe your prayers, pay the required alms, and lend Allah a generous loan. Whatever good deeds you perform will be waiting for you with Allah. This will be the best and richest reward. Ask Allah for forgiveness. Certainly, Allah is forgiving and merciful.*

THE FIRST MALES TO ACCEPT ISLAM

I159 A famine overtook the Quraysh and Mohammed's uncle Abu Talib had a large family. Abu Talib was a well respected tribal leader, but had fallen on hard times. Mohammed went to another uncle, Al Abbas, and they both went to Abu Talib and offered to help raise two of his children. Ali went into Mohammed's house to be raised by him and Khadija. When Ali turned ten he joined with Mohammed in his new religion, Islam.

I160 Mohammed and Ali used to go to the edge of town to practice their new ritual prayers. One day Abu Talib came upon them and asked what were they doing? Mohammed replied, "Uncle, this is the religion of Allah, His angels, His prophets and the religion of Abraham. Allah has sent me as an apostle to all mankind. You, my uncle, deserve that I should teach you the truth and call you to Islam." His uncle said that he could not give up the religion of his ancestors, but that he would support Mohammed.

The native Arabic religions were tribal in that every tribe had its deities, but the ceremonies and traditions were passed down by oral tradition, not in writing.

Mohammed lived in Mecca, which had been a religious center for many generations. It had a stone building that was roughly shaped like a cube and was called a Kabah. There were at least five other Kabahs in other towns in Arabia. The Kabah was a religious center for many of the native religions. Some sources say that there were as many as 360 deities worshipped in Mecca, a city that was profoundly polytheistic and tolerant. There were religious festivals that involved pilgrimages to Mecca, so at different times of the year, many tribes would gather to trade and do religious ceremonies.

One of the many gods in Mecca was Allah, a moon god. The native religions did not have any formal structure to the many deities, but Allah was a high god. Allah was the primary god of the Quraysh tribe of Mohammed, and Mohammed's father was named Abdullah, slave of Allah.

The idea of having an Arabian prophet was new. The sources of the native religions were unknown, but the new religion of Islam had a self-declared prophet. The Jews had prophets, and now the Arabs had a prophet in Mohammed.

> 87:1 ***Praise the name of your Lord, the Most High, who has created and proportioned all things, who has determined man's destinies and guided them, who brought forth the pasture, and reduced it to dusty stubble.***
> 87:6 ***We will teach you to recite [the Koran] so that you do not forget, unless Allah wishes. He knows everything manifest and secret, and We will make it easy for you [Mohammed] to attain a state of ease. Therefore***

give warning because the warning is profitable. He who fears Allah will receive the warning, and only the most unfortunate ones will avoid it. They will be flung into Hellfire, in which there is no death or life.

Since Mohammed was a prophet, it was natural that the Koran should pick the thread of the history of the Jews and their prophets, such as Abraham and Moses.

87:14 *Happy is the man who is purified [by Islam] and who remembers the name of his Lord and prays.*
87:16 *You prefer this present life, though the hereafter is better and more enduring.*
87:18 *This is certainly contained in the earlier scriptures of Abraham and Moses*

Stories about Abraham:

51:24 *Have you heard the story of Abraham's honored guests? They went to him and said, "Peace!" And he replied, "Peace, strangers." And he went among his household and brought out a fatted calf, and he set it before them and said, "Do you want to eat?" They did not, and he became afraid of them. They said to him, "Do not be afraid," and gave him the news that he was going to father a wise son. Abraham's wife came forward with a cry, striking her face, and said, "But I am old and barren!"*
51:30 *They said, "Your Lord says it is true, and he is wise and knowing."*
51:31 *Abraham said, "What errand are you on, messengers?" They replied, "We are sent to a wicked people, to shower them with stones of clay, sent by your Lord for their excesses."*
51:35 *We went to evacuate the believers in the city, but We only found one Muslim family, and We left signs warning those who fear the painful punishment. Moses was another sign. We sent him to Pharaoh with manifest authority. But Pharaoh was confident of his might and turned his back and said, "You are a magician, or insane." So We seized him and his army and cast them into the sea, and he had only himself to blame.*

Stories about Moses:

79: 15 *Have you heard the story of Moses? How his Lord called to him in the sacred valley of Tuwa, saying, "Go to Pharaoh. He has rebelled, and say, 'Do you want to be purified?' Then I will guide you to your Lord so that you may fear Him."*
79:20 *And Moses showed Pharaoh a great miracle. But Pharaoh denied it and disobeyed. Furthermore, he turned his back and rebelled against Allah. He gathered an army and made a proclamation, saying, "I am your lord, the most high." So Allah punished him and made an example*

of him in this life and the hereafter. Surely this is a lesson for those who fear Allah.

Mohammed preached the doctrine of the Day of Judgment.

80:11 *No, this [the Koran] is a warning! Let him who is willing, keep this in mind. It is written on honored pages, exalted and purified, by the hands of scribes, honorable and righteous.*
80:16 *Cursed be man! What has made him reject Allah? From what thing did Allah create him? He created him and molded him from a drop of sperm; then He made an easy path for him from the womb then caused him to die and put him in his grave. Then when He pleases, He will resurrect him. But man has not yet fulfilled Allah's commands.*
80:24 *Let man consider his food. First, We poured down the rain in abundance; then split the earth apart and caused the grain to grow along with grapes and healing herbs, the olive and the palm; and enclosed gardens dense with trees, and fruits and vegetables for man's use and for his cattle.*
80:33 *But when the trumpet blast sounds, a man will flee from his brother and his mother and his father and his wife and his children. That day, every man will be focused on his own concerns. There will be radiant faces that day, laughing and joyous, but other faces that day will have dust upon them and blackness will cover them. These are the unbelievers, the wicked.*

101:1 *The disaster! What is the disaster? Who will teach you what the disaster is?*
101:4 *The Day when men will be like scattered moths, and the mountains will be like carded wool then, the man whose balance of good deeds is heavy will have a pleasant life.*
101:8 *The man whose balance of good deeds is light will dwell in the pit. Who will teach you what the pit is? A raging Fire!*

When is the Day of Resurrection?

75:1 *I swear by the Day of Resurrection. I swear by the self-examining soul.*
75:3 *Does man think that We will be unable to reunite his bones? Yes! We can restore him down to the finger tips. Man chooses to deny that which is in front of him. He asks, "When is the Day of Resurrection?"*
75:7 *But when the eye becomes dazzled, and when the moon is eclipsed, and when the sun and the moon are united, on that day men will cry, "Where can we hide?" But they cry vainly, because there is no place to hide—the only asylum that day is with your Lord. On that day men will be told of everything they did and everything they did not do. Yes! Man is evidence against himself, even if he makes excuses.*

75:16 *(While reciting this revelation, do not hasten carelessly because it is Our responsibility to collect and recite it. When We recite it, carefully follow the recital, and surely, We will clarify everything afterwards.)*
75:20 *Yes! Men love the present life and neglect the life to come. Some faces will be joyous that day, looking toward their Lord; and some faces that day will be despondent, as if they sensed an imminent disaster. Yes! When the soul comes up into the throat, and people cry, "Who has magic that can save us?"*
75:28 *When the man is sure that his time has come, and when one leg is laid over the other [in the death struggle], on that day he will be driven to your Lord, because he did not believe, and he did not pray. Instead he called the truth a lie and turned his back. Then he paraded back to his people with haughty attitude.*
75:34 *That hour is getting closer and closer. It constantly gets closer and closer.*
75:36 *Does man think that he has no purpose? Did he not begin as a drop of sperm? Later he became a clot of blood that Allah formed and fashioned and made from him a pair, the male and female.*
75:40 *Do you think that He does not have the power to resurrect the dead?*

The Wicked Will be in Hell

82:1 *When the sky splits in half, and when the stars disperse, and when the oceans burst forth, and when the graves are thrown open, every soul will know what it has done and what it did not do. Man, what led you away from your generous Lord, Who created you and molded you and gave you form? He made you in any form He chose, but you deny the Day of Judgment.*
82:10 *Surely there are guardians looking over you—honorable recorders—who know and write everything you do. The righteous will dwell in happiness, but the wicked will be in Hell. They will burn there on Judgment Day, and there is no way for them to avoid it. Who will teach you what the Judgment Day is? It is the day when no soul has control over another; on that day only Allah has power.*

99:1 *When the earth is shaken with quakes and the earth casts up her burdens, man will ask, "What does this mean?"*
99:4 *On that day she will tell her news, because your Lord inspired her. On that day men will come forward in droves to witness their deeds, and whoever has done even an atom's weight of good will see it, and whoever has done even an atom's weight of evil will see it.*

Drink from a Fiercely Boiling Fountain

88:1 *Have you heard the news of the overwhelming event?*

88:2 *Some faces will be downcast that day, troubled and weary, burnt at the scorching Fire, forced to drink from a fiercely boiling fountain, with only bitter thorns for food, which neither nourishes nor satisfies hunger.*
88:8 *Other faces that day will be joyous, and in a lofty Garden, very pleased with their past efforts. No vain talk will be heard there. There will be gushing fountains. There will be raised couches, and goblets placed nearby, and cushions arranged, and carpets spread out.*
88:17 *Will they consider the camels and how they were made? Or consider how the sky was upraised, and how the mountains are rooted, and how the earth is spread?*
88:21 *Warn them, because you [Mohammed] are merely a warner. You have no authority over them, but whoever turns back and disbelieves, Allah will punish them terribly.*
88:25 *Truly they will return to Us. Then it will be time for Us to settle their accounts.*

After the Day of Doom would come Paradise and Hell.

52:7 *Truly, a punishment from your Lord is coming, and no one can stop it. That day heaven will heave from side to side, and the mountains will shake to pieces. Woe on that day to those who called the messengers liars, who wasted their time in vain disputes.*
52:13 *On that day they will be thrown into the Fire of Hell. This is the Fire that you treated like a lie. What! Do you think that this is magic? Or, do you not see it? Burn there! Bear it patiently, or impatiently. It will all be the same to you, because you will certainly get what you deserve.*
52:17 *But those who have feared Allah will live pleasantly amid Gardens, rejoicing in what their Lord has given them, and what their Lord has protected them from, saying, "Eat and drink in health as a reward for your good deeds." They will recline on arranged couches, and We will marry them to dark-eyed houris [beautiful companions of pleasure].*
52:21 *And the believers, whose children have accepted the faith, We will reunite with their descendents. We will not cheat them of their reward. Every man is pledged to Allah for his actions and his rewards. We will give them abundant fruit and meat. There they will share a cup that holds no idle discourse or motivation to sin. They will be waited on by young boys as beautiful as hidden pearls, and some will gather together and ask one another questions.*
52:26 *"There was a time when we were filled with concerns about the future of our families, but Allah has been kind to us, and He has kept us safe from the torments of Hell, truly. We called upon Him before. He is bountiful and merciful."*

Try to Trick Me

77:8 *Until what day will that time be deferred when the stars lose their light, and when the heaven is split in two, and when the mountains are reduced to dust and scattered, and when the messengers are gathered at their appointed time? To the Day of Judgment! And who will teach you what the Day of Judgment is? Woe on that day to those who reject the truth! Did We not destroy the former generations? We will make the later generations follow them. This is how We deal with evil doers. Woe on that day to those who reject the truth!*

77:20 *Did We not create you from a cloudy fluid that We kept in a safe place [the womb] until an appointed time? This is Our power! Our power is unmatched! Woe on that day to those who reject the truth!*

77:25 *Did We not design the world to contain the living and the dead and place on it tall strong mountains and sweet water to drink? Woe on that day to those who reject the truth!*

77:29 *They will be told, "Go to that Hell that you deny. Go to the shadows of smoke that rise in three columns, where there is no relief or shelter from the flame." The sparks flying out are like towers, yellow like tawny camels. Woe on that day to those who reject the truth!*

77:35 *They cannot speak that day, and they will not be allowed any excuses. Woe on that day to those who reject the truth!*

77:38 *This is the day of sorting, when We will collect you and your ancestors. If you have any tricks, try to trick Me. Woe on that day to those who reject the truth!*

77:41 *Because of your efforts, the righteous will be in a cool, shaded place, with anything they desire to eat and drink contentedly. This is how We reward the good. Woe on that day to those who reject the truth!*

77:46 *Eat and drink a little while. Surely you are sinners. Woe on that day to those who reject the truth!*

77:48 *When they are told to bow down, they do not bow down. Woe on that day to those who reject the truth! After this what revelation will they believe in?*

We Have Specially Made for Them Houris

56:1 *When the inevitable day of terror arrives, no one will treat its sudden arrival as a lie. That day many will be crushed! That day some will be exalted!*

56:4 *When the earth is shaken to its core, and the mountains crumble to powder and become scattered dust, and the people are divided into three groups, the people of the right hand—Oh, how happy the people of the right hand will be!*

56:9 *The people of the left hand—Oh, how wretched they will be!*

56:10 *The people who were foremost on earth [the first to follow Mohammed], they will be foremost in the hereafter. A large number of those who lived before are the people who will be brought close to Allah, in Gardens of delight. A few of those who lived later [after Islam was well established] will be on decorated couches, reclining on them face to face. They will be waited on by immortal young boys with goblets and ewers and a cup of pure wine that gives no headache nor muddles the mind, and with fruits that are most pleasing, and with the flesh of birds that they desire. In compensation for their past good deeds, they will have houris [heavenly companions of pleasure] with big, dark eyes like pearls peeking from their shells. They will not hear any vain or sinful talk, only the cry, "Peace! Peace!"*

56:27 *The people of the right-hand—Oh! How happy the people of the right-hand will be resting on raised couches amid thornless sidrahs [plum trees] and talh trees [banana trees], thick with fruit, and in extended shade and constantly flowing waters, and abundant fruits, neither forbidden nor out of reach. And We have specially made for them houris, companions, chaste and pure virgins, lovers and friends of equal age with them for the people of the right hand, a large number of the people of old, and a large number of the people of the latter generations.*

56:41 *The people of the left-hand—Oh, how wretched the people of the left-hand will be amid scorching winds and scalding water, and in the shade of black smoke, neither cool nor refreshing. Formerly they were blessed with worldly pleasures, yet they persisted in terrible sin and used to say, "What will be resurrected after we have died and crumbled to bone and dust? What about our fathers, the men of old?"*

56:49 *Say: Yes, the former and the latter. They will all be gathered at the appointed hour.*

56:51 *Then those who denied [Mohammed was a prophet] and erred will certainly eat from the Ez-zakkoum tree [a tree of Hell], and they will gorge themselves with it. Then they will drink scalding water and will drink like a thirsty camel. This will be their feast on the Judgment Day!*

Which of Your Lord's Blessings Would You Deny?

55:33 *Oh, assembly of jinn and men, if you can cross the bounds of the heavens and the earth, then cross them. You will never cross them without Our permission. Which of your Lord's blessings would you deny?*

55:35 *A flash of Fire and molten brass will be hurled at both of you, and you will have no defense against it. Which of your Lord's blessings would you deny?*

55:37 *When the sky is split in two and becomes red like stained leather, which of your Lord's blessings would you deny?*

55:39 *On that day neither man nor jinn will be asked about his sin. Which of your Lord's blessings would you deny?*

55:41 *The guilty will be recognized by their marks [dark faces], and they will be grabbed by their forelocks and their feet. Which of your Lord's blessings would you deny?*
55:43 *This is the Hell that the guilty deny. They will wander around between it and boiling hot water. Which of your Lord's blessings would you deny?*
55:46 *But there will be two Gardens for those who fear to stand before their Lord. Which of your Lord's blessings would you deny?*
55:48 *Gardens with branches spreading out from every kind of tree. Which of your Lord's blessings would you deny?*
55:50 *In them (each) will be two springs flowing (free): Which of your Lord's blessings would you deny?*
55:52 *In them will be two kinds of every fruit. Which of your Lord's blessings would you deny?*
55:54 *They will recline on couches lined with silk brocade, and the fruit of both Gardens will be within arms reach. Which of your Lord's blessings would you deny?*
55:56 *There will be bashful virgins who gaze modestly, who have never been touched by either man nor jinn. Which of your Lord's blessings would you deny?*
55:58 *As lovely as rubies and pearls: which of your Lord's blessings would you deny?*
55:60 *Should the reward for goodness be anything but goodness? Which of your Lord's blessings would you deny?*
55:62 *And besides these there are two other gardens, dark green with foliage. Which of your Lord's blessings would you deny?*
55:66 *With gushing fountains in each. Which of your Lord's blessings would you deny?*
55:68 *In each, fruits and palms and pomegranates. Which of your Lord's blessings would you deny?*
55:70 *In each, fair and beautiful virgins. Which of your Lord's blessings would you deny?*
55:72 *With large dark eyes, they are closely guarded in pavilions. Which of your Lord's blessings would you deny?*
55:74 *They have never been touched by either man nor jinn. Which of your Lord's blessings would you deny?*
55:76 *They recline on green cushions and beautiful carpets. Which of your Lord's blessings would you deny?*
55:78 *Blessed be the name of your Lord, full of majesty and glory.*

I161 There was added a new element to the religion. Any person who rejected the revelations of Mohammed would be eternally punished. The culture of religious tolerance in Mecca now had a new religion which preached the end of tolerance. Only Islam was acceptable.

68:42 *On the day when men's legs will be laid bare, and they are called upon to bow in adoration, they will not be able. Their eyes will be downcast. Shame will overwhelm them, because when they were protected, they were called to bow down in worship, but they refused.*
68:44 *Leave Me alone to deal with those who reject this revelation. We will lead them by degrees to their ruin by ways they will be unaware of. I will bear with them a long time, because My plan is firm.*
68:46 *Do you [Mohammed] demand payment from them so that they are burdened with debt? Do they have knowledge of secret things? Have they written them down?*
68:48 *Wait patiently for your Lord's Judgment, and do not be like him [Jonah] who was swallowed by the whale, when he cried out in distress to Allah. If his Lord's favor had not reached him, he would have been cast forth on the naked shore, overwhelmed with shame. But his Lord chose him and placed him among the just.*
68:51 *The unbelievers will practically kill you with their eyes when they hear the warnings [of the Koran], and they will say, "He is certainly insane."*
68:52 *But it is a warning to all creation.*

1166 Since the word was out, Mohammed began to openly preach his new doctrine. He had been private for three years before he went public.

The first of many parables was given:

68:17 *Surely, We have tried them [the Meccans] as We tried the owners of the garden, when they swore they would harvest its fruit in the morning; but added no exception [by saying, "If it is the will of Allah"]. Then an encompassing plague from your Lord swept through it while they slept, and by the morning the garden was barren, as if all its fruit had been cut.*
68:21 *At dawn they called to each other, "Go to your fields early if you want to cut your dates." So they went, quietly whispering to each other, "No poor man will enter your garden today." And so they went out at dawn to their fields with this purpose in mind.*
68:26 *But when they saw the garden, they said, "Surely we have gone astray. Indeed, our harvest is destroyed." The best among them said, "Did I not say to you, 'Why do you refuse to praise Allah?'" They said, "Glory to our Lord! Surely we have done wrong."*
68:30 *Then they began to blame one another, and they said, "Woe to us! We were insolent! Perhaps our Lord will give us a better garden in exchange. Surely we beg this from our Lord."*
68:33 *This has been their punishment, but the punishment of the hereafter is even greater, but they did not know this. Surely the Allah-fearing will be in Gardens of Delight in the presence of their Lord. Should We*

> *deal with those who have submitted to Allah like We do those who offend him? What has happened to you [unbelievers] to make you judge as you do? Do you have a Scripture from which you can learn how you can have the things that you choose? Or have you received an oath from Us, binding until Judgment Day, that you will have everything you demand? Ask them [the unbelievers] who will guarantee this? Or do they have other gods? Let them bring their other gods if they are telling the truth.*

The qualities of Allah were given:

> 56:57 *We created you, will you refuse to give Us credit? Have you thought about the sperm that you produce? Did you create it, or did We? We have decreed that death be a part of your life; yet that does not prevent Us from replacing you with others, either like yourselves, or in forms that you can not imagine! You know of the first forms of creation: do you not reflect? Have you considered what you sow? Do you cause it to grow, or do We? If We wished We could make your harvest so dry and brittle that you would be amazed and say, "Truly we are indebted, but we are denied our harvest."*
> 56:68 *Have you considered the water that you drink? Do you send it down from the clouds, or do We? We could make it brackish if We wished. Would you be thankful then?*
> 56:71 *Have you considered the fire that you obtain by friction? Did you make the trees, or did We? We made it for a memorial and to benefit the desert travelers, therefore praise the name of your Lord, the Great.*

> 112:1 *Say: He is the only god: Allah, the Eternal!*
> 112:3 *No one is born of Him, and He is born of no one; and there is no one like Him.*

The Arabs had always believed in jinns, invisible beings created from fire. Now they appeared in the Koran.

> 114:1 *Say: I seek protection with the Lord of men, the king of men, the judge of men, and from the mischief of gossips, who whisper into the hearts of men tales against the jinn and men.*

> 51:56 *I created jinn and man only to worship me. I need no livelihood from them, and I do not need them to feed me. Truly, Allah is the sole sustainer, the possessor of power, and the unmovable!*
> 51:59 *Let those who injure you share the fate of the sinners of old. They should not challenge Me to hasten it. Woe to the unbelievers, because of the day they are threatened with.*

The other deities in Mecca were attacked.

> 53:19 *Do you see Al-Lat and Al-Ozza, and Manat [Arabic deities] the third idol? What? Do you have male children and Allah female children [Arabs called angels the daughters of Allah]? That is an unfair division!*
> 53:23 *These are mere names. You and your fathers gave them these names. Allah has not acknowledged them. They follow only their own conceits and desires, even though their Lord has already given them guidance.*
> 53:24 *Will man have everything he desires? The future and the present are in Allah's hands. No matter how many angels are in the heavens, their intercession will do no good, until Allah has permitted entry to whom He pleases and whom He will accept.*
> 53:27 *Surely, the ones who give female names to the angels are the ones who do not believe in the hereafter, but of this they have no knowledge. They are following a guess, and a guess can not replace the truth.*
> 53:29 *Stay away from those who turn their backs on Our warnings and desire only the present life. This is all that they know. Truly, your Lord knows everything about those who stray from his path, and He knows everything about those who have accepted his guidance. Whatever is in the heavens and on the earth belongs to Allah. He may reward evildoers according to their own deeds and those who do good will be rewarded with good things.*
> 53:32 *Surely, your Lord is filled with forgiveness for those who avoid great sins and shameful acts and only commit minor sins. He knew you well when He brought you out of the earth and when you were in your mother's womb. Do not try to justify yourself. He knows the Allah-fearing people the best.*

The early Koran of Mecca is marked by many oaths by Allah.

> 92:1 *By the night when she spreads her veil, by the day when it shines bright and by Him who made man and woman – certainly you strive for many goals!*

> 86:1 *By the heaven and the morning star! Who will teach you what the morning star is? It is the star of piercing brightness. A guardian is set over every soul.*

> 86:11 *I swear by the heaven that completes its cycle and by the earth that bursts with new growth, that this [the Koran] is the final word, and it is not an amusement.*

> 91:1 *By the sun and its midday brightness! By the moon when she follows him! By the day when it reveals his [the sun's] glory! By the night when it [the moon] covers him [the sun]! By the heaven and Him who built it! By the earth and Him who spread it! By the soul and by Him who formed it, and breathed into it its perception of right and wrong. Blessed is he who has kept it pure, and cursed is he who has corrupted it!*

95:1 *I swear by the fig and the olive, by Mount Sinai, and by this inviolate land [Mecca]! We have created man in a noble image then reduced him to the lowest of the low, except those who believe and do the right things, because their reward will never fail.*

51:1 *By the winds that move far and wide and carry their load of laden clouds, and by those that speed and those that distribute blessings by command!*

52:1 *By Mount Sinai, and the Scriptures written on an outspread scroll, and by the often-visited house [the Kabah in Mecca], and by the lofty roof [the sky], and by the swollen sea,*

56:75 *It is not necessary for me to swear by the setting of the stars. That is a great oath, if you know it, that this is indeed the honorable Koran, written in the guarded book which only the purified may touch. It is a revelation from the Lord of the worlds.*

103:1 *I swear by the declining day!*
103:2 *Certainly, man's fate is cast amidst destruction, except for those who believe and do good and urge others to the truth and to be steadfast.*

85:1 *By the star-sprinkled heaven! By the promised Day of Judgment! By the witness and the witnessed!*

77:1 *By the winds sent forth, one after another; by the raging hurricanes, which scatter clouds then separate them from one another; and by those that bring forth the word either to excuse or warn; surely, that which you have been promised is coming.*

89:1 *I swear by the daybreak and ten nights [the first ten nights of a sacred month], by the even and the odd, and by the night when it departs. Is this not an oath for a sensible man?*

Mohammed's task in Mecca was difficult.

52:29 *Therefore, continue to warn men. By the grace of your Lord, you are neither insane, nor a soothsayer.*
52:30 *Will people say, "He is a poet! Let us wait until his fortunes turn." Say: "Wait," because truthfully, I will wait with you.*
52:32 *Is it their dreams that cause them to do this? Or is it because they are a perverse people? Will they say, "He has written it [the Koran] himself?" No! It is because they did not believe. If that is true, let them write a book like it.*
52:35 *Were they created from nothing? Did they create themselves? Did they create the heavens and the earth? No! It is because they have no faith. Do they possess your Lord's treasures? Do they have absolute power? Can they communicate with the angels? If so, let them bring proof.*

52:39 *Does Allah have daughters while you have sons? Do you ask them for a payment so that they are weighed down with debt? Do they have secret knowledge that they can write down? Do they try to set traps for you? The unbelievers are the ones that are ensnared. Do they have any gods besides Allah? Glory be to Allah above the false gods they join with Him. If they saw a piece of the sky falling, they would say, "It is only a dense cloud."*

52:45 *Ignore them until they meet the day when they will swoon with terror—a day when their tricks will avail them nothing and no help will come their way. Truly, there is another punishment for the evildoers, but most of them do not know it.*

52:48 *Wait patiently for your Lord's Judgment, because you are in Our eye. Sing Allah's praises when you rise up, and give Him praise at night and when the stars are setting.*

And Your Companion [Mohammed] Is Not Insane

81:1 *When the sun ceases to shine and the stars fall; when the mountains fall to pieces; when the she-camels are abandoned; when the wild animals are herded together; when the seas boil; when souls are rejoined with their bodies; when the female child that had been buried alive is asked for what crime was she killed; when the books are opened; when the sky is torn away; when Hell is ignited; when Paradise is brought near, every soul will know what it has done,*

81:15 *It does not matter that I swear by the planets that rise and set, and by the night as it slips away, and by the dawn as it brightens. This is the word of an honorable messenger [Gabriel], powerful and influential with the Lord of the throne, obeyed by angels, trustworthy, and your companion [Mohammed] is not insane. He saw him [Gabriel] clearly on the horizon. Neither does he conceal heaven's secrets, nor does he teach Satan's doctrine.*

81:26 *Where then are you going? Surely, this is nothing except a warning to all creatures who are willing to walk the straight path, but you will not, unless Allah, the Lord of the worlds, wills it.*

The Koran contains encouragement for Mohammed:

94:1 *Did We not open your heart for you [Mohammed] and relieve you of the burden that hurt your back? And did We not improve your reputation? So, certainly, with every hardship there is relief. Certainly, with every hardship there is relief.*

94:7 *When you are through with prayers, you should continue to work. Do everything you can to please your Lord.*

Mohammed worked on a daily basis to convert others. One day he had brushed off a blind man as he tried to convert a rich man.

> 80:1 *He [Mohammed] frowned and turned his back, because the blind man came to him. But what convinced you that he would not be purified by the faith, or be warned, and the warning might profit him?*
> 80:5 *As for the wealthy man, you give him all your attention, but it is not your concern if he is not purified. Not only that, but you neglect the man who comes to you striving earnestly, and full of fears.*

Mohammed spent a great deal of time arguing with the Meccans and telling them that they were doomed to Hell if they rejected him and his message.

> 84:1 *When the sky is split in half and obeys its Lord, as it must; when the earth is flattened, and has cast out everything it contains and is empty [the graves deliver the dead], and obeys its Lord, as it must; then certainly those who want to meet their Lord will meet Him.*
> 84:7 *He who receives his book [of life's deeds] in his right hand [saved in Paradise], his account will be taken by a quick and easy reckoning and he will return joyously to his people. But those who receive their book behind their backs [damned to Hell] will invite destruction. They will burn in the Fire. They lived joyously among their people because they did not believe that they would return to Allah, but their Lord is always watching them.*
> 84:16 *So I do not need to swear by the glow of sunset, and by the night and everything it conceals, and by the moon at its fullest. You will certainly travel from stage to stage.*
> 84:20 *What is wrong with those who do not believe? When the Koran is read to them, why do they refuse to bow down? The unbelievers call it a lie.*
> 84:23 *But Allah knows their secrets, so announce to them a painful punishment. Those who believe and do good deeds, they will have a reward that never ends.*

Hell Lies in Wait

> 78:1 *What do they ask one another? About the great news [the Koran], the source of their disputes? No, but they will learn the truth! No! No, but they will learn the truth!*
> 78:6 *Did We not make the earth a great tent and the mountains its tent-pegs? We created you with two sexes, and created sleep so that you may rest. We created the night as a covering, and created the day to seek a livelihood, and built above you seven substantial heavens, and placed on it a burning lamp. We send down from the clouds abundant rainwater to produce fruits and vegetables and thickly wooded gardens.*
> 78:17 *Surely, the day of decision is fixed, when a trumpet will sound and you will come in droves, and heaven will be opened with countless gates, and the mountains will vibrate and vanish into thin air. Hell lies*

in wait, the home of transgressors, where they will live for ages. They will taste nothing cool and drink nothing except boiling and freezing water. A just reward!
78:27 *They did not think about their account, and they did not believe Our revelations, but We paid attention and wrote everything down, so taste the fruit of your actions. You will get nothing else except torment.*
78:31 *But the Allah-fearing will be fulfilled with enclosed Gardens and vineyards and voluptuous women of equal age [houris] and a full cup [of wine that produces no hangover]. No vain or false talk will be heard there. A reward from your Lord and a fitting gift!*
78:37 *Lord of the heavens and of the earth, and of all that lies between, the merciful Allah! None will be able to speak with him. On the day that the spirit and the angels will stand in ranks, none will speak unless Allah permits, and then only those who speak rightly. This is the sure day. Whoever will, let him take the path back to his Lord.*
78:40 *Surely, We warn you that punishment is near. The day is near when men will see the deeds that their hands have done and when the unbeliever will say, "Oh, I wish I were dust!"*

Their Entertainment Will Be Scalding Water

56:81 *Will you scorn this announcement? Will you make denial your livelihood?*
56:83 *Why, then—when the soul of a dying man comes up his throat, and you are staring at him, though We are closer to him than you, although you do not see Us—why then, if you are to escape Judgment, cause that soul to return? Tell Me, then, if you speak the truth.*
56:87 *As for him that is brought near Allah, he will live in pleasure and repose in a Garden of Delights. If he is one of the people of the right hand, he will be greeted by others of the right hand with, "Peace be with you."*
56:92 *But those who mistakenly treat the prophets as deceivers, their entertainment will be scalding water, and the broiling of Hellfire. Surely this is a certain truth. Therefore, praise the name of your Lord, the Great.*

70:36 *But what has happened to the unbelievers that causes them to rush madly around you, on the right and left-hand, in droves? Does every one of them hope to enter the Garden of Delight? Certainly not! We have created them, and they know from what.*
70:40 *It does not matter that I swear by the Lord of the East and the West that We have the power to replace them with others better than themselves, and We will not be stopped.*
70:42 *So let them gossip and play until they come face to face with the day they are promised, the day when they hastily rise from their graves like men rushing toward a goal with their eyes downcast and disgrace covering them. That is the day they are promised.*

This Is a Warning

73:10 *Listen to what they [unbelievers] say with patience, and leave them with dignity. Let me deal with the wealthy and those who deny the truth. Bear with them for a while, because We have strong shackles and a raging Fire and food that chokes and a painful punishment. The day will come when the earth and the mountains will be shaken, and the mountains will become dust.*

73:15 *Certainly We have sent an apostle to bear witness against you [the world], just as We sent an apostle to Pharaoh, but Pharaoh rejected the apostle, and We punished him severely. If you refuse to believe, how will you protect yourself from the day that will turn your children's hair gray? The heavens will be torn apart. His promise will be fulfilled. This is a warning. Let those who will, find a path to his Lord.*

The Meccans said that there was no Day of Doom. The Koran:

79:1 *I swear by those angels who snatch out the souls of the wicked, and by those who gently draw out the souls of the blessed, by those who glide along, by those who race forward; and by those who govern the universe!*

79:6 *On the day when the first trumpet sounds and a second blast follows, men's hearts will pound, and their eyes will be downcast. The unbelievers will ask, "Will we be brought back to life even after we have become dust and bones?" They will say, "What is the good in that?" But there will be only one shout, and they will be awakened.*

79:27 *Which is harder to create, you, or the heaven that He built? He has raised it high and given it order. He gave darkness to the night and brought out its light. Afterwards He spread the earth and produced from it the water and the pastures and set the mountains firmly for you and your cattle to enjoy.*

79:34 *But when the great disaster comes, the day when men will reflect upon their efforts and Hell is in full view of everyone, then for those who rebelled and preferred the life of this world, surely, Hell will be their home.*

79:40 *But those who fear to stand before their Lord and have restrained their souls from lust, surely, Paradise will be their home. They will ask you about the Hour and when it will come. But what knowledge do you have of it?*

79:44 *Its arrival is known only to your Lord, and you are only responsible for warning those who fear it. On the day when they see it, it will seem to them that they had been waiting only an evening, or maybe until the following morning.*

Woe on That Day to Those Who Deny Our Signs

83:1 *Woe to the cheaters who always demand full measure from others, but skimp when they measure out or weigh to others. What! Do they*

believe that they will not be resurrected on the great day when all men
will stand before the Lord of the worlds? Yes! The register [a record of
actions] of the wicked is in Sidjin [a place in Hell where the sinners'
records are kept]. And who will make you understand what Sidjin is? It
is a complete record.
83:10 *Woe on that day to those who deny Our signs, who regard the Judg-*
ment Day as a lie! No one regards it as a lie except the transgressor or the
criminal, who, when Our signs are recited to him, says, "Old wives tales!"
No! Their habits have become like rust on their hearts. Yes, they will be
veiled from their Lord's light that day. Then they will be burned in Hell.
They will be told, "This is what you called a lie."
83:18 *No! But the register of the righteous is in Illiyoun [a place in Para-*
dise where the actions of the righteous are recorded]. And who will make
you understand what Illiyoun is? It is a complete record, attested to by
the angels nearest Allah.
83:22 *Surely, the righteous will live among delights! Seated on bridal*
couches they will gaze around. You will see the delight in their faces. Fine
wines, sealed with musk, will be given them to drink. For those who have
aspirations, aspire for wine mixed with the waters of Tasnim, a fountain
where those close to Allah drink.
83:29 *Sinners used to jeer at the believers and wink at one another when*
one passed by, and they jested as they returned to their own people. When
they see believers, they say, "Those people have gone astray." And yet they
were not sent to be the guardians of those people.
83:34 *On that day the faithful will mock the unbelievers, while they sit on*
bridal couches and watch them. Should not the unbelievers be paid back
for what they did?

Cursed Are the Liars

51:5 *Truly, that which threatens you [the Meccans] is real. The Judgment*
will certainly happen. I swear by the star-tracked heaven!
51:8 *You [Mohammed] are confused as what to say, but those who turn*
from the truth are turned aside by divine decree.
51:10 *Cursed are the liars, who stumble along in the depths of ignorance!*
They ask, "When is the Judgment Day?" They will be tormented by the
flames that day. "Have a taste of your torment, whose imminent arrival
you denied."
51:15 *But the Allah-fearing will live in Paradise amid gardens and foun-*
tains, enjoying what their Lord has given them, because they lived a good
life. They slept little at night, and at dawn they prayed for forgiveness,
and they gave a proper share of their wealth to the poor and outcast.
51:20 *There are signs on earth for men of strong belief, and also in our-*
selves. Will you not see them? In heaven there is sustenance for you and a

warning. By the Lord of the heaven and the earth, I swear that this is the truth, as surely as you speak.
51:22 *By the Lord of the heaven and the earth, I swear that this is the truth, as surely as you speak*

Not only were the present day Meccans going to Hell if they did not follow Mohammed, history was full of those who were doomed to Hell for ignoring the message of Allah.

91:11 *The tribe of Thamud [Thamud was a trade town in ruins north of Mecca] proudly rejected the message of the Lord. When the greatest sinner among them rushed forward, the apostle of the Lord said to them, "It is the she-camel of Allah! Let her drink." But they called him a liar and hamstrung her, so their Lord destroyed them for their crime, one and all, and He did not fear the consequences.*

The Sky Will Be Split in Two

69:1 *The Inevitable! Who will make you understand what the Inevitable is?*
69:3 *The people of Thamud and Ad [Ad lay on an old trade route north of Mecca. It was abandoned in Mohammed's day] regarded the Judgment Day as a lie. The people of Thamud were destroyed by crashing thunderbolts. The people of Ad were destroyed by a roaring blast of wind. The wind did Allah's bidding against them for a full week. During that time you could have seen the people laid low, as if they had been the trunks of hollow palms. Could you have seen any of them surviving?*
69:9 *Pharaoh, too, and those who thrived before him, and the overthrown cities, all committed sin, and disobeyed the messenger sent by their Lord. That is why He punished them with an accumulated punishment.*
69:11 *When the flood rose high, We carried you in the ark so We could use that event to warn you and so the hearing ear might hear it. But when one blast is sounded on the trumpet, and the earth and the mountains are shaken, and both are simultaneously crushed into powder, on that day the woe that must come suddenly will come, and the sky will be split in two, because it will be fragile that day. The angels will align on the edges of the sky and over them. Eight will carry up the throne of your Lord.*
69:18 *On that day you will be brought before Him and none of your secrets will remain secret. Those who receive their book in their right hand will say to their friends, "Take my book and read it. I always knew that I would come to my reckoning." And he will have a life of bliss, in a lofty Garden, with clusters of fruit nearby. Eat and drink with satisfaction. This is the reward for the good acts that you performed in the past.*
69:25 *But those who receive their book with their left hand will say, "Oh, I wish that I were never given my book and that I had never heard of my*

reckoning! I wish that death had been the end of me! My wealth has done me no good! My power has fled from me!"
69:30 *Take him, and chain him, and cast him into Hell. Then fasten him to a seventy-yard chain, because he did not believe in Allah, the Greatest, and did not help to feed the poor. He will have no friends here that day, no food, only the pus that runs from sores, which only the sinners eat.*
69:38 *I do not need to swear by what you see and by that which you do not see—that this is surely the word of an honored messenger! It is not the word of a poet—you have so little faith! It is also not the word of a soothsayer—you heed little of Our warning! It is a message from the Lord of the worlds.*
69:44 *If he [Mohammed] had invented any of Our revelations, We would have grabbed him by the right hand, and cut his throat, and We would not have protected him from any of you.*
69:48 *But, surely, the Koran is a warning for the Allah-fearing. We know many think it is a lie. But it will cause grief for the unbelievers, because it is the absolute truth.*
69:52 *Praise the name of your Lord, the Greatest.*

I Am Sent by Him to Warn You.

51:41 *When We sent a desolating blast against Ad, it left nothing in its wake, but turned everything to dust. And in Thamud, they were told, "Enjoy yourself while you still have time." But they rebelled against their Lord's command, and so the tempest overtook them as they stood by and watched. They were powerless and unable to stand. Before them, We had destroyed the people of Noah because they were wicked.*
51:47 *We have built the heaven with Our might and raised it up high and made it vast. We have built the earth and stretched it out like a great carpet. How smooth We have spread it out! We created everything in pairs—you should remind yourselves of that.*
51:50 *Run to Allah. I am sent by Him to warn you. Do not worship other gods beside Allah. I am sent by Him to warn you.*
51:52 *Every apostle that came before was denied and called, "Sorcerer," or "insane." Have these people made a tradition of their mockery? Yes, they are rebellious people. Turn away from them, and you will not be blamed. Instead warn them, because, truthfully a warning will help the believers.*

On That Day When the Earth Is Crushed to Powder

89:6 *Have you thought about how your Lord dealt with the people of Ad, at Irem with the many unique pillars? Or with the people of Thamud who hewed out the rocks in the valley? [Ad, Thamud and Irem were destroyed because they did not listen to their prophets] Or with Pharaoh who impaled his victims on a stake? All of them committed excesses in the lands and increased wickedness there. This is the reason your Lord poured on them the scourge of chastisement. Your Lord is always watchful.*

89:15 *As for man, when his Lord tries him and honors him and is generous to him, he says, "My Lord honors me." But when He tries him and limits his gifts to him, he says, "My Lord despises me." No, but you do not honor the orphan, and you do not urge others to feed the poor, and you devour inheritances with insatiable greed, and you love riches with inordinate love.*

89:21 *No, on that day when the earth is crushed to powder, and Your Lord comes, and the angels are arranged by rank, and Hell is brought near, men will remember, but will that memory help them? He will say, "Oh, I wish that I had spent my life preparing for this!" On that day none will punish like Allah will punish, and none can bind like Allah will bind.*

89:27 *Oh, soul that rests, return to your Lord, pleased, and pleasing Him. You may enter among My servants and enter into My Paradise.*

Surely, Your Lord's Punishment Is Terrible

85:4 *The makers of the pit of the fuel-fed Fire are cursed because they sat by it witnessing what they inflicted on the believers! These witnesses tormented the believers only because of their faith in Allah, the mighty. The heavens and the earth are his kingdom; Allah is the witness of all things.*

85:10 *Certainly, those who persecuted the believers, men and women, and did not repent, await the torments of Hell, and the torments of burning. But those who believe and do good things shall have the Gardens [Paradise] where underground rivers flow. This is the great triumph.*

85:12 *Surely, your Lord's punishment is terrible! It is He who produces all things and causes them to be reproduced. He is the indulgent, the loving, the possessor of the glorious throne, the builder of all He wills.*

85:17 *Have you not heard the story of the armies of Pharaoh and Thamud? No! The unbelievers live in denial, but Allah surrounds them all. It is a glorious Koran written on an eternal tablet.*

I166 The Muslims went to the edge of Mecca to pray in order to be alone. One day a group of the Quraysh came upon them and began to mock them and a fight started. Sad, a Muslim, picked up the jaw bone of a camel and struck one of the Quraysh with it and bloodied him. This violence was the first blood to be shed in Islam.

I167 When Mohammed spoke about his new religion, it did not cause any problems among the Meccans. Then Mohammed began to condemn their religion and rituals and worship. This was a new phenomena. New religions could be added and had been, but not to the detriment to others. The Meccans took offense and resolved to treat him as an enemy. Luckily, he had the protection of his influential uncle, Abu Talib.

I168 Some of the Quraysh went to Abu Talib, Mohammed's tribal protector, and said to him, "Your nephew has cursed our gods, insulted our religion, mocked our way of life, criticized our civilization, attacked our virtues, and said that our forefathers were ignorant and in error. You must stop him, or you must let us stop him. We will rid you of him." Abu Talib gave them a soft reply and sent them away.

I169 The Quraysh saw that Abu Talib would not help. Mohammed continued to preach Islam and attack them and their lives. Mecca was a small town, everybody knew everybody. Islam had split the town of Mecca and divided the ruling and priestly tribe. The Quraysh were attacked at the very ground of their social being.

I170 Things got much worse. Now there was open hostility in the town. Quarrels increased, arguments got very heated. Complete disharmony dominated the town. The tribe started to abuse the recently converted Muslims. But Mohammed's uncle Abu Talib was a respected elder and was able to protect them from real harm.

THE FAIR

Mecca was a town with two sources of money from the outside. The first was trading, and Mohammed had made his money in the caravan trade. The other was the fees from the pilgrims to the shrine of the Kabah. Fairs combined a little of both. All the tribes came for a fair. People would see old acquaintances and buy, sell or trade goods. Since Mecca was one of several sacred or pilgrim sites, rituals for the different tribal gods were performed around the Kabah and Mecca.

I171 It was time for the fair and the Quraysh were in turmoil. They were desperate that the divisions and rancor that had come with Mohammed's preaching not spread to the other clans outside Mecca. So a group of concerned Quraysh talked and decided to meet with Al Walid, a man of respect and influence. He told them that all the visitors would come to them and ask about this man Mohammed and what he was preaching. It was a foregone conclusion that Mohammed would preach and people would ask.

I171 But what could they agree on to tell the visitors so that there could be one voice. What would they call him? Was he possessed? Crazy? A ecstatic poet? A sorcerer? Who was he? What was he? Finally they agreed upon Mohammed being a sorcerer since he separated a son from his father or brother or wife or from his family.

> 68:1 *NUN[1]. By the pen and by what the angels write, by the grace of your Lord, you [Mohammed] are not possessed! Certainly, a limitless reward awaits you, because you have a noble nature, but you will see and they ewill see, which of you is insane.*
> 53:1 *By the star when it sets, your companion [Mohammed] is not wrong, nor is he misled, and he does not speak out of his own desire.*
> 53:4 *This [the Koran] is a revelation only to him. The Lord of mighty power filled it with wisdom and taught it to him. Allah appeared in a stately form in the highest part of the horizon. He approached and came nearer, at a distance of about two bow-lengths, or even closer, and he gave his revelation to his servant.*
> 53:11 *His heart did not invent what he saw. What! Will you dispute with him what he saw? He had seen Gabriel before, near the Sidrah-tree [a shade tree], which marks the boundary near the Garden of repose. When the Sidrah-tree was mysteriously covered, his eye did not turn away, nor did it wander because he saw his Lord's greatest sign.*

> 81:23 *He saw him [Gabriel] clearly on the horizon. Neither does he conceal heaven's secrets, nor does he teach Satan's doctrine.*
> 81:26 *Where then are you going? Surely, this is nothing except a warning to all creatures who are willing to walk the straight path, but you will not, unless Allah, the Lord of the worlds, wills it.*

I171 So the Meccans split up and went out on the roadsides of town to speak with the travelers before they even arrived at Mecca.

I171 Mohammed delivered a message from Allah about Al Walid, the leader of the unbelievers. Indeed, many of the rich and powerful, who resisted Mohammed, earned their place in the Koran. The Koran gives such precise details and direct quotes of their arguments that if you were a Meccan of that day, you would know exactly who the person was.

> 96:6 *No, man is certainly stubborn. He sees himself as wealthy. Certainly, all things return to your Lord.*
> 96:9 *What do you think of a man [Abu Jahl] who holds back a servant of Allah [Mohammed] when he prays? Do you think that he is on the right path, or practices piety? Do you think that he treats the truth as a lie and turns his back? Does he not know that Allah sees everything?*
> 96:15 *No! Certainly if he does not stop, We will grab him by the forelock [cutting off or holding by the forelock was a shame in Arabic culture], the lying, sinful forelock! Let him call his comrades [the other Meccans]. We will call the guards of Hell. No, do not obey him, rather, adore and get closer to Allah.*

---

1. Several chapters begin with Arabic letters such as NUN. Their meaning is not known.

This Is Nothing but Old Magic

74:11 *Let Me deal with My creations, whom I have given great riches and sons to sit by their side, and whose lives I have made smooth and comfortable. And still he [Al Walid] wants me to give him more. No, I say. He is an enemy of Our revelations. I will impose a dreadful punishment on him because he plotted and planned.*

74:19 *Damn him! How he planned. Again, Damn him! How he planned.*

74:21 *Then he looked around and frowned and scowled and turned his back with vain pride and said, "This is nothing but old magic; it is the work of a mere mortal."*

74:26 *We will certainly throw him into Hell.*

74:27 *What will make you realize what Hell is? It leaves nothing, and it spares nothing. It chars the skin.*

74:30 *Nineteen angels oversee it. The angels are the only guardians of Hell, and We have set their number to confuse the unbelievers and to give the believers certain knowledge of the truth of the Koran so the believers will increase their faith. So the believers and the others who have received the Scriptures have no doubts. The weak of heart and the unbelievers will ask, "What does Allah mean by this parable?"*

74:34 *This is how Allah confuses whom He will and how He guides whom He chooses: no one knows the armies of your Lord except Allah himself. This is nothing but a warning to men.*

74:35 *No, by the moon and by the night as it retreats and by the dawn as it breaks, Hell is one of the most dreadful woes filled with warning to men, to any who choose to go forward [believers] or to any who choose to stay behind [unbelievers].*

74:41 *Every soul is pledged for its own deeds except those that stand on Allah's right hand. In their gardens they will ask the wicked: "What has brought you to Hell?"*

74:44 *They will say, "We did not pray, we did not feed the hungry, we argued with the small-minded, and we denied the Judgment Day until our dying day."*

74:49 *No mediation or intercession will help them. What is wrong with them that they reject Our warning like a frightened donkey fleeing a lion? Each of them wants to have everything spelled out, but that cannot be. They do not fear the hereafter.*

74:54 *No! The Koran is warning enough. Anyone who chooses shall be warned. Only if Allah pleases will the people be warned. He is to be feared and often forgiving.*

They Are the People of the Left-Hand

90:1 *No, I swear by this city [Mecca], this city in which you [Mohammed] dwell, and by the father and the child!*

90:4 *Certainly, We have created man to be tried by afflictions. Does he think that no one has power over him? He says, "I have wasted great wealth." Does he think that no one sees him? Have we not given him eyes, and tongue, and lips, and guided him to the two highways?*

90:11 *But he did not attempt the steep road. Who will teach you what the steep road is? It is to free a slave, or to give food during famine to the orphan of a relative, or to the pauper who lies in the dust. It is also, to be a believer and to urge perseverance and compassion upon one another. These are the people of the right hand.*

90:18 *But those who reject Our signs, they are the people of the left-hand. Hellfire will close around them.*

Fables of the Ancients

68:6 *Your Lord knows the man who strays from His path, and He knows who has been guided. Do not listen to those who treat you like a liar. They want you to compromise with them so that they may compromise with you.*

68:10 *Do not listen to the despicable person, who readily swears oaths, a defamer, going about with slander, enemy of the good, a transgressor, a criminal. He is cruel and impure from birth, though wealthy and blessed with sons. When Our wonderful verses are recited to him, he says "Fables of the ancients." We will brand him on the nose.*

53:33 *Have you considered him who turns his back on the faith? Who is stingy and covets? Does he have secret knowledge, or vision? Has he not been told what is in the book of Moses, and about Abraham and his faithful pledge? Namely, that no bearer of burdens can bear the burden of another.*

53:39 *Man can have nothing except what he works for. Nothing will be credited to a man which he did not earn. His effort will be noted. Then he will be rewarded, totally, justly, and completely. That is the goal of your Lord. He causes laughter and crying, and He causes death and life, and He created the male and female sexes from the fertilized sperm. He has promised a resurrection, and He gives wealth and satisfaction. He is the lord of Sirius [the Dog star]. He destroyed the tribe of Ad, and the people of Thamud, and before them, the wicked and perverse people of Noah, and left no survivors. He destroyed the two overthrown cities of Sodom and Gomorrah so that they were ruins.*

53:56 *Which of your Lord's blessings would you doubt?*

Allah Is the Lord of the Ladders

70:1 *A skeptic asked about the punishment soon to befall the unbelievers. No one can prevent Allah from inflicting it. Allah is the Lord of the ladders that the angels and the spirit ascend in a day that lasts fifty thousand years.*

70:5 *So be patient with admirable patience. They think that day is far away, but We see that it is near. The day when the heavens will become like molten brass, and the mountains will become like tufts of wool, and friends do not care about friends, though they are in plain sight of one another. To save himself from the punishment of that day, the wicked would give his children and his wife and his brother and all of his relatives who loved him and everyone on earth, if that could save him.*
70:15 *But no. Because the Fire, dragging him by the scalp, will claim him who turned his back and fled from the truth and amassed and hoarded wealth. Man is truly an impatient creation. He is impatient when evil touches him and miserly when good reaches him.*

111:1 *Let the hands of Abu Lahab [Mohammed's uncle and an opponent] die and let him die! His wealth and attainments will not help him. He will be burned in Hell, and his wife will carry the firewood, with a palm fiber rope around her neck.*

And Slay the Sacrificial Victims

108:1 *Certainly We have given an abundance to you [Mohammed]. Therefore pray to the Lord, and slay the sacrificial victims [ritual killing of animals].*
108:3 *Surely those who hate you will be childless.*

105:1 *Did you not see how your Lord dealt with the army of the elephant?*[1] *Did He not cause their plans to fail? He sent flocks of birds against them, which pelted them with stones of baked clay, and He made them like the stubble in a field that had been devoured.*

109:1 *Say: Oh you unbelievers!*
109:2 *I do not worship what you worship, and you do not worship what I worship. I will never worship what you worship, and you will never worship what I worship. You to your religion, me to my religion.*

104:1 *Woe to every slanderer and backbiter who gathers wealth and hordes it for the future. He certainly thinks he will keep his wealth forever. No! He certainly will be flung into Hell, and who will teach you what Hell is?*
104:6 *It is the Fire kindled by Allah that will rise above the hearts of the damned and close over them in towering columns.*

I172 The plan of hurting Mohammed by warning the visitors made everyone more curious. When they heard Mohammed's soaring words from the Koran many visitors were impressed. When they left they took all the

---

1. In 570 AD an army with an elephant attacked Mecca. The army caught smallpox and retreated.

stories from Mecca, the Quraysh, the new Muslims and then, of course, Mohammed. Soon all of that part of Arabia was talking.

I178 In what would be very fortuitous for Mohammed, the Arabs of Medina were attracted to Mohammed's message. Since half of their town were Jews, the Arabs of Medina were used to the talk of only one god.

PUBLIC TEACHING

CHAPTER 4

3:32 Say: Obey Allah and His messenger, but if they reject it, then truly, Allah does not love those who reject the faith.

At first Mohammed had only told close friends and relatives about his message. Now he began to move more into the public. The Koran condemns those who argue with Mohammed.

> 36:77 *Does man not see that We created him from a drop of sperm? But still, he is a sworn enemy. And he makes substitutes for Us and forgets the facts of his creation saying, "Who will resurrect these bones when they are rotten?" Say: He gave them life in the beginning, and He will return it to them because He has knowledge of all creation. He makes fire from the green tree for you and allows you to kindle flame. Is the creator of the heavens and the earth not able to create the likes of them? Certainly He is the supreme creator, the knower. If He intends something, His command is, "Be," and it is! So glory to Him in whose hands is the kingdom of all things! All things will return to Him.*

> 25:32 *Those who disbelieve say, "Why was the Koran not revealed to him all at once?" It was revealed one part at a time so that We might strengthen your heart with it and so that We might rehearse it with you gradually, in slow, well-arranged stages.*
> 25:33 *They will not come to you with any difficult questions for which We have not provided you the true and best answers. Those who will be gathered together face down in Hell will have the worst place and will be the farthest away from the right path.*

The reaction of the Meccans was with false arguments.

> 18:54 *In this Koran We have given to man every kind of example, but man is, in most respects, contentious. Nothing prevents men from believing when guidance comes to them nor from asking their Lord's forgiveness, unless it is that they wish that the same fate which befell the ancients should also befall them—that they come face to face with doom.*
> 18:56 *We do not send messengers except as bearers of glad tidings and to give warnings. Yet the unbelievers make false contentions so that they may refute the truth. They mock Our signs just like they do Our warnings. Who is more unjust than he who is reminded of His Lord's signs*

but turns away from them and forgets what His hands have done? Truly We have placed veils over their hearts so that they do not understand, and deafness over their ears. Even if you give them guidance, they will not follow.

18:58 *Your Lord is most forgiving, the Lord of mercy. If He were to give them what they deserve, He would certainly have hastened their punishment, but they have an appointed time which they cannot escape. The same could be said for the cities. We destroyed them when they behaved wickedly, and We appointed a set time for their destruction.*

The native religions that had been practiced for time out of mind were all false and condemned in every way.

The Damned Knew That the Religion of Their Fathers Was Wrong

37:11 *Ask the Meccans whether they or the angels are the stronger creation? We created men from firm clay.*

37:12 *Truly you [Mohammed] are amazed when they mock. When they [the Meccans] are warned, they pay no attention. When they see a sign, they begin to mock and say, "This is obviously magic. What? Will we be resurrected after we are nothing but dust and bones? And what about our ancestors?"*

37:18 *Tell them, "Yes! And you will be disgraced." There will be a single cry, and they will look around and say, "Oh, woe to us!" This is the day of reckoning. This is the Judgment Day that you said was a lie.*

37:22 *Gather together the unjust, their consorts [the demons], and the false gods they worshiped besides Allah and point them down the road to Hell. Stop them because they must be questioned. "What is wrong with you that you do not help each other?"*

37:26 *But on this day, they will submit to Allah and blame one another. They will say, "You [the demons] used to come to us from the right-hand side [the side of a good omen]." But they [the demons] will answer, "No, it was you who did not believe. We had no power over you. No, you were a wicked people. Our Lord's sentence has been passed upon us, and we will surely taste our punishment. We misled you because we were lost." Therefore, they will be partners in punishment that day.*

37:34 *Truly, that is how We deal with the guilty, because when they were told that there is no god but Allah, they swelled with pride and said, "Should we abandon our gods for a crazy poet?"*

37:37 *No! He [Mohammed] comes truthfully and confirms the prophets of old. You will surely taste the painful punishment, and you will be punished for what you have done, all except the sincere servants of Allah! They will have a fixed banquet of fruits; and they will be honored in the Garden of delight, facing one another on couches. A cup filled from a gushing spring will be passed among them, crystal clear and delicious to those who drink. It causes neither pain nor intoxication. And with them are companions [houris] with large eyes and modest glances, fair like a sheltered egg. They will ask one another questions. One of them will say, "I had a close friend who said, 'Are you one of those who accept the truth? What? When we have died, and become dust and bones, will we really be judged?'"*

37:54 *He will say to those around him, "Will you look?" Looking down, he saw his friend in the depths of Hell. And he will say to him, "By Allah, you almost destroyed me. Except for my Lord's favor, I surely would have been one of those who came with you into torment."*

37:58 *"Is it not true that we will not die," say the blessed, "except for our first death and that we have escaped the torment?" Certainly this is the supreme achievement! For something like this, a striver should strive!*

37:62 *Is this a better feast than the Zaqqum tree [the tree of Hell]? We have certainly made the tree to torment the wicked. It grows at the bottom of Hell. Its fruit is like the heads of vipers. The damned will certainly eat it until their bellies fill. Then they will drink a mixture of boiling water. Then they will return to the Fire.*

37:69 *The damned knew that the religion of their fathers was wrong, but they still followed the old religion. Even before them, most of the ancients erred, though We had sent messengers to warn them. See what happened to these warned ones except for Allah's true servants?*

Would They Hasten Our Vengeance?

37:149 *Ask them [the Meccans] whether their Lord has daughters [the Meccans said that angels were the daughters of Allah], while they have sons. Did they watch as We created the angels female? Is it not a lie of their own making when they say, "Allah has begotten children?" They are certainly liars. Would he have preferred daughters to sons? What reasons do you have for thinking that?*

37:156 *Will you listen to this warning, or do you have a clear authority? Produce your scripture if you are telling the truth. And they imagine him to be kin with the jinn, but the jinn have long known that they will appear before Allah.*

37:159 *Glory to Allah. He is free from what they falsely attribute to him. His faithful servants are sincere and devoted. Surely, you [the Meccans] and what you worship can not stir up anyone against Allah, except those who will burn in Hell. Everyone of us [the believers] has an appointed place, and we range ourselves in ranks and declare Allah's glory.*

37:167 *And if those unbelievers say, "If we had a revelation sent to us from the men of old, we would surely have been one of Allah's faithful servants." They do not believe the Koran, but they will learn its truth eventually. Our word went out long ago to Our servants, the messengers so they would be helped and so Our armies would be victorious.*

37:174 *So turn away from them [the Meccans] for a while and watch them, because they will soon see their doom. Would they hasten Our vengeance? When it comes home to them, those who have been warned will have an evil morning. So turn away from them for a while, and watch them, because they too will see their doom.*
37:180 *The glory of Allah, the Lord of all greatness, is far above what they ascribe to him. Peace be on His apostles! Praise be to Allah, the Lord of the worlds.*

We Will Defend You against Those Who Scoff

15:90 *We will punish those who foster division and break up the Koran into parts. By your Lord, We will certainly call them to account for all their deeds, so openly proclaim what you are commanded, and turn away from the polytheists.*
15:95 *Surely, We will defend you against those who scoff, who set up other gods with Allah. But they will come to know. We know that your heart is troubled at their words, but celebrate the praises of your Lord, and be one of those who bow down in adoration. And serve your Lord until death overtakes you.*

Leave the Wicked upon Their Knees

19:66 *Man says, "What? When I am dead, will I then be resurrected?" Does man not remember that We created him before out of nothing?*
19:68 *I swear by your Lord, We will certainly gather them together with the devils; then We will force them to their knees around Hell; then We will take from each group those who were most stubbornly rebellious against beneficent Allah.*
19:70 *Certainly, We know better than any who is most deserving of being burned there. There is none among you who will avoid it; this is an inevitable decree of your Lord. We will rescue those who guard against evil and leave the wicked upon their knees. When Our clear signs are recited to them, the unbelievers will say to those who believe, "Which of our two sides is in the better position? Which has the stronger assembly? "How many generations have We destroyed before them that were more wealthy and more splendid looking? "*
19:75 *Say: As for those who are in error, Allah will prolong their days—until they see what they were threatened with, whether it is worldly punishment, or the Hour of Judgment—then they will realize who is in the weaker position and who has the weaker force. Allah increases the guidance of those already guided. Lasting good works are better in your Lord's eyes for reward and give a better return.*
19:77 *Have you seen someone who rejects Our signs and says, "I will certainly be given wealth and children?" Does he have knowledge of the unseen, or has he made peace with Allah? No! We will certainly record*

what he says and prolong his period of punishment. We will inherit the things he speaks of, and he will come before Us, poor and alone.

19:81 *They have taken other gods besides Allah to give themselves power and glory. Instead, they [the false gods] will soon reject their [the unbelievers] worship and will become their enemies. Do you not see that We send the devils against the unbelievers to urge them into sin? Do not rush hastily against them, because We allot them only a limited number of days.*

19:85 *One day We will gather the righteous and bring them before Allah to receive honors, and We will drive the guilty into Hell like a thirsty herd of cattle driven to water; none will have the power to intercede except those who have received Allah's permission.*

19:88 *They [the Christians] say, "Allah has fathered a son." Certainly you have said a monstrous thing! It might almost tear the heavens apart, and split the earth in two, and cause the mountains to crumble to pieces, that they ascribe a son to Allah. It is not consistent with Allah's majesty that He should father a son!*

19:93 *There is no one in the heavens or earth that does not approach Allah as a servant. He has taken note of them and numbered them exactly. Each of them will come alone to Him on Judgment Day. But Allah will certainly show love to those who believe and do good deeds.*

19:97 *So We have made this Koran easy in your language [Arabic] so that you may use it to give glad tidings to the righteous and warnings to the contentious. How many generations have We destroyed before them? Can you find a single one of them now, or hear as much as a whisper from them?*

Truly, This Religion of Yours Is the Only Religion

21:92 *Truly, this religion of yours is the only religion, and I am your Lord, so worship Me. But they have broken their religion [Christianity] into sects, and yet they will all return to Us. Whoever does good things and believes will not have his efforts denied. We will record everything.*

21:95 *There is a ban on those cities We have destroyed. They will not return until Gog and Magog [barbarians who figure in the Final Days] are let loose and they hurry from every hillside and the true promise draws near. Then the unbelievers will stare in horror and say, "Oh no! We lived in ignorance. No, we were unjust."*

21:98 *Surely you and those you worship besides Allah are nothing but fuel for Hell. You will be sent there. If these were gods, they would not be sent down into it, but all of them will live there forever. There they will do nothing but weep, and that will be the only thing that they hear.*

21:101 *But those for whom We have ordained, good things will be far away. They will not hear the slightest sound from Hell as they live according to their soul's desire. The great Terror [Judgment Day] will cause them no grief. Instead, the angels will greet them every day by saying, "This is your day, the day that you were promised, the day when We roll the heavens up like a scroll. Just as We made the first creation, so We will reproduce it. This is a promise We are bound to. Truly it is something We will fulfill. After the message was given to Our servants We wrote in the Psalms, My righteous servants will inherit the earth." Surely there is a message here for those who worship Allah.*

My Lord Does Not Care for You or Your Prayers

25:56 *And We have sent you only to bring good news and to warn. Say: I do not ask any reward from you except that those who will, may follow the straight path to his Lord. Put your trust in Him who lives and never dies. Celebrate His praise. He fully knows the faults of His servants. He, who created the heavens and the earth and everything in between in just six days is firmly established on the throne of authority. Allah, most gracious! Ask any wise person about Him. But when it is said to them, "Bow down before the merciful Allah," they say, "Who is merciful Allah? Should we bow down to what you tell us to?" It adds to their aversion.*
25:61 *Blessed is He who placed the constellations in the heavens and placed there the sun and moon. It is He who made the night and the day to follow each other for the benefit of those who desire to consider Allah, or who desire to be grateful.*
25:63 *The servants of Allah are those who walk humbly on the earth, and when the ignorant speak to them, they say, "Peace!" The servants of Allah are those who spend the night worshiping their Lord, bowing down and standing. They say, "Lord, turn away from us the wrath of Hell because its torment is endless. It is certainly an evil abode and a terrible resting place." They are neither extravagant nor miserly in their spending, but instead keep a just balance between the two. They do not call upon other gods along with Allah and do not kill those whom Allah has forbidden to be killed [other Muslims] except for just cause. They do not fornicate. The unbelievers not only pay the penalty, but their punishment on the Day of Reckoning will be doubled, and they will remain disgraced in Hell forever, unless they repent, believe, and do good works.*
25:70 *Allah is forgiving and merciful, and whoever repents and does good has truly turned to Allah with an acceptable and true conversion. The believers do not bear false witness and pass by frivolity with dignity. They, when reminded of their Lord's revelations, do not act like they are deaf and blind. They say, "Lord, make our wives and children the apples of our eyes, and make us examples for those who fear you." The believers will be rewarded with the highest places in Paradise because of their steadfast patience. They will be greeted there with greetings and salutations, and they will live there forever. What a happy abode and resting place!*

25:77 *Say to the unbelievers: My Lord does not care for you or your prayers. You have rejected the truth, so sooner or later, a punishment will come.*

Truly, You Say a Dreadful Thing

17:40 *What? Has your Lord honored you by giving you sons while He has taken for Himself daughters from among the angels [the Meccans said that angels were the daughters of Allah]? Truly, you say a dreadful thing.*

17:41 *In this Koran, We have explained things in several ways so that they [the Meccans] may take heed, but it only increases their aversion. Say: If, as they say, there were other gods besides Allah, then they would have tried to find a way to the Lord of the throne. Glory to Him! He is exalted far above what they say. The seven heavens, the earth, and everyone in them celebrates His glory. There is not a single creature that does not celebrate His glory. But you do not understand their celebrations of glory. He is kind and forgiving.*

The Wicked Will See the Fire

18:47 *One day we will remove the mountains, and you will see the earth as a level plain. We will gather mankind together, and We will omit no one. They will be brought before Allah, in ranks and it will be said to them, "You have been brought before Us naked like We created you in the beginning. You thought that We would not keep the appointment We promised you."*

18:49 *And the book of life's deeds will be placed before each, and you will see the wicked become alarmed at what it contains. They will say, "Woe to us! What kind of book is this? It omits nothing, either small or large, but instead records everything." They will discover all of their actions there to confront them, and your Lord will not deal unjustly with anyone.*

18:50 *Recall when We said to the angels, "Bow down to Adam." They all bowed down except Iblis [Satan]. He was a jinn, and he rebelled against his Lord's command. Will you choose him and his offspring as your protector instead of Me when they are your sworn enemies? This is an evil exchange for the wicked!*

18:51 *I did not make them to witness the creation of the heavens and the earth or their own creation. Nor do I choose seducers to be My helpers. One day I will say, "Call to those whom you thought were My partners." They will call to their false gods, but they will get no response, and We will place a deadly barrier between them. The wicked will see the Fire, and they will realize that they are about to fall into it, and they will not find any escape.*

The Meccans had many leaders who resisted Mohammed.

38:55 *But the evil have a terrible place waiting for them—Hell—where they will be burned. What a wretched bed to lie on! Let them taste boiling water and icy fluid and other vile things. Their leaders will be told, "This group will be thrown head first into the fire with you. There is no welcome for them. They will burn in the fire!"*
38:60 *They will say to those who misled them, "No! There is no welcome for you. You brought this wretched place upon us!" They will say, "Lord, double the punishment for those who brought this upon us." They will say, "Why do we not see the people who we thought were wicked, whom we mocked? Were we mistaken, or have our eyes missed them?" Truly, that is fitting and just—the mutual accusations of the people of the fire.*
38:65 *Say: I am here to warn you. There is no god but Allah, the One, the Almighty! Lord of the heavens and the earth, and everything in between, the mighty, the most forgiving! Say: This is an important message that you turn away from! I had no knowledge of the dispute between those on high. Nothing has been revealed to me except that I am here to warn you.*

I183 Mohammed continued to preach the glory of Allah and condemn the Quraysh religion. He told them their way of life was wrong, their ancestors would burn in Hell, he cursed their gods, he despised their religion and divided the community, setting one tribesman against the others. The Quraysh felt that this was all past bearing. Tolerance had always been their way. Many clans, many gods, many religions. Another religion was fine, why did Mohammed demean them?

44:7 *Lord of the heavens and of the earth and everything in between if you are firm in your faith. There is no god except him! He gives life and causes death! Your Lord and the Lord of your ancestors!*

We Throw the Truth at Falsehood, and It Crushes Its Head

21:16 *We did not create the heavens and the earth and everything in between for entertainment. If We had wanted a diversion, We could have found amusement in Our presence, as if We would ever do such a thing! No, We throw the truth at falsehood, and it crushes its head. There you have it: falsehood is destroyed! Woe to you for the lies you say about Us!*
21:19 *Every creature in the heavens and on earth belongs to Him. Those in His presence are not too proud to serve Him, nor do they get tired of the service. They praise Him day and night. They never stop.*
21:21 *Have they found earthly gods that can raise the dead? If there had been other gods besides Allah, then there would be utter confusion in the heavens and on the earth. Glory to Allah, the Lord of the throne, far beyond their lies! He cannot be questioned about His actions, but they shall be made to answer for theirs.*

21:24 Have they taken other gods besides Allah? Say: Bring your proof. This is my Message and the Message that was brought by the prophets before me. But most of them do not know the truth and turn away. Even before you, We have never sent a messenger to whom We did not reveal that there is no god but Me; therefore, worship and serve Me.
21:26 Men look to the angels and say, "Merciful Allah has children." Glory to Him! But no, the angels are honored servants. They speak only when spoken to, and they follow only His command. He knows their future and their past. They can not intercede for anyone without His approval, and they tremble in fear of Him. If an angel should say, "I am a god like Him," We would punish it with Hell. That is how We repay the wicked.
21:30 Do not the unbelievers realize that the heavens and the earth were a single mass before We cut them apart? We made every living creature from water. Why will they not believe? We placed the mountains firmly on the earth to prevent them from shaking, and We made broad gaps between them to act as paths for the people to be guided. We have made the sky like a secure canopy and still they turn away from the signs. It is He Who created the night and the day and the sun and the moon. Each floats along in its celestial orbit.
21:34 We have never given immortality to a human. If you [Mohammed] have to die, should they [the Meccans] live forever? Every soul shall taste death, and to judge you, We will test you with good and evil. You must return to Us.

25:1 Blessed is He who sent down to His servant [Mohammed] a standard of behavior so that he might warn all people. His is the kingdom of the heavens and the earth. He has never begotten a son, nor has He any equal. He has created all things and has decreed all destinies.

The Unbeliever Is Satan's Ally

25:45 Have you considered how your Lord makes the shadow grow? If He wished, He could make it stationary. But We have made the sun its guide; then We bring it to Ourselves, a gradual retreat. It is He who makes the night like a covering for you and sleep a repose and makes the day a resurrection.
25:48 He sends the winds bearing good news before His mercy, and We send down pure water from heaven so that We may give life to a dead planet and quench the thirst of Our creations, animals and great numbers of people. We distribute it among them so that they celebrate Our praises, but most men refuse to be anything except ungrateful. If We had wished, We could have sent a messenger to every city. So do not listen to the unbelievers, but instead strive against them with all your might.
25:53 He let loose the two seas, one sweet and refreshing, the other salty and bitter. Between the two He has set a barrier, an impassible obstruction. He

has created man from water and made blood and marriage relationships for him because your Lord is all powerful. And still they worship others besides Allah who can neither help nor hurt them. The unbeliever is Satan's ally against his Lord.

18:109 ***Say: If the sea were ink for the words of my Lord, it would dry up before His words were exhausted, even if We added an equally-sized sea to the first.***
18:110 ***Say: I am only a man like you. It has been revealed to me that your Allah is the only god. Therefore, whoever hopes to meet his Lord should do good deeds and not join another in worship besides Allah.***

I183 One day at the Kabah the Meccans were discussing Mohammed and his enmity towards them, when Mohammed arrived. He kissed the Black Stone of the Kabah and started past them as he circumambulated [walk around the Kabah and repeat prayers] the Kabah. Each time he passed by them they insulted him. On the third round, he stopped and said, "Listen to me, by Allah I will bring you slaughter." The Quraysh were stunned at his threat. They said, "Mohammed, you have never been a violent man, go away."

I184 The next day many of the Quraysh were at the Kabah when Mohammed arrived. They crowded around him and said, "Are you the one who condemned our gods and our religion?" Mohammed answered that he was the one. One of them grabbed him and Abu Bakr, Mohammed's chief follower, pressed forward and said, "Would you kill a man for saying that Allah is his Lord?" They let him go. This was worst treatment that Mohammed received in Mecca.

But Mohammed was not afraid. He was on a divine mission.

21:107 ***We have sent you only to be a mercy for all people. Say: It has been revealed to me that Allah is the only god. Will you submit to Him? If they turn their backs, then say, "I have truthfully warned you alike. I do not know if Judgment Day will come sooner or later. Allah knows what is said openly and what you hide. I only know that you will be tried and that you may enjoy yourself for awhile." Say: My Lord judges with truth. Our Lord is the beneficent Allah Whose help is sought against lies you ascribe to Him.***

He continued to speak of Allah and the Koran. Many times in the Koran we find self-proofs of the validity of the Koran and the proof of Allah.

26:1 ***TA. SIN. MIN. These are the verses of the Book that make things clear.***

26:3 *You may torment yourself [Mohammed] if they do not believe. If We wanted, We could send them a sign from the sky that would force them to humbly bow their heads, but every new warning they receive from Allah is ignored. They have rejected the message, but they will learn the truth of what they mocked! Do they not see the earth and how much of so many noble things We have made there? Truly, there is a sign there, but most do not believe. And surely, your Lord, He is the mighty, the merciful.*

Embrace the Fire This Day

36: 45 *When they are told, "Beware of what is in front of you and what is behind you so that you might receive mercy," they pay no attention. All of the many signs sent by their Lord were met with rejection. When they are told, "Give alms from the bounty you receive from Allah," the unbelievers say to the believers, "Should we feed those whom Allah could feed if he wished? You are clearly mistaken."*

36:48 *And they say, "If you are telling the truth, when will this promise be fulfilled?" They wait for a single blast, which will surprise them as they argue amongst themselves. They will have no chance to settle affairs or to return to their families. When the trumpet is blown, they will pour from the graves and hasten to their Lord.*

36:52 *They will say, "Oh, woe to us! Who has raised us from our sleep? This is what the gracious Allah promised. The messengers told us the truth." It will only be a single blast, and they will be immediately brought before Us. On that day, no soul will be wronged in the least, and everyone will get what they deserve. Surely on that day, the dwellers of Paradise will be busy with their joys. They and their wives will recline on thrones in pleasant shade. Every fruit will be there for their enjoyment, and they will have everything they ask for. "Peace!" A word of salutation from the most merciful Lord.*

36:59 *But you sinners will be set apart this day! Did I not order you, the sons of Adam [humanity], that you must not worship Satan because he was your sworn enemy and that you should worship Me because that was the right path? But he led a great many of you astray. Did you not, then, understand? This is the Hell you were promised. Embrace the Fire this day, because you did not believe.*

36:65 *We will seal up their mouths that day. Their hands will speak to us, and their feet will testify to everything they did. If We had wished, We could have certainly blinded them; then they would grope to find the way. How could they see? If We had wished, We certainly could have fixed them in place, unable to move or retreat.*

36:68 *If We grant long life, We demand a return to the earlier, weaker condition. Do they not understand? We have not taught the prophet poetry; it is not good enough for him. This is nothing but a warning and a clear Koran, to warn the living and to justly indict the unbelievers.*

36:71 *Do they not see that Our hands created cattle to be under their mastery and that We have subjected them for man's use so that some are used for transport and others for eating? Man enjoys many beneficial uses and nourishment from them. Why will he not be thankful?*
36:74 *And they take other gods to worship beside Allah hoping that they might help. The false gods do not have the power to help them but will instead be gathered together and brought to judgment. Do not let their words cause you grief. We know what they do secretly and what they do openly.*

Only Merciful Allah Could Keep Them Aloft

67:6 *The torment of Hell waits for those who do not believe in their Lord, and the journey there is terrible! When they are thrown in, they will hear the Fire roaring as it boils. It will almost burst with fury. Every time another group is thrown in, its keepers will ask them, "Did someone not warn you?"*
67:9 *They will say. Yes. Someone came to warn us, but we rejected him and said, 'Allah has revealed nothing to us. You are deluded.'"*
67:10 *They will say, "If we had listened or understood, we would not have been among the prisoners of the Fire." They will acknowledge their sins, but mercy is far away from the prisoners of the Fire.*
67:12 *However, forgiveness and a great reward waits for those who secretly fear their Lord. Whether you speak openly or secretly, He knows everything in your heart. Should He not know His creations? He is the subtle, the aware. He smoothed the earth for you, so walk its paths and eat the food He provides. Everything will return to Him after death.*
67:16 *Are you confident that Allah in heaven will not open the earth and swallow you in an earthquake? Are you sure that Allah in heaven will not send a hurricane against you? You will understand My warning then! It is true that your ancestors rejected their prophets. Was not My wrath terrible?*
67:19 *Do they not see the birds above, spreading and folding their wings? Only merciful Allah could keep them aloft. He watches over everything.*
67:20 *Who could help you like an army except merciful Allah? The unbelievers are totally deluded. Who would provide for you if He withheld His provisions? Still, they continue to be proud and reject Him. Is the person groveling along on his face better than those who walk upright on a straight path?*
67:23 *Say: He created you and gave you the gifts of sight, hearing, and feeling. Still, few are grateful. Say: He has sown you in the ground, and He will gather you. And they say, "If you are telling the truth, when will this promise be fulfilled?"*
67:26 *Say: Only Allah has knowledge of the time. I am only sent to publicly warn. But when they see it approach, the faces of the unbelievers will*

grieve. It will be said, "This is what you have been predicting." Say: What do you think? Whether Allah destroys me and my followers, or grants us mercy, who will protect the unbelievers from a terrible punishment? Say: He is the merciful. We believe in Him and trust Him, and you will learn later who is clearly in error. Say: What do you think? If all water sank into the earth, who would bring you clear running water?

But Their Hearts Are Ignorant and Confused about the Koran

23:62 *We do not place upon any soul a burden that is beyond its ability, and We possess a record which speaks the truth. They will never be wronged.*

23:63 *But their hearts are ignorant and confused about the Koran, and there are actions in which they will persist until the time Our punishment overtakes them when they will cry for help. It will be said to them, "Do not cry for help today, because We will certainly not help you. My signs were recited to you, but you turned your back on them in arrogance, talking nonsense about the Koran, like someone telling fables at bedtime."*

23:68 *Do they not consider the Word of Allah, or has nothing new come to them since the time of their ancestors? Is it that they do not recognize their messenger and so reject him? Or do they say, "He is possessed."? No, he has brought the truth to them, but most of them hate the truth. If the truth did not contradict their desires, then the heavens and the earth and everything contained in them would have been corrupted and ruined. No! We have brought them their warning, but they turn away.*

23:72 *Is it because you ask them for some reward? Your Lord's reward is best. Of all who reward, He is best. Certainly, you call them to the straight and narrow way. Those who deny the afterlife are straying from that way. If We were to show them mercy and relieve them of their troubles, they would still persist in their wickedness, blindly wandering on. We have already punished them, but still they do not submit to their Lord, and they do not humble themselves. When We open the gate leading to their severe punishment, they will despair at the thought.*

23:78 *He created and gave you the senses of sight, hearing, feeling, and reason. Little thanks do you give Him. He has caused you to multiply across the earth, and you will be gathered and returned to Him. It is He who gives life and death, and He changes the night into the day. Do you not understand?*

23:81 *On the contrary. They [the Meccans] say the things that their ancestors said. They say, "When we are dead and have become dust and bones, will we really be resurrected? We and our fathers before us have been promised such a thing. This is nothing except an ancient fable."*

23:84 *Say: If you know, to whom does the earth and everything on it belong?*

23:85 *They will say, "Allah." Say: Will you not, then, reflect?*

23:86 *Say: Who is the Lord of the seven heavens and the Lord of the glorious throne?*

23:87 *They will say, "They belong to Allah." Say: Will you not, then, refrain from evil?*

23:88 *Say: In Whose hands is the kingdom of all things, He Who protects everything but is not protected by any? Tell me if you know.*

23:89 *They will say, "Allah's." Say: Then why are you deceived? We have brought the truth to them, but they are liars.*

23:91 *Allah has never begotten a son, nor is there another god besides Him. If there were, then each god would have made its own kingdom, and some would have certainly overpowered others. Glory to Allah! He is far above the powers attributed to Him. He knows what is seen and unseen. He is exalted high above those whom some call his equal.*

How Could There Be Another God besides Allah?

27:59 *Say: Praise be to Allah and peace be on His servants whom He has chosen for His message. Who is better, Allah or the false gods they associate with Him? Is He not the best, Who created the heavens and the earth, and Who sends rain down from heaven for you, which We then cause to grow luxurious gardens? You do not have the power to cause trees to grow. How could there be another god besides Allah? Still, they try to say that there are equals to Him! Is He not the best Who set the earth firmly in place and placed rivers and immovable mountains there and placed a barrier between the two seas [fresh water and salt water]? How could there be another god besides Allah? Still, they try to say that there are equals to Him! Is He not the best Who answers the cries of distressed souls when they call to Him and relieves their suffering and makes you the inheritors of the earth? How could there be another god besides Allah? How few keep this in mind! Is He not the best Who guides you through the darkness of the land and the sea and sends the winds as heralds of His mercy? How could there be another god besides Allah? Allah is far above what they associate with Him.*

27:64 *Is He not the best Who created life and then repeats it, and Who provides for you from the heavens and the earth? How could there be another god besides Allah? Say: If you are telling the truth, then bring your proof. Say: No one in heaven or earth, no one except Allah, knows the unseen. They do not know when they will be raised from the dead. They know even less about the hereafter. No, they have great doubts about it. No, they are blind to it.*

27:67 *The unbelievers say, "What? Will we really be raised from the dead when we have become dust like our fathers? It is true that we were promised this, ourselves and our fathers, too. This is nothing but ancient fables."*

27:69 *Say: Travel through the land and see what becomes of the wicked. Do not grieve over them and do not be distressed because of their plots against you. They say, "If you are telling the truth, when will this promise come to pass?"*
27:72 *Say: Perhaps some of what you seek to hurry towards is near. Your Lord is filled with goodness toward men, but most are not thankful. Your Lord knows full well what is hidden in their hearts, as well as everything they reveal. There is nothing hidden in the heavens or earth that is not recorded in a clear book.*

86:15 *They plot and scheme against you [Mohammed], and I plot and scheme against them. Therefore, deal calmly with the unbelievers and leave them alone for a while.*
36:37 *The night is a sign for them. We withdraw it from the day and plunge them into darkness, and the sun runs its mandated course. That is the decree of Allah, the Powerful, The All-Knowing. Consider the moon; it follows the regulated course We set until it returns again to the beginning, like the rebirth of an old withered palm-stalk. The sun may not outreach the moon, and the night may not pass the day—each floats along in its own orbit.*
36:41 *Bearing their race away through the flood in a heavily-laden ark [Noah] is a sign for them. We have created other, similar vessels [ships] which they voyage. If We wished, we could drown them with none to hear their cries. They cannot be saved except through Our mercy, and so they may enjoy themselves for a little longer.*

Do You See a Crack in the Sky?

67:1 *Blessed is He whose hands hold the kingdom and has power over all things; Who created life and death to determine who conducts themselves best; and He is the mighty, the forgiving! He created and raised seven heavens, one above the other. You can not see one defect in merciful Allah's creation. Do you see a crack in the sky? Look again and again. Your vision will blur from looking, but you will find no defects.*

27:86 *Do they not realize that We have made the night for them to rest in and the day to give them light? Surely here is a sign to people who believe. And on the day that the trumpet sounds, everyone in the heavens and the earth will be stricken with terror except those whom Allah is pleased to save and all will come humbly to Him. And you will see the mountains, which you think are solid, float away like so many clouds. Such is the work of Allah, who orders all things. He is aware of everything that you do.*

A TRIBAL CHIEF TRIES TO CUT A DEAL

I186 One day while the Quraysh were in council one of the chiefs, Utba, decided to approach Mohammed and see if he could make a deal that would please everybody. Things were only getting worse about Mohammed and the others said to go and try. So he went to the Kabah and there was Mohammed. "Nephew, you have come to us with an important matter. But you have divided the community, ridiculed our customs, and insulted our forefathers. See if any of my suggestions can help in this matter. If you want money, we will give you money. If you want honor we will make you our king. If you are possessed we will get you a physician."

I186 Mohammed said that he represented the only Allah. His teachings were beautiful, and then he began to recite the glorious poetry and imagery of the Koran. The tribal chief was impressed with the beauty of Mohammed's words and left.

I186 When the tribal chief returned to the Quraysh, he said, "Leave him alone, his words are beautiful. If other Arabs kill him, your problem is solved. If he becomes sovereign over all, you will share in his glory. His power will become your power and you can make money off his success." They replied that Mohammed had bewitched him.

Mohammed spoke beautiful words about Islam.

> 76:1 ***Have not eons of time passed over man when he was not even a thought? We have created man from the sexual union so that We could test him, and We have gifted him with senses. Whether he is thankful or ungrateful, We taught him to do the right thing.***

We Protect Them from Every Cursed Devil

> 15:16 ***We placed the constellations in the heavens and made them beautiful for all to see, and We protect them from every cursed devil [uncertain, perhaps the jinns], except, perhaps, those few who sneak to listen. Those are pursued by fiery comets. And We have spread the earth out like a carpet and set strong mountains upon it and caused every possible thing to grow there. And We have given it the means to provide for you and those who are not dependent upon you. There is nothing that does not come from Us. And We will not send it down, except in preordained measure. We send the winds to fertilize and cause the rain to fall from the sky, giving you abundant water to drink, even though you are not the guardian of its stores. We are the givers of life and death and are the heirs of all things. We know who of you hurries forward, and who lags behind. Certainly, your Lord will gather them all together because He is wise and knowing.***

15:85 *We created the heavens and the earth and everything in between for a just end. And, certainly, the Hour will come. So forgive with gracious forgiveness because your Lord is the creator of all things, the all-knowing.*

We Can Certainly Take It Away

23:12 *We created man from fine clay, which We firmly placed as a seed in a safe home [the womb]. Then We shaped the seed into a clot of blood. From the clot of blood We fashioned a lump of tissue, and from the lump We created bones that We then clothed with flesh, which We caused to grow into another creation. So blessed be Allah, the best of creators. After creation, and after some time, you will certainly die. You will be resurrected on the Judgment Day.*

23:17 *We have made the seven heavens over you. We are never careless with creation. We sent water down from heaven according to a proper measure, and We caused it to sink into the earth, and We can certainly take it away. With water, We grow gardens with palm trees and vineyards for you. In them you have abundant fruit, which you eat, and a tree [the olive tree] that grows on Mount Sinai, which produces oil and an edible relish. And the cattle are a lesson for you. We give you the milk to drink, as well as the other benefits you gain from their bodies and their meat, which you use for food. You are carried on both them and ships.*

And Truly Your Religion Is the One Religion

23:49 *And We gave the Book to Moses so that they might be guided.*

23:50 *And We made the son of Mary and his mother a sign, and We gave them a lofty abode for shelter, quiet and well provided with meadows and springs.*

23:51 *Oh messengers! Eat the things that are good, and do the right thing. I am aware of what you do. And truly your religion is the one religion, and I am your Lord, so fear and obey Me. But mankind has broken religion into sects, each rejoicing at that which they have retained. So leave them in their confusion and ignorance for a while.*

23:55 *Do they think that because We have given them an abundance of wealth and sons that We would rush to them with every blessing? No, they do not understand. But those who live in awe for fear of their Lord; and who believe in their Lord's signs; and who accept no other gods with their Lord; and who give charitably with fear in their hearts because they know they will return to their Lord—these will rush for the good things, and they will be the first to attain them.*

23:62 *We do not place upon any soul a burden that is beyond its ability, and We possess a record which speaks the truth. They will never be wronged.*

17:80 *Say: Lord, cause me to have a good birth and a good death and give me from your presence the power to assist me. And say: Truth has come and falsehood has perished. Falsehood is, by its nature, a thing that perishes. And We send down in the Koran things which are a healing and a mercy to believers, but it only adds to the ruin of the wicked. Yet when We give Our favors to man, he turns away and acts arrogantly, and when evil afflicts him, he despairs. Say: Every one acts according to his own nature, and your Lord knows best who is best guided in his path.*

17:85 *They will ask you about the spirit [probably the angel Gabriel]. Say: The spirit is commanded by my Lord, and you are given only a little knowledge about it. If We wished, We could take Our revelations away from you. Then you would find no one to intercede with us on your behalf except as a mercy from your Lord. Surely His kindness to you is great.*

They will be thrown face down into the Fire

27:89 *Those who do good deeds will be rewarded beyond their due. They will be safe from terror that day. And if any do evil, they will be thrown face down into the Fire. Should your reward not reflect your actions?*

27:91 *Say: I am commanded only to worship the Lord of this land who has made it sacred, and to whom all things belong. I am commanded to be a Muslim, one who has surrendered to Allah, and to recite the Koran. If anyone does good things, they do so only for the good of their souls, and if any go astray, say: I am only here to warn.*

27:93 *And say: Praise be to Allah who will soon show you His signs so that you shall know them. Your Lord is not unaware of what you do.*

18:45 *Tell them a parable about the life of this world. It is like the rain which We send down from the skies. The earth's plants absorb it, but soon they become dry and broken and scattered on the wind. Allah has power over all things. Riches and children are decorations of the life in this world. Good deeds, which endure, are better in the eyes of your Lord as rewards and the best foundation for hope.*

There were frequent references in the Koran about the Koran.

44:1 *HA. MIM. By the book that makes everything clear!*

44:3 *We revealed it on a blessed night—because We are always warning man—on a night when every command is made clear by Our command. We are always sending Our messengers as a mercy from your Lord. He hears and knows everything.*

43:1 *HA. MIM. I swear by the Book that makes everything clear We have made it a Koran in Arabic so that you may understand. It is the perfect transcript of the original Book kept by us: lofty and full of wisdom.*

17:105 *"In truth We have revealed the Koran, and in truth has it descended. We have sent you to be nothing but a bearer of good news and to warn sinners. It is a Koran that We have revealed in sections so that you may read it to the people in intervals. We have revealed it by stages."*

17:107 *Say: Whether you believe in it or not, those who have previously received its knowledge have fallen on their faces, worshipping when it is recited to them and saying: Glory be to Allah! Our Lord's promise has been fulfilled. They fall down on their faces weeping, and it adds to their humility.*

A *Book That Makes Things Clear*

27:1 *TA. SIN. These are the revelations of the Koran, a book that makes things clear, a guide and good news for the believers. The believers observe prayers and pay the poor tax and are convinced of the hereafter.*

27:4 *As for those who do not believe in the hereafter, We have made all of their actions seem desirable in their minds, so they stray from the right path. Terrible punishment waits for these people, and in the hereafter, these will be the biggest losers.*

27:6 *As for you [Mohammed], the Koran was given to you by the wise, the knowing Allah.*

20:112 *But those who believe and have done the right things will have no fear of wrong or loss. This is why We sent to you an Arabic Koran and explained in detail Our warnings so that they may fear Allah and heed them. Exalted above all is Allah, the King, the Truth! Do not hurry through its recital before its revelation is made complete to you. Instead say, "Lord, increase my knowledge."*

This Is How We influenced the Hearts of the Wicked

26:192 *This Book has come down from the Lord of the worlds. The faithful spirit [Gabriel] has come down with it upon your [Mohammed's] heart so that you may warn others in the clear Arabic language. Truly, it is foretold in the ancient scriptures. Is it not a sign that the learned men of the Israelites recognized? If We had revealed it to any of the non-Arabs and he had recited it to them, they would not have believed in it.*

26:200 *This is how We influenced the hearts of the wicked. They will not believe in it until they see the painful punishment. And it will come upon them suddenly when they do not expect it. They will say, "Can we have a reprieve?"*

Mohammed continued to make it clear that not believing the words he brought from Allah would lead to a violent and painful eternity.

54:1 *The Hour of Judgment is near, and the moon is split in two. If they [unbelievers] see a miracle, they just turn away and say, "This is just an illusion." They reject the warning and follow their own cravings, but everything is settled in its own time. They have received warnings—profound wisdom—that should deter them, but warnings do no good.*

54:6 *[Mohammed] Turn your back on them. On Judgment Day, when the summoner calls them to a terrible thing, they will come out of their graves with downcast eyes like wandering locusts scurrying to the summoner. The unbelievers will say, "This is the dreaded day!*

They Will Be Waited on by Eternally Young Boys

76:4 *We have prepared chains, fetters, and a blazing fire for the unbelievers.*

76:5 *The righteous, however, will drink cups filled from a camphor fountain—the fountain Allah's servants drink from—as it flows from place to place rewarding those who perform their vows and fear a day whose evil will spread far and wide. Even when they were hungry they gave their food to the poor, the orphan, and the prisoner. "We feed you for Allah's sake. We are not looking for reward or thanks from you. We are afraid of suffering and punishment from Allah."*

76:11 *But Allah saved them from the evil of that day and brought them happiness and joy. He rewarded their patience with Paradise and silk robes. Reclining on couches, none will suffer from extreme heat or cold. Trees will shade them, and fruit will dangle near by. Silver cups and crystal goblets will pass among them: silver cups, transparent as glass, their size reflecting the measure of one's deeds. They will be given ginger-flavored wine from the fountain called Salsabil. They will be waited on by eternally young boys. When you look at them you would think they were scattered pearls. When you see it, you will see a vast kingdom of delights. They will wear richly brocaded green silk robes with silver bracelets on their arms, and they will quench their thirst with a pure drink given them by their Lord. This will be your reward. Your efforts will not go unnoticed.*

76:23 *We have sent the Koran to you in stages to be a revelation. Wait patiently for Allah's command, and do not obey the wicked and the unbelieving. Celebrate your Lord's name in the morning, in the evening, and at night. Adore him and praise him all night long.*

76:27 *But men love the fleeting present and ignore the dreadful day ahead. We have created them, and We built them strong. When We want to, We will make others to replace them. This is certainly a warning. Whoever chooses, will take a straight path to his Lord. But unless Allah wills it, because he is knowing and wise, you will not succeed. You will receive his mercy if he chooses to give it, but he has prepared a terrible punishment for the wicked.*

Made It without Any Cracks

50:1 *KAF. By the glorious Koran: They [the Meccans] wonder that one of their own people should come to warn them. "This," say the unbelievers,*

"is a strange thing. What? When we are dead and turned to dust will we be resurrected? That is not possible."
50:4 *We know how many have been consumed by the earth; we have a record of accounts. They are confused, because they have denied the truth. Why do they not look at the sky and notice how We raised it and decorated it and made it without any cracks?*
50:7 *And the earth, We have spread it out and built the mountains and grew every kind of beautiful plant to be a vision and a reminder for every servant who turns to Allah. We sent down the rain with its blessings from heaven to irrigate the gardens and grow the harvest, and the tall palm trees, thick with date-bearing branches, for man's sustenance. This is how We give life to a dead country. The resurrection will happen the same way.*
50:12 *Other men before these rejected their prophets: the people of Noah and the men of Ar-Rass [unknown city] and the tribe of Thamud [the people of a ruined Nabatean city near Medina] and Ad [an ancient people of southern Arabia] and Pharaoh and the brethren of Lot and the people of the forest and the people of Tubba [the people of Himyar in Arabia]. All rejected their prophets; therefore, they were justly punished.*
50:15 *Were We so fatigued by the first creation that they doubted that We could make another? We created man, and We know what his soul says to him because We are closer to him than his jugular vein.*
50:17 *When the two angels [one angel will drive the person, and the other angel recorded the deeds of life] receive him for his accounting, one will sit on the right hand, the other on the left. He will not say a word that escapes a nearby watcher, and the stupor of certain death will bring him to a realization: "This is what you were trying to escape."*
50:20 *And a trumpet will sound. This is the threatened day! Every soul will come, each accompanied by an angel to drive [like cattle] and another to bear witness. (It will be said) "You paid no attention to your warnings, but your vision will be sharp today because We have removed the veil from your eyes." And his witnessing angel will say, "His record is here with me." And Allah will say, "Throw into Hell every ungrateful, rebellious, hinderer of the good, and every transgressor and doubter who worshiped other gods besides Allah. Throw them into the terrible torment."*
50:27 *His companion [the devil chained to the unbeliever] will say, "Allah, I did not lead him astray, but he was already in great error." Allah will say, "Do not argue in front of Me. I had warned you before. My sentence cannot be changed, and I am not unjust to man."*
50:30 *We will cry out to Hell that day, "Are you full?" And it will respond, "Are there more?" And Paradise will be brought close to the righteous. "For those who have repented and kept Allah's laws, this is what you*

have been promised. Those who secretly feared Allah, the merciful, and came contritely to him enter it in peace. This is the day of eternal life." There they will have everything they desire, and We can add still more.

How Many Generations We Have Destroyed before Them?

20:127 *This is how We will reward those who transgressed and did not believe in the sign of his Lord. Surely the punishment of the next world will be more terrible and more enduring. Are not they who walk over the ancient dead cities aware of how many generations We have destroyed before them? Surely there are signs here for reasonable men. If a respite had not already been granted by your Lord and a time fixed, their punishment would have already begun.*

20:130 *So be patient with what they say, and constantly celebrate your Lord's praise before the sun rises and before it sets, and for part of the night and at both ends of the day so that you may please Him. Do not strain your eye longing for the things We have given to others—the pleasures of the material world—so that We may test them. Your Lord's provision is better and more enduring.*

20:132 *Urge your people to pray, and urge them continually. We do not ask you to provide sustenance—We will provide for you, and the pious will be rewarded in the Hereafter. But they say, "If only he had come to us with a sign from his Lord!" But did clear proof not come to them from earlier scriptures?*

20:134 *If We had destroyed them with our punishments before it was time, they would have surely said, "Lord! How could we believe if you did not send an apostle to guide us before we were humbled and disgraced." Say: All of us are waiting, so wait. You will learn who has followed the straight and even path and who has received guidance.*

38:27 *We did not create the heavens and earth and everything in between for nothing. That is what the unbelievers think, but woe to the unbelievers because the fire of Hell awaits! Should We treat those who believe and do the right thing the same as those who spread evil over the world? Should We treat the Allah-fearing like the wicked?*

38:29 *We have sent a holy Book to you so that men may ponder its verses and that men of understanding may reflect. And We gave David a son, Solomon. He was an excellent servant because he constantly turned toward Us in repentance.*

He Does Not Share His Secret with Anyone except His Messenger

72:22 *Say: Surely, no one but Allah can protect me. Nor can I find any refuge except Him. My only task is to convey Allah's truth and His message. Those who rebel against Allah and His apostle have the fire of Hell, and they will remain there forever! They will doubt until they see with their own eyes what they are promised. Then they will know who is weaker in allies and fewer in number.*

72:25 *Say: I do not know whether the scourge you are promised is near, or whether Allah has assigned it to a distant day. He knows the secret. He does not share His secret with anyone except His messenger. He makes a guard march before and behind him [the messenger]. He will know if His apostles have delivered their Lord's messages. He knows everything about them and pays close attention to everything that concerns them.*

Repel Evil with What Is the Best

23:93 *Say: Oh my Lord! If it is your will that I witness what you have promised, then, Oh my Lord, do not place me with the unjust. Certainly, We are able to show you with what We have threatened them. Repel evil with what is the best. We are well aware of what they say about you.*

23:97 *And say: Oh my Lord! I seek refuge with You from the suggestions of the evil ones. And I seek refuge with you, my Lord, from their presence.*

23:99 *When death overtakes one of the wicked, he says, "Lord, send me back again so that I may do the good things that I have left undone." But, no, they are nothing but empty words. There is a barrier around the wicked that will remain until the Judgment Day. When the trumpet is blown, there will be no ties of kinship connecting them, nor will they ask about one another.*

23:102 *Those whose balance is heavy will attain salvation, but those whose balance is light will have lost their souls, and they will abide in Hell. The Fire will burn their faces, and their lips will twitch in pain. It will be said, "Were My signs not recited to you? Did you not reject them?"*

23:106 *They will say, "Lord, misfortune defeated us, and we were led astray. Lord, take us from here. If we return to evil, then surely we are unjust.*

23:108 *Allah will say, "Do not speak to Me, but instead be gone into the flames. Some of My servants would say, 'Lord, we believe. Forgive us and have mercy on us, because you are the most merciful.' But you ridiculed them so much that you forgot My warning while you were mocking them. I have rewarded them for their patience and constancy. They are the blissful."*

23:112 *Allah will ask, "How many years did you stay on earth?"*

23:113 *They will say, "We stayed a day or part of a day. Ask those who keep count."*

23:114 *Allah will say, "You stayed only a little while; if you had only known. Did you think that We had created you in vain and that you would not be brought back to us for judgment?"*

23:116 *Let Allah be exalted, the true king! There is no god but Him, the Lord of the throne of grace. If anyone invokes another god besides Allah, he does so without proof. His reckoning is with Allah, alone. Surely the unbelievers will not succeed.*

23:118 *Say: Oh my Lord! Forgive and have mercy on us, because you are the most merciful.*

They Do Nothing but Mock You

21:36 *When the unbelievers see you, they do nothing but mock you. They say, "Is this the man who talks so much about your gods?" But they reject any mention of the beneficent Allah.*
21:37 *Man is an impatient creature. Soon, when I show you My signs, you will not be in such a hurry. They say, "If you are telling the truth, when will this promise be fulfilled?" If only the unbelievers knew the time when they will be unable to keep the flames from their faces and backs when they cannot be saved. No. It will come upon them suddenly and will confound them. They will be unable to prevent it or to stop it. Other prophets have been mocked before you. Their mockers were destroyed by the same doom that they laughingly denied.*
21:42 *Say: Who will protect you from the wrath of gracious Allah? And still they turn away from the mention of their Lord. Do they have gods besides Us who can protect them? They have no power to help themselves, and they can not be defended from Us. No, We have given the good things to these men and their fathers for the term of their lives. Do they not see that We come to their land like conquerors and reduce the land under their control? Will they be the winners? Say: I only warn you of what has been revealed to me. But the deaf will not hear the call, even when they are warned!*
21:46 *If only a breath of your Lord's wrath should touch them, they would surely say, "Oh no! We have certainly been wicked." We will set up scales of justice on Judgment Day so that no soul is treated unjustly. If there is an act as small as a mustard seed, We will consider it, and We are capable of judging.*

Unbelievers Whose Eyes Were Veiled from My Signs

18:99 *On that day We shall let them surge against one another like waves. The trumpet will be blown, and We will gather them all together. On that day We shall present Hell for all the unbelievers to see—unbelievers whose eyes were veiled from My signs and who could not even hear. What? Do the unbelievers think that they can take My servants to be guardians besides me? We have prepared Hell to entertain the unbelievers.*
18:103 *Say: Shall We tell you whose actions will make them the biggest losers? Those whose efforts are lost in this world's life even while they thought that they were doing good deeds. These are the people who disbelieve in their Lord's revelations and who do not believe they will meet Him in the afterlife. Their deeds will have been done in vain, and on the Judgment Day, We will not give them any weight. Their reward is Hell, because they disbelieved and mocked Our revelations and Our*

messengers. As for those who believe and do good deeds, they have the Gardens of Paradise for their entertainment where they will dwell forever, never wishing to leave.

When We Decide to Destroy a City

17:8 *Perhaps your Lord will have mercy upon you but if you revert to wickedness, then We will repeat Our punishment, and We have made Hell a prison for those who disbelieve.*

17:9 *This Koran leads to that which is most righteous and gives guidance to the believers who do good deeds that they will have a great reward. It says that We have prepared a terrible punishment for the unbelievers. Man prays for evil like he ought to pray for good because man is hasty.*

17:12 *We have made the night and the day two signs. We have obscured the sign of the night, but we have made the sign of the day shine brightly so that you may seek bounty from your Lord and so that you may calculate the years and days. We have explained everything clearly.*

17:13 *We have tied every man's fate about his neck. On the Judgment Day We will bring out an open book [the book of life's deeds kept by an angel] for him. It will be said to him, "Read your book. Your own soul is sufficient testimony against yourself." Whoever acts righteously does so for his own soul. Whoever goes astray harms only himself. No soul may bear the burden of another, and We never punish until We have sent a messenger with a warning.*

17:16 *When We decide to destroy a city, We first send Our commands to their affluent leaders but when they act wickedly, justifying its doom, then we destroy them completely. How many generations have We destroyed since Noah? Your Lord is able to know and see the sins of His servants.*

17:18 *Whoever desires this present life, We will quickly grant what We please for whomever We please. Later, We will assign him to Hell where he will burn, disgraced and rejected.*

17:19 *Any believer who desires the afterlife and strives for it as he should, will find his efforts are acceptable to Allah. We freely give the bounties of your Lord to everyone. The bounties of your Lord are not denied to anyone. Notice how we have given more to some than to others. The afterlife is greater in degrees and greater in excellence.*

17:22 *Do not equate Allah with any other god, or you will sit down despised and helpless. Your Lord has ordered that you must not worship any besides Him and that you be kind to your parents. If either or both reach old age, do not speak to them with contempt or reject them, but instead speak to them with respect. With tenderness, submit humbly to them and say, "Lord, have mercy on them because they raised me when I was a child."*

Showered with Water That Is Like Molten Brass

18:27 *Recite and teach what has been revealed to you about your Lord's Book. No one can alter His words, and you will not find any refuge besides Him. Be patient with those who call upon their Lord morning and night seeking His good will. Do not take your eyes from them looking for the pomp and distraction of this life. Do not obey someone whose heart We have allowed to forget Us and who chases his own desires and whose soul cannot be saved.*
18:29 *Say: The truth is from your Lord. Let those who will, believe. Let those who will, be unbelievers. We have prepared a Fire for the unbelievers that is like the walls and roof of a tent. It will enclose them. If they cry for relief, they will be showered with water that is like molten brass which scalds their faces. What a dreadful drink and resting place!*
18:30 *As for those who believe and who have done what is right, We will certainly not waste the reward of anyone who does even a single good deed. There will be eternal gardens for the righteous. Rivers will flow beneath them. They will be decorated with gold bracelets and will wear fine green silk garments with heavy brocade. They will lie on elevated couches. Wonderful is the reward! Beautiful is the couch!*

20:99 *This is why We tell you stories of what happened before; We have sent you Our personal message. Whoever turns away from it will surely carry a burden on Judgment Day. They will remain under it, and the burden will be grievous for them to bear on Judgment Day. There will be a blast from a trumpet that day, and We will gather the wicked together, and their eyes will be blue with terror [the enemies of the Arabs were the Greeks, many of whom had blue eyes]. They will say to one another in muted voices, "You stayed only ten days on earth." We know best what they will say when the best among them say, "You did not stay longer than a day." They will ask you about the mountains that day. Tell them, "My Lord will scatter them like dust and leave them smooth like a level plain where you will see nothing crooked or uneven."*
20:108 *On that day they will follow their summoner who never deceives. Voices will be low before merciful Allah. Only slight whispers will be heard. No intercession will help that day except him that Allah allows to intercede and whose words are approved. He knows their future and their past, but they have no idea.*
20:111 *Their faces will be humble before Him—the living, the self-subsisting and eternal. Whoever is burdened by iniquity is certainly a failure. This is why We sent to you an Arabic Koran and explained in detail Our warnings so that they may fear Allah and heed them. Exalted above all is Allah, the King, the Truth! Do not hurry through its recital before its revelation is made complete to you. Instead say, "Lord, increase my knowledge."*

Mecca was a small town and there were meetings about what to do about Mohammed.

> 43:68 *My servants, there is no fear for you that day, nor will you grieve, because you have believed in Our signs and surrendered your will to Allah. You and your wives shall enter the Garden rejoicing. Trays and goblets of gold will be passed around to them, and they will have everything they desire. They will dwell there forever. This is the Garden that will be given you because of your good deeds in life. There is an abundance of fruit there for you to enjoy.*
> 43:74 *The guilty, however, will dwell forever in the torment of Hell. The punishment will not be lightened for them, and they will be overwhelmed with despair. We were not unjust toward them. It was they who were unjust. They will cry, "Malik [an angel who is a keeper of Hell], let your Lord put us out of our misery." He will respond, "No! You will remain here." Surely, We have brought the truth to you, but most of you hate the truth.*
> 43:79 *Do they make plots against you? We also make plots. Do they think that We do not hear their secrets and their private conversations? We do, and Our messengers are there to record them.*

The Koran records some of the resistance of the Meccans to Mohammed.

> 38:1 *SAD. I swear by the Koran, full of warning! Truly, the unbelievers must be filled with arrogant pride to oppose you. How many earlier generations did We destroy? In the end, they cried for mercy when there was no time to escape!*
> 38:4 *They are skeptical that a messenger would come to them from their own people, and the unbelievers say, "This man is a sorcerer and a liar! Has he combined all the gods into one Allah? That is an amazing thing!" And their chiefs [the leaders of the opposition to Mohammed in Mecca] went about and said, "Walk away. Remain faithful to your gods. This is a plot. We have never heard of such a thing in the earlier religion. This is nothing but an invented tale!"*
> 38:8 *They say, "Why, of all people, has the message been sent to him [Mohammed]?" Yes! They doubt My warnings because they have not tasted My vengeance. Do they possess the blessings of the mighty, your Lord's mercy? Is the kingdom of the heavens and the earth and everything in between in their hands? If so, let them climb up to the heavens if they can! Any allies [Mohammed's opponents] remaining here will be defeated.*
> 38:12 *Before them the people of Noah and Ad and Pharaoh, the impaler, rejected their prophets. The people of Thamud [the people of a ruined Nabatean city near Medina] and Lot and the people who lived in the forest also rejected their prophets. They all called My messengers liars; therefore, their punishment was justified.*

> 38:15 *The unbelievers of Mecca today are only waiting for a single trumpet blast [announcing the Final Day] to happen soon. They will say, "Oh, our Lord, hurry our fate to us. Do not make us wait until the Judgment Day."*

MORE ARGUMENTS WITH THE MECCANS

I188, 189 Another group of Meccans sent for Mohammed to see if they could negotiate away this painful division of the tribes. They went over old ground and again Mohammed refused the money and power that was offered. He said they were the ones who needed to decide whether they wanted to suffer in the next world and he had the only solution. If they rejected him and his message, Allah would tend to them. One of the Quraysh said, "Well, if you speak for and represent the only true god, then perhaps his Allah could do something for them."

"This land is dry. Let his Allah send them a river next to Mecca."

"They were cramped being next to the mountains. Let his Allah open up some space by moving the mountains back."

"Our best members are dead. Let your Allah renew them to life and in particular send back the best leader of our tribe, Qusayy. We will ask Qusayy whether or not you speak truly."

I189 Mohammed said that he was sent as a messenger, not to do such work. They could either accept his message or reject it and be subject to the loss. Then one of them said, "If you won't use your Allah to help us, then let your Allah help you. Send an angel to confirm you and prove to us that we are wrong. As long as the angel was present, let him make Mohammed a garden and fine home and present him with all the gold and silver he needed. If you do this, we will know that you represent Allah and we are wrong." The Quraysh wanted miracles as a proof.

> 25:7 *They say, "What kind of messenger is this? He eats food and walks the streets! Why has an angel not been sent down with him to assist in warning the people? Why has he not been given a great treasure or a rich garden to supply his needs?" The unjust say, "You are merely following a madman." See what kind of comparisons they make to you. They have gone astray and cannot find their way.*
>
> 25:10 *Blessed is He who, if He pleases, can give you things even better than that of which they speak. He can give you gardens with flowing rivers and palaces to live in.*
>
> 25:11 *But no, they deny the Hour of Judgment. Well, We have prepared a raging Fire for those who deny the coming Hour. When it sees them from a distance, they will hear its raging fury. When they are thrown, and bound together into a cramped cell, they will beg for immediate*

destruction. "Do not pray for a single destruction that day, but instead pray for many destructions.
25:15 *Say: Which is better, this or the eternal Garden that is promised to the righteous as a reward and a final destination? They will live there forever and have everything they desire! It is fitting to pray to your Lord for such a thing.*
25:17 *And on the day when He assembles them and their false gods, He will say, "Did you [the false gods] lead My servants astray, or did they become lost on their own?"*
25:18 *The false ones [false gods] will say, "Glory be to You! It was not fitting that we worshiped other gods besides You, but You allowed them and their fathers to enjoy the good things until they forgot the message and became a lost people."*
25:19 *Allah will say to the idolaters, "They have proven that you are liars, so you cannot avert your doom, nor be helped." We will force the wicked to taste a terrible punishment.*
25:20 *All of the messengers whom We sent before you were also men who ate food and walked the streets. We have made some of you a test for others. Will you be steadfast? Your Lord is watching everything.*
25:21 *Those who do not look forward to Our meeting say, "Why have angels not been sent down to us and why may we not see our Lord?" Obviously, they think too highly of themselves. Their impiety is insolent and scornful!*
25:22 *There will be no joy for the guilty on the day they see the angels. The angels will say, "Here is a barrier that you may not pass." Then We will examine their actions and leave them like so much scattered and floating dust.*
25:24 *The inhabitants of the Garden will be happier that day. They will dwell in their home, the best resting place.*
25:25 *On the day the heavens will be split, the angels will be sent down in ranks. The kingdom will belong completely to merciful Allah. It will be a terrible day for the unbelievers. On the day when the wicked bite their nails, they will say, "Oh, if only I had followed the same path as the messenger! Oh no! I wish that I had never taken such people as my friend! He led me astray from Allah's message after it had come to me. Satan is a traitor to man!"*
25:30 *Then the messenger will say, "My Lord, truly my people have treated the Koran as a joke." Even so, We have given every prophet an enemy from among the sinners; but Allah is a sufficient guide and helper.*

We Do Not Send the Angels without Good Reason

15:1 *ALIF. LAM. RA. These are the verses of the Scripture, a recital that makes things clear.*

15:2 *The unbelievers will often wish they were Muslims. Let them enjoy themselves, and let false hope beguile them. They will eventually learn the truth.*
15:4 *We never destroy a city whose term was not preordained. No nation can delay or change its destiny. They say: "You [Mohammed] to whom the message was revealed, you are surely insane. If you were telling the truth, why did you not bring angels to us?"*
15:8 *We do not send the angels without good reason. If We did, the unbelievers would still not understand. Surely, We have sent down the message, and surely, We will guard it. Before your time, We sent apostles to the sects of the ancient peoples, but they mocked every messenger. Similarly, We allow doubt to enter the hearts of the sinners. They do not believe it, even though the example of the ancients has preceded them. Even if We opened a gate into heaven for them the entire time they ascended, they would say, "Our eyes are playing tricks on us. No, we are bewitched."*

I189 Mohammed did not do miracles, because such things were not what Allah had appointed him to do.

I189 Then one of the Quraysh said, "Then let the heavens be dropped on us in pieces as you say your Lord could do. Then if you do not we will not believe." Mohammed said that Allah could do that if Allah wished or he might not if he wished.

I189 They then said, "Did not your Lord know that we would ask you these questions? Then your Lord could have prepared you with better answers. And your Lord could have told you what to tell us if we don't believe. We hear that you are getting this Koran from a man named Al Rahman from another town. We don't believe in Al Rahman. Our conscience is clear. We must either destroy you or you must destroy us. Bring your angels and we will believe them."

I190 Mohammed turned and left. A cousin chased him and fell in beside him to talk. He said, "Mohammed, your tribe has made you propositions and you have rejected them. First, they asked you for things for themselves that they might see if you are true. Then they would follow you. You did nothing. Then they asked you for things for yourself so they could see your superiority over them and prove your standing with Allah. You did nothing. Then they said to bring on the punishments that your Allah has told you about and you have frightened us with his threats. You did nothing. Personally, I will never believe until you get a ladder up to the sky, you will climb it while I watch, and four angels will come and testify that you are truthful. But you know, even if you did all that, I still don't know if I would believe you."

1190 Mohammed went home and was sad and depressed. He had hoped when they sent for him it was to announce their submission to his Allah and his teachings. Instead, it was resistance and questions.

> 26:204 *What! Do they seek to hasten Our punishment? What do you think? If after giving them their fill for years and their punishment finally comes upon them, how will their pleasures help them? We have never destroyed a city that We did not warn first with a reminder. We did not treat them unjustly.*
> 26:210 *The devils were not sent down with the Koran. It does not suit them, and they do not have the power because they are banned from hearing it. Do not call upon any god but Allah, or you will be doomed. Rather, warn your close relatives,*
> 26:215 *And be kind to the believers who follow you. If they disobey you, say, "I will not be responsible for your actions." Put your trust in Him who is mighty and merciful, Who sees you when you stand in prayer, and your demeanor among the worshippers, because He hears and knows everything.*
> 26:221 *Shall I tell you who Satan will descend upon? He will descend upon every lying, wicked person. They speak of what they hear, but most of them are liars. It is the poets that the erring follow. Do you see how they wander distractedly around every valley, and that they do not practice what they preach? But not so for the believers, who believe, do good works, and remember Allah often, and who defend themselves when unjustly treated. But those who treat them unjustly will find out what a terrible fate awaits them.*

The Koran had advice for Mohammed in these difficult times.

> 15:87 *We have given you seven of the often-repeated verses [Sura 1] and the great Koran. Do not strain your eyes coveting the good things that We have given to some of the unbelievers, and do not grieve for them, but instead take the believers tenderly under your wing. Say: " I am the one who gives plain warning."*
> 17:54 *Your Lord knows you best. If He pleases, He will have mercy upon you, or if He wishes, He will punish you. We have not sent you [Mohammed] to watch over them [the Meccans]. Your Lord has absolute knowledge of everything in the heavens and the earth. We have made some prophets excel others, and We gave the Psalms to David.*

> 25:41 *When they see you, they mock you, saying, "Is this the man whom Allah sends as a messenger? He would have led us far from our gods if we had not been so loyal to them!" When they see the punishment that is waiting, they will soon realize who was more misled. What do you think of someone who worships his own passion like a god? Would you*

be a guardian for such a person? Or do you think that most of them even hear or understand? They are just like cattle. No, they stray even further from the path.

17:75 *In that case, We should have given you a double taste of punishment in this life and in the hereafter. You would have found no one to help you against Us. Their intent was to scare you off of the land [the Jews told Mohammed that Syria was the land of prophets and that he should go there] in order to expel you. In that case, they would not have stayed but a bit longer than you.*
17:77 *This was Our method with the prophets that We sent before you. You will find no change in Our methods. Establish regular prayers—at sunset until the dark of night and the prayer and recitation at dawn because the morning prayer and recitation is watched. And pray during some part of the night. This would be beyond what is required, but perhaps your Lord will raise you to a higher station.*

I191 Mohammed would come to the Kabah and tell the Meccans what terrible punishments that Allah had delivered to the others in history who had not believed their prophets. That was now one of his constant themes. Allah destroyed others like you who did not listen to men like me.

My Vengeance and Warning Was Terrible

54:9 *Before them, Noah's people rejected the truth. They rejected Our servant and called him insane and drove him away. So he cried out to his Lord, "I am defeated. Help me!"*
54:11 *We opened heaven's gates and water gushed out, and We caused springs to erupt all over the earth and their waters [waters of heaven and springs of earth] met by preordained plan. We carried Noah away on a boat made with planks and nails. It floated away under Our watchful eye. A reward for someone who was rejected—We left it [the ark] as a sign, but will anyone pay attention? My vengeance and warning was terrible!*
54:17 *We have made the Koran easy to remember, but will any one pay attention?*
54:18 *The people of Ad [an ancient people of southern Arabia] rejected the truth, but My vengeance and warning was terrible because We sent a roaring wind against them on a day of constant disaster sweeping men away like the stumps of uprooted palms. My vengeance and warning was terrible!*
54:22 *We have made the Koran easy to remember, but will any one pay attention?*
54:23 *The people of Thamud [Thamud was a trade town in ruins north of Mecca] rejected the warning, and they said, "Should we follow one man*

just like ourselves? That would be wrong and insane. Is he the only one of us to be trusted with such a warning? No! He is an arrogant liar." Tomorrow they will learn who the foolish liar is.
54:27 *We will send them a she-camel as a test. Watch them and be patient. Tell them that their water must be divided between themselves and the she-camel, and they must take equal, alternating turns. Instead, they called their companion, who killed her. My vengeance and warning was terrible! We sent a single blast against them and they became like dried sticks.*
54:32 *We have made the Koran easy to remember, but will any one pay attention?*
54:33 *Lot's people rejected his warning, but We sent a shower of stones against them, except for Lot and his family, whom We saved at dawn as a favor. This is how We reward those who give thanks. He certainly warned them of Our punishment, but they doubted the warning. They even tried to get him to turn out his guests, but We blinded their eyes and said, "Taste My vengeance and My warning!" In the morning a relentless punishment struck them.*
54:40 *We have made the Koran easy to remember, but will any one pay attention?*
54:41 *Warnings also came to the people of Pharaoh. They rejected all of Our signs, but We grasped them with the grasp of the mighty and the powerful.*
54:43 *Are your unbelievers better men than these? Is there an exception for you [the Meccans] in the scriptures? Or do they say, "We can defend ourselves if we stand together?" They will be routed and will turn their backs and run. No! The Hour of Judgment is their promised time, and that hour will be terrible and bitter.*
54:47 *Surely, the wicked are wrong and crazy. They will be dragged on their faces into the fire that day. "Feel the fury of Hell." We have created everything according to a preordained plan. Our command is a single word, as quick as the wink of an eye. We have destroyed men like you [the Meccans] in the past, but is any one warned?*
54:52 *Everything they do is written down in the books [records kept by recording angels]—every act, both small and great, is recorded. Surely, the righteous will live among the Gardens with rivers, in the seat of honor, in the presence of a mighty king.*

He Is Insane

44:9 *They [the Meccans] fool around in doubt, but watch them the day the sky emits a visible smoke that will cover mankind. This will be a terrible punishment. They will cry, "Lord, take away our punishment. We are believers." But how did warning them help when Our messenger went to them, and they rejected him and said, "He learned it from others, he is insane!"? If We were to give you any respite, you would surely revert to wickedness. On the day when We seize you with a terrible onslaught, We will certainly inflict punishment!*

44:17 *Long ago, before their time, We tried with the people of Pharaoh when We presented a noble apostle [Moses] to them. "Return the servants of Allah to me because I am an apostle worthy of all trust. Do not exalt yourself against Allah because I come to you with clear authority. I rely on the protection of my Lord and your Lord that you will not stone me. And if you do not believe me, then leave me alone." Finally he cried to his Lord, "These are wicked people."*

44:23 *Allah said, "Take my servants away during the night because you will be pursued. Leave the sea split behind you. Their army will be drowned." They left many gardens and fountains behind them and many cornfields and noble buildings and many good things that they enjoyed. We gave those things as an inheritance to another people. Neither the heaven nor the earth cried for them, and they received no reprieve, but We did rescue the Children of Israel from a shameful punishment by Pharaoh, who was haughty and excessive.*

44:32 *We chose them, in Our wisdom, above all other peoples, and We gave them miracles that contained a clear choice. And still, these unbelievers say, "There is nothing after our death, and we will not be resurrected. If you are telling the truth, then bring back our fathers." Are they better than the people of Tubba [possibly Yemen], and those that came before them whom We destroyed because of their wickedness?*

44:38 *We did not create the heavens and the earth and everything in between as a game. We created them for a just end, but most of them do not understand. Surely they will have a time set aside on Judgment Day, a day when the master will not be helped by his servant, and the servant will not be helped by the master—except for those who have Allah's mercy. He is the mighty, the merciful.*

44:43 *Surely the Zaqqum tree [the tree of Hell] will be food for the sinners. Like molten brass, it will boil in their bellies like the boiling of scalding water. (It will be said) "Seize him and drag him down to the middle of Hell. Torment him by pouring boiling water on his head. (Say) Taste this: You thought that you were powerful and honorable! This is the thing that you doubted."*

44:51 *The righteous, however, will live in a protected place among gardens and fountains, facing one another and dressed in richly brocaded fine silk. This is how it will be. We will marry them to beautiful virgins with big dark eyes [houris]. There they can call for any kind of fruit in comfort and safety. They have only the first death there, and Allah will save them from the pains of Hell. It is the gracious gift of your Lord! This is the supreme achievement.*

44:58 *We have made this Koran in Arabic so it will be easy to understand and so that you will take warning. So watch and wait, because they are also waiting.*

We Have Bound Their Necks with Chains That Reach the Chin

36:1 *YA. SIN. I swear by the wise Koran that you are surely one of the messengers on a straight path, a revelation of the mighty, the merciful, sent to warn a people whose fathers were not warned, and consequently remain heedless.*
36:7 *Our sentence against them is just because they do not believe. We have bound their necks with chains that reach the chin, forcing their heads up. We have placed barriers in front, behind, and over them, so they can not see. It does not matter whether you warn them or not, because they will not believe. You can only warn those who follow the message and fear merciful Allah in private. Give them glad tidings of forgiveness and a generous reward. It is true We will give life to the dead and that We record what they will do and what they have done. We have recorded everything in Our perfect ledger.*
36:13 *Use a parable to tell them the story of the people of the city [Antioch] when the messengers visited. When We first sent two messengers to them, the people rejected them, but We sent a third to strengthen their numbers. They said, "We are messengers sent to you by Allah."*
36:15 *The people said, "You are merely men just like us. Allah has sent no revelation. You only tell lies."*
36:16 *The messengers replied, "Our Lord knows that we have been sent to you. Our only duty is to proclaim the clear message."*
36:18 *They said, "We predict evil from you. If you do not stop, we will certainly stone you and inflict a terrible punishment."*
36:19 *The messengers said, "Your prediction of evil comes from within. Is it because you are warned? No! You are a people in error."*
36:20 *A man [Habib, the carpenter] came running from the outskirts of the city and said, "My people, listen to the messengers! Obey those who do not ask any reward and who follow the right path. It would be unreasonable of me not to serve Him who created me, and to Whom we will all return. Should I worship other gods besides Him? If Allah wished to afflict me their intercession could not help me at all, nor could they save me. If I did worship other gods, I would be in clear error. I believe in your Lord, so listen to me." It was said to him, "Enter the Garden of Paradise." The man replied, "Oh, if only my people knew how gracious Allah has been to me and that He has made me one of the honored ones!"*
36:28 *After the man [Habib] from the outskirts died, We sent no army down from heaven against his people. We did not need to do so. It was nothing more than a single cry, and they were extinct. Oh! The misery that falls upon My servants! Every messenger sent to them has been mocked. Do*

they not see how many earlier generations We have destroyed? Everyone of them will be brought before Us for judgment.

36:33 *The dead earth is a sign for them. We give it life which produces grain for them to eat. And We have placed gardens of palms and grapes there with springs gushing water so they might enjoy the fruit of Our artistry. Their hands did not make this. Why will they not be grateful?*

How Many Generations Did We Destroy before Them?

50:36 *How many generations did We destroy before them who were mightier than they are in strength so they filled the land? Was there any place for them to hide? Certainly, there is a reminder here for those who have hearts or who listen and give witness to the truth. We created the heavens and the earth and everything in between in six days, and We did not get tired.*

50:39 *Therefore, be patient with what they say, and sing the praises of your Lord before sunrise and before sunset. Praise him at night and after the prayers. Listen for the day when the crier calls from near by. The day men hear that shout will be the Judgment Day.*

50:43 *Surely, We give life and cause death. Everything will return to Us. The day that the earth quickly splits open as the dead emerge from their graves will be an easy gathering for Us to make. We know exactly what the unbelievers say, and you should not compel them. Use the Koran to warn those who fear my threat.*

According to the Koran the ancient towns of Arabia were destroyed because they did not believe their prophet.

You Are Certainly One of the Bewitched

26:141 *The people of Thamud rejected the messengers. Their brother Salih said to them, "Will you not fear Allah? I am a faithful messenger worthy of all trust. Fear Allah and obey me. I ask for no reward. My reward comes only from the Lord of the worlds. Will you be left safely to enjoy all you have among gardens and fountains and corn-fields and palm-trees, heavy with fruit, and—insolent as you are—your homes carved from the mountain stone? Fear Allah and obey me. Do not obey the bidding of the extravagant who make mischief in the land, and do not reform."*

26:153 *They said, "You are certainly one of the bewitched. You are only a man like us. Give us a sign if you are telling the truth."*

26:155 *He said, "Here is a she-camel. She has a right to drink from the well, and you have a right to drink from the well, each at a scheduled time. But do not harm her, or the punishment of a terrible day will overtake you."*

26:157 *But they hamstrung her, and then regretted it, so the punishment overtook them. Surely, there is a sign here, but most of them do not believe.*

We Also Plotted

27:45 *Long ago We sent to the Thamud their brother Salih saying, "Worship Allah." But they became two quarrelling factions. He said, "My people, why do you embrace evil, rather than good? Why do you not ask Allah's forgiveness so that you may receive mercy?"*

27:47 *They said, "We predict that you and your followers will bring us evil." He said, "The evil that you sense will befall you, will come from Allah. You are a people on trial."*

27:48 *In the city there were nine men from one family who made mischief in the land and would not reform. They said, "Swear to one another by Allah that we will attack Salih and his family at night, and we will tell his vengeance-seeking heirs that we did not see the murder of his family, and we will be telling the truth." They plotted and planned, but We also plotted, even though they did not realize. See how their plotting turned out. We destroyed them and their entire people. You may still see their ruined homes which were destroyed because they were wicked. Surely this is a sign for those who understand. We saved those who believed and acted righteously.*

This Is Just an Ancient Myth

26:123 *The people of Ad rejected the messengers. Their brother Hud said to them, "Will you not fear Allah? I am a faithful messenger worthy of all trust. Fear Allah and obey me. I ask for no reward. My reward comes only from the Lord of the worlds. What? Do you build monuments on every high place to amuse yourselves? Do you acquire fine buildings in the hope that you will live there forever? When you exert your power, do you do so like a tyrant? Fear Allah and obey me. Fear Him who has generously given you everything you know. Fear Him who has generously given you cattle, and children, and gardens, and fountains. Truly, I fear that you will have the punishment of a terrible day."*

26:136 *They said, "It does not matter to us if you warn us or not. This is just an ancient myth. We are not the ones who will be punished."*

26:139 *So they rejected him, and We destroyed them. Surely, there is a sign here, but most of them do not believe. Truly, your Lord, He is the mighty, the merciful!*

They Were Overtaken by the Punishment of Overshadowing Gloom

26:176 *The people who lived in the forest of Madian rejected the messengers. Their brother Shuaid said to them, "Will you not fear Allah? I am a faithful messenger worthy of all trust. Fear Allah and obey me. I ask for no reward. My reward comes only from the Lord of the worlds. Give just measure, and do not be one of those who give less than is due. Weigh with an exact balance. Do not cheat men of their goods, and do*

not do evil on the earth by making mischief. Fear Him who created you and your ancestors."
26:185 *They said, "You are certainly one of the bewitched. You are only a man like us, and we think you are a liar. If you are telling the truth, make part of the sky fall down upon us."*
26:188 *He said, "My Lord knows everything you do."*
26:189 *When they rejected him, they were overtaken by the punishment of overshadowing gloom. This was surely the punishment of a terrible day! There is a sign here, but most of them do not believe. Truly, your Lord, He is the mighty, the merciful!*

25:38 *And Ad and Thamud, and the people of Rass [an unknown reference], and many generations between them: to each of them We sent parables and warnings, and We utterly destroyed each of them. Certainly the unbelievers must have passed by the city that We destroyed with a deadly rain. Have they not seen it with their own eyes? They do not hope to be resurrected.*

The Cry Overtook Them in the Morning

15:78 *The people who lived in the forest [perhaps Midian] were also sinners, so We took vengeance upon them, and they both were on an open road, and plain to see.*
15:80 *The people who lived in the rocky place [the people of Thamud] also rejected Allah's messengers. We sent Our signs to them, but they turned away from them. They cut their homes into the rock, feeling secure, but the cry overtook them in the morning, and all their efforts did nothing to help them.*

The parable of the vineyard:

18:32 *Tell them a parable of two men. We gave one man two gardens of grapevines and enclosed them with date palms. Between the two, We placed corn fields. Both of these gardens produced their fruits and did not fail in the least. We caused a river to flow through the middle of them.*
18:34 *The first man possessed very much and during the course of an argument with his companion said, "I am wealthier than you and have a larger number of servants." When the first man went to his gardens, his state of mind was harmful to his soul. He said, "I do not think this will ever perish, and I do not think that the Hour of Judgment will ever come. Even if I am returned to my Lord, I will certainly be given something even better than this in exchange."*
18:37 *The other man said, "Do you reject Him Who created you first from dust and then from a drop of sperm before finally shaping you into a man? As for me, He is Allah my Lord, and I do not associate any my with Lord. Why did you not say when you entered your gardens, 'It is the will*

of Allah. There is no power except with Allah!' If you believe that I am your inferior in wealth and sons, it may be that Allah will give me something better than your gardens and may send His thunderbolts against them so that the next morning there will nothing but bare ground. Or perhaps one morning the water in the garden will sink into the earth so that you will be unable to reach it."

18:42 *And the first man's wealth was destroyed. He wrung his hands at the thought of all the money he had spent on his garden, which lay about him in ruins, and he said, "Oh, if only I had not worshiped other gods besides Allah!" He had no large number of servants to help him against Allah nor was he able to defend himself. Protection can only come from Allah, the True One. He gives the best reward, and He causes the best consequences.*

I191 One of the Quraysh, Al Nadr, had been to Persia and had learned many tales and sagas from the story tellers there. The traveler would announce, "I can tell a better tale than Mohammed." Then he would proceed to tell them ancient sagas and stories of Persia. "In what way is Mohammed a better story teller than me?"

But Mohammed's stories were straight from Allah. Here are stories about David, a king of the Jews:

38: 17 *Be patient with what they say, and remember Our servant David, a powerful man, who always looked repentantly to Allah. We made the mountains sing the praises of Allah in unison with him in the morning and the evening, and the birds gathered together; all joined him in praise of Allah. We made his kingdom strong and gave him wisdom and sound Judgment.*

38:21 *Have you heard the story of the two disputing men who climbed the wall of David's private chamber? David was frightened when they entered his room. They said, "Do not be afraid. We have a dispute, and one of us has certainly wronged the other. Judge where the truth lies between us, and do not be unjust, but guide us to the right way. My brother has ninety-nine ewes [female sheep], and I have only one. He pressured me and said, 'Let me have her.'"*

38:24 *David replied, "Certainly he has wronged you by insisting that you give him your ewe. It's true that many partners wrong one another the exception being those who believe and behave correctly. There are few of those." David realized that We had tried him. He asked forgiveness from his Lord, fell down bowing, and repented.*

38:25 *So We forgave him this sin; truly he is honored and well received by Us and has an excellent place in Paradise. It was said to him, "David, We have indeed made you a vice-regent on earth. Use truth and justice when judging between men, and do not follow your passions because they may cause you to stray from Allah's path. Those who stray from Allah's path will meet a terrible punishment because they have forgotten the Judgment Day.*

Stories about Noah:

71:1 *We sent Noah to his people and said to him, "Warn your people before a terrible punishment befalls them." He said, "My people, I come to you as a plain-speaking warner. Serve and fear Allah and obey me. He will forgive you your sins and give you respite until the appointed time, because when Allah's appointed time has come, it can not be delayed. If only you knew this!"*
71:5 *He said, "Lord, I have cried to my people day and night; and my cries only increase their aversion. Whenever I cry to them so that you may forgive them, they cover their ears and cover themselves in their cloaks, and persist stubbornly in their error. Then I called loudly to them. Then I spoke plainly, and I spoke to them privately and I said, 'Beg your Lord for forgiveness because he is ready to forgive. He will open the sky and send down rain in abundance. He will increase your wealth and children and will give you gardens and rivers. What is the matter with you that you refuse to seek goodness from Allah's hand when it was Him who made you in diverse stages?'"*
71:15 *"Do you not see how Allah created the seven heavens and set them one above another? He placed the moon there and made it a light, and made the sun a lamp and placed it there, and Allah caused you to spring out of the earth like a plant. Later he will turn you back into the earth and bring you out again. Allah has spread the earth for you like a carpet so that you may walk there along spacious paths." Noah said, "Lord, they rebel against me and follow those whose wealth and children add only to their troubles."*
71:22 *And they devised a great plot. They said, "Do not forsake your gods; do not forsake Wadd, or Sowah, or Yaghuth nor Yahuk or Nesr [names of Semitic gods]." They have led many astray and have added only error to the ways of the wicked. Because of their sins, they were drowned and forced into the fire, and they discovered that Allah was their only shelter.*
71:26 *And Noah said, "Lord, do not leave one family of unbelievers alive on earth. Because if you do, then they will trick your servants and will only breed more sinners and unbelievers. Lord, forgive me and my parents and every believer that enters my house and all the male and female believers. Give nothing but destruction to the wicked."*

We Drowned the Rest

37:75 *Noah called upon Us long ago, and We promptly listened, and We saved him and his family from the great flood, and We made his offspring*

the survivors. We left for him honor through posterity, "Peace be on Noah throughout the worlds!"
37:80 *This is how We reward the good, because he was one of Our believing servants, and We drowned the rest.*

26:105 *The people of Noah rejected the messengers when their brother Noah said to them, "Will you not fear Allah? I am a faithful messenger worthy of all trust. Fear Allah and obey me. I ask no reward from you for this because my reward comes only from the Lord of the worlds. Fear Allah and obey me."*
26:111 *They said, "Should we believe you when only the lowest people follow you?"*
26:112 *He answered, "I have no knowledge of their actions. Their account is only with my Lord if you could only understand this. I will not turn away those who believe, because I am only sent to publicly warn."*
26:116 *They said, "Noah, if you do not stop, you will certainly be stoned to death."*
26:117 *He said, "Lord, my people reject me. Judge between us, and save me and those believers with me."*
26:119 *So We saved him and those who went with him in the laden ark, and later We drowned the rest. Surely, there is a sign here, but most of them do not believe. Truly, your Lord, He is the mighty, the merciful!*

He [Noah] Is Only a Madman

23:23 *It can not be disputed that We sent Noah to his people, and he said, "Oh, My people! Serve Allah. You have no other god but Him. Will you not fear Him?" But the chiefs of the unbelievers said, "He is a mere mortal, just like yourselves, who wishes to make himself superior to you. If Allah wished to send a message, then He would have sent angels. We have never heard of such a thing from our ancestors." Others said, "He is only a madman; be patient with him for a while."*
23:26 *Noah said, "My Lord, help me. They accuse me of lying." So We inspired him with Our revelation: "Make an ark under Our eye and guidance. When We command and when the oceans overflow, load onto the ark pairs of every creature and your followers except those who have already been damned. Do not plead with Me on behalf of the wicked because they will be drowned.*
23:28 *When you and your followers are on the ark, say, "Praise be to Allah, who has rescued us from the wicked." And say, "Oh, my Lord! Allow me to disembark at a blessed landing-place because you are best able to bring us to safety." In this there are signs for men to recognize. We are always testing man.*
23:31 *After them, We created another generation. And We sent to them a messenger from their own people saying, "Worship Allah! You have no*

other god but Him. Will you not fear Him?" And the chiefs of his people were unbelievers who called the afterlife a lie. We had given them the pleasures of this life, and they said, "He is a man, just like yourselves; he eats what you eat, and he drinks what you drink. If you obey a mortal like yourselves, then you will certainly be doomed. Does he promise that you will be resurrected after you have died and become dust and bones? That which you are threatened with is very, very far from reality. There is nothing beyond our life in this world. We live and we die, and we will not be raised up again. He is merely a man who has invented a lie about Allah. We will not believe him."

23:39 *He said, "My Lord, help me. They accuse me of lying."*

23:40 *Allah said, "In a short time they will quickly repent." Then the justice of the awful blast overtook them, and We turned them into so much rubbish swept away by a flood. So away with the wicked.*

23:42 *After them, We created other generations. No people may either hasten or delay their appointed time. Then We sent Our messengers one after another. Every time a messenger went forth to a nation, its people accused him of lying, so We caused them to follow one another into disaster, and We made them examples. So, away with the unbelievers.*

23:45 *Then We sent Moses and his brother Aaron with Our signs and a clear mandate to Pharaoh and his chiefs, who scorned them. They were an arrogant people. They said, "Shall we believe two mere mortals like ourselves whose people are our slaves?" So they denied them, and we made them another destroyed people. So away with the Pharaoh.*

25:35 *Long ago, We gave Moses the Book, and appointed his brother Aaron as his aide. We commanded them, "Both of you go to the people who have rejected Our signs." We absolutely destroyed those people. And the people of Noah, when they rejected the messengers, We drowned them and made them a sign for all men. We have prepared a terrible penalty for all the wicked.*

They Were an Evil People

21:76 *Remember Noah when, long ago, he cried to us. We heard his prayer and saved him and his family from disaster. We saved him from the people who rejected Our signs. They were an evil people, and we drowned all of them.*

21:78 *Remember David and Solomon when they judged a dispute over strayed sheep and a pasture? We witnessed their judgment. We gave Solomon understanding of the dispute, and We gave each of them wisdom and knowledge. We made the mountains and the birds join with David in Our praise. We did all these things. We taught David the art of making coats of battle armor to protect you from one another's violence. Why will you not be thankful?*

> 21:81 *We made the wind subject to Solomon. At his bidding it flowed to the land We had blessed, because We know all things. We subdued the devils forcing them to dive for pearls for Solomon and do other work besides, and We kept close guard over them.*
> 21:83 *Remember Job when he cried to his Lord, "I am seized by evil, but You are the most merciful of the merciful." We heard his prayer, removed his distress, and returned his family to him doubled in size. This was a mercy from Us and a memorial for those who serve Us.*
> 21:85 *Remember Ishmael, Idris, and Zul-kifl [prophets of old, the identity of Zul-kifl is uncertain], all steadfast and patient men. We admitted them into Our mercy because they were righteous.*

Other Jewish references:

> 38:41 *Do you remember Our servant Job when he cried to his Lord, "Satan has afflicted me with distress and torment." We said to him, "Stamp the ground with your foot. Here is a spring, a cool washing place, and water to drink." And We gave him back his family and doubled their number as an example of Our mercy and as a reminder for men of understanding. We said to him, "Take up in your hand a branch and strike her with it, and do not break your oath.[1] " Truly, We found him to be full of patience and constant. He was an excellent servant, because he constantly turned toward Us in repentance.*
> 38:45 *And remember Our servants Abraham, Isaac, and Jacob, men of power and vision. Surely We purified and chose them for a special purpose, proclaiming the message of the afterlife. They were, in Our eyes, truly some of the select and the good.*
> 38:48 *And remember Ishmael, Elisha, and Zul-Kifl [Ezekiel]: all of them belong among the chosen.*
> 38:49 *This is a reminder, and, surely, the righteous will have an excellent home in the afterlife, the Gardens of Eternity whose doors will always be open for them. They can recline and call at their leisure for abundant fruit and drink. They will have virgins of their own age, who glance modestly. This is what you are promised on the Judgment Day. This is Our gift to you. It will never fail.*

Stories about Abraham:

> 37:83 *Truly, Abraham shared this faith when he brought a perfect heart to his Lord and he said to his father and to his people, "What are you worshiping? A lie! Do you want gods besides Allah? And what do you think about the Lord of the worlds?"*

---

1. Job swore to beat his wife with one hundred blows. Later he softened, and, to fulfill his oath, he put one hundred small twigs in his hand and hit her once.

37:88 *Then he looked up and gazed at the stars and said, "Truly, I am ill." [Abraham's peoples' worship involved the stars] And they turned their backs on him and left. He turned to the images of their gods and said, "Do you not eat? What is wrong with you? Why do you not speak?" He began to attack them, striking them with his right hand.*
37:94 *As his tribesmen came running back to him, he said, "Do you worship what you have carved when Allah has created you and what you make?" They said, "Build a pyre for him, and throw him into the blazing fire." They tried to plot against him, but We spoiled their plans. And Abraham said, "Truly, I will go to my Lord, and he will guide me. Oh Lord, give me a righteous son." We gave him the good news of a gentle son.*
37:102 *When the son [Ishmael] grew tall enough to work, his father said to him, "Son, a dream tells me that I should sacrifice you. What do you think?" He said, "Father, do what you are commanded. If Allah wills, you will find me patient."*
37:103 *After they had surrendered themselves to the will of Allah, he laid his son [Ishmael] face down . We cried out to him, "Abraham! You have satisfied the vision." See how We reward the righteous. This was obviously a clear test. And We ransomed his son with an impressive victim [a ram], and We left this for him to be honored through posterity.*
37:109 *"Peace be on Abraham!" This is how We reward the good, because he was one of Our believing servants.*
37:112 *And We gave him the good news of the birth of Isaac—a righteous prophet—We bestowed Our blessing on him and Isaac. Among their descendents [the Jews] are some that do good and others that do harm to their souls.*

A Punishment from Allah, the Merciful

19:41 *And mention Abraham in the Scripture because he was a man of truth and a prophet. When he said to his father, "Father, why worship something that does not see, hear, or help you in the least? Father, knowledge has come to me that has not come to you. Follow me and I will lead you onto a straight and even path. Father, do not worship Satan because Satan is a rebel against Allah, the merciful. Father, I am afraid that a punishment from Allah, the merciful, will fall upon you and that you will become Satan's slave."*
19:46 *Abraham's father replied, "Do you reject my gods, Abraham? If you do not stop, I will certainly stone you. Go away from me for a long time."*
19:47 *Abraham said, "Peace be with you. I will pray to Allah for your forgiveness because He is always gracious to me. But I will turn away from you and the gods you pray to besides Allah. I will call upon my Lord. Perhaps my prayers will not go unanswered."*

19:49 *When he had separated himself from them and that which they worshiped besides Allah, We gave him Isaac and Jacob and made both of them prophets. In Our mercy, We gave gifts to them and gave them an exalted and true lasting reputation.*

19:51 *And mention Moses in the Scripture because he was a pure man. More than that, he was an apostle and a prophet. We called to him from the right side of the mountain and caused him to come close to Us for a secret conversation. In Our mercy, We gave to him his brother Aaron, a prophet.*

19:54 *And mention Ishmael in the Scripture because he was true to his promise and an apostle and a prophet. He urged his people to pray and give alms and was pleasing to his Lord. And mention Idris [an uncertain reference] in the Scripture. He was a man of truth and a prophet. We raised him to a lofty station.*

43:26 *Consider when Abraham said to his father and his people: "I am innocent of what you worship. I worship only Him who created me, and He will certainly guide me." And he left it as a sign to endure among his descendents so that they might return to Allah.*

Fire, Be Cool and a Place of Safety for Abraham

21:51 *Long ago We gave Abraham his direction because We knew he was worthy. When he said to his father and his people, "What are these idols that you are so devoted to?"*

21:53 *They said, "We found our fathers worshiping them."*

21:54 *Abraham said, "Obviously, you and your fathers have made a mistake."*

21:55 *They said, "Are you being serious, or are you some kind of fool?"*

21:56 *He said, "No, I'm telling the truth. Your Lord is the Lord of the heavens and the earth and their creator, and I am a witness to this. And, by Allah, I will act against your idols after you have turned your backs and gone away." So he smashed them all to pieces, except the main one, so that they would return to it seeking answers. They asked, "Who has done this to our gods? Surely he must be a wicked man."*

21:60 *Others said, "We heard a young man called Abraham speaking of them."*

21:61 *They said, "Bring him before the eyes of the people so that they may testify against him."*

21:62 *They asked, "Abraham, did you do this to our gods?"*

21:63 *He replied, "No. It was done by the chief of the gods. Ask the others, if they can speak."*

21:64 *They spoke amongst themselves and said, "Surely, you are the ones who are mistaken!" Then they became confounded with shame and said, "You know that these idols can not speak."*

21:66 *Abraham said, "So do you worship, along with Allah, things that can not help or harm you? Curses to you and the idols you worship besides Allah! Do you not understand?"*
21:68 *They said, "If you are going to do something, burn him and protect your gods."*
21:69 *We said, "Fire, be cool and a place of safety for Abraham!" They tried to plot against him, but We made them the sufferers.*
21:71 *We rescued him and his nephew Lot and brought them safely to the land We have blessed for all mankind. We gave him Isaac and, as a grandson, Jacob, and We made them both righteous men. We made them leaders who guided others by Our command; and We inspired them to do good deeds, to establish regular prayers, and to regularly give to charity; and they worshiped us, exclusively.*

Jonah

37:139 *Jonah was also one of those sent to warn. When he ran away to a laden ship, he agreed to cast lots with them and was condemned, and the fish swallowed him because he had committed wrong. But if he had not been one of those who glorify Allah, he would surely have stayed in its belly until Judgment Day. And We cast him sickly on the naked shore, and We caused a gourd-vine to grow above him, and We sent him to a hundred thousand people or more [in Ninevah, in Syria]. Because they believed, We allowed them to enjoy their lives for a while.*

21:87 *Remember Zun-nun [Jonah], when he went away in anger and thought that We had no power over him. In the darkness, he cried, "There is no god but Allah. Glory to You. I was certainly wrong!" We heard his prayer, and we rescued him from his distress. This is how we save the faithful.*

Lot

15:51 *Tell them about Abraham's guests when they entered his home and said, "Peace." He said, "We are afraid of you."*
15:53 *They said, "Do not be afraid. We bring you the good news of a wise son."*
15:54 *He said, "Now that I am an old man, how can you be bringing me good news of a son? What, then, is your good news?"*
15:55 *They said, "We give you good news, truthfully, do not despair."*
15:56 *He said, "Who despairs of his Lord's mercy except those who go astray?"*
15:57 *Abraham said, "Then what brings you to me, you messengers of Allah?"*

15:58 They said, "We have been sent to a guilty people except Lot's family whom We will save but for his wife. We have decreed that she will be among those who lag behind."
15:61 When the messengers came to Lot's family, he said to them, "You people are strangers to me."
15:63 They said, "Yes, we have come to you on a mission that your people doubt. We have come to you with the truth, and we are certainly truthful. Take your family from here in the dead of night and follow close behind. Do not let any of them turn around, and go to the place you are commanded." We gave him this command so that the sinners would be destroyed in the morning.
15:67 The people of the city came rejoicing at the news of Lot's visitors. He said to them, "These are my guests. Do not disgrace me. Instead, fear Allah and do not put me to shame."
15:70 They said, "Did we not forbid you to talk with anyone?"
15:71 Lot said, "If you must act like that, here are my daughters." By your life, they wandered blindly about in intoxicating lust. But an explosion overtook them at sunrise, and We turned their city upside down, and We rained down upon them stones of baked clay. Surely, there are signs in this for those who pay attention. And these cities were on a road that still exists. Surely, there is a sign in this for the believers.

37:133 And truly Lot was one of those sent to warn. We saved him and his family, all except an old woman who lagged behind. Then We destroyed the others. If you ever pass their ruined city in the morning or at night, will you not understand?

We Saved Him from the City That Practiced Sexual Abominations

21:74 And We gave wisdom and knowledge to Lot, and We saved him from the city that practiced sexual abominations [homosexuality] because they were an evil and perverse people. And We admitted him into Our mercy because he was one of the righteous.
27:54 And remember what Lot said when We sent him to his people, "What? Will you act wickedly even though you see that it is wrong? Will you really lust after men rather than women? You are certainly an ignorant people." And the only answer that his people gave was: "Expel Lot and his family from your city. They wish to remain pure!" But We saved him and his family except his wife. We decreed that she would be one of those who lingered behind. And We rained down a shower of brimstone upon the others, and this rain was fatal for those who had been warned, but who did not take heed.

Will You Have Sexual Relations with Men

26:159 Truly, your Lord, He is the mighty, the merciful!

26:160 *The people of Lot rejected the messengers. Their brother Lot said to them, "Will you not fear Allah? I am a faithful messenger worthy of all trust. Fear Allah and obey me. I ask for no reward. My reward comes only from the Lord of the worlds. What? Of all the creatures of the world, will you have sexual relations with men? Will you ignore your wives whom Allah has created for you? You people exceed all limits!"*
26:167 *They said, "Lot, if you do not stop, you will certainly be banished."*
26:168 *He said, "I detest your behavior. My Lord, save me and my family from what they do."*
26:170 *So We delivered him and his entire family except one old woman who lingered behind. Then We destroyed the rest. We rained down on them a shower of brimstone. And the rain was fatal to those We had warned. Surely, there is a sign here, but most of them do not believe. Truly, your Lord, He is the mighty, the merciful!*

Solomon

27:15 *In the past We gave knowledge to David and Solomon, and they said, "Praise be to Allah, Who has favored us over many of His believing servants!" Solomon was David's heir, and he said, "People, we have been taught the language of the birds, and have been given everything. This is clearly a blessing from Allah!"*
27:17 *Armies of men, jinns, and birds were gathered together before Solomon and arranged in battle order, and they marched until they reached the Valley of Ants. One ant said, "Ants, go into your homes so Solomon and his armies do not unwittingly crush you under foot." Solomon smiled at her words and said, "Lord, let me be thankful for your blessings which you have given me; and my parents; and that I should do good things, which are pleasing to you; and include me in the numbers of your righteous servants."*
27:20 *He reviewed the birds and said, "Why do I not see the lapwing [hoopoe]? Is he one of those absent? I will certainly punish him severely or even kill him if he does not have a good excuse." But the lapwing was not far behind, and he said, "I have discovered something you are unaware of, and I come to you from Saba [a kingdom of South Arabia] with good news. I have found out that they are ruled by a woman, and she has been given great wealth and has a mighty throne. I discovered her and her peoples worshipping the sun instead of Allah. Satan has made their actions seem pleasing in their minds and has prevented them from finding the true path so they receive no guidance. They do not worship Allah, Who brings forth what is hidden in the heavens and the earth, and Who knows what you hide and what you admit. There is no god, but Allah! Lord of the glorious throne!"*

27:27 *Solomon said, "We shall soon see whether you are telling the truth, or not. Take and deliver my letter to them; then turn away from them and wait for their answer."*

27:29 *The queen said, "My chiefs, a noble letter has been delivered to me. It is from Solomon and it says, "In the name of Allah, most gracious, most merciful. Do not be arrogant against me, but instead come and submit to me."*

27:32 *She said, "My counselors, give me advice. I never decide an issue without your advice."*

27:33 *They said, "We are strong, willing, and brave, but the power is in your hands. Tell us what you want us to do."*

27:34 *She replied, "Typically, when kings enter a city, they pillage and humiliate its leading citizens. These people will do the same. I will send them a gift and wait until my ambassadors return with their response."*

27:36 *When Sheba's envoy came before Solomon, the king said, "What? Will you try to bribe me with riches? What Allah has given me is better than what He has given to you. You are impressed with your gift, but I am not. Return to your people. You had better believe that we will come to them with forces which they cannot resist, and we will drive them from their land shamed and humbled."*

27:38 *He said to his officers, "My chiefs, which one of you will bring me her throne before they come to me and submit to Allah?"*

27:39 *An evil jinn said, "I will bring it to you before you get out of your chair. I am capable and trustworthy."*

27:40 *But one who knew the Scripture said, "I will bring it to you in the blink of an eye." When Solomon saw it set before him, he said, "This is done by the grace of Allah to see whether or not I would be grateful. If someone is grateful, his gratitude benefits only him. If someone is ungrateful, then he harms only himself. Truly my Lord is self-sufficient, bountiful."*

27:41 *He said, "Disguise her throne so that it is unrecognizable. We will see whether or not she has guidance."*

27:42 *When she arrived, she was asked, "Is this your throne?" She replied, "It seems to be the same." Solomon said, "We received knowledge long before she, and we have submitted to Allah." And he persuaded her from worshiping others besides Allah because she came from a people who had no faith.*

27:44 *It was said to her, "Enter the palace." When she saw it, she thought it was a pool of water, and she pulled up her garment and bared her legs. Solomon said, "It is a palace paved with glass." She said, "Lord, I have sinned against my soul. I submit with Solomon to the Lord of the worlds."*

He Began to Hack and Slash Their Legs and Necks

38:31 *Do you remember the evening the prancing horses were displayed before David? He said, "It is true that I have preferred the good things of this world over the remembrance of my Lord until they leave my sight. Bring them back to me." When they were again brought before him, he began to hack and slash their legs and necks [with his sword].*
38:34 *We also tried Solomon by placing a lifeless replica on his throne, which caused him to repent. He said, "Lord, forgive me and give me a kingdom that will be ruled by no other besides me, because you are truly the bountiful giver." So We subjected the wind to his power. At his bidding it flowed softly wherever he directed. And we subjected the devils, who build and dive in the seas, and the others bound together in chains to his power. We said, "This is Our gift. Whether you share them with others, or withhold them, We will ask for no compensation." Solomon also ranks highly with Us, and he has an excellent place in Paradise.*

Adam

20:115 *Long ago We made a pact with Adam, but he forgot it, and We did not find any resolve in him. When We said to the angels, "Fall down and worship Adam," all of them worshiped him except Iblis [Satan] who refused. We said, "Adam, he is truly an enemy to you and your wife. Do not let him drive you from the garden so that you become miserable. There is enough in the garden to provide you with food and clothing forever.*
20:120 *But Satan whispered to him, "Adam, would you like me to show you the tree of immortality and the power that never decreases?" Adam and Eve both ate from the tree, and their nakedness became apparent, so they began to sew clothing made from garden leaves to hide their nakedness. This is how Adam disobeyed Allah and went astray.*
20:122 *Later his Lord chose him and turned toward him again and guided him. And Allah said, "Both of you go down from here enemies to one another. You will receive more guidance from Me later. Whoever follows My guidance will not go wrong and will not be wretched, but whoever turns away from My message will truly have a life of misery. We will resurrect him and the others, blind, on Judgment Day." He will say, "Lord, why have You gathered me here with the others, blind, when before I could see?" He will reply, "Because Our signs came to you and you ignored them, so you will be ignored today."*

Zacharias

19:1 *KAF. HA. YA. AIN. SAD. This is a recital of your Lord's mercy to his servant Zachariah when he secretly called to his Lord praying, "Oh Lord, certainly my bones are weak and the gray hairs glisten on my head, but my prayers to you, my Lord, have never gone unanswered. But now I fear what my relatives will do after me since my wife is barren. Give me, as your special gift, a successor who will be my heir and an heir to the house of Jacob, and make him, Lord, acceptable to you."*

19:7 *It was said to him, "Zachariah! We bring you good news of a son whose name will be John, a name We have given to no one before."*

19:8 *He said, "Lord, how can I have a son when my wife is barren and I am an old man whose powers have failed him?"*

19:9 *Allah said, "It will happen. Your Lord says, 'For Me this is easy. Before this, I created you out of nothing.'"*

19:10 *He said, "Lord, give me a sign." Allah said, "Your sign will be that you will not speak for three nights, even though you are not mute."*

19:11 *So he went to his people from his sanctuary and signified to them that they should praise Allah morning and evening.*

19:12 *And it was said to his son, "John, receive the Book with strong purpose." And We gave him wisdom while he was still a child and tenderness and purity from Us. He was devout, and kind to his parents, and he was neither arrogant nor rebellious. And peace was on him on the day he was born, until the day he died, and on the day he will be resurrected.*

21:89 *Remember Zacharias when he called upon his Lord saying, "Oh Lord, do not leave me without a child, though You are the best of heirs." We heard him and gave him John for a son and made his wife fit to bear a child. They rivaled each other in goodness and called upon us with love and reverence and humbled themselves before Us.*

21:91 *Remember the virgin woman [Mary] into whom We breathed Our spirit and made her and her son a sign to all people.*

They Became the Conquerors

37:114 *Long ago We bestowed Our favors on Moses and Aaron. We saved them and their families from the great distress. We helped them, so they became the conquerors. We gave them each the book that makes everything clear. We guided both of them onto the right path. We left this for each of them to be honored through posterity.*

37:120 *"Peace be on Moses and Aaron!" This is how We reward the good, because they were two of Our believing servants.*

37:123 *And Elias was one of those sent to warn when he said to his people, "Do you not fear Allah? Do you call the name of Baal and forsake the most skillful Creator, Allah your Lord, and the Lord of your ancestors?" But they treated him like a liar and will therefore be called up for punishment, except Allah's faithful servants. And We left this for him to be honored through posterity.*

37:130 *"Peace be on Elias!" This is how We reward the good, because he was one of Our believing servants.*

Who Neglect Prayer and Pursue Their Lusts

> 19:58 *These were among the prophets of the descendents of Adam and among those whom We carried with Noah, and among the descendents of Abraham and Israel, and among those whom We have guided and chosen, to whom Allah has shown favor. When the signs of Allah the merciful were recited to them, they fell down worshipping and weeping.*
>
> 19:59 *But others have come after them who neglect prayer and pursue their lusts; in the end, they will face destruction, except those who repent and believe and do good. These will enter the Garden, which Allah, the merciful, has promised to His servants, and will not be wronged in the least. His promise will certainly come to pass. They will not hear any idle talk there, but only the greeting of "Peace," and food will be given them morning and evening. This is the Garden that We will give as an inheritance for Our servants who fear Us.*

And then there were the many stories of Moses

> 20:1 *TA-HA. We did not send the Koran to you to cause you sadness, but as a warning for those who fear Allah. It is a message from Him who made the earth and the heavens above, Allah, the merciful, who sits on His throne. Whatever is in the heavens and the earth, everything in between, and under the ground is His! You do not need to speak loudly, because He knows the most secret whisper and what is even more hidden. Allah! There is no god but Him! He is known by the most beautiful names!*
>
> 20:9 *Have you heard the story of Moses? He saw a fire and said to his family, "Wait here. I see a fire. Maybe I can bring an ember from it, or find a guide there."*
>
> 20:11 *When he came to it, a voice called out, "Moses! I am your Lord. Take off your shoes. You are in the sacred Tuwa valley. I have chosen you. Listen to what I say. I am Allah. There is no god but Me. Worship Me and observe prayer to celebrate My praise. The Hour [Judgment Day] is certainly coming. I plan to keep it a secret so that all souls may be rewarded for their actions. Therefore do not let those who disbelieve and follow their lusts turn you away from the truth and cause your destruction.*
>
> 20:17 *What is that in your right hand, Moses?" He said, "It is my staff. I lean on it and beat the leaves down with it for my sheep, among other things." Allah said, "Throw it down, Moses!" He threw it down, and it turned into a slithering serpent. Allah said, "Grab it and do not be afraid. We will change it back to its former state. Now put your hand under your arm. It will come out white [with leprosy], but unhurt. Another sign so that We may show you Our greatest signs. Go to Pharaoh, because he has exceeded all limits."*
>
> 20:25 *Moses said, "My Lord, relieve my mind and make my task easy. Untie my tongue so they can understand what I say. Give me an assistant*

*from my family—Aaron, my brother—add his strength to mine, and
make him share my task. We will glorify you without pause, because you
are always watching." He said, "Moses, your request is granted. We have
shown you favor before. Our message to your mother inspired her saying:
'Put him into a chest and throw it in the river; the river will leave him on
the bank where he will be found by an enemy to Me and to him.' But I cast
my love down upon you so that you might be raised under my eye."*
20:40 *"Your sister went and said, 'May I bring you someone to nurse him?'
Then We returned you to your mother so that her tears would be dried,
and so she would not grieve. When you killed a man, We saved you from
trouble, and tried you severely. You stayed with the Median [a city on the
Red Sea] people for many years, and then you came here by My decree. I
have chosen you for Myself. You and your brother go with My signs and
do not fail to remember Me. Go to Pharaoh, because he has exceeded all
limits, but speak gently to him; hopefully, he will listen or be afraid."*
20:45 *They said, "Lord, we are afraid that he will be arrogant toward us,
or try to harm us."*
20:46 *He said, "Do not be afraid, because I am with the both of you. I will
listen and watch over you. Go to him and say, 'Surely we have been sent
by your Lord. Let the Children of Israel go with us and do not torment
them. We bring you a sign from your Lord, and peace to him who follows
His guidance. It has been revealed to us that those who reject him and
turn away will be punished.'"*
20:49 *And Pharaoh said, "Who is your Lord, Moses?"*
20:50 *Moses said, "Our Lord is the One who created everything and gave
it all purpose."*
20:51 *Pharaoh replied, "What is the state of the previous generations?"*
20:52 *Moses said, "That knowledge is with My Lord, recorded in His book.
My Lord never errs and He never forgets. He has spread the earth for you
like a carpet and made paths for you to follow. He has sent down the rain
from heaven, and from that we produce the various herbs: (Saying) 'Eat
and feed your cattle. Surely, there are signs here for a thinking man. We
created you from it, we will return you to it, and from it we will raise you
a second time.'"*
20:56 *We showed him all of Our signs, but he rejected and refused them.
He said, "Moses, have you come to drive us from our land with your magic? We will surely produce magic to match your own. Let us schedule a
contest—which neither of us should miss—in a neutral location."*
20:59 *Moses said, "Let us meet on the day of the feast. Gather the people
together at mid-day."*
20:60 *So Pharaoh and his magicians made their plans and came to the
meeting.*

20:61 *Moses said to them, "Woe to you! Do not invent a lie against Allah, or He will destroy you with His punishment. A liar is always destroyed."*

20:62 *The magicians discussed their plans in secret. They said, "These two are expert magicians who plan to drive you from your land with their magic and to destroy your way of life. Make your plans and come and form ranks. Whoever wins today will gain the upper hand." They said, "Moses, will you throw down your rod first, or shall we?" He said, "You cast first." Then, through their magic, their ropes and rods appeared to run, and Moses became afraid.*

20:68 *We said, "Do not be afraid, you will have the upper hand. Cast down what is in your right hand. It will swallow up what they have made because it is nothing but a magicians trick, and a magician, no matter how good, will not be successful."*

20:70 *The magicians threw themselves down and worshipped. They said, "We believe in the Lord of Moses and Aaron." Pharaoh said, "Will you believe in him before I give my permission? This must be the master who taught you your magic. I will cut off your hands and feet on opposite sides and crucify you on the trunks of palm trees, and you will surely learn then which of us gives the more terrible and long-lasting punishment."*

20:72 *They said, "We will never have more regard for you than we do for the clear signs that have been revealed to us, or than we have for our creator. So decree whatever you will decree. Your decrees are only good in this life. We believe in our Lord that He may forgive our sins and magic which you forced upon us. Allah is better and more lasting than you. Hell surely waits for the guilty who come before their Lord. There they will neither live nor die, but lofty positions wait for the believers who come righteously before their Lord! They will dwell in eternal gardens with underground rivers. This is the reward of the pure."*

20:77 *We revealed to Moses, "Take away My servants and travel by night. Cleave a dry path through the sea for them. Do not be afraid of being overtaken and have no fear." Pharaoh and his army followed, but the sea overwhelmed them, because he misled his people by not guiding them.*

20:80 *Children of Israel! We saved you from your enemies, and We made a pact with you on the sacred side of the mountain and sent down to you manna and quails. We said, "Eat the good things that We have given you, but not to excess, or My wrath may fall on you, and whoever My wrath falls upon will surely perish. I will surely forgive him who turns to Allah and believes and does good deeds, and listens to guidance."*

20:83 *(Allah said) "Moses, why have you hurried ahead of your people?"*

20:84 *Moses said, "Lord, they are right behind me, but I have hurried to be with you to please you."*

20:85 *He said, "We have tested your people while you were gone, and Samiri [The identity of Samiri is not known] has led them astray."*

20:86 *Moses returned to his people angry and sad. He said, "My People, did your Lord not promise you a good promise? Was I gone from you too long, or did you break your promise with me because you wanted to anger your Lord?"*
20:87 *"We did not want to break our promise with you, but we had to carry the people's ornaments, so Samiri suggested we throw them in the fire." Then he brought out of the fire the image of a lowing calf. They cried, "This is your god and the god of Moses, but he has forgotten."*
20:89 *What! Did they not see that it could not reply to them and could not help or hurt them?*
20:90 *Aaron had already told them, "People, You are being tested. Surely your Lord is the god of Mercy: Follow and obey me."*
20:91 *They said, "We will not stop worshiping it until Moses returns."*
20:92 *Moses said, "Aaron, when you saw that they had gone astray, why did you not come and get me? Did you disobey my order?"*
20:94 *He said, "Son of my mother! Do not grab me by the beard or the head. I was afraid that you would say that I caused a division among the Children of Israel, and did not wait for your word."*
20:95 *Moses said, "Samiri, what was your motive?" He replied, "I saw what they did not. My soul prompted me, so I took a handful of dust from the footprint of Allah's messenger and flung it into the calf."*
20:97 *Moses said, "Go away. Surely your punishment in this life will be to say, 'Do not touch me.' And there is a sentence against you that you cannot avoid. Now look at the god that you are so devoted to. We will certainly burn it to ashes and scatter them on the sea. Your god is Allah. There is no god, but Allah. He knows all things."*

Go to the Wicked People

26:10 *Remember when your Lord said to Moses, "Go to the wicked people, the people of Pharaoh. Will they not fear me?" He said, "My Lord, truthfully, I am afraid they will reject me, and I will be embarrassed, and I may not speak clearly. Send for Aaron to help me. They have charged me with a crime [Moses had killed an Egyptian], and I'm afraid that they will kill me." Allah said, "Certainly not. Both of you go with Our signs. We will be with you, listening. Go to Pharaoh and say, 'Truly, we are the messengers of the Lord of the worlds. Let the Children of Israel go with us."*
26:18 *Pharaoh said, "Did we not raise you among us when you were a child? Did you not spend many years of your life among us? And still you have done what you have done! You are one of the ungrateful."*
26:20 *Moses said, "I did it then when I was in error. I fled from you, because I was afraid, but My Lord has given me wisdom and has made me one of His apostles. And what is this favor you remind me of—that you have enslaved the Children of Israel?"*
26:23 *Pharaoh said, "Who is the Lord of the worlds?"*

26:24 *Moses replied, "The Lord of the heavens and of the earth and everything in between if you only believed."*

26:25 *Pharaoh said to those near him, "Do you hear this?"*

26:26 *"Your Lord," said Moses, "and the Lord of your ancestors."*

26:27 *"Truly, the apostle that has been sent," said Pharaoh, "is insane."*

26:28 *Moses said, "He is the Lord of the east, and the west, and everything between, if only you understood."*

26:29 *Pharaoh said, "If you worship any god beside me, I will certainly imprison you."*

26:30 *Moses replied, "Even if I give you proof of my mission?"*

26:31 *Pharaoh said, "Show your proof if you are telling the truth." He then threw down his staff, and it clearly became a snake. He drew his hand out from under his cloak and it was white [with leprosy] for all to see. Pharaoh said to his nobles surrounding him, "This is truly a skillful sorcerer. His plan is to drive you from your land with his magic. What do you suggest?" They said, "Put him and his brother off for awhile, and send messengers to all the cities, to bring you every skilled magician."*

26:38 *So the magicians were all gathered together at a set time on an appointed day. And it was said to the people: "Is everyone here?" "Yes, and we will follow the magicians if they win."*

26:41 *"When the magicians arrived, they said to Pharaoh, "Will we be rewarded if we win?" He said, "Yes, certainly. If you do, you will be among those who are near my person."*

26:43 *Moses said to them, "Throw what you have to throw." So they threw down their ropes and staffs and said, "By the might of Pharaoh, we will certainly win." Then Moses threw down his staff, and it swallowed up the false illusions. The magicians threw themselves down in awe. They said, "We believe in the Lord of the worlds, the Lord of Moses and Aaron."*

26:49 *Pharaoh said, "So, you believe in him before I give you permission? Certainly, then, he is your master and the one who taught you your magic. But you will soon know my power. I will cut off your hands and feet on opposite sides and then crucify all of you." They said, "It cannot harm us, we will return to our Lord. We hope that our Lord will forgive our sins since we are the first of the believers."*

26:53 *We then revealed to Moses, "Take away My servants, and leave at night because you will be pursued." And Pharaoh sent messengers throughout the cities: "These Israelites are only a small band. They may rage against us, but we are a vigilant, great army."*

26:58 *So we expelled them from gardens, and fountains, and treasures, and fine buildings. So it happened, and we gave their things to the children of Israel as an inheritance. At sunrise the Egyptians followed them. When the two groups saw each other, the people of Moses said, "We are sure to be caught." He said, "Certainly not. My Lord is with me. He will guide*

me." We then revealed to Moses, "Strike the sea with your staff." It split in two, each part like a huge mountain. We made the others follow them to that place. We saved Moses and all of his followers, but We drowned the others. Surely this is a sign, but most of them did not believe.
26:69 *But truly, your Lord, He is mighty and merciful!*
26:70 *Recite to them the story of Abraham. When he said to his father and his people, "What do you worship?"*
26:72 *They said, "We worship idols and give them constant devotion."*
26:73 *He said, "Do they hear you when you call to them? Do they help you, or do you harm?"*
26:74 *They said, "No, but it is what our fathers did."*
26:75 *He said, "Do you see what you have been worshiping? You and your ancestors are my enemies, but not the Lord of the worlds. He created me and guides me, and He gives me food and drink. When I am sick, He heals me, He causes me to die and then gives me rebirth, and, I hope, He will forgive me my sins on the Judgment Day."*
26:83 *"My Lord, give me wisdom and unite me with the righteous, give me a good name in posterity, and make me an heir of the Garden of Delight. Forgive my father because he was one of those who have gone astray. Do not let me be disgraced when men are raised up, on the day when neither riches or children will help, except for those who come to Allah with a sound heart. Paradise will be brought close to the righteous and Hell opened for those who have gone astray. It will be said to them, 'Where are the gods whom you worshipped besides Allah? Can they harm you or help themselves?'"*
26:94 *"And they will be cast into the fire—the seducers and the seduced and all the hosts of Iblis [Satan]. They will say, as they quarrel among themselves, 'Allah, we were plainly in error when we made our deities equal with the Lord of the worlds. It was the wicked who misled us, and we have no one to plead for us and no friend who cares for us. If we could only return, we would be believers.'"*
26:103 *Surely, there is a sign here, but most of them do not believe. Truly, your Lord, He is mighty and merciful!*

Why Have Angels Not Accompanied Him on His Mission?

43:46 *Earlier We sent Moses with Our signs to Pharaoh and his chiefs, and he said, "I am a messenger of the Lord of the worlds." But when he came to them with Our signs, they laughed at them. We showed them many signs, each greater than the last, and We punished them so that they might turn to Us. And they said, " Oh, sorcerer, for our sake call upon your Lord. You have a covenant with Him. We will certainly follow the right guidance." But when We removed the punishment, they broke their word.*
43:51 *And Pharaoh made a proclamation to his people saying, "My people, doesn't the kingdom of Egypt belong to me, as well as the rivers that*

flow at my feet? Do you not see? I am certainly better than this man, who is a contemptible wretch and who can barely make himself understood. Why hasn't he been given gold bracelets, and why have angels not accompanied him on his mission?" This is how he incited his people to mock Moses, and they obeyed him. They were truly an evil people. Then, when they angered Us, We punished them by drowning them all. We made them a people of the past and an example for the future.

21:48 *A long time ago We gave Moses and Aaron the standard We would use for judgment,. It was a light and a warning for those who want to do right, those who fear their Lord in their inner most thoughts, and those who dread the Hour of Judgment. What We have revealed is a blessed reminder. Will you reject it?*

25:35 *Long ago, We gave Moses the Book, and appointed his brother Aaron as his aide. We commanded them, "Both of you go to the people who have rejected Our signs." We absolutely destroyed those people. And the people of Noah, when they rejected the messengers, We drowned them and made them a sign for all men. We have prepared a terrible penalty for all the wicked.*

This Is Obviously Witchcraft

27:7 *Recall when Moses said to his family, "I see a distant fire. I will go there and bring news or, if nothing else, a burning ember so that you may warm yourselves. When he came upon the fire, a voice said to him, "Blessed are those in the fire and those near by. Glory to Allah, the Lord of the worlds! Moses, throw down your staff!" But when he saw it writhing like a snake, he turned to run away. A voice called out, "Moses, do not be afraid. Truly, a prophet has nothing to fear in My presence, even he who has done wrong but afterwards does good instead of evil, because I am the forgiving, the merciful. Place your hand inside the bosom of your cloak. It will come out white [like a leper] but uninjured. This will be one of nine signs that you will take to Pharaoh and his people; they are certainly a wicked people."*
27:13 *But when Our signs were brought to them, they said, "This is obviously witchcraft!" And they unjustly and arrogantly rejected those signs, even though their souls were convinced of their truth. Consider the consequences for the wicked.*

17:101 *We gave Moses nine clear signs. Ask the children of Israel how it was when he came to them and Pharaoh said to him, "I think that you are a madman." Moses said, "Truly you know that no one but the Lord of the heavens and the earth has sent these signs as clear proof, and truly I think that you are a lost soul." So Pharaoh wished to wipe them from the face of the earth, but We destroyed him and all of his followers. After his death, We said to the Children of Israel, "Dwell safely here in the land of promise, but when the promise of the hereafter comes to pass, We will assemble you and the other nations together in judgment.*

And there was one Moses story never referred to in the Torah.

18:60 *Recall when Moses said to his servant, "I will not give up until I reach the junction of the two rivers, even though I travel for many years." When they reached the junction of the rivers, they forgot about the fish that swam their course to the sea. After they had gone further, Moses said to his servant, "Bring us our breakfast. Our journey makes us tired."*
18:63 *The servant replied, "What do you think? When we rested at the rock, I forgot about the fish. No one except Satan could make me forget to mention it. However, it simply followed its course to the sea in a wonderful way."*
18:64 *Moses said, "That is what we were seeking." So they returned by retracing their steps. They found one of Our servants to whom We had given Our mercy and instructed with Our knowledge.*
18:66 *Moses said to him, "May I follow you so that you may teach me the lessons that have been taught to you?"*
18:67 *The man said, "You will not have the patience to learn from me! How can you have patience with things that you do not understand?"*
18:69 *Moses said, "Allah willing, you will find me patient, and I will not disobey you in any way."*
18:70 *The man said, "If you wish to follow me, then do not ask me any questions unless I speak to you about it first."*
18:71 *They proceeded in his way until they embarked on a ship when the man made a hole in its bottom. Moses cried, "What? Are you scuttling the ship to drown everyone on it? You have certainly done a terrible thing."*
18:72 *He replied, "Did I not tell you that you would not have the patience to deal with me?"*
18:73 *Moses said, "Do not scold me for forgetting, and do not be so hard on me because of my fault."*
18:74 *They proceeded on until they met a young boy whom the man killed. Moses said, "Have you killed an innocent person who has killed no one? You have certainly done a evil thing."*
18:75 *The man said, "Did I not tell you that you would not have the patience to deal with me?*
18:76 *Moses said, "If I question you about anything after this, do not keep me in your company. You will then have an excuse to dismiss me."*
18:77 *They proceeded on until they reached a city where they asked the citizens for some food but were refused. There they found a wall about to fall, which the man repaired. Moses said, "If you had wished, you could have been paid for your work."*

18:78 *The man said, "This is where you and I part company. Now I will tell you the significance of those things which you had not the patience to wait for. As for the ship, it belonged to poor men who worked upon the river. I wished to damage it because there is a king behind them who is seizing any ship that he can by force. As for the boy, his parents were believers, and we were afraid that he would oppress them by rebelling and by disbelieving. We desired that Allah should exchange him for a son who was more virtuous and more compassionate. As for the wall, it belonged to two orphaned youths of the town, and their treasure was buried beneath it. Their father was a righteous man, so your Lord intended that when they became adults, they would recover their treasure through the mercy of Allah. I did not do it of my own accord. This explains those things which you were so impatient to learn."*

I192 Since Mohammed and the Koran claimed Jewish roots, the Quraysh decided to send their story teller to the Jews in Medina and ask for help. This was not a causal quest, as it took the better part of a month for the trip and questions. So Al Nadr went to Medina and asked the rabbis what questions to ask Mohammed. He told the rabbis about Mohammed, what he did, what he said and that he claimed to be a prophet. Since they had had prophets they must know more about the subject than the Meccans.

I192 The rabbis said, "Ask him these three questions. If he knows the answer then he is a prophet, if not then he is a fake."

"What happened to the young men who disappeared in ancient days."

"Ask him about the mighty traveler who reached the ends of the East and the West."

"Ask him, What is the spirit?"

I192 Back in Mecca, they went to Mohammed and asked him the three questions. He said he would get back to them tomorrow. Days went by. Finally, fifteen days had passed. Mohammed waited on Gabriel for the answers. The Meccans began to talk. Mohammed did not know what to do. He had no answers. Finally, he had a vision of Gabriel.

19:64 *The angels say, "We descend from heaven only by Allah's command. Everything that is before us and everything that is behind us and whatever is in between belongs to Him. And Your Lord never forgets. Lord of the heavens and the earth and everything in between! Worship Him and remain steadfast in your praise of Him. Do you know any that is worthy of the same name?"*

The Koran answered all the questions and statements of the Quraysh. With regards to the question about what happened to the young men in ancient times:

18:9 *Do you believe that the Sleepers of the Cave and the Inscription
[an unknown reference] were among Our signs? When the youths [the
Sleepers] took refuge in the cave, they said, "Lord, give us Your mercy
and cause us to act rightly." We drew a veil over them depriving them of
their senses for many years. Then We roused them so that We could know
which would best determine the number of years they lived in the cave.*
18:13 *We tell you their story truthfully. They were youths who believed
in their Lord, and We increased their ability to guide others. We gave
strength to their hearts. Recall when they stood up and said, "Our Lord
is the Lord of the heaven and the earth. We will worship no other god
besides Him. If we did, then we would have certainly said an outrageous
thing. Our people have taken other gods to worship besides Allah. Why
do they not prove their existence? Who is more wicked than a person who
makes up lies about Allah? When will you turn away from them and the
things they worship besides Allah? Seek refuge in the cave. Your Lord will
extend His mercy to you and cause your affairs to turn out for the best."*
18:17 *You may have seen the sun, when it rose, pass to the right of their
cave and set to their left while they were in its spacious middle. This is
one of signs of Allah. Whomever Allah guides is rightly guided. Whomever He allows to stray will not find a friend to guide him.*
18:18 *While they were sleeping, you would have thought that they were
awake [they slept with their eyes open]. We turned them on their right side
and their left side. Their dog lay in the entrance with its paws stretched
out. If you had come upon them, you would have certainly run away
filled with terror of them. This was their condition before We awakened
them so that they might question one another. One of them asked, "How
long have you lingered here?" Some said, "We have been here a day or so."
Others said, "Your Lord knows exactly how long you have lingered. One
of you should take your money into the city find and buy the best food
possible. He should be courteous and should not let anyone know about
you. If they should come upon you, they would either kill you or force you
to return to their religion, in which case you would never prosper."*
18:21 *We made their existence known to the city so that they would know
that Allah's promise is true and that there is no doubt about the Hour of
Judgment. The people of the city argued amongst themselves about the
affair. Some said, "We should construct a building over them. Their Lord
knows all about them." The winners of the debate were those who said,
"We will certainly build a temple over them."*
18:22 *Some say, "There were three, the dog being the forth." Others say,
"Five, the dog was the sixth." Still others say, "There were seven, and
a dog made eight." Say: My Lord knows the exact number. Only a few
know the truth. So do not become involved in arguments about them except on matters that are clear, and do not consult any of them about the
Sleepers.*

> 18:23 *And do not say, "I will do it tomorrow," without adding, "Allah willing." Remember your Lord when you forget and say, "I hope that Allah will guide me even closer than this to the right path."*
>
> 18:25 *They remained in their cave for three hundred years, though some say three hundred and nine. Say: Allah knows exactly how long they stayed. He knows the secrets of the heavens and the earth. Man has no guardian besides Him. He does not allow any to share His power.*

As to the question about the mighty traveler:

> 18:83 *They will ask you about Zul-Qarnain [Alexander, the Great]. Say: I will recite to you an account of him. We established his power in the land and gave him the means to achieve any of his aims. So he followed a path, until, when he reached the setting of the sun, he found it setting in a muddy pond. Near by he found a people. We said, "Zul-Qarnain, you have the authority to either punish them or to show them kindness."*
>
> 18:87 *He said, "Whoever does wrong, we will certainly punish. Then he will be returned to his Lord, Who will punish him with a terrible punishment. But whoever believes and does good deeds shall be given a wonderful reward, and We will give them easy commands to obey."*
>
> 18:89 *Then he followed another path, until, when he came to the rising of the sun, he found that it rose upon a people to whom We had given no protection from it. He left them as they were. We knew everything about him. Then he followed another path until, when he reached a place between two mountains, he found a people living in a valley who could scarcely understand a single word. They said, "Zul-Qarnain, the people of Gog and Magog are terrorizing the land. May we pay you tribute so that you will build a strong barrier between us and them?"*
>
> 18:95 *He said, "The power which my Lord has given me is better than your tribute. Help me, therefore, with manpower. I will build a strong barrier between you and them. Bring me blocks of iron." Later, when he had filled the gap between the two mountains, he said, "Blow with your bellows!" When it had become as red as fire, he said, "Bring me molten lead to pour over it." So the people of Gog and Magog were unable to climb over the barrier or to go through it. He said, "This is a mercy from my Lord, but when my Lord's promise comes to pass, He will destroy it, because my Lord's promises always come true."*

The question—what is the spirit?

> 17:85 *They will ask you about the spirit [probably the angel Gabriel]. Say: The spirit is commanded by my Lord, and you are given only a little knowledge about it. If We wished, We could take Our revelations away from you. Then you would find no one to intercede with us on your behalf except as a mercy from your Lord. Surely His kindness to you is great.*

The Quraysh had questions about proof of Mohammed's messages. Here is the Koran's restatement of their questions about angels coming, creating rivers, creating wealth and any other miracle to prove Mohammed's validity. The Koran's response:

> 17:88 *Say: If men and jinn were assembled to produce something like this Koran, they could not produce its equal, even though they assisted each other. And certainly in this Koran We have explained to man every kind of argument, and yet most men refuse everything except disbelief. They [the Meccans] say, "We will not believe in you until you cause a spring to gush forth from the earth for us; or until you have a garden of date trees and grape vines, and cause rivers to gush abundantly in their midst; or when you cause the sky to fall down in pieces, as you claim will happen; or when you bring us face-to-face with Allah and the angels; or when you have a house of gold; or when you ascend into heaven; and even then we will not believe in your ascension until you bring down a book for us which we may read." Say: Glory be to my Lord! Am I nothing except a man, a messenger?*
>
> 17:94 *What keeps men from believing when guidance has come to them but that they say, "Has Allah sent a man like us to be His messenger?" Say: If angels walked the earth, We would have sent down from heaven an angel as Our messenger. Say: Allah is a sufficient witness between you and me. He is well acquainted with His servants and He sees everything.*
>
> 17:97 *Whoever Allah guides, he is a follower of the right way, and whoever He causes to err, they shall not find any to assist them but Him. We will gather them together on the Resurrection Day, face down, blind, deaf, and dumb. Hell will be their home. Every time its flames die down, We will add fuel to the Fire. This is their reward because they did not believe Our signs and said, "When we are reduced to bones and dust, will we really be raised up as a new creation?"*
>
> 17:99 *Do they not realize that Allah, Who created the heavens and the earth, is able to create the likes of them? He has appointed a duration for them that can not be denied, but the wicked deny everything except disbelief. Say: If you controlled the treasures of the mercy of my Lord, you would be afraid to spend them because man is miserly.*

As regards to the old Persian stories that are as good as Mohammed's:

> 25:3 *Still they have worshiped other gods, besides Him, who have created nothing and were themselves created. They are powerless to work good or evil for themselves, nor can they control life or death or resurrection. But the unbelievers say, "This [the Koran] is nothing but a lie which he [Mohammed] has created with the assistance of others producing slander and injustice."*

> 25:5 *They say, " These are ancient fables that he has written down. They are dictated to him morning and night."*
> 25:6 *Say: The Koran was revealed by Him who knows the secrets of the heavens and the earth. He is truly forgiving and merciful.*

As for following the religion of their forefathers:

> 43:21 *Are they clinging to a scripture that We had given them earlier? No! They say, "Our fathers followed a certain religion, and we are guided by their footsteps." And so, whenever We sent a messenger before you to an erring people, their wealthy said, "Our fathers followed a certain religion, and we are guided by their footsteps." The messenger said, "What! Even if I bring you better guidance than your fathers had?" They replied, "We do not believe what you say." So We punished them. Now see what comes to those who reject truth!*

After the Jewish leaders in Medina helped the Meccans with questions to ask Mohammed, the Koran has its first negative comments about the Jews.

> 27:76 *Surely this Koran explains to the Children of Israel most of the issues upon which they disagree. Certainly it is a guide and a mercy for those who believe. Surely your Lord will use His wisdom to judge between them. He is the mighty and the all-knowing. So put your trust in Allah. Surely, you are on the path to the plain truth.*
> 27:80 *You can not make the dead listen or the deaf to hear, when they have turned to flee, nor can you guide the blind from their errors. You can not make any listen except those who believe our revelations and who have submitted to Islam. When the Word against them is fulfilled, We will send a monster created from the earth to speak to them because mankind did not believe Our signs. One day We will gather together, from all peoples, a group of those who rejected Our signs and organize them into ranks until, when they come before their Lord, He will say, "Did you reject My signs because you could not understand them? What was it that you were doing?" And the Word will be fulfilled against them, because of their wickedness. They will be unable to speak in their own defense.*

> 17:2 *We gave the Book [the Torah] to Moses and made it a guide for the Children of Israel, commanding, "Do not take another guardian besides me." You descendents of the people We carried to safety with Noah! He was a grateful servant. In the Book We gave clear warning to the Children of Israel that they would twice commit wickedness on the earth and be filled with arrogance. Upon the first warning we sent Our mighty and war-like servants against you [the Syrians conquered the Jews]. They went from house to house, and Our warning was completely fulfilled. Later, in turn, We made you masters over them and increased your*

> *resources and children and made your armies much larger. We said, "If you do well, you will do well for yourselves; if you do evil, you will do it against yourselves." So, when the second warning came, We sent another people to bring grief to you [the Romans conquered the Jews], and to enter the temple as they did before and to utterly destroy all that came under their control.*

THE QURAYSH LISTEN TO MOHAMMED'S READING

I203 Three of the Meccans decided, each on their own, to sit outside Mohammed's house and listen to him recite the Koran and pray. As they left they ran into each other. They said that they should not do it again as someone might think that they cause others to listen. But on the next night they all three did the same thing. And so on the third night as well. They then talked among each other. One said, "I heard things I know and know what was meant by them. And I heard things I don't know and I don't know what was intended by them." The other agreed. The third said that he had always had a competition with one of Mohammed's recent converts. They had both fed the poor and helped the oppressed. They had always been as equals, but now his friendly rival claimed that he had a prophet and his friend did not. Hence, he was now superior. He said, "But I can never believe in this man, Mohammed."

I204 So the next time Mohammed called upon them to submit to Islam, they said, "Our hearts are veiled; we don't understand what you say. There is something in our ears so we can't hear you. A curtain divides us. You go follow your path and we will go ours."

The Koranic response:

> 17:45 *When you recite the Koran, We place an invisible barrier between you and the unbelievers. We place veils over their hearts and deafness in their ears so that they do not understand it, and when you mention only your Lord, Allah, in the Koran, they turn their backs and flee from the truth. We know absolutely what they listen to when they listen to you, and when they speak privately, the wicked say, "You follow a mad man!" See what they compare you to. But they have gone astray and cannot find the way.*
>
> 17:49 *They say, "When we are nothing but bones and dust, will we really be raised up from the dead to be a new creation?" Say: Yes, whether you be stones, or iron, or any other thing which you conceive to be harder to resurrect." When they say, "Who will bring us back to life?" Say: He who created you the first time. They will shake their heads at you and say, "When will this happen?" Say to them, "Perhaps it will be soon—a day*

when He will call you, and you will answer by praising Him, and you will think that you have waited only a little while!"

Mohammed's opponents are frequently quoted and paraphrased:

43:5 *Should We take the message away from you [the Meccans] because you are sinners? How many prophets did We send among the ancient peoples? They mocked every prophet that came to them. We destroyed nations mightier than these today, and the example of the older generations has passed away.*
43:9 *If you were to ask them [the Meccans] who created the heavens and the earth, they would say, "The mighty, the knowing One has created them." He made the earth a resting place for you and laid out paths for you to find your way. He sends down measured amounts of rain from the sky, which We use to resurrect a dead land just as you will be resurrected. He created all the mated pairs and made ships and animals to carry you along so that you may sit squarely and firmly on their backs. When you are firmly mounted, remember to celebrate your Lord's blessing. Say: Glory to Him that has subjugated these animals for our use when we were incapable of doing so. Surely, we will all return to Our Lord.*
43:15 *And yet, they say some of His servants are really His children [Jesus]! Certainly man is clearly ungrateful. What? Has Allah adopted daughters from among His creations [the Meccans said that angels were the daughters of Allah] and chosen sons for you? Allah's face darkens and He becomes filled with anger when He hears that one of His servants is set up as His likeness.*
43:18 *What? Can they say that a being, brought up among trinkets [the idols were bedecked with jewelry] and unreasonably contentious, is the child of Allah? And they say that the angels that personally serve Allah are females. Did they witness their creation? Their testimony will be recorded, and they will be questioned. And they say, "We would not have worshipped such idols if it was Allah's will." They have no knowledge of this. They only lie.*

We Assign a Devil as a Companion

43:29 *I have allowed these men and their fathers to enjoy the pleasurable things of this life until the truth comes to them and a messenger makes things clear.*
43:30 *But when the truth came to them, they said: "This is trickery, and we reject it." And they say, "Why was this Koran not revealed to a great man of one of the two cities [Mecca and Taif]?"*
43:32 *Will they distribute Allah's mercy? We distribute among them their worldly success, and We exalt some of them above the others in ranks, subjecting some to others. Your Lord's mercy is greater than the wealth they amass. And if it were not probable that all humanity might become*

a single nation of unbelievers, We would have given silver roofs and staircases to everyone, and silver doors for their homes, and silver couches on which to recline, and ornaments of gold, but these are merely luxuries of this world's life. The afterlife with your Lord is for the righteous.

43:36 *We assign a devil as a companion for those who turn their backs and neglect to remember Allah. Satan will certainly turn man from the way of Allah, even though he believes he is being guided correctly. On the day when man comes before Us, he will say, "Satan, I wish that the distance between east and west separated us." Satan is a wretched companion. But that realization will not help you that day, because you were unjust, and you will share the punishment. Can you make the deaf listen or guide the blind and those clearly in error?*

43:41 *Even if We took you [Mohammed] away, We would surely take vengeance upon them; even though We showed you what We have promised them, We would still have total control over them. So keep a firm hold on the revelation sent to you; surely you are on the right path. The Koran is indeed the message for you and your people, and you shall all be soon brought to account.*

43:45 *And ask Our messengers that We sent before you [Mohammed]: have We ever appointed gods to be worshipped along with the merciful Allah?*

He Is Just a Crazy Poet

21:1 *Man's final reckoning draws ever closer to him, and yet he heedlessly continues to turn away. Every new warning that comes to him from his Lord is ridiculed. The wicked confer secretly and say, "Is he a man like you, or something more? Will you succumb to witchcraft with your eyes wide open?"*

21:4 *Say: My Lord knows what is spoken in the heavens and on earth. He is the hearer and the knower of all things.*

21:5 *They say, "No, This is nothing but jumbled dreams. He made it up. He is just a crazy poet! We want him to bring us a sign similar to those given to the prophets of the past!" Up to their time, despite Our warnings, not a single city that We destroyed believed. Will these people believe?*

21:7 *Before you, Our messengers were also men to whom We sent a revelation. If you do not know this, you should ask someone who has received the Message. We did not give them bodies that did not need food, and they would not live forever. In the end, We kept Our promise, and We saved whom We pleased and destroyed the sinners. Now We have given you a book [the Koran] that contains the message for you. Now will you understand?*

21:11 *How many wicked cities have We destroyed and replaced with another people? And still, when they sensed Our punishment, they began to run. It was said to them, "Do not run. Return to your homes and easy lives so that you may be called to account for your actions." They said, "Oh no! We were certainly wicked!" This cry of theirs did not stop until We mowed them down and left them like reaped corn.*

Follow Our Way, and We Will Bear Your Sins

29:12 *The unbelievers say to the faithful, "Follow our way, and we will bear your sins." They cannot bear anyone's sins—they are liars. They will bear their own burdens, and they will bear burdens beside their own. On Judgment Day they will be called into account for their inventions.*

29:14 *We sent Noah to his people, and he was with them a thousand years save fifty, and the flood overtook them for they were wrongdoers. We rescued him and those who were in the ark, and We made it a sign to all men. And remember Abraham when he said to his people, "Worship Allah and fear Him. This will be best for you if you understand."*

29:17 *You only worship idols besides Allah and are the authors of a lie. Those you worship besides Allah can give you no sustenance. Seek sustenance from Allah and serve Him and give Him thanks. You will return to Him. If you reject the truth, there were nations before you who treated Allah's messenger as a liar. The only duty of the messenger is to convey the message clearly. Do they not see how Allah conceives the creation and can recreate it? This truly is easy for Allah.*

The Koran introduces stories about Mary and Jesus.

19:16 *And mention Mary in the Scripture, when she withdrew from her family to a place in the East. She took a veil to screen herself from them. Then We sent Our spirit [Gabriel] to her in the form of a perfect man. She said, "I seek protection from you with Merciful Allah. If you fear Him, then do not come near me."*

19:19 *He said, "I am merely your Lord's messenger. I come to announce to you the gift of a holy son."*

19:20 *She said, "How can I have a son when no man has touched me, and I am chaste?"*

19:21 *He said, "Even so, it will happen. Your Lord says, 'That is easy for Me.' We will make him a sign for all men and a mercy from Us. It is something that is decreed." And she conceived him, and she withdrew with him to a remote place. When the pain of childbirth drove her to the trunk of a palm-tree, she said, "If only I had died before this."*

19:24 *But a voice from below her said, "Do not grieve; your Lord has provided a stream beneath you. Shake the trunk of the palm-tree towards yourself; it will drop fresh ripe dates upon you. So eat and drink and dry your eyes. And if you should see any man, say, 'I have promised a fast to Allah. I will speak to no one today.'"*

19:27 *Later, she brought the baby to her people, carrying him in her arms. They said, "Mary, you have come with an amazing thing. Sister of Aaron,*

> *your father was not a wicked man, and your mother was not unchaste." But she merely pointed to the baby. They said, "How can we speak with an infant in a cradle?" The child said, "Surely, I am the servant of Allah. He has given me the Book and has made me a prophet. He has made me blessed wherever I am; and has urged me to pray and give alms, as long as I live; and to be dutiful to my mother; and He has not made me arrogant or miserable. The peace of Allah was on me the day I was born, and will be on me the day that I die; and on the day I will be resurrected."*
> 19:34 *This was Jesus, the son of Mary; this is a statement of truth about which they [Christians] dispute. It does not befit the majesty of Allah to father a son. Glory be to Him! When He decrees something, He only needs to say, "Be," and it is. Surely, Allah is my Lord and your Lord, so serve Him. That is the right path.*
> 19:37 *The sects differ among themselves about Jesus. Woe to the unbelievers because of the upcoming judgment of a momentous day. They will see and hear clearly on the day they come before Us. But today the unjust are clearly in error. Warn them of the day of distress when the matter is decided. They are negligent, and they do not believe. We will inherit the earth and everyone on it, and they will be returned to Us.*

And then there are arguments that give the Koranic view of Christianity:

> 43:57 *When Jesus, the son of Mary, is held up as an example, your people laugh out loud and say, "Are our gods better, or is he?" They raise the question merely to provoke you [Mohammed]. They are a contentious people. He was nothing but a servant upon whom We granted favor and of whom We made an example for the children of Israel. If it were Our Wish, We could make angels from among you to be your successors on the earth. Jesus will be a sign for the Hour of Judgment. Therefore have no doubts about it, but instead follow Me. This is the right path. Do not let Satan deter you. Surely he is your sworn enemy.*
> 43:64 *When Jesus came with clear proof of Allah's sovereignty, he said, "I come to you with wisdom and to clear up some things which you dispute. Therefore fear Allah and obey me. Allah is my Lord and yours. Worship Him. This is the right path."*
> 43:65 *But the factions among them [Christians] fell into disagreement, so woe to wrong-doers from the punishment of a terrible day. Do they wait only for the Hour of Judgment that it should come upon them suddenly when they least expect it? On that day, friends will become enemies to one another, except those who kept faith with Allah.*

So Leave Them to Chatter On

> 43:81 *Say to the Christians: If Allah, the most gracious, had a son, I would be the first to worship. Glory to the Lord of the heavens and the earth, the Lord of the throne! He is free from the things attributed to*

Him! So leave them to chatter on and play with words until they meet the day they are promised.
43:84 *Allah rules the heavens and the earth. He is the wise, the knowing. Blessed is He whose kingdom is the heavens and the earth and everything in between. He has knowledge of the Hour of Judgment, and you will be returned to Him.*
43:86 *Those whom they invoke for protection besides Allah have no power to intercede. Only He who bears witness to the truth may do that, and they know Him. If you asked them who their creator is, they would certainly say, "Allah." Then, how are they turned from the truth? And the Prophet will cry, "My Lord, truly these are people who do not believe." So turn away from them and say, "Peace." They will soon find out.*

18:1 *Praise be to Allah Who has revealed the Book to His servant and Who has not placed into it any deceit.*
18:2 *He has made it very clear in order to warn of a terrible punishment from Him and to give good news to the righteous believers of a substantial reward of Paradise, where they will remain for ever after.*
18:4 *Warn those [Christians] who say, "Allah has fathered a son." They do not have any proof about that and neither did their fathers. It is a terrible thing that comes from their mouths. They say nothing but lies. You may worry yourself to death fretting because they do not believe this message.*
18:7 *The things which are on the earth are mere decorations so We may test mankind and determine who has acted best. But We will soon reduce everything on it to dust.*

The Koran continued to teach about the spirit world of Satan (Ilbis) and the jinns.

I Am Forgiving and Merciful, and My Punishment Is the Most Terrible Punishment

15:26 *We created man from potter's clay, from black mud molded into shape. We earlier created the jinn from a blazing fire. Remember, your Lord said to the angels, "I will create man from dry clay, from black mud molded into shape. When I have fashioned him and breathed My spirit into him, you must fall down and worship him."*
15:31 *And the angels bowed down together to worship him, except Iblis. He refused to bow down.*
15:32 *Allah said, "Iblis, why did you not bow down and worship with the others?"*
15:33 *He said, "I am not the kind to bow down and worship man, whom you have created from clay, from shaped mud."*

15:34 *Allah said, "Then get out of here, because you are cursed, and you will remain cursed until the Judgment Day."*
15:36 *He said, "Allah, give me a reprieve until the day man is raised from the dead."*
15:37 *Allah said, "You are granted a reprieve until the preordained time."*
15:39 *He said, "Because You have led me astray, I will make evil seem to be fair to those on the earth, and I will mislead all of them, except those who are Your devoted servants."*
15:41 *Allah said, "This way leads straight to Me. You will have no power over My servants, except those wrongdoers who will follow you." Surely, Hell is the promised place for all of them. It has seven gates, and each of those gates has an assigned group.*
15:45: *The righteous will live among gardens and fountains. They will be told: "You may enter in peace and security." We will remove all rancor from their hearts, and they will sit together like brothers, facing each other on couches. Fatigue will not touch them there, and they will never be asked to leave. Tell My servants that I am forgiving and merciful, and My punishment is the most terrible punishment.*

We Terrorize and Warn Them

17:56 *Say: Call on those whom you claim to be gods besides Allah. They have neither the power to remove your troubles, nor to change them.*
17:57 *Those whom they call upon themselves seek access to their Lord and strive to be closest to Him. They, too, hope for His mercy and fear His punishment. Certainly, your Lord's punishment is something to be afraid of. There is not a single city that We will not destroy or punish before the Resurrection Day. This is written in the Book. We have refrained from sending Our signs because the men of earlier generations have rejected them as lies. We gave the she-camel to Thamud [the people of a ruined Nabatean city near Medina] as a sign, but they mistreated her. We send signs only to make men fear.*
17:60 *Remember when We said to you, "Your Lord encompasses mankind." We created the vision which We showed you and also the cursed tree [the tree of Hell] in the Koran to be a trial for men. We terrorize and warn them, but it only increases their great wickedness.*
17:61 *Recall what We said to the angels, "Bow down before Adam." All except Iblis [Satan] bowed down. He said, "Why should I bow down to someone whom You created from clay? Do You see this creature whom You have honored above me? If you will give me respite until the Resurrection Day, I will destroy all except a few of his descendents."*
17:63 *Allah said, "Go! If any of them follow you, then Hell will be a fitting payment for all of you. Beguile any of them that you can with your voice, urge your infantry and cavalry against them, be their partner in wealth and children, and promise them anything. But Satan promises only to*

deceive. As for My servants, you will have no authority over them." Your Lord is sufficient to be their protector.

17:66 *It is your Lord who speeds the ship across the sea for you so that you might seek His bounty. He is most merciful to you. When distress comes upon you at sea, those whom you call upon [false gods] cannot be found. Only Allah is there. When He delivers you safely to land, you turn away from Him. Man is ungrateful. Are you confidant that He will not cause you to be swallowed by the earth or that He will not send a deadly storm against you? You will have no protector if He does. Or do you feel secure that He will not send you to sea a second time and cause a fierce gale to drown you because of your ingratitude? You will have no one to help you against Us, if He does.*

17:70 *We have honored the children of Adam. We carry them over the land and sea and have provided them with the good things, and We have given them special favors far beyond what We have given most of Our other creations.*

17:71 *One day We will summon all men and their leaders. Those who receive their record [the book of life's deeds recorded by an angel] in their right hand will read it and will not be harmed in the least. But those who were blind in this world will be blind in the next and even further from the path. Their [the Meccans'] purpose was to turn you away from Our revelation and to substitute an invention [soften the condemnation of the ancient Arabic religion and customs] the in Our name. If this had occurred, then they would certainly have accepted your friendship. If We had not given you strength, then you would have been apt to be a little sympathetic towards them.*

The Shooting Stars Guard against Every Rebellious Satan

37:1 *By the angels drawn up in ranks, and by those who repel wickedness with admonition, and by those who recite the Koran as a reminder, Allah is the one true god, Lord of the heavens and earth and everything between and Lord of the east.*

37:6 *We have adorned the lower heavens with ornaments. The shooting stars guard against every rebellious Satan so that they can not eavesdrop on the heavenly assembly. They are driven off and damned to perpetual torment by pelting them from all sides. If one slyly sneaks and listens, he is chased away by a meteor.*

My Curse Is on You until the Judgment Day

38:71 *When your Lord said to the angels, "I am about to create man from clay, and when I have shaped him and breathed My spirit into him, then fall down and worship him." And all of the angels prostrated themselves except Iblis. He was proud and became an unbeliever.*

38:75 *Allah said, "Iblis, what prevents you from prostrating yourself to him whom I have created with My hands? Are you too proud, or are you one of the exalted ones?"*
38:76 *He replied, "I am better than he is. You created me from fire, and you made him from clay."*
38:77 *Allah said, "Then get out of here because you are cursed, and My curse is on you until the Judgment Day."*
38:79 *He said, "Lord, give me respite until the Judgment Day."*
38:80 *Allah said, "Then you will be reprieved until the Judgment Day."*
38:82 *He said, "I swear by your power. I will seduce all of them to evil, except your sincere servants."*
38:84 *Allah said, "Then it is true, just, and fitting, and I speak the truth when I say that I will certainly fill Hell with you and every one of your followers."*
38:86 *Say: I do not ask any reward for this, and I am no pretender. This is nothing but a reminder to all men. And after a while, you will come to realize the truth.*

Those Who Try to Listen Find an Ambush of Shooting Stars Waiting

72:1 *Say: It has been revealed to me that a group of jinn listened [to Mohammed recite the Koran] and said, "Truly, we have heard a wonderful recital. It guides us to the truth. We believe in it, and we will never again worship another god. Exalted is the majesty of Our Lord! He has neither a wife nor a child. The foolish among us speak of a god that is unjust. We believed that no man or jinn would utter a lie against Allah."*
72:6 *Indeed there are men who have taken refuge among the jinn, and they have increased their folly. They thought, as you do, that Allah would not resurrect any of the dead. And we [the jinns] sought heaven's secrets but found that it was protected by strong guards and blazing meteors. We used to listen to the wisdom of heaven and sat on some of the seats. But now those who try to listen find an ambush of shooting stars waiting. And it is true that we do not know whether this means evil for those on earth or means to guide them. There are good among us and others who are not. We follow different paths.*
72:12 *It is true we think that no one can frustrate Allah on earth or frustrate Him by fleeing. As soon as we heard the guidance, we believed it. Whoever believes in his Lord, does not need to fear either loss or injustice. Some of us are Muslims; others have gone astray. Whoever submits to Islam pursues the way of truth; but those who go astray will be fuel for Hell. If the unbelievers walk the right path, We will give them abundant waters to drink so we may test them. Those who turn away from remembering their Lord will be sent by Him into a severe torment.*
72:18 *The places of worship are only for Allah, so do not pray to anyone else besides Him.*

> 72:19 *When Allah's servant [Mohammed] stood up to call upon Him, the jinn crowded densely around him. Say: I pray only to Allah, and I ascribe Him no equal.*
> 72:21 *Say: I have no power to help or hurt you.*
>
> 67:5 *We adorned the sky with lights. We will use them as missiles [shooting stars] against the evil ones [jinns who try to listen to the words of heaven]. We have prepared a torment of Fire for them.*

Now verses in the Koran began to form the basis of the legal system (the Sharia) of Islam.

> 23:1 *The successful ones will be the believers who are humble in their prayers who avoid vain conversation, who contribute to the needy, and who abstain from sex (except with their wives or slaves [slaves are bought or taken in battle], in which case they are free from blame, but those who exceed these limits are sinners). Those who honor their promises and contracts and who pay strict attention to their prayers will inherit Paradise. They will dwell there forever.*

Do Not Kill Anyone Whom Allah Has Forbidden to Be Slain [a Muslim]

> 17:25 *Your Lord knows everything in your souls. He knows if you are righteous. He is forgiving to those who frequently turn to Him. Render to your kin their due rights and also to the needy and the traveler. Do not squander your wealth wastefully. The wasteful are brothers of the evil ones, [satans] and the evil ones are always ungrateful to their Lord. And if you turn away from them seeking your Lord's mercy, which you hope for, speak kindly to them. Do not let your hand be tied to your neck like a miser, and do not stretch it out to its limits so that you become rebuked and destitute. Surely, your Lord will abundantly provide sustenance for whom He pleases, and He provides in a just measure. He is always aware of His servants.*
> 17:31 *Do not kill your children because you fear poverty. We will provide for them as well as for you. Surely, killing them is a terrible sin.*
> 17:32 *Have nothing to do with adultery. It is a shameful act and an evil path that leads to other evils.*
> 17:33 *Do not kill any one whom Allah has forbidden to be slain [a Muslim] unless it is for a just cause [apostasy, retribution for a killing]. Whoever is unjustly slain, We have given their heirs the authority to either forgive or demand retribution, but do not allow him to exceed limits in slaying because he will be helped by the law.*
> 17:34 *Do not use the property of the orphan, except to improve it, until he reaches maturity. Fulfill your promise because every promise will be investigated.*

17:35 *Give full measure when you measure, and weigh with an honest scale. This is fair and much better in the end. Do not follow that of which you have no knowledge. Every act of hearing, seeing, or feeling will be investigated on the Day of Reckoning.*
17:37 *Do not walk arrogantly upon the earth because you cannot split the earth in two, and you cannot become as tall as the mountains. All of this is evil and hateful in the sight of your Lord. This is part of the wisdom that your Lord has revealed to you [Mohammed]. Do not worship another god with Allah, or you will be thrown into Hell, condemned and abandoned.*

17:110 *Say: Call upon Allah, or call upon the Merciful, whatever name you use is all the same. He has the best names. Do not say your prayer too loud, nor say it in low tones, but seek a middle way. Say: Praise be to Allah, Who has not begot a son and who has no partner in the kingdom and Who has no need of a protector to save Him from disgrace. Magnify Him by proclaiming His greatness.*

6:117 *The Lord knows best who strays from his path, and He knows best who follows the right course.*
6:118 *Only eat what has been consecrated in Allah's name. Do not eat what He has forbidden you except of necessity. But many are led astray by their own appetites and lack of knowledge. The Lord knows those who exceed the limits. Abandon all sin, open or secret. Those who sin will be rewarded for what they have gained. Do not eat that on which the name of Allah has not been pronounced for that is a crime, and the evil ones will inspire their friends to dispute with you, but if you obey them, you will be unbelievers.*
6:122 *Can he who was raised from the dead and given light so he can walk among men be like he who is in permanent darkness? Thus has the conduct of the unbelievers been made to seem fair to them.*

This Is My Straight Path

6:152 *And do not approach the property of the orphan, but to improve it, until he reaches maturity, and give full measure and weight with justice. We will not place any burden on a soul beyond its ability, and whenever you speak, speak justly, even though it be the affair of a kinsman, and fulfill the covenant of Allah. He commands you that you may remember. This is My straight path. So follow it, and do not follow other paths. They may lead you from His path. This He commands that you may ward off evil.*
6:154 *Then We gave the Book to Moses—complete for him who would do good, explaining all things in detail, and a guidance and a mercy—that they might believe in the meeting with their Lord. And this is a blessed*

Scripture which We have revealed, so follow it and fear Allah that you may find mercy.

Allah Will Test You

16:90 *Allah commands that you practice justice, righteousness, and generosity to relatives. He forbids lewdness, shameful behavior, injustice, and rebellion. He warns you so that you will pay attention.*
16:91 *Fulfill your agreement when you have made a covenant with Allah, and do not break your oaths after confirming them. You have made Allah your surety. Allah knows everything that you do.*
16:92 *Do not be like a woman who unravels her yarn after it is spun and strong. Do not use your oaths to deceive anyone lest one group becomes more numerous than another. Allah will test you, and on the Judgment Day, He will resolve your arguments.*

Seek Refuge in Allah from the Accursed Satan

16:98 *When you recite the Koran, seek refuge in Allah from the accursed Satan. He has no authority over those who believe and put their trust in their Lord. Satan has authority only over those who befriend him and those who worship others besides Allah.*
16:110 *Surely your Lord will be forgiving to those who flee persecution [left Mecca], who struggle hard, and who are patient. Your Lord is forgiving and merciful.*
16:111 *One day, every soul will come, pleading for itself, and everyone will be repaid in full for what it has done, and none will be unjustly dealt with.*
16:112 *Allah gives a parable about a city [Mecca] that is safe and secure, abundantly supplied with everything it needs, and yet, it is ungrateful for the favors of Allah. Allah gives it a taste of hunger and fear because of the evil it has done. A messenger from themselves came to them, but they rejected him and a punishment overtook them while they were unjust.*
16:114 *Therefore eat the lawful and good things Allah has given you, and be grateful for His favor if you serve Him. He has only forbidden you to eat carrion, blood, pork, and any food that has been blessed by the name of a false god. However, if one is forced to eat any of these things, unwillingly and not excessively, Allah is forgiving and merciful.*

30:38 *Give what is due to your kinsmen and to the poor and to the traveler. This is best for those who seek Allah's favor, and it will be them who prosper.*
30:39 *Whenever you loan money at excessive interest rates you will not be blessed by Allah. However, whatever you give in alms, seeking Allah's pleasure, will surely multiply.*

Prostrate Themselves before Him

7:204 *And when the Koran is read, listen to it with attention and hold your peace that mercy may be shown to you. Remember the Lord humbly within yourself in a low voice in the mornings and the evenings [prayer]. Do not be one of the neglectful ones. Those who are with the Lord are not too proud to serve Him. They celebrate His praises and prostrate themselves before Him.*

16:104 *Allah will not guide those who do not believe, and they will have a painful punishment. Those who do not believe in Allah's revelations forge lies. They are the liars.*

16:106 *Those who disbelieve in Allah after having believed [became apostates], who open their hearts to disbelief, will feel the wrath of Allah and will have a terrible punishment. (But there is no punishment for anyone who is compelled by force to deny Allah in words, but whose heart is faithful) This is because they love the life in this world more than the afterlife and because Allah does not guide unbelievers. Allah has sealed the hearts, ears, and eyes of those people, and so they are heedless. Undoubtedly, they will be the losers in the afterlife.*

STRUGGLES

CHAPTER 5

8:20 Believers! Be obedient to Allah and His messenger, and do not turn your backs now that you know the truth. Do not be like the ones who say, "We hear," but do not obey.

I217 Each of the clans of the Quraysh began to persecute those Muslims that they had any power over. If Mohammed attacked them, they would attack him through his converts. One slave, Bilal (to become famous later) was physically abused by being placed in the hot sun with a huge rock on his chest and being told to deny Islam. He refused. This was repeated until Abu Bakr, a chief Muslim, took notice and asked how long the owner would abuse him. The owner said, "You are one of those who corrupted him, you save him." So Abu Bakr offered to trade a stronger black, non-Muslim slave for Bilal. Then Abu Bakr freed Bilal. Abu Bakr did this with six other Muslim slaves as well.

MIGRATION TO ETHIOPIA

I208 Since the Quraysh were resisting Islam and being harsh to the Muslims, Mohammed decided to send many of his followers to Ethiopia as the Christian king there would not bother them. So eighty to ninety Muslims left Arabia to cross the Red Sea to Ethiopia.

In these times of stress, the Koran has advice for Mohammed.

> 28:85 *He who sanctioned the Koran for you [Mohammed] will certainly bring you home [to Mecca] again. Say: My Lord best knows who brings guidance and who is in error.*
> 28:86 *You never expected that the Book would be given to you except as a mercy from your Lord. So do not lend support to the unbelievers. Do not let them divert you from the signs of Allah after they have been sent down to you, but invite men to your Lord, and do not be in the company of unbelievers. Do not call on any other god with Allah. There is no god but Allah. Everything perishes except Him. Judgment is His, and you will return to Him .*
> 7:157 *Those who follow the Messenger—the Prophet who neither reads nor writes, whom they shall find described in the Torah and the Gospel, who commands good and forbids evil; allows the pure and healthful and*

prohibits the impure; releases them from the burdens and shackles that were upon them—those who believe in him, honor and help him and follow the light [the Koran] that was sent down with him, they are the successful.
7:158 *Say: Oh, people, I am sent to you as the messenger of Allah, whose kingdom is the heavens and the earth. There is no god but He. He gives both life and death. So believe in Allah and His messenger, the unlettered Prophet, who believes in Allah and His word. Follow Him so that you may be led aright.*

29:45 *Recite the portions of the Book that have been revealed to you and establish regular prayer for prayer restrains one from indecency and unjust deeds. The remembrance of Allah is the gravest duty, and Allah knows what you do.*

42:51 *It is not fitting for man that Allah should speak with him except by inspiration or from behind a veil or by a messenger sent to reveal what He wills with His permission. He is exalted and wise. So We have sent, by Our command, the spirit Gabriel to you [Mohammed] with a revelation. You did not know what the Scripture was or what the faith was, but We have made it a light by which We will guide whichever servants We will. You will guide them into the right way, the path of Allah. All affairs return to Allah, to whom belongs heaven and earth.*

7:1 *ELIF. LAM. MIM. SAD. A Book has been revealed to you [Mohammed], so do not hold any heaviness in your heart so that you may warn the unfaithful and remind the believers.*

This (Koran) Is Only a Lie.

34:39 *Say: My Lord will be liberal or sparing in supplies with whom He pleases of his servants, and whatever you spend for good, He will replace it; He is the best provider. One day He will gather His angels all together, and He will say, "Did these men worship you?" They will say, "Glory to you. You are our guardian, not them. No, they worshipped the jinn. Most of them believed in them." So on this day they will not have power over one another for profit or harm, and We will say to the evildoers, "Taste the torment of the Fire, which you called a lie."*
34:43 *For when Our clear signs are recited to them, they say, "This is merely a man who would turn you away from your father's religion." They say, "This (Koran) is only a lie." And when they hear the truth, the unbelievers say, "This is nothing but clear sorcery." Yet We did not give them any books to study deeply, nor have We sent them a messenger with warnings. Those before them rejected the truth, but they have not given Us a tenth of what We have given to them. When they rejected My messengers, My vengeance was terrible.*

34:46 *Say: I advise you in one thing: that you stand up before Allah and reflect. There is no madness in your fellow citizen [Mohammed]. He is only your warner before a severe punishment.*
34:47 *Say: I do not ask any reward from you. Keep it for yourselves. My reward is from Allah alone. He is witness to all things. Say: Truly my Lord sends the truth. He knows the unseen. Say: The truth has come, and falsehood will vanish and not return. Say: If I am wrong, it will cost my own soul. If I am guided, it is because of what my Lord reveals to me for He Hears all things and is near.*
34:51 *If you could see them when they are seized with terror. There will be no escape, and they will be taken from their graves. And they will say, "We believe in the truth," but how can they reach faith in this life? They rejected faith before, and they aimed slanders at the mysteries. A barrier will be placed between them and their desires as was done with those who doubted.*

We Know What They Say Grieves You

6:33 *We know what they say grieves you [Mohammed], but it is not you whom they charge with lies; the wicked condemn the signs of Allah. Messengers before you [Mohammed] were rejected, but they were patient with the rejection until Our help reached them for none can change the words of Allah. And certainly some news of the messengers have reached you already. If their turning away is hard on you [Mohammed], find a tunnel into the earth or a ladder up to heaven so that you can bring them a sign. If Allah desired, He would bring them all to the true guidance, so do not be one of the foolish. Allah will answer only those who listen. As for the dead, Allah will raise them up. Then they will return to Him.*

Whom the Devils Have Made into a Fool

6:66 *But your people call it [the Koran] a lie, though it is the truth. Say: I am not in charge of you. For every prophecy there is a set time, and you will soon know it. And when you see men ridiculing with Our revelations, turn away from them until they turn to other talk. And if Satan makes you forget, as soon as you remember, leave the scoffers.*
6:69 *Those who fear Allah are not to pass judgment upon the unjust, but their duty is to remind them so that they may fear Him and guard themselves from evil. Avoid those who make their religion a pastime and a mockery and are deceived by life in this world, but warn them that every soul is damned by its own actions. They will have no protector beside Allah, and if they offered the fullest ransom, it would not be accepted. They will perish by their own acts. The unbelievers will drink only boiling water and suffer grievous torment.*
6:71 *Say: Should we call on gods besides Allah—those who can neither help nor hurt us—a and turn on our heels after Allah has guided us?*

Do not be some bewildered man whom the devils have made into a fool, blundering over the earth, while his friends call him to the right path saying, "Come to us?" Say: Allah's guidance is the true guidance. We submit to the Lord of the worlds.
6:72 *Establish regular prayers, and be dutiful to Allah for it is to Him that we shall be gathered. It is He who created the heavens and the earth, in truth. The day He says "Be," it is. His word is the truth. His is the kingdom on the day when the trumpet will blow. He knows the visible and the invisible, alike. He is wise and knowing.*

1235 A Meccan met Mohammed and said, "Mohammed, you stop cursing our gods or we will start cursing your Allah." So Mohammed stopped cursing the Meccan gods. An ongoing theme of Mohammed's was of ancient civilizations who did not listen to their prophets and the terrible downfall of that country.

11:50 *We sent their brother Hud to the Ad people. He said, "Oh, my people, worship Allah. You have no god beside Him. You only invent your other gods. Oh, my people, I ask you for no payment for this message. My reward is only with Him who made me. Will you not understand? Oh, my people, ask pardon of your Lord. Turn to Him and repent. He will send clouds with ample rain and will give you additional strength. Do not turn back with deeds of evil."*
11:53 *They said, "Oh, Hud, you have not brought us clear proofs of your mission. We will not abandon our gods at your word because we do not believe you."*
11:54 *They said, "We can only say that some of our gods may have seized you with evil."*
11:55 *Hud said, "With Allah as my witness and you as witnesses also, I am innocent of your joining other gods to Allah. So conspire against me all of you, and do not grant me a delay. I trust in Allah, my Lord and yours. There is not a single beast that He does not hold by the hairs on its head. My Lord is truly on the right path. If you turn back, at least I have already delivered my message to you. My Lord will put another people in your place. You cannot hurt Him. My Lord is guardian over all things." When We inflicted Our doom, We rescued Hud and those who believed with Him by Our special mercy. We rescued them from a severe penalty.*
11:59 *The men of Ad [an ancient people of southern Arabia] rejected signs of their Lord, rebelled against His messengers, and followed the bidding of every proud, defiant person. They were cursed in this world, and on Resurrection Day it will be said to them, "Did Ad not reject their Lord?" The people of Ad were cast far away.*

We Decimated the Cities around You

46:21 *Keep in mind the brother of Ad; he warned his people in the sand dunes. There have been others who have warned people saying, "Worship none but Allah. I fear a great day of punishment for you."*
46:22 *They said, "Have you come to turn us away from our gods? Then bring on the scourge if you're telling the truth."*
46:23 *"Only Allah knows that," he said, "I merely deliver the message, but I see that you are ignorant."*
46:24 *Then they saw a cloud coming into their valley. They said, "The cloud is bringing us rain." No, it is the scourge you sought, a wind that carries agonizing retribution. Everything was destroyed by the command of the Lord. Morning rose on empty houses—the reward of the guilty.*
46:26 *We had empowered them while We have not empowered you. We had given them ears, eyes, and hearts, but their ears, eyes, and hearts did nothing to aid them while they spurned the signs of Allah. The punishment they had mocked encompassed them on all sides. We decimated the cities around you then renewed our message so that they might return to Us. But why did not their other gods besides Allah help them? No, those gods withdrew from them. That was their delusion and scheme.*

29:38 *Remember that We destroyed the Ad [an ancient people of southern Arabia] and the Thamud [Thamud was a trade town in ruins north of Mecca]. This is apparent to you in the ruins of their dwellings. For Satan made their deeds seem fair to them and drew them from the right path, even though they could see clearly.*
29:39 *Remember too, Korah, and Pharaoh, and Haman. Moses came to them with clear proof of his mission, and they were arrogant, but they were powerless. We seized every one of them for his sin. Against some We sent a stone-charged wind. Some of them were surprised by the terrible cry of Gabriel. For some of them We opened up the earth, and some of them We drowned. It was not Allah who dealt wrongly with them, they wronged themselves.*

Receive the Punishment of the All-Encompassing Day

11:84 *We sent their brother Shuaib to Midian. He said, "Oh, my people, worship Allah. You have no other god than He. Do not give short weight and measure. I see you are prosperous, but I fear you will receive the punishment of the all-encompassing day. "Oh, my people, give to others their due in full weight and measure; do not withhold from people what is rightly theirs, and do not commit injustice on the earth causing corruption. "That which Allah leaves with you is better for you if you are believers. But I am not your keeper."*
11:87 *They said to him, "Oh, Shuaib, does your religion of prayer command that we leave the gods our fathers worshipped or that we should*

not do what we please with our property? You are the patient one, the right-minded."
11:88 *He said, "Oh, my people, see if I have a clear revelation from my Lord and if He supplies me in abundance. I do not desire to do what I forbid you to do; I seek only your betterment. My sole help is Allah. In Him I trust, and to Him I turn. "Oh, my people, do not let your opposition to me cause you to sin so you suffer a similar fate to that of the people of Noah, or the people of Hud, or the people of Salih, and the people of Lot are not too distant from you. Ask forgiveness of your Lord and turn to Him. Surely, my Lord is merciful and loving."*
11:91 *They said, "Oh, Shuaib, we do not understand much of what you say, and we clearly see that you are powerless among us. If it were not for your family, we surely would have stoned you, and you could not have prevailed against us."*
11:92 *He said, "Oh, my people, do you think more highly of my family than Allah? Do you put Him behind you, neglected? My Lord surrounds you. And, Oh, my people, do whatever you have the power to do. I will do my part, too, and soon you will know who will receive the penalty that will disgrace him and who is the liar. Watch, and I, too am watching with you."*

They Were Found Dead on the Floors of Their Homes

29:36 *To the Midian people, We sent their brother Shuaib. He said, "Oh, my people, worship Allah and fear the last day. Do not commit deeds of harmful excess." But they rejected him, and an earthquake assailed them. At morning, they were found dead on the floor of their homes.*

7:85 *Then We sent their brother Shuaib to Midian. He said, "Oh, my people, worship Allah. You have no other god than Him. Now you have a clear sign from your Lord. Give full measure and weight, do not take from man his due, and do not commit corruption on the earth after it has been reformed. It is better for you if you are believers. Do not lie in wait by every road to threaten or mislead those who believe in Allah or seek to make the way crooked. Remember that there were few of you and He multiplied you, and remember what became of those who did mischief. And if some of you believe in the messages I bring and some of you do not believe, then have patience until Allah judges between us for He is the best judge."*
7:88 *The chiefs of his people were full of pride and said, " Oh, Shuaib, we will surely drive you and those who believe with you out from our cities unless you return to our faith." He said, "What? Even though we detest it? It would be a lie against Allah if we return to your religion after Allah has rescued us from it, and we will not go back to it unless Allah wills it. Our Lord comprehends all things in his knowledge. We put our trust in Allah.*

Oh, our Lord, decide between us and our people, with truth, for You are the best One to decide."

7:90 *And the leaders said, "If you follow Shuaib, you will surely be ruined."*

7:91 *Then an earthquake surprised them, and they were found in the morning dead on their faces in their homes. The men who had rejected Shuaib became as though they had never lived in their homes. Those who rejected Shuaib were ruined. So Shuaib left them saying, "Oh, my people, I delivered my Lord's messages to you, and I gave you good advice. How can I be sorry for a people who would not believe?"*

We Annihilated the Unbelievers

7:65 *And to the tribe of Ad, We sent their brother Hud. He said, "Oh, my people, worship Allah, you have no other god than Him. Will you not fear Him?"*

7:66 *The leaders among his people who were unbelievers said, "We see you involved in foolishness, and we think that you are a liar."*

7:67 *He said, "Oh, my people! There is no foolishness in me, but I am a messenger from the Lord of the worlds. "I convey the messages of my Lord to you, and I am your faithful advisor. Do you not marvel that a message has come to you from your Lord through one of yourselves that He may warn you? Remember how He made you the successors of the Noah's people and gave you stature? Remember then the bounty of Allah that you may be successful."*

7:70 *They said, "Have you come to us so that we may worship Allah exclusively and give up what our fathers worshipped? Then bring to us that which you threaten if you are a man of truth."*

7:71 *He said, "Punishment and wrath have already lighted on you from your Lord. Do you dispute with me about names that you and your fathers have given your idols without authority from Allah? Wait then, and I too will wait with you." And We saved him and those who were with him by Our mercy, and We annihilated the unbelievers who had treated Our signs as lies.*

A Blast Overtook the Wicked

11:61 *We sent their brother Salih to the Thamud. He said, "Oh, my people, worship Allah. You have no other god than Him. He raised you up out of the earth and settled you there, so ask pardon of Him then, and humbly turn to Him for your Lord is near, ready to answer."*

11:62 *They said, "Oh, Salih, you have been among us, and we placed our hopes in you. Are you asking us not to worship the gods that our fathers worshipped? Truly, we are in doubt about what you are asking us."*

11:63 *He said, "Oh, my people, what do you think? If I have a clear revelation from my Lord that supports me, and if He has shown His mercy on me, who could protect me from Allah if I were to rebel against Him? You would only cause me an increase of ruin."*

11:64 *"Oh, my people, this she-camel of Allah is a sign to you. Let her feed on Allah's earth, and do not harm her, for a speedy punishment will overtake you." Yet they killed her, and he said, "Enjoy yourselves in your dwellings for three more days. There is a promise Allah must keep."*

11:66 *When Our sentence came to pass, We rescued Salih and those who believed with him from humiliation on that day by Our mercy. Your Lord is strong and mighty. A blast overtook the wicked, and they were found motionless in their homes in the morning, as though they had never lived in there. The Thamud disbelieved their Lord, and the Thamud were utterly cast off.*

We Reject the Signs in Which You Believe

7:73 *And to Thamud's people [Thamud lay on an old trade route, north of Mecca. It was abandoned in Mohammed's day] We sent their brother Salih. He said, "Oh, my people! Worship Allah. You have no other god than Him, and clear proof has come to you from the Lord. This she-camel of Allah is a sign to you, so let her graze on Allah's earth and do not harm her, or you will be seized with a grievous punishment.*

7:74 *"Remember how He made you inheritors to the Adites and settled you in the land so that you build castles on the plains and build houses into the hills? So remember the benefits of Allah, and refrain from evil and corruption on the earth."*

7:75 *The chiefs of his people, who were scornful, said to those whom they thought were weak, even to those of them who believed, "Do you know for certain that Salih is sent by his Lord?" They said, "We do believe in the signs that have been sent through him."*

7:76 *Those who were scornful said, "We reject the signs in which you believe."*

7:77 *So they killed the she-camel and revolted against their Lord's command and said, "Oh, Salih, bring about your threats if you are a messenger sent by Allah." Then the earthquake seized them, and in the morning they were found dead on their faces in their homes.*

7:79 *So he turned away from them and said, "Oh, my people! I delivered my Lord's message to you, and I gave you good advice, but you do not love good advice."*

We Turned Those Cities Upside Down

11:69 *Our messengers came to Abraham with glad tidings. "Peace," they said. He said, "Peace," and he did not delay but brought a roasted calf to his guests. When he saw that they did not touch it, he became mistrustful and fearful of them. They said, "Do not fear, for We are sent against the people of Lot."*

11:71 *Abraham's wife was standing by and laughed, and We gave her news of the birth of Isaac and after Isaac, Jacob. She said, "Ah, woe is me. Will I bear a son when I am old and when my husband is an old man? This would be a wondrous thing."*
11:73 *They said, "Do you wonder at Allah's command? Allah's mercy and blessing be on you, Oh, people of this house. He is worthy of praise and glory."*
11:74 *When Abraham's fear had passed away and these glad tidings had reached him, he pleaded with Us for the people of Lot. Abraham was patient, compassionate, and penitent.*
11:76 *"Oh, Abraham, desist from this, for the command of Allah has already gone forward. As for them, a punishment is coming to them that cannot be held back."*
11:77 *When Our messengers came to Lot, he was distressed for them, because he lacked the strength to protect them. He said, "This is a difficult day." And his people came rushing towards him, for they had long been committing abominations. He said, "Oh, my people, here are my daughters. They will be purer for you to marry. Fear Allah, and do not put me to shame regarding my guests. Is there not one right-minded man among you?"*
11:79 *They said, "You know that we do not need your daughters. You know well what we desire."*
11:80 *He said, "I wish that I had the strength to resist you or that I could find refuge with someone among you who is powerful."*
11:81 *The angels said, "Oh, Lot, we are the messengers of your Lord; they will not touch you. Leave with your family and friends tonight, and do not let any one of you look back, but your wife will remain behind. Whatever happens to them will happen to her. Morning is the appointed time; is the morning not near?"*
11:82 *When Our decree came to pass, We turned those cities upside down, and We rained down upon them blocks of clay one after another, marked by the Lord Himself [each block of clay had the name of the person who was to be destroyed]. They are never far from the wicked.*

His Seizing Is Painful, Terrible

11:94 *When our decree came to pass, We saved Shuaib and his companions in faith by Our mercy, and the mighty blast overtook the wicked. In the morning they were found motionless in their houses, as if they had never lived in them. Midian [a city on the Red Sea] was swept off even as Thamud [the people of a ruined Nabatean city near Medina] had been swept off.*
11:96 *We sent Moses with Our signs and Authority to Pharaoh and his nobles, who followed the commands of Pharaoh, and Pharaoh was not a good guide. He will go to his people on Judgment Day and lead them*

into the Fire like cattle to water. It is a wretched place to which they will descend. They were followed by a curse in this life, and on the Day of the Resurrection a woeful gift will be given to them.
11:100 *These are the stories of some of the cities that We relate to you. Some of them are standing; others have been ruined. We were not unfair to them, but they were unjust to themselves and their gods. The ones they called besides Allah did not avail them at all when your Lord's command came to pass. They only added to their ruin. Such is the Lord's reach when He seizes the cities that have been wicked. His seizing is painful, terrible.*

Lot, his wife and family:

7:80 *We also sent Lot. He said to his people, "Will you commit indecencies [homosexuality] as no creature ever has before you? You lust for men instead of women? You are indeed a people given up to excess."*
7:82 *But his people could only answer, "Turn them out of your city, surely they want to purify themselves." So We saved him and his family except his wife; she was of those who stayed behind. We rained rain brimstone upon them. See the end of the evildoers.*

A Vengeance from Heaven

29:20 *Say [Allah to Abraham]: Travel throughout the earth, and see how Allah brought forth created beings. So will Allah cause them to be born again for Allah has power over all things. Allah will punish whom He pleases, and He will have mercy on whom He pleases. You will be taken back to Him. You will not escape Him in the earth or in the heavens nor will you have any protector or helper beside Allah. Those who disbelieve the signs of Allah or doubt that they will ever meet him, will despair of My mercy. They will suffer a most grievous penalty.*
29:24 *The answer of the people of Abraham was to say, "Slay him or burn him." But Allah saved him from the Fire. These are signs to those who believe. Abraham said, "You have taken idols instead of Allah out of friendship you have between you in this world, but on the Day of Resurrection you will deny the others, and some of you will curse the others. Your abode will be the Fire, and you will have no help."*
29:26 *But Lot believed in him and said, "I will leave home for the sake of my Lord for He is mighty and wise."*
29:27 *And We bestowed on him [Abraham] Isaac and Jacob and gave them the gift of prophecy and revelation. We gave him his reward in this world, and in the next he shall be among the just.*
29:28 *Remember when Lot said to his people, "You surely are guilty of an indecency [homosexuality], which no nation has ever done before you. Do you go, even to men, and do you commit robbery on the highway, and*

do you practice crime in your assemblies?" But the only answer of his people was to say, "Bring the wrath of Allah if you are telling the truth."
29:30 *He cried, "My Lord, help me against a corrupt people."*
29:31 *And when Our messengers came to Abraham with the tidings of good news, they said, "We are going to destroy the people in this city for they are criminals."*
29:32 *He said, "Lot is there." They said, "We know full well who is there. We will deliver him and his family, except his wife. She is one of those who will stay behind."*
29:33 *When our messengers came to Lot, he was troubled on account of them for he could not protect them. They said, "Do not fear nor grieve for you and your family will be saved except your wife. She will remain behind. We are going to bring down on the people of this city a vengeance from heaven for the excesses they have committed." And that will be a clear sign to men of understanding.*

14:5 *We sent Moses with Our signs saying to him, "Bring your people out from the darkness into the light, and remind them of the days of Allah's favors." There are signs here for every patient and grateful person.*
14:6 *Remind them that Moses said to his people, "Remember Allah's kindness to you when He freed you from the tyranny of the family of Pharaoh. They afflicted you with severe torments and slaughtered your male children while they spared your females." This was a great trial from your Lord. Remember. Your Lord made it known: "If you give thanks, then I will surely give you more and more, but if you are thankless, my chastisement is terrible." And Moses said, "If you and all who are on the earth are thankless, still Allah is self-sufficient and worthy of all praise."*
14:9 *Has the story not reached you of those who came before you, the people of Noah, and Ad [an ancient people of southern Arabia], and Thamud [Thamud was a trade town in ruins north of Mecca], and of those who lived after them? No one knows them but Allah. Their messengers came to them with clear proofs of their mission, but they put their hands on their mouths and said, "We do not believe in your mission, and we are suspicious about you say."*
14:10 *Their messengers said, "Is there any doubt about Allah, maker of the heavens and of the earth? It is He who invites you so that He may pardon your sins and give you a reprieve until an appointed time." They said, "You are just men like us. If you desire to turn us away from our fathers' worship, then bring us some clear proof."*
14:11 *Their messengers said to them, "Yes, we are only men like you, but Allah gives His favors to whom He pleases. It is not in our power to bring you any special proof except by the permission of Allah. Let the believers put their trust in Allah. What reason do we have for not putting our trust*

in Allah since He has already guided us in our ways? We will certainly bear with patience the harm you would do to us. Let the trusting put their trust in Allah."

14:13 *And those who did not believe said to their messengers, "We will surely drive you from our land unless you return to the religion of our ancestors." Then their Lord revealed to them, "We will certainly destroy the unjust. We will certainly cause you to dwell in the land after them. This for him who dreads the time he will stand at My judgment-seat and who dreads My threats!" They sought a decision that moment, and every rebellious unbeliever perished.*

14:16 *Hell is before him, and for drink he will have boiling, stinking water. He will drink it in gulps, but he will not swallow it because he detests it. Death will come at him from every side, but he cannot die. Before him will be an unrelenting doom.*

1235 A story teller boasted that he could tell better old stories and would tell them in competition with Mohammed. But the story teller was an unbeliever and the Koran condemned him, as well as all unbelievers.

31:6 *There are men who engage in idle tales [A Persian story-teller in Mecca said that his stories were better than Mohammed's] without knowing, and they mislead others from the way of Allah and turn it to scorn. There will be a shameful punishment for them. When Our signs are revealed to him, he turns away in arrogance as if he had not heard them, as though there were deafness in his ears. Give him tidings of a terrible punishment. Those who will believe and do good works, will enjoy the Gardens of Bliss, where they will abide forever. It is Allah's true promise, and He is mighty and wise.*

31:10 *He created the heavens without pillars that can be seen and put mountains firmly on the earth so that they would not move. He scattered over it animals of every sort. He sent down rain from the heavens and caused every kind of noble plant to grow. This is the creation of Allah. Now show me what others beside Him have created. The wrongdoers are in obvious error.*

Repel Evil with What Is Best

41:33 *Who speaks better than he who prays to Allah while doing good deeds, and says, "I am among those who bow in submission."*

41:34 *Goodness and evil are not equal. Repel evil with what is best; then your enemy will seem like your friend. No one will be granted such goodness except those who are patient and practice self-restraint. Only the most favored are given this. When Satan tempts you, seek refuge in Allah because He hears and knows.*

41:37 *The night and the day and the sun and the moon are among His signs. But if you worship Allah, then do not bow down to the sun and the moon. But if the unbelievers are too proud, it does not matter because those who are with your Lord praise Him night and day. Also among His signs is His sending down the rain to renew the parched earth. Surely He who gives the earth life will give life to the dead because His power extends over everything.*

41:40 *Those who distort our revelations are not hidden from Us. Who is in the better position: the person who will be thrown into the Fire, or the person who is safely delivered on the Judgment Day? Do what you wish; surely He sees everything that you do. Certainly the person who rejects the message will be punished. This is a mighty Book. Lies cannot come near it from any direction. It is a revelation from the wise and the praiseworthy.*

41:43 *Nothing has been said to you that was not said to the messengers who came before you. Truly, forgiveness is with your Lord and also with Him is a terrible punishment. If We had sent a Koran in a language other than Arabic, they would have said, "Why are its verses not easy to understand? Why is the message in a strange language and the messenger an Arab?" Say: For those who believe, it is a guide and a healing. Those who do not believe are deaf and blind. It is as if they are called from a great distance.*

The Curse of Allah Is on the Unjust

11:18 *Who does more wrong than he who invents a lie concerning Allah? They will be brought back before their Lord, and the witnesses will say, "These are the ones who lied against their Lord. Surely the curse of Allah is on the unjust and whoever lures others from the way of Allah and seeks to make it crooked. They do not believe in a life to come." They will not weaken Allah's power on earth, and they have no protector beside Allah. Their torment will be doubled because they could not bear to hear, and they were not able to see. These are the ones who have lost their own souls, and the gods they had invented have left them. In the hereafter, they will be the lost ones.*

11:23 *Believers who do the right things and humble themselves before their Lord are the rightful owners of the Garden. They will abide there forever.*

11:24 *These two kinds of people can be compared to a blind and deaf man in contrast to a seeing and hearing man. Can you call these two alike? Will you not understand?*

The Hatred of Allah Is More Grievous

40:1 *HA. MIM. The revelation of this Book is from Allah the almighty, the all-knowing, who forgives sins, accepts penitence, is strict in punishment, and has a long reach. There is no god but Allah. All things return to him.*

40:4 *Only the unbelievers dispute the signs of Allah. Do not let their worldly prosperity deceive you.*
40:5 *The people of Noah, and the factions after them, denied their messengers before these, and every nation schemed against their messenger to destroy him. They argued falsely to refute the truth. Then I seized them, and how great was my punishment. So the word of the Lord proved true against the unbelievers. They truly are companions to the Fire.*
40:7 *Those who bear the throne and those who encircle it sing the praise of their Lord, believe in Him, and implore forgiveness for the believers. Oh, our Lord, your reach is over all things in mercy and knowledge. Forgive those who turn to you and follow your path. Save them from the pains of Hell. Oh, our Lord, bring them into the Gardens that you have promised them and their fathers, wives, and children who do right, for you are the all-mighty and the all-wise.*
40:9 *"And keep them from evil deeds for the one You keep from evil on that day, You have shown great mercy, and this will be the supreme triumph for them. A voice will cry out to the unbelievers: "Surely the hatred of Allah is more grievous to you than your hatred of yourselves when you were called to the faith and refused it."*
40:11 *They shall say, "Oh, our Lord, twice You gave us death, and twice You gave us life. Now we recognize our sins. Is there any escape?"*
40:12 *This has befallen you because when only Allah was proclaimed to you, you did not believe, but when false gods were joined with him, you believed. The judgment belongs to Allah, the high, the great. He shows you signs and sends down supplies to you from heaven, but none will receive warning except he who turns to Allah. Call on Allah, then, offering Him sincere devotion, though the unbelievers detest it.*

Teaches by Repetition

39:17 *There is good news for those who reject false gods and turn to Allah, so give good tidings to My servants who listen to My word and follow the best of it. These are the ones Allah has guided, and these are men of insight. If one has justly been sentenced to punishment and doom, can he be helped or rescued?*
39:20 *Those who fear their Lord will have storied pavilions, and rivers will flow beneath them. It is the promise of Allah. Allah will not fail in his promise.*
39:21 *Can you not see that Allah sends down water from heaven and guides it along to form springs in the earth? Then He brings forth food of varied sorts. Then He causes it to wither, become yellow, and crumble away. This is a remembrance for men of insight.*
39:22 *Is he whose heart Allah has opened to Islam and who has light from his Lord, the same as one who disbelieves? Woe to those whose hearts are hardened against the remembrance of Allah. They plainly err.*

39:23 *Allah has revealed the best of messages in a Book, in a uniform style, and teaches by repetition. For those who fear their Lord, the words make them tremble. Their skins and hearts soften at the remembrance of their Lord. This is Allah's guidance. He guides whom He pleases, and sends astray whom He pleases, and then no guide will there be for him.*
39:24 *Is he who will have only his face to shelter him against punishment on Judgment Day the same as he who does right? It will be said to the evil doers, "Taste what you have earned." Those before them denied the revelation, but a punishment came to them when they were not looking for it. So Allah made them taste humiliation in this present life, but the punishment in the life to come will surely be greater. If only they knew.*

Whomever Allah Sends Astray Will No Longer Have a Protector

42:35 *Those who argue about Our signs should know that there will be no escape for them. Whatever you receive is but a passing comfort for this life. What is better with Allah and more enduring for those who believe and put their trust in their Lord is to avoid greater crimes and shameful deeds, and when they are angered, forgive.*
42:38 *Those who listen to their Lord and observe regular prayer are those whose affairs are guided by mutual counsel, who spend from what We have given them, and who, when a wrong is done them, defend themselves. Let the punishment for evil be equal to the evil, but he who forgives and is reconciled will be rewarded by Allah himself for He does not love those who act unjustly.*
42:41 *Whoever defends himself after being wronged will bear no blame against him. The blame is only against those who unjustly wrong others and rebel on earth disregarding justice. These will have a grievous punishment. Whoever bears wrongs and is patient and forgiving shows courage in their acts.*
42:44 *Whomever Allah sends astray will no longer have a protector. And you will see the wrongdoers when they see the doom saying, "Is there any way to return?" And you will see them brought before the Fire made humble by disgrace, and looking with stealthy glances. The believers will say, "Truly, they are losers who have lost themselves and their families on Resurrection Day. Now the wrongdoers will be in lasting torment." They have no protectors other than Allah, and there is no road for him whom Allah causes to err.*
42:47 *Listen to your Lord before the day comes when you cannot turn back. You will have no refuge on that day, nor will you be able to deny your sins.*
42:48 *If they turn aside from your [Mohammed's] message, We have not sent you to guard over them. Your duty is only to deliver the message. When we cause man to taste Our gifts of mercy, he will rejoice in it, but if evil afflicts him for deeds he has done, then man is ungrateful.*

There Is a Terrible Penalty for Those Who Reject Allah

35:3 *Oh, men, call to mind Allah's grace toward you. Is there a creator other than Allah who provides for you from heaven and earth? There is no god but Allah. How are you turned away from Him? If they reject you [Mohammed], then messengers have been rejected before you, but to Allah all things will return.*

35:5 *Oh, men, surely the promise of Allah is true. Do not let the life of the world deceive you or the chief deceiver [Satan] deceive you about Allah. Yes, Satan is your enemy, so treat him as an enemy. He invites his followers to him so they may become companions of the Flame.*

35:7 *There is a terrible penalty for those who reject Allah, but for those who believe and do good works, there is forgiveness and a great reward. Is he who works the devil's deeds, while being convinced that he is good, to be treated as if he is right? Allah misleads whom He will and guides whom He will. Do not grieve after them. Allah knows all their doings.*

Unbelievers Will Have the Fire of Hell

35:33 *They will enter the Gardens wearing bracelets of gold and pearl, and their garments will be made of silk. They will say, "Praise be to Allah who has removed sorrow from us. Our Lord is forgiving and bountiful. Allah has placed us in the eternal mansions. No toil or weariness will reach us."*

35:36 *Unbelievers will have the Fire of Hell, but it will not let them die nor will the torment be lightened for them. So We punish the ungrateful. They will cry for help from there saying, "Take us out, our Lord. We will do good deeds and not the deeds we used to do." Did We not grant you a life long enough to thoughtfully reflect, and the warner was there among you? So taste the fruit of your deeds. The wrongdoers have no help.*

35:38 *Allah truly knows the hidden things of heaven and earth for He knows what is in men's hearts. He made you inherit the earth. If any reject Allah, the rejection works against themselves. In the sight of their Lord, this rejection acts to increase His hatred, and their unbelief multiplies the loss for the unbelievers.*

We Have Neglected Nothing in the Book

6:37 *They say, "Why has a sign not been sent down to him from his Lord?" Say: Allah certainly has power to send down a sign, but most of them will not know it." There is not a beast on earth nor fowl that flies on two wings but they are a community like yourselves. We have neglected nothing in the Book, and they will all be gathered to their Lord in the end. They who reject Our signs are deaf, dumb, and blind. Allah will mislead whomever He pleases, and He will put on the straight path whomever He pleases.*

6:40 *Say: Tell me, if the punishment of Allah came upon you or the Hour were to come upon you, would you call any others besides Allah? Answer that, if you are truthful. No. You would only call Him, and He will answer your prayer if He wills it, and you would forget the false gods you joined with Him.*

6:42 *We have already sent messengers to many nations before you [the Meccans], and We seized them with terror and suffering that they might humble themselves. If only they had been humbled when Our disaster came on them. On the contrary, their hearts were hardened, and Satan made their sinful acts seem good to them. And when they had forgotten the warning they had received, We opened the gates of all good things to them until, as they were rejoicing in Our gifts, We seized them, and they were plunged into despair. So the unbelievers were annihilated. All praise be to Allah, the Lord of the worlds!*

6:46 *Say: Have you imagined if Allah should take away your hearing and your sight and set a seal upon your hearts? What god besides Allah could restore them to you? See how We repeat the signs, yet you still turn away from them?*

6:47 *Say: Have you considered when the punishment of Allah comes on you suddenly or is preceded by a sign, will any perish besides the wrong-doers? We send the messengers to bring good news and to warn so those who believe and mend their ways will have neither fear nor grief. But those who deny Our revelations will be punished for their errors.*

This Is a Blessed Scripture

6:90 *These are the men to whom We gave the Scripture and wisdom and prophecy, but if their descendants reject them, We will entrust their charge to a new people who will not disbelieve them. These are the men whom Allah guided, so follow their guidance. Say: I ask for no payment. It is only a reminder to all men."*

6:91 *They do not know Allah when they say, "Allah has not revealed anything to man." Say: Who sent down the Book [the Torah] which Moses brought, a light and guidance to man? But you have put it down in scattered writings for show while you conceal much of it. Has it not taught you what neither you nor your fathers knew? Say: Allah sent it down. Then leave them in their chatter. And this is a blessed Scripture which We have sent down confirming that which was before it so you might warn the mother of towns [Mecca] and those around her. Those who believe in the next life will believe in it [the Koran] and attend to their prayers constantly.*

6:93 *Who is more wicked than he who devises a lie against Allah or says, "I have been inspired [at this time in Arabia there were others who said they were prophets]," when he has not, or who says, "I can reveal the like of that which Allah revealed"? If you could see how the ungodly fare in the flood of confusion at death, and the angels reach forth their hands saying, "Yield up your souls. This day you will receive your reward of humiliating punishment because you told lies against Allah and proudly rejected His signs! And now you have come back to Us bare and alone, as We created you at first, and you leave behind all the good things that We had given you. We do not see your false gods. Now the bonds between you have been severed, and those whom you regarded as partners with Allah have deserted you."*

Allah Gives Either Generously or Little to Whomever He Pleases

13:18 *Those who obey Allah will be richly rewarded. But those who ignore Him, if they had all the riches of heaven and earth and much more, they would willingly offer it as ransom. The unbelievers will encounter an evil reckoning. Hell will be their home, in a bed of misery. Is one who recognizes the truth revealed to you by your Lord the same as the one who is blind?*

13:20 *Only those who are wise will take heed—those who keep Allah's pledge of faith and unite that which Allah has commanded to be joined. The wise fear their Lord and dread a terrible reckoning and seek their Lord's will and pray regularly and give gifts, in secret and openly. The wise overcome evil with good and will be rewarded with eternal Paradise. They will enter the Garden along with the righteous among their parents, spouses, and children. The angels will greet them from every gate saying, "May you receive peace for all that you have patiently endured! You are blessed with the reward of Paradise!"*

13:25 *But those who break their pledge to Allah, after having promised it, and break apart those things that Allah has commanded to be joined and bring about corruption in the land, they will be cursed, and the terrors of Hell await them.*

13:26 *Allah gives either generously or little to whomever He pleases. The unbelievers rejoice in their lives here on earth, but their present life on earth is only a temporary joy compared to the life that is to come.*

They Will Live in Paradise Forever

46:13 *Whoever says, "Our Lord is Allah," and firmly follows His guidance will not be tested by fear or grief. They will live in Paradise forever—rewarded for their good deeds.*

46:15 *We command man to show kindness to his parents. His mother bore and gave birth to him in pain. From birth to weaning is thirty months; when he reaches full strength at forty years of age, he says, "My Lord, open my heart so that I may be grateful for the favor You have given me and my parents and so that I will do the good works that please You. Be gracious to me in my offspring; I have turned to you and do surrender to Islam." From these We will accept their best work and pass over their evil deeds. They shall dwell in Paradise, a promise of truth that was made to them in life.*

46:17 *But he who rebukes his parents, "Are you promising that I will be resurrected when generations have passed before me?" And they cry to Allah for help telling their son, "Woe to you! Believe! The promise of Allah is true!" But he says, "This is nothing but old men's fables." These are the ones who prove the sentence passed on all nations, jinn and men, who have passed away before them. They are the losers. They will be rewarded according to their works so that Allah may pay them back fully, and they will be dealt with fairly.*

46:20 *And the unbelievers will be set before the Fire. "You gathered your precious wealth during your life on earth and enjoyed it. Today you will be rewarded with the penalty of shame because you were proud and unjust on earth without cause and you transgressed.*

1238 A Meccan took an old bone to Mohammed, crumbled it up and blew the dust towards Mohammed. He asked, "Will your Allah revive this bone?" Mohammed said, "Yes, I do say that. Allah will resurrect this bone and you will die. Then Allah will send you to Hell!"

The Koran gives the details of Judgment Day and Hell.

40:45 *So Allah preserved him from the evils they plotted while a dreadful punishment over took the Pharaoh's people. They will be brought in front of the Fire morning and evening, and on Judgment Day, when the hour comes to pass, it will be said, "Cast Pharaoh's people into the severest punishment."*

40:47 *When they will argue with each other in the Fire, the weak ones will say to those who were so arrogant, "We were only following you. Will you take a larger share of the Fire?"*

40:48 *And the arrogant ones will say, "We are all in this Fire; for now, Allah has judged between his servants."*

40:49 *Those in the Fire will say to the keepers of Hell, "Entreat your Lord to relieve us of one day of this torment."*

40:50 *They shall say, "Did your messengers not bring you clear signs?" "Yes," they will reply. They shall say, "Then pray for help," but the prayers of the unbelievers will be in vain.*

40:51 *Assuredly, We will help Our messengers and the believers in this present life, and on the day when the witnesses arise, the day on which their excuses will not profit them, they will only have a curse and the woe of a home in Hell.*

40:53 *We did, of old, give Moses the guidance—a guidance and warning to men of understanding—and We made the Children of Israel the inheritors of the Book. Then patiently persevere for the promise of Allah is true. Seek pardon for your faults, and celebrate the praises of your Lord at evening and at morning.*

40:56 *As to those who dispute the signs of Allah without authority having reached them, there is nothing in their hearts but a desire to become great, which they will never attain. So take refuge in Allah for He is the hearer, the beholder.*
40:57 *Greater surely than the creation of man is the creation of the heavens and of the earth, but most men do not know it. The blind man and the seer are not alike, and neither is the evildoer equal with the believer who does things that are right. How few think of this. The Hour will surely come. There is no doubt of it, but most men do not believe it.*
40:60 *And your Lord says, "Call on me, and I will answer your prayer, but those who are too arrogant to serve Me will enter Hell with shame."*

Allah Is Swifter to Plot

10:1 *ELIF. LAM. RA. These are the signs of the wise Book.*
10:2 *Is it a matter of wonderment to the men of Mecca that We have inspired a man among them saying, "Warn the people, and give good tidings to those who believe so that they will stand firm with their Lord." The unbelievers say, "This is a manifest sorcerer."*
10:3 *Your Lord is Allah who created the heavens and the earth in six days and is firmly established on the throne governing all things. No one can intercede with him without his permission. This is Allah your Lord, so serve him. Will you obey? You will all return to Him. The promise of Allah is true. He produces a creature then reproduces it that He may reward those who believe and do the good things, but those who disbelieve will drink boiling water and suffer a terrible torment because they have not believed.*
10:5 *He made the radiant sun and the moon a light. They measure periods so that you may know the number of years and the count of time. Allah created this only for the truth. He explained His signs clearly for those who understand. In the alternations of night and of day, and in all that Allah created in the heavens and in the earth, there are signs for those who fear Him.*
10:7 *They who hope they do not meet Us and who find their satisfaction in this world's life and rest on it, and who neglect Our signs—their home will be the Fire because of what they earned. For those who believe and do good things, their Lord will direct them aright because of their faith. Rivers shall flow at their feet in Gardens of Bliss. Their cry will be, "Glory be to thee, Allah." "Peace" will be their greeting, and the close of their cry will be, "Praise be to Allah, Lord, of all creatures."*
10:11 *If Allah were to hasten evil to men for the ill they have earned, as they wish Him to hasten their good, their doom would be known. So We leave those who do not hope for Our meeting blindly wandering on. When trouble touches man, he cries to Us to be on his side sitting or standing. When We remove his troubles, he goes on his way as though he had not*

cried to Us because of his troubles. That is how their deeds are made to seem fair to them.

10:13 *We have destroyed generations before you when they acted wickedly. Messengers came to them with clear signs from Allah, but they would not believe. This is how We reward the wicked. Then We caused you to succeed them on the earth to see how you would act. But when Our clear signs are recited to them, those who do not want to meet Us say, "Bring a different Koran than this, or make some change in it." Say: I [Mohammed] do not have the authority to change it as I see fit. I follow what is inspired in me. If I disobey my Lord, I fear the punishment of a great day. Say: If Allah desired, I would not have recited it to you, nor would He have taught it to you. I have dwelt among you a lifetime before it came to me. Do you not understand? And who is more unjust than he who invents a lie against Allah, or rejects His signs as lies? But the guilty will never prosper.*

10:18 *They worship gods besides Allah who will neither hurt nor help them and say, "These are our intercessors with Allah." Say: Would you inform Allah of something in the heavens and in the earth that He does not know? Glory be to Him. He is exalted above the deities they associate with Him.*

10:19 *Men were of one nation, but they fell into differences, and if a decree had not gone out from the Lord, their differences would have surely been decided between them.*

10:20 *They say, "Why is there not a sign sent down from his Lord?" Say: The unseen is with Allah, so wait. I, too, will be with you among those who wait. When We grant men a mercy after an adversity has afflicted them and We cause this people to taste of mercy, they start plotting against Our signs. Say: Allah is swifter to plot. Our messengers record all the plots you make.*

He Would Not Leave a Single Living Creature on the Earth

35:40 *Say: Have you ever seen the idols whom you call on beside Allah? Show me the part of earth they have created, or did they help create the heavens? Have We given them a Book so they can act on clear proof? No, the wrongdoers promise one another only delusions. It is Allah who upholds heaven and earth or they would cease to function. If they were failing, no one could hold them up but He for He is patient and forgiving.*

35:42 *They [Jews and Christians] swore their strongest oaths by Allah that if a warner came to them, they would follow his guidance more than any people had, but when the messenger came to them, it only increased their flight from good deeds. Their arrogance on earth and their plans for evil will only entrap the arrogant men who created the plans. Do they remember the way Allah dealt with the peoples of old? You will not find*

any change in the course of Allah. Have they not traveled through the land and seen what was the end of those before them, though they were stronger than these? Nothing in the heavens or on earth escapes Allah for He is knowing and almighty.
35:45 *If Allah should punish men according to what they deserve, He would not leave a single living creature on the earth, but He waits until the appointed term. When their term expires, then Allah will have His sight on His servants.*

The Koran gives the qualities of Allah.

40:61 *Allah made the night so you could rest and the day to give you light for seeing. Allah is rich in bounties to men, but most men do not give thanks. Such is Allah your Lord, creator of all things. There is no god but Allah. Why then are you turned from the truth? Those who deny the signs of Allah are turned aside.*
40:64 *Allah made the earth for you as a resting place and built up the heavens over it. He formed you and made your forms beautiful, and provided you with good things. This is Allah your Lord. Blessed be Allah, Lord of the worlds. He is the living one. There is no god but Allah. Call on Him with sincere devotion. Praise be to Allah, Lord of the worlds.*
40:66 *Say: I am forbidden to worship any beside Allah after the clear signs that have come to me from my Lord, and I am commanded to submit to the Lord of the worlds.*
40:67 *It is He who created you from dust, then from a drop of sperm, then a clot. That you may understand, He brought you forth as a child, let you reach your full strength, let you become an old man (but some die first), and then you reach the appointed term. It is He who gives life and death, and when He decrees a thing, He only says of it, "Be," and it is.*
40:69 *Do you not see those who dispute the signs of Allah and how are they turned aside?*
40:70 *Those who reject the Book and the revelations with which We have sent our messengers will soon know the truth. When the yokes and the chains are on their necks, they will be dragged into the boiling waters then they will be thrust into the Fire and burned. Then it will be said to them, "Where are the ones whom you made partners with Allah?" They will say, "They have gone away from us. Before, we did not call on anyone." This is how Allah leads the unbelievers astray. This is because you rejoiced in other things than the truth on the earth. Enter the gates of Hell to live there forever. Evil is the abode of the arrogant ones.*
40:77 *Have patience, for the promise of Allah is true. Whether We let you [Mohammed] see part of the woes We promise them, or We cause you to die first, they will all return to Us. We have already sent messengers before you. We have told you the stories of some of them, and of others We have told you nothing. But no messenger had the power to work a miracle*

unless by the permission of Allah. When the command of Allah comes, judgment is given with truth. Those who treat it as a lie perish.
40:79 *It is Allah who gave you the cattle. On some of them you may ride, and of some you may eat. There are other advantages in them. You may carry burdens. And on ships and on cattle you are carried. He shows you His signs. Which of the signs of Allah will you deny?*
40:82 *Have they not traveled in this land and seen what was the end of those who came before them? They were more numerous than these and mightier in power and in the fortifications they left on the land, yet all they accomplished was no profit to them. When their messengers came to them with clear signs, they exulted in the knowledge they possessed, but the very wrath that they mocked encompassed them. And when they saw Our vengeance they said, "We believe in Allah alone, and we reject the partners we once associated with Him."*
40:85 *But their professions of faith, when they had seen our vengeance, did not profit them. Such has been the procedure of Allah with regard to his servants. Then the unbelievers perished.*

It Is Not in My Power to Hasten the Punishment

6:54 *And when those who believe in Our signs come to you, Say: Peace be on you. The Lord hath prescribed for himself a law of mercy so that if any one of you does evil through ignorance and repents afterwards and does right, He will be forgiving and merciful. This is why We clearly explain the signs so that the sinners might be made known.*
6:56 *Say: I am forbidden to worship any gods you call on besides Allah. Say: I will not follow your wishes for then I will go astray and will not be one of the guided. Say: I act on clear proof from my Lord while you reject Him. It is not in my power to hasten the punishment you desire; that decision is with Allah only. He declares the truth, and He is the best of judges.*
6:58 *Say: If I had the power to hasten what you desire, the matter between me and you would be settled, but Allah knows best those who do wrong. With Him are the keys of all secrets, treasures no one knows but He. He knows whatever is on the earth and in the sea. Not a leaf falls without His knowledge. There is not a grain in the darkness of the earth nor anything green or dry but it is clearly in His records. It is He who takes your souls at night and knows what you have done by day. Then He wakes you up again by day so that your appointed term can be fulfilled. In the end, you will return to Him, and then He will show you the truth of what you were doing. He is Supreme over his servants, and He sends guardians [angels] to watch over you until, when death comes and Our unfailing messengers [angels] receive him, then are they returned to Allah, their protector, the true One. He judges and He is swift in judging.*

6:63 *Say: Who delivers you from the darkness of the land and of the sea when you humbly call on Him both openly and secretly saying "If You rescue us from this, we will surely be thankful?" Say: Allah rescues you from this and from every distress, yet afterwards you worship false gods! Say: He has the power to send disasters on you from above and below, or He can throw you into confusion causing dissension among you. See how We explain the signs so they might understand.*

Thus Have We Given Every Messenger Evil Ones among Men

6:95 *It is Allah who causes the seed-grain and the date stone to sprout. He brings the living from the dead and the dead from the living. This is Allah! Why, then, are you turned away from Him? He causes the dawn to appear and has made the night for rest and the sun and the moon for counting time. This is the arrangement of the mighty, the wise! And it is He who made the stars for you that they might guide yourselves in the darkness of the land and of the sea. We have made our signs clear to men who know. It is He who has produced you from a single soul, and here is an abode and a place of rest. We have made our signs to men of insight. And it is He who sends down rain from the skies, and We use it to grow plants of every kind. We grow the green foliage and the grain, and from the date palms grow clusters of dates. And We grow gardens of grapes, olives, and pomegranates, each alike and unlike. Look on their fruit and the ripening. In these things are signs for those who believe.*

6:100 *They make the jinn equal to Allah, though He created them, and they falsely attribute to Him, in ignorance, sons and daughters. Praise and glory be to Him, for He is above their imaginations. Originator of the heavens and of the earth. How can He have a son when He has no mate? He himself created everything, and He knows everything. This is Allah your Lord. There is no god but He, the creator of all things. Worship Him; He has charge of all things. No vision can grasp Him, but his grasps reaches all vision. He is above all comprehension and knows all things. Clear proofs have come to you from your Lord. Whoever will see, it is for the good of his soul. Whoever is blind to them, it will be to his harm. I am not your keeper. That is why We explain Our signs by various means so that they can say, "You [Mohammed] have studied deeply," and so We can make it clear to people of understanding.*

6:106 *Follow that which is inspired in you by the Lord. There is no god but Allah, and turn from those who join other gods with Him. If it had been Allah's plan, they would not have taken false gods. But We have not made you a keeper over them, neither are you responsible for them.*

6:108 *Do not revile those whom they call on other than Allah in case they, out of spite, revile Allah in their ignorance. Thus for all people We have We made their actions seem fair. Then they will return to their Lord, and He will tell them the truth of what they did. They have sworn by*

Allah with their most solemn oath that if a sign comes to them, they will certainly believe it. Say: Signs are in the power of Allah alone. What will make you realize that even if the signs come, they still will not believe? We will confuse their hearts and their eyes because they refused to believe the first instance, and We will let them wander blindly in their rebellion.
6:111 *Even if We had sent down the angels to them, the dead had spoken to them, and We had gathered all things before their eyes, they would not believe unless Allah had willed it, but most of them are ignorant. Thus have We given every messenger evil ones among men and jinns inspiring each other with flowery talk to deceive, and had your Lord planned it, they would not have done it. So leave them and their vain imaginings alone. Let the hearts of those who do not believe incline to such deceit, and let them find their content in it, and let them earn what they may.*
6:114 *Say: Shall I [Mohammed] seek for a judge other than Allah when it is He who sent down the Book fully explained? Those to whom We have given the Book know that it is sent down from your Lord with truth. So do not be a doubter. The words of the Lord are perfect in truth and in justice. No one can change His word. He hears and knows.*

These Are Signs for Those Who Reflect

45:1 *HA. MIM. This revelation is sent down from Allah, the mighty, the wise. Surely in the heavens and the earth are signs for those who believe. Your own creation and that of the animals, which are scattered over the earth, are signs for those with strong faith.*
45:5 *The succession of night and day, and the rain which Allah sends down from the heavens that revives the barren earth, and the changing of the winds are signs for wise people. These are among the signs of Allah, which We truthfully recite to you. What teachings will they believe in if they reject Allah and his signs?*
45:7 *Woe to every sinful liar who hears the signs of Allah and still persists in vanity and pride as if he had never heard them. Tell him of a terrible punishment. When he becomes aware of Our signs he takes them for a joke. There will be a shameful penalty for people such as this. Hell is waiting for them. Neither their possessions nor the false gods can protect them in the least. They shall have a grievous punishment. Those who reject the signs and guidance of their Lord will receive a punishment of painful torment.*
45:12 *It is Allah who has made you master of the sea so that ships may sail over them by His command so you may seek His bounty, and so that, perhaps, you may be thankful. He has made you master over all that is in the heavens and on the earth. Everything is from him. Surely, these are signs for those who reflect.*

Among His Signs

30:17 *So give glory to Allah in the evening and the morning. Let there be praise for him in the heavens and the earth at dusk and at noon. He brings forth the living from the dead and brings the forth the dead from the living. He revives the earth when it is lifeless. In the same way will you be brought back to life.*

30:20 *Among His signs is that He created you from dust. Then, suddenly, you are a race of men scattered far and wide.*

30:21 *Among His signs is that He created mates for you from your own bodies that you may find rest and contentment with them, and He has placed love and compassion in your hearts. Truly, there are signs here for those who reflect.*

30:22 *Among His signs is the creation of the heavens and the earth and the many languages and colors. Truly, there are signs here for knowledgeable people.*

30:23 *Among His signs is your slumber during the night and day, and your quest for His bounties. Truly, there are signs here for those who listen.*

30:24 *Among His signs is that He shows you the lightning as a source for fear and hope. He sends the rain down from heaven and uses it to give life to the barren earth. Truly, there are signs here for those who understand.*

30:25 *Among His signs is that the heavens and the earth stand firm at his command. Later, with a single call, He will summon you from the earth, and you will come. Everything in the heavens and the earth belong to Him. Everything is obedient to Him. He began the process of creation, and he repeats it, and it is very easy for Him. He has the finest qualities in the heavens and the earth. He is mighty and wise.*

I239 Some Meccans approached Mohammed and said, "Let us worship what you worship. Then you worship what we worship. If what you worship is better than what we worship, then we will take a share of your worship. And if what we worship is better, then you can take a share of that." The Koran's reply:

10:94 *If you are in doubt as to what We have revealed to you, ask those who have read the Scriptures [Jews, Christians] before you. The truth has come to you from your Lord. Do not be one of those who doubts. And do not be one of those who rejects the signs of Allah, or you will be one of those who will perish. Those against whom the decree of your Lord is pronounced shall not believe until they see the painful doom, though every kind of sign was brought to them. Why were the people of Jonah the only city that believed when We warned them? When they believed, We delivered them from the penalty of shame in this world and gave them comfort for a while.*

> 10:99 *But if the Lord had pleased, all men on earth would have believed together. Would you compel men to become believers? No soul can believe without the permission of Allah, and He will place doubt on those who do not understand. Say: Consider whatever is in the heavens and on the earth, but neither signs nor warners profit those who do not believe.*
> 10:102 *What do they expect, then, but what happened in the days of men who passed before them? Say: Wait. I, too, will wait with you. We save Our messengers and those who believe. It is binding on Us to deliver the faithful. Say: Oh, men, if you are in doubt of my religion, I do not worship whom you worship beside Allah, but I worship Allah who will cause you to die. I am commanded to be a believer.*
> 10:105 *And set your face toward the true religion, sound in faith, and do not be of those who revere other gods besides Allah. Do not call on gods besides Allah who cannot help or hurt you. If you do this, you will be one of the wrongdoers. And if Allah afflicts you with harm, there is no one who can remove it but Him, and if He intends good for you, no one can hold it back. He strikes whichever servant He pleases, and He is the gracious and the merciful.*
> 10:108 *Say: Oh, men, now truth has reached you from your Lord. He who receives the guidance will be guided only for his own soul, and he who strays does so at his own loss, and I am not your guardian. Follow what is revealed to you, and be patient until Allah judges for He is the best of judges.*

Islam means submission and that is what all must do. The only religion in Allah's eyes is Islam.

> 41:47 *He alone has knowledge of the Hour. No fruit grows, nor does any female conceive or deliver without His knowledge. On the day when He calls men to return to Him saying, "Where are the other gods?" they will say, "We confess that none of us can testify for them." The gods they used to worship will fail them, and they will realize that there is no escape for them.*
> 41:49 *Man never tires of praying for good, but if evil touches him, he becomes despondent and hopeless. If We show mercy after some affliction touches him, he will surely say, "This is due to my own virtues. I do not believe that the Hour of Judgment will ever occur, but if I am returned to my Lord, I will certainly receive my highest good." But We will show the unbelievers everything that they have done, and We will give them a taste of a terrible punishment. When We show favor to man, he turns away and withdraws from Allah, but when evil touches him, he becomes full of long prayers.*
> 41:52 *What do you think? If this Book is really from Allah and you deny it, who will have done a greater wrong than he who openly rejects Allah? We*

will show them Our signs all over the earth and in their own souls, until it becomes clear to them that it is the truth. Is it not enough that your Lord is a witness to all things? Do they doubt that they will meet their Lord? Does He not encompass all things?

Satan Made Their Actions Seem Good

16:53 *Any favor that is given you comes from Allah. You call to him when any misfortune befalls you. After He removes your troubles, some of you worship other gods besides Him so that they are ungrateful for what We have given them. Enjoy yourselves because you will soon know your mistake. They give credit to false gods for some of the things that We have given. By Allah, you will be asked about the things that you invent.*
16:57 *Glory be to Him! They wish for sons, and they say that Allah has daughters [the Meccans considered the angels to be the daughters of Allah]. If they receive news that they have a daughter, their face darkens and they are filled with anguish. They hide themselves from their people in shame. Should they keep the child in shame or simply bury it? What an evil choice they make for themselves.*
16:60 *It is an evil characteristic to not believe in the afterlife. Allah is sublime. He is mighty and wise. If Allah punished men for their wickedness, He would not leave a single living creature on the earth, but he gives them reprieve until an appointed time. When their doom comes, they will not be able to postpone it even an hour just as they can not cause it to come sooner. They give to Allah the things that they hate, and their tongues tell the lie that they will have the good. They will undoubtedly be sent to Hell and abandoned.*
16:63 *By Allah, We have sent messengers to nations before you, but Satan made their actions seem good to them, so today he is their guardian, and they will have a terrible punishment. We have revealed the Scripture to you so that you might explain to them those things that they question and as a guide and a mercy for people who believe.*

But Their Gods Will Reply, "You Are Liars!"

16:82 *However, if they [the Meccans] turn away, your only duty is to preach the clear message. They recognize the favors of Allah and then deny it. Most of them are ungrateful.*
16:84 *One day We will raise up a witness from every nation; then no excuses will be accepted from unbelievers, and they will not be allowed to make amends. When the wicked see the penalty waiting for them, it will not be made lighter for them nor will they be reprieved.*
16:86 *When those who ascribe partners to Allah see their false gods, they will say, "Lord, these are the equals to whom we used to pray rather than You." But their gods will reply, "You are liars!" They will openly submit to Allah that day, and all of their inventions will desert them. Because they*

have spoken against Allah, We will add punishment to their punishment for all those who rejected Allah and kept men from the way of Allah.
16:89 *One day We will raise up from every people a witness who will testify against his own people. We will bring you [Mohammed] to testify against your people. We have revealed the Scripture to you as a way of explaining everything, and as a guide, a mercy, and good news for those who submit to Allah.*

He Sends the Spirit of Inspiration to Any Servant He Pleases

40:15 *Possessor of the highest rank, Lord of the Throne, He sends the spirit of inspiration to any servant He pleases so He may warn of the day of meeting.*
40:16 *On that day every soul will be rewarded for what it has earned. There will be no injustice on that day. Allah will be swift to reckon. Warn them, then, of the approaching day when men's hearts will rise up to their throats, choking them. There will be no friend or intercessor who will prevail for the wrongdoers. Allah knows the deceitful eye and what men's hearts conceal. Allah will judge with justice and truth while those gods they call on beside Him will not judge at all. Allah hears and knows all.*
40:21 *Have they not traveled this land to see what has been the end of those who disbelieved before them? They were even mightier than these in strength and in their traces left in the land; yet Allah destroyed them for their sins, and they had no protector against Allah. That was because messengers came to them with clear proofs, but they rejected them, so Allah took them in hand for He is mighty and vehement in punishing. We had sent Moses of old with Our signs and with clear authority to Pharaoh, and Haman, and Karun, and they said, "Sorcerer, impostor."*

Allah Guides Whom He Will

28:55 *And when they hear idle talk, they withdraw from it and say, "Our deeds are for us and your deeds are for you. Peace be on you. We do not seek fools."*
28:56 *You [Mohammed] truly cannot guide everyone whom you desire, but Allah guides whom He will. He knows best who follows His guidance. But they say, "If we follow your guidance, we will be driven from our land." Have We not settled them in a sacred, secure territory where fruits of every kind are gathered together—Our gift for their support? But most of them do not understand. And how many communities have We destroyed that were thankless for the livelihoods We provided? These dwellings have not been inhabited since their time save by a few, and We are their inheritors. Your Lord did not destroy the cities until He had sent a messenger to their city to recite Our signs to its people. We never destroy cities unless its people are unjust.*

28:60 *The material things you have been given are merely for enjoyment of this present life, but that which is with Allah is better and more lasting. Will you not be wise? Is the man to whom We have made a good promise, which he will fulfill, the same as the man to whom We have given the enjoyments of this present life, and who on Judgment Day will be brought up for punishment? On that day Allah will cry to them and say, "Where are those gods you associated with me?"*

28:63 *The doomed will say, "Oh, our Lord, these are the ones we led astray, even as we had been led astray ourselves. We are blameless before You. They did not worship us." And it will be said, "Call your false gods now." They will call them, but they will have no answer. They will see the punishment and wish that they had been guided aright. On that day Allah will call to them and say, "How did you answer the messengers?" On that day they will be too blinded with confusion to give an account, nor will they question one another.*

28:67 *As to him who will turn to Allah, believe, and do the right thing, it may come to pass that he will be among those who achieve salvation. Your Lord creates and chooses what He will, but the false gods have no power to choose. Glory be to Allah. He is above all whom they associate with Him.*

There Is No Guide for Him Whom Allah Sends Astray

39:32 *Who does more wrong than one who lies against Allah and rejects the truth when it comes to him as a lie? Is there not a home in Hell for the blasphemers? The dutiful bring the truth and believe it to be the truth. They will have whatever they desire from their Lord. This is the reward of the good. Allah will disregard the worst of what they did and reward them for the best they did.*

39:36 *Is Allah not sufficient for His servant? They try to scare you with other gods besides Him, but there is no guide for him whom Allah sends astray. Whomever Allah guides, no one can lead astray. Is not Allah, almighty, able to enforce His will?*

39:38 *If you ask them who created the heavens and the earth, they will surely answer, Allah. Say: Do you think that those you call besides Allah could remove His affliction? If Allah chose to afflict me, or if He showed me mercy, could they withhold His mercy? Say: Allah is sufficient for me; the trusting put their trust in Him. Say: Oh, my people, do whatever you can. I too will do my part, and in the end you will know who will receive the penalty that will shame him, and who will receive a lasting punishment.*

39:41 *We have revealed the Book to you for mankind and for the ends of truth. Whoever receives the guidance, will benefit his own soul, and whoever rejects it, will injure his own soul, but you are not entrusted as a custodian over them.*

39:42 *Allah takes men's souls at the time of their deaths, and those who do not die, He takes during their sleep. He keeps those on whom he has passed a decree of death but sends the others back until the appointed time. These are signs for those who reflect.*
39:43 *Do they take others for intercessors besides Allah? Say: Even though they have no power over anything, do they understand? Say: Intercession is wholly with Allah. His is the kingdom of the heavens and of the earth. You will be brought back to Him in the end. When Allah alone is named, the hearts of those who do not believe in the life to come shrivel up, but when gods other than Allah are named, they are filled with joy.*
39:46 *Say: Oh, Allah, creator of heaven and earth, who knows the visible and invisible, You will judge between your servants in matters of their disputes. Even if the wicked possessed all that is in the earth and then again as much, they would offer it as ransom for themselves from the pain of the punishment on Judgment Day, and things they had never reckoned on will appear to them from Allah. They will clearly see the evil of their own ill deeds, and the Fire they mocked will encircle them on every side.*

Follow What Allah Has Sent Down

31:20 *Do you not see how Allah has made all that is in the heavens and all that is on the earth subservient to you and has made His generous bounties flow to you, both seen and unseen? Yet there are those who dispute Allah without knowledge nor a Scripture to enlighten them. And when it is said to them, "Follow what Allah has sent down," they say, "No, we will follow the path that we found our fathers following." Even if it is Satan inviting them into the doom of Fire?*
31:22 *Whoever submits himself completely to Allah and is a doer of good has grasped a firm handhold for with Allah lies the end and decision of all affairs. If any reject faith, do not let their rejection grieve you. They will return to Us, and We will tell them of their deeds for Allah knows well what is in men's hearts. We grant them pleasure for a little while, and afterwards, We will drive them to an unrelenting punishment.*
31:25 *If you ask them who created heaven and earth, they will certainly say, Allah. Say: Praise be to Allah. But most of them do not know.*

He Has Invented It Himself

10:24 *This present life is like the water that We send down from heaven, and the produce of the earth, of which men and cattle eat, grows abundantly until the earth is draped in its golden ornaments, and people think they have power over it. We command it by night or by day, and We lay it to waste, as if it had not flourished just yesterday. This is how We make Our signs clear for those who reflect.*

10:25 *Allah calls to the abode of peace [Paradise], and He guides whom He pleases to the right path. Those who do good find the best reward. No darkness or shame will cover their faces. These are the rightful owners of the Garden. They will abide there forever.*

10:27 *Those who have made evil will have a reward of like evil, and humility will cover their faces. No one will protect them from Allah, as though their faces were covered with the cloak of darkness of the night. They are companions of the Fire. They will abide there forever. On that day We will gather them all together. Then We will say to those who revered other gods besides Allah, "To your place—you and those other gods of yours." We will separate them both [men from their gods] one from the other, and We will say, "You did not worship Us. Allah is a sufficient witness between us and you: We cared nothing for your worship." There every soul will become acquainted with what it did before, and they will be brought back to Allah, their true Lord, and the deities of their own devising will vanish from them.*

10:31 *Say: Who provides for you from the heaven and the earth? Who has power over hearing and sight? And who brings forth the living from the dead and the dead from the living? And who rules all things? They will surely say, Allah. Then say: Will you not keep your duty to Him? This is Allah, your true Lord, and when the truth is gone, what remains but error? How is it that you are turned away? So is the word of the Lord proved true against those who do wrong, and they will not believe. Say: Are there any of the gods you revere besides Allah who can originate creation then repeat it? Say: Allah produces a creature then causes it to return to Him. How are you misled?*

10:35 *Say: Do any of the gods you prefer to Allah guide you to the truth? Say: Allah gives guidance to the truth. Who is more worthy to be followed? He who guides to the truth, or he who himself must be guided to find the truth? What is the matter with you? How are you judging things? Most of them follow nothing but guesses, but a guess cannot replace the truth. Allah is aware of all that they do.*

10:37 *The Koran could not have been created by any but Allah, but it confirms what was revealed before it and is a fuller explanation of the Scriptures [Old and New Testaments]. There is no doubt in it of the Lord of all creatures.*

10:38 *Do they say, "He has invented it himself"? Say: Then bring a sura [chapter of the Koran] like it, and call anyone for help you can besides Allah if you are truthful. But that which they cannot understand, they have called inventions, though the explanation of it has not yet been given them. Those before them rejected the truth, but see what was the end of the unjust! And there are some of them who believe in it and some who do not, but the Lord knows the mischief makers.*

10:41 *If they call you a liar, say, "My work is for me, and your work is for you. You are innocent of what I do, and I am innocent of what you do." Some of them will listen to you, but can you make the deaf hear even though they do not understand? Some of them look toward you, but can you guide the blind even though they cannot see?*
10:44 *Allah does not do injustice to men, but men will wrong themselves.*

Allah's Is the Final Argument

6:132 *There will be ranks for all according to their deeds. Your Lord is aware of all that they do. And your Lord is self-sufficient and merciful. If it were His will, He could destroy you and choose your successors as He raised you up from the offspring of other people. That which is promised you will surely come to pass. You cannot escape it.*
6:135 *Say: Oh, my people! Act according to your ability. I verily will act my part. Soon you will come to know who will be happy in the hereafter. The unjust will not prosper.*
6:136 *They set apart a portion of the fruits and cattle for Allah, Who created all things, and say, "This for Allah," so they assert," and this for our other gods, whom we revere along with Him." [The Arabs set aside part of their crops for their chief god, the moon god, Allah. They set aside another part of their crops for the lesser gods.] The lesser god's shares do not reach Allah, but Allah's share reaches the lesser gods. This is evil. They have made it seem fair to kill their children in order to lead them to their own destruction and cause confusion in their religion. But if Allah had willed against it, they would not have done this. Therefore, leave them alone with their devices. They also say there are cattle and crops that are forbidden asserting that We have said that none may taste them but whom We choose. And they say there are cattle that should be exempt from labor and cattle over which they should not pronounce the name of Allah. All is a lie against Him, and He will reward them for their inventions. They say that which is in the wombs of these cattle is allowed to our males and forbidden to our wives, but if it is still-born, then both partake of it. Allah will reward them for their false attribution of this law to Him. He is wise and aware. They are lost who, in their ignorance, have slain their children and have forbidden food, which Allah has given them, devising a lie against Allah. Now have they erred, and they were not following the right course.*
6:141 *It is He who produces the gardens of the vine, the date-palm, and crops of all kinds, and olives, and pomegranates, like and unlike. Eat of their fruit, and pay the due at harvest time. Do not waste by means of excess for Allah does not love the wasters. There are cattle for burdens and for food. Eat what Allah has given you, and do not follow in the steps of Satan for he is your avowed enemy.*

6:143 *Take eight sorts of cattle in four pairs: two pairs of sheep, and two pairs of goats. Say: Has He forbidden the two males or the two females or that which the wombs of the two females enclose? Tell me with knowledge if you speak the truth. Of camels a pair, and of oxen a pair. Say: Has He forbidden the two males or the two females or what is in the wombs of the two females? Were you present when Allah ordered such a thing? Who does more wrong than one who creates a lie against Allah to mislead men? Allah truly does not guide the wicked.*
6:145 *Say: In what has been revealed to me I do not find any forbidden food except that which died itself; or blood that poured forth; or swine's flesh for that is an abomination, being slain in the name of other than Allah. But whoever is forced to eat by necessity, not desiring or exceeding the limit, the Lord is forgiving and merciful.*
6:146 *To the Jews We forbade every beast with an undivided hoof and the fat of both oxen and sheep, save what might be on their backs, or their entrails, or the fat attached to the bone. With this have We rewarded them for their rebellion for We are true in our laws. If they give the lie to you, then say, "Your Lord is of all-embracing mercy, but His severity will not be withdrawn from the guilty."*
6:148 *Those who are polytheists will say, "If Allah had pleased, neither we nor our fathers would have revered others nor should we have had any taboos." Even their ancestors before them argued falsely until they had tasted Our punishment. Say: Do you have any knowledge that you can produce for us? You follow nothing but opinion and tell nothing but lies. Say: Allah's is the final argument. If He had pleased, He would have guided you all.*
6:150 *Say: Bring your witnesses forward who can prove that Allah has forbidden these animals, but if they bear witness, do not bear witness with them nor follow the whims of those who deny Our revelations, and do not believe in the hereafter for they make others equal to Our Lord.*
6:151 *Say: Come, I will recite what Allah has prohibited to you. Remember that you will not place false gods alongside Him, that you will be good to your parents, and that you will not slay your children because of poverty. We provide for you and for them. Do not commit indecencies openly or concealed, and do not take a life, which Allah has made sacred, except by way of justice and law. This He commands of you that you will learn wisdom.*

Keep Us from the Punishment of the Fire

3:14 *Tempting is the lure of women and children, of stored up treasures of gold and silver, of well-bred horses, cattle and farmland. These are the pleasures of this world, but a more excellent home is found with Allah. Say: Should I tell you about things better than these, prepared for those who fear Allah? They will live forever in Gardens underneath which rivers flow with spouses of perfect purity, for Allah shows grace to his servants.*

3:16 *Believers are those who say, "Our Lord! Surely we believe in You. Forgive us of our sins and keep us from the punishment of the Fire." The patient, the honest, the obedient, and the generous, are those who ask for forgiveness each morning.*

We Have Cast Veils over Their Hearts

6:21 *And who is more unjust than he who conceives a lie concerning Allah or who rejects Our signs? The wrongdoers will not prosper.*

6:22 *On the Day We will gather them all together, We will say to those who praised other gods than Allah, "Where are those make-believe gods of yours?" Then they will have no other excuse but to say, "By Allah, our Lord, we were not unbelievers." See how they lie against themselves, and the gods they invented failed them!*

6:25 *Some among them listen to you [Mohammed], but We have cast veils over their hearts and a heaviness to their ears so that they cannot understand our signs [the Koran]. If they see every sign, they will not have faith in them, but when they come to you, they will dispute with you, and the unbelievers will say, "This is only the fables of the old ones."*

6:26 *And they prohibit others from it [the Koran] and depart from it themselves, but they only destroy their own souls, while they do not perceive it. If you could see when they will be set over the Fire. They will say, "Oh, if we could return we would not deny the signs of the Lord, and we would be one of the believers." Yes, they will clearly see what they had concealed from themselves, but if they returned, they would return to forbidden things, for surely they are liars.*

6:29 *And they say, "There is only our life in this world, and we will not be raised up again." If you could see them when they will stand before their Lord. He will say to them, "Is this not the truth [the Resurrection and Judgment]?" They will say, "Yes, by our Lord!" He will say, "Taste then the punishment because you rejected faith."*

6:31 *They are lost who deny that they will meet with Allah until, suddenly, the Hour comes upon them, and they cry "Oh, woe to us that we neglected it." They shall bear their evil burdens on their backs. Life in this world is but a pastime and amusement, but best is the mansion in Paradise for those who do their duty! Do you not understand?*

THE SATANIC VERSES

T11921 Mohammed was always thinking of how he could persuade all the Meccans. It came to him that the three gods of the Quraysh could intercede with Allah. Mohammed said, "These are the exalted high

1. The T references are to Al Tabari's *History of Prophets and Kings.*

flying cranes whose intercession is approved." The Meccans were delighted and happy. When Mohammed lead prayers at the Kabah, all the Meccans, Muslim and non-Muslim, took part. The Quraysh hung about after the combined service and remarked how happy they were. The tribe had been unified in worship, as before Islam.

T1192 When the news reached Ethiopia, some of the Muslims started for home. But then, trouble. The Koran revealed that Mohammed was wrong. Meccan gods could have no part in his religion. Satan had made him say those terrible words about how the other gods could help Allah. The retraction by Mohammed made the relations between Islam and the Meccans far worse than it had ever been.

> 22:52 ***Never have We sent a prophet or messenger before you whom Satan did not tempt with evil desires, but Allah will bring Satan's temptations to nothing. Allah will affirm His revelations, for He is knowing and wise. He makes Satan's suggestions a temptation for those whose hearts are diseased or for those whose hearts are hardened. Truly, is this is why the unbelievers are in great opposition so that those who have been given knowledge will know that the Koran is the truth from their Lord and so that they may believe in it and humbly submit to Him. Allah will truly guide the believers to the right path.***
> 22:55 ***But the unbelievers will never stop doubting until the Hour of Judgment comes upon them unaware or until the punishment of a disastrous day. On that day Allah's rule will be absolute. He will judge between them. And those who believed and did good works will be led into Gardens of delight. As for the unbelievers who treated Our signs as lies, they will receive a shameful punishment.***

THE POET'S SUBMISSION

I252 Al Dausi was a poet of some standing in Arabia and when he visited Mecca he was warned to stay away from Mohammed. Mohammed had hurt the Quraysh and broken the harmony of the tribe. He was warned that Mohammed could bring such divisions to his own family. But Al Dausi went to the mosque and there was Mohammed. Since he had been warned about Mohammed this made Al Dausi more curious to hear what Mohammed said when he prayed. He liked what he heard and followed Mohammed home. They spoke for some time and Al Dausi decided to submit to Islam.

I253 He returned home. His father was old and came to greet his son. Al Dausi said to him, "Go away father, for I want nothing to do with you or you with me." His father said, "Why, my son?" Al Dausi said, "I have become a Muslim." The father replied, "Well, then I shall do so as well."

1253 He then entered his home and told his wife, "Leave me, I want nothing to do with you." She cried, "Why?" Al Dausi said, "Islam has divided us and I now follow Mohammed." She replied, "Then your religion is my religion." He then instructed her in Islam.

The Koran is constant in its admonitions about whom a Muslim should be friends with.

> 9:23 *Oh, Believers, do not make friends of your fathers or your brothers if they love unbelief above Islam. He who makes them his friends does wrong. Say: If your fathers, and your sons, and your brothers, and your wives, and your kin-folks, and the wealth which you have gained, and the merchandise that you fear you will not sell, and the dwellings in which you delight—if all are dearer to you than Allah and His Messenger and efforts on His Path, then wait until Allah's command comes to pass. Allah does not guide the impious.*

> 3:28 *Believers should not take unbelievers as friends in preference to other believers. Those who do this will have none of Allah's protection and will only have themselves as guards. Allah warns you to fear Him for all will return to Him.*

> 3:118 *Believers! Do not become friends with anyone except your own people. The unbelievers will not rest until they have corrupted you. They wish nothing but your ruin. Their hatred of you is made clear by their words, but even greater hatred is hidden within their hearts. We have made Our signs clear to you. Therefore, do your best to comprehend them.*

> 4:89 *They would have you become unbelievers like them so you will all be the same. Therefore, do not take any of them as friends until they have abandoned their homes to fight for Allah's cause. But if they turn back, find them and kill them wherever they are. Do not take any of them as a friend or a helper except those who seek asylum among your allies and those who come to you because their hearts have forbidden them from fighting against you or their own people. If it had been Allah's will, He would have given them power over you so they would have certainly fought you. Therefore, if they leave you and do not wage war against you and seek peace with you, Allah commands you not to injure them.*

> 4:138 *Warn the hypocrites that torturous punishment awaits them. The hypocrites take unbelievers as friends rather than believers. Do they look for honor at their hands? Truly all honor belongs to Allah.*

Do Not Take Unbelievers as Friends over Fellow Believers

4:144 *Believers! Do not take unbelievers as friends over fellow believers. Would you give Allah a clear reason to punish you?*

60:1 *Oh, you who believe, do not take My enemy and yours for friends by showing them kindness. They reject the truth that has come to you. They drive out the messengers and yourselves because you believe in Allah, your Lord. If you continue to fight for Allah's cause [jihad] and from a desire to please Me, would you show them kindness in private? I know best what you conceal and what you reveal. Whoever does this among you has already strayed from the right path.*

60:13 *Oh, Believers, do not enter into friendship with those against whom Allah is angered. They have despaired of the hereafter, even as the unbelievers despair of those who are in graves.*

5:57 *Oh, you who believe, do not take those who have received the Scriptures [Jews and Christians] before you, who have scoffed and jested at your religion, or who are unbelievers for your friends. Fear Allah if you are true believers. When you call to prayer, they make it a mockery and a joke. This is because they are a people who do not understand.*

I260 There was one Christian in Mecca in whom Mohammed took an interest. In the market there was a Christian slave who ran a booth. Mohammed would go and speak with him at length. This led to the Quraysh saying that what Mohammed said in the Koran, came from the Christian slave. The Koran's response:

16:101 *When We exchange one verse for another, and Allah knows best what He reveals, they say, "You are making this up." Most of them do not understand.*
16:102 *Say: The Holy Spirit [Gabriel] has truthfully revealed it from your Lord so that it may confirm the faith of those who believe and be a guide and good news for those who submit. We know that they say, "It is a man that teaches him." The man [his name is uncertain] they point to speaks a foreign language while this is clear Arabic.*

11:12 *You may feel like abandoning part of what was revealed to you, and you will be distressed at heart for fear of them, saying, "Why has there not been a treasure or an angel sent down with him?" You are there only to warn. Allah has all things in his charge. Or they might say, "He invented the Koran." Say: Then invent ten suras [chapters] of your own, and call whomever you can to help you besides Allah if you are men of truth. If your false gods do not answer you, then know that this has been sent to you with the awareness of Allah and that there is no Allah but He. Will you submit to Islam, then?*

32:1 *ALIF. LAM. MIM. This Book is without a doubt a revelation sent down from the Lord of the worlds. Do they say, "He [Mohammed] has made it up"? No. It is the truth sent from your Lord so that you may warn a people who have not yet been warned so that they may be guided.*

41:1 *HA. MIM. A revelation from the most gracious, Most merciful Allah, a Book whose verses are explained in detail, a recital in Arabic for people of understanding.*

11:1 *ELIF. LAM. RA. This is a book whose verses are established in wisdom and explained in detail from the wise and the all-informed so that you should worship none but Allah. I am sent by Him to you as a warner, and I bring good news.*

14:1 *ELIF. LAM. RA. We have sent down these Scriptures to you [Mohammed] so that you may bring men out of darkness into light and into the path of the mighty and the glorious—with the permission of Allah, to whom all things in the heavens and on the earth belong. Misery to the unbelievers for they will receive a terrible punishment.*

12:1 *ELIF. LAM. RA. These are signs of the clear Book. We have sent down an Arabic Koran so that you might understand it.*

39:27 *Now we have set forth for men in this Koran every kind of parable for their warning, an Arabic Koran, free from tortuous wording so they may guard against evil.*

31:1 *ELIF. LAM. MIM. These are the verses of the wise Book, a guidance and a mercy to the righteous who observe prayer, pay the poor tax, and believe firmly in the hereafter. The believers have guidance from their Lord, and they will be successful.*

46:1 *HA-MIM. This Scripture is revealed by Allah, the powerful, the wise. We have created the heavens and the earth and everything between them in truth and for a fixed term, but the unbelievers ignore the warnings.*

30:58 *In this Koran We have used every kind of parable, but if you bring any sign to them, the unbelievers will say, "You are only saying lies." This is how Allah seals up the hearts of those who have no knowledge. So be patient. Surely Allah's promise is true. Do not let those who have no firm beliefs unsettle you.*

THE NIGHT JOURNEY

17:1 *Glory to Allah, Who took His servant on a night time journey from the Sacred Mosque in Mecca to the furthest Mosque [Jerusalem], whose neighborhood We have blessed so that We might show him Our signs: He, and only He, hears and sees all things.*

I264 One night as he lay sleeping, Mohammed said that the angel nudged him with his foot. He awoke, saw nothing, and went back to sleep. This happened again. Then it happened a third time. Mohammed awoke, saw Gabriel and took his arm. They went out the door and found a white animal, half mule and half donkey. Its feet had wings and could move to the horizon at one step. Gabriel put Mohammed on the white animal and off they went to Jerusalem to the site of the Temple.

I264 There at the temple were Jesus, Abraham, Moses, and other prophets. Mohammed led them in prayer. Gabriel brought Mohammed two bowls. One was filled with wine and the other was filled with milk. Mohammed took the one with milk and drank it. That was the right choice.

I265 When Mohammed told this story at the Kabah, the Quraysh hooted at the absurdity of it. Actually, some of the Muslims found it too hard to believe and left Islam. One of them went to Abu Bakr and told him that Mohammed had gone to Jerusalem the night before. Bakr said they were lying. They told him to go and hear for himself. Mohammed was at the mosque telling of his story. Abu Bakr said, "If he says it, then it is true. He tells me of communication with Allah that comes to him at all hours of the day and night. I believe him."

I265 Aisha, Mohammed's favorite wife, said that Mohammed never left the bed that night, however, his spirit soared.

I266 Mohammed reported that Abraham looked exactly like him. Moses was a ruddy faced man, tall, thin, and with curly hair. Jesus was light skinned with reddish complexion and freckles and lank hair.

I268 After the prayers had been done in Jerusalem, Gabriel brought a fine ladder. Mohammed and Gabriel climbed the ladder until they came to one of the gates of heaven, called Gate of the Watchers. An angel was in charge there and had under his command 12,000 angels. And each of those 12,000 angels had 12,000 angels under them. The guardian angel asked Gabriel who Mohammed was. When Gabriel said it was Mohammed, the angel wished Mohammed well.

I268 All the angels who greeted Mohammed, smiled and wished him well, except for one. Mohammed asked Gabriel who was the unsmiling angel. The unsmiling angel was Malik, the Keeper of Hell. Mohammed asked Gabriel to ask Malik if he would show him Hell. So Malik removed the lid to Hell and flames blazed into the air. Mohammed quickly ask for the lid to be put back on Hell.

I269 At the lowest heaven, a man sat with the spirits of men passing in front of him. To one he would say, "A good spirit from a good body." And to another spirit he would say, "An evil spirit from an evil body."

Mohammed asked who the man was. It was Adam reviewing the spirits of his children. The spirit of a believer excited him and the spirit of an infidel disgusted him.

1269 Mohammed saw men with lips like a camel. In their hands were flaming hot coals. They would shove the coals into their mouths and the burning coals came out of their ass. These were those who had stolen the wealth of orphans. Then he saw the family of the Pharaoh with huge bellies. Then he saw women hanging from their breasts. These women had fathered bastards on their husbands. Mohammed said that Allah hates women who birth bastards. They deprive the true sons of their portion and learn the secrets of the harem.

1270 Then Mohammed was taken up to the second heaven and saw Jesus and his cousin, John, son of Zakariah. In the third heaven he saw Joseph, son of Jacob. In the fourth heaven, Mohammed saw Idris. In the fifth heaven was a man with a long beard and white hair. He was a very handsome man who was Aaron, son of Imran. In the sixth heaven was a dark man with a hooked nose. This was Moses. In the seventh heaven was a man sitting on a throne in front of a mansion. Every day 70,000 angels went into the mansion, not to come out until the day of resurrection. The man on the throne looked just like Mohammed; it was Abraham. Abraham took Mohammed into Paradise and there was a beautiful woman with red lips. Mohammed ask who she belonged to, for she was very attractive to him. She was Zayd. When he got back, Mohammed told her of this.

1271 When Gabriel took Mohammed to each of the heavens and asked permission to enter he had to say who he had brought and whether they had a mission. They would then say, "Allah grant him life, brother and friend." When Mohammed got to the seventh heaven his Lord gave him the duty of fifty prayers a day. When he returned past Moses, Moses asked him how many prayers Allah had given him. When Moses heard that it was fifty, he said, "Prayer is a weighty matter and your people are weak. Go back and ask your Lord to reduce the number for you and your community. Mohammed went back and got the number reduced to forty. When he passed Moses, the same conversation took place. And so on until Allah reduced the number to five. Moses tried to get Mohammed to go back and get the number reduced even further, but Mohammed felt ashamed to ask for more.

In the Night Journey we see Mohammed as the successor to the Jewish prophets.

Joseph

12:3 *We reveal to you [Mohammed] one of the most beautiful stories in this Koran, though before this, you were one of those who did not know.*
12:4 *When Joseph said to his Father [Jacob], "Oh, my Father, I saw in a dream eleven stars and the sun and the moon, and I saw them prostrate themselves to me."*
12:5 *He said, "Oh, my son, do not tell your brothers of your vision unless they conspire in a plot against you, for Satan is an open enemy of man. So your Lord will choose you and will teach you the interpretation of stories and will perfect His favors to you and to the family of Jacob, even as He perfected it for your fathers Abraham and Isaac. The Lord is knowing, wise."*
12:7 *Surely in Joseph and his brothers are signs for the seekers of truth. [Jacob had twelve sons out of two wives and two slaves. Rachel was the mother of Joseph and Benjamin.] They [the other ten brothers] said, "Joseph and his brother [Benjamin] are better loved by our Father than we, but we are more in number. Our father is wrong. Let us kill Joseph or drive him to some other land so that your father's favor will be for you alone. After that you can live as upright persons."*
12:10 *One of them said, "Do not kill Joseph, but cast him down to the bottom of the well, if you must, so some travelers will take him up."*
12:11 *They said, "Oh, our Father, why do you not trust us with Joseph since we are his sincere friends? Send him with us tomorrow so he may enjoy himself and play. We will guard him well."*
12:13 *Jacob said, "It grieves me that you will take him away, and I fear that the wolf may devour him while you are not paying attention."*
12:14 *They said, "If the wolf were to devour him with so many of us there and when we are so strong, we would have perished first."*
12:15 *When they went away with him, they agreed to place him at the bottom of the well, and We revealed to Joseph, "You will tell them of this deed when they shall not know you." And they came weeping to their father at nightfall. They said, "Oh, our Father, truthfully, we went to run races, and we left Joseph with our things, and the wolf devoured him, but you will not believe us even though we speak the truth." They brought his shirt with fake blood upon it. Jacob said, "No, you have arranged this affair, but patience is good, and I will pray for the help of Allah so I may bear what you tell me."*
12:19 *There came a caravan of travelers, and they sent their water-carrier for water, and he let down his bucket. He said, "Ah, there, good news; this is a fine youth." They hid him like a treasure to make merchandise of him, but Allah knew what they did. They sold him for a small price, a few pieces of silver. They attached no value to him. An Egyptian who bought him said to his wife, "Treat him hospitably. He may be useful to*

us, or we may adopt him as a son." This is how We settled Joseph in the land [Egypt], and We instructed him in the interpretation of stories, for Allah is master of His affairs, but most men do not know it. When Joseph had reached full maturity, We gave him wisdom and knowledge, for this is how We reward the well doers.

12:23 *The mistress of his home developed a passion for Joseph, and she shut the doors and said, "Come here." He said, "Allah keep me! Your husband has given me a good home and treated me honorably no good comes to wrongdoers." Still, she desired him, and he would have longed for her if he had not seen the signs from his Lord. So We ordered that We might turn him away from all evil and indecency for he was one of Our sincere servants.*

12:25 *They both raced to the door, and she tore his shirt from behind, and they met her husband at the door. She said, "What is the punishment to him who would do evil to your wife? Prison or a painful doom?"*

12:26 *Joseph said, "It was she who asked me to commit an evil act." One from her own family bore witness: "If his shirt is torn in front, then she speaks truth, and he is a liar. But if his shirt be torn behind, she lies and he is true."*

12:28 *So when his lord saw his shirt torn behind, he said, "This is a device of you women. Your devices are great, "Joseph, leave this affair. Wife, ask pardon for your crime, for you have sinned."*

12:30 *The women in the city said, "The wife of the Prince is trying to seduce her servant. He has inspired her with his love, but we clearly see she is going astray." And when she heard of their spiteful talk, she sent for them and prepared a banquet for them and gave each one of them a knife. She said, "Joseph, show yourself." When they saw him, they were amazed and cut their hands and said, "Allah keep us. This is no man. This is a noble angel." She said, "This is the man about whom you blamed me. I tried to seduce him from his true self, but he stood firm. Now, if he does not obey my command, he will surely be cast into prison and become one of the despised."*

12:33 *He said, "Oh, my Lord, I prefer the prison to that which they invite me, but unless you turn away their snares from me, I will feel inclined to play the youth with them and become one of the foolish." So his Lord heard him and turned aside their snares from him for he is the hearer and the knower.*

12:35 *It occurred to the men, even after they had seen the signs of his innocence, to imprison him for a time. And two youths entered into the prison with him. One of them said, "I had a dream that I was pressing grapes." The other said, "I dreamed that I was carrying bread on my head that the birds did eat. Tell us what this means, for we see you are good to all."*

12:37 *Joseph said, "Before any food comes to feed either of you, I will acquaint you with the truth and meaning of your dreams. This is a part of what my Lord has taught me, for I have abandoned the religion of those who do not believe Allah and who deny the life to come. I follow the religion of my fathers, Abraham, Isaac, and Jacob. We could never join false gods with Allah. This is because of Allah's bounty towards us and towards mankind, but most men do not give thanks. Oh, my two fellow prisoners, are various lords best or Allah, the one, the mighty? Those you worship beside Him are mere names that you and your fathers have named without authority. This decision is for Allah, alone. He has commanded that you worship none but Him. This is the right faith, but most men do not know it.*

12:41 *"Oh, my two fellow prisoners, one of you will pour wine for his Lord to drink, but the other will be crucified, and the birds will eat from his head. So the matter is decreed concerning your question." Joseph said to the one whom he judged would be released, "Mention me in the presence of your lord, " but Satan caused him to forget to mention Joseph to his lord, so he stayed in prison a few years.*

12:43 *The King of Egypt said, "I saw seven fat cows in a dream being eaten by seven lean cows, and seven green ears of corn and seven others withered. Oh, nobles, explain to me my dream if you are able to explain dreams."*

12:44 *They said, "They are confused and mixed dreams, and we do not interpret dreams."*

12:45 *Then Joseph's freed prisoner companion said, "I will tell you the interpretation. Let me try." He went to Joseph in prison and said, "Joseph, truthful one, explain to us the dream of the seven fat cows which seven lean ones devoured, and of the seven green ears with the others withered that I may return to the men and that they may be informed."*

12:47 *He said, "You will sow seven years as usual, and the corn you reap you will leave in its ear except a little of which you will eat. After that will come seven grievous years when you will eat what you have stored except that which you will have kept. A year after this, men will have rain, and they will press wine and oil."*

12:50 *The King said, "Bring him to me." And when the messenger returned, Joseph said, "Go back to your lord, and ask him what is the case of the women who cut their hands, for my lord well knows the snare they laid."*

12:51 *The King sent for the women and asked, "What happened when you tried to seduce Joseph?" They said, "Allah keep us. We do not know any evil against him." The wife said, "Now the truth appears. It was I who tried to seduce him. He is most surely one of the truthful ones."*

12:52 *Joseph said, "I asked for this so that my lord may know that I was*
not false in his absence, and that Allah does not guide the snares of the
false ones. Yet I do not absolve myself, for the human heart is prone
to evil except that my Lord has mercy on us, for my Lord is forgiving
and merciful."
12:54 *So the King said, "Bring him to me. I will take him for my special*
service." And when he had spoken with Joseph he said, "Be assured that
from this day you will be with us, confirmed in rank and trusted."
12:55 *Joseph said, "Set me over the granaries of the land, and I will guard*
over them wisely." So We gave Joseph power in the land. He was the own-
er of it as he pleased. We give our favors to those We will, and We will
guard the reward of the righteous. The reward of the life to come is better
for those who have believed and feared Allah.
12:58 *Joseph's brothers came before him. He knew them, but they did not*
know him. And when he had provided them with their provision, he said,
"Bring me your brother [Benjamin] from your father. Do you not see
that I fill the measure and am the best of hosts? If you do not bring him to
me, there will be no measure of corn for you from me, nor will you come
near me."
12:61 *They said, "We will try to obtain him from his father [Jacob], and*
we will surely do it."
12:62 *Joseph told his servants, "Put their money into their camel-packs so*
they will see it when they have returned to their family so they will come
back to us."
12:63 *When they returned to their father, they said, "Oh, our father, the*
grain has been denied us unless we return with our brother [Benjamin],
so send our brother with us, and we will have our measure. We will guard
him well."
12:64 *He said, "Should I trust you with him as I trusted you before with his*
brother? Allah is the best guardian, and He shows the most compassion
of the compassionate."
12:65 *When they opened their goods, they found their money had been*
returned to them. They said, "Oh, our father, what more can we desire?
Our money has been returned to us. We will provide corn for our families
and will take care of our brother and will receive a camel's burden of
more corn. What we bring now is a light quantity."
12:66 *He said, "I will not send him with you but on your oath before*
Allah that you will bring him back to me unless you are surrounded."
When they had given him their pledge, he said, "Allah is witness of
what we say."
12:67 *And he said, "Oh, my sons! Do not enter by one gate, but enter by*
different gates. Yet I cannot help you against anything decreed by Allah.

Judgment belongs to Allah, alone. I put my trust in Him, and let all who
trust put their trust in him."
12:68 *And when they entered as their father commanded, it did not pro-*
tect them from anything decreed by Allah. It was a desire of Jacob's soul,
which he satisfied. He was possessed of knowledge, which we had taught
him, but most men do not know. When they came to Joseph, he took his
brother to him. He said, "I am your brother, so do not grieve at what they
did." When he had provided them with their provisions, he placed his
drinking cup in his brother's camel-pack. Then a crier cried after them,
"Oh, travelers, you are surely thieves."
12:71 *They turned back to them and said, "What is that you are*
missing?"
12:72 *"We miss," they said, "the King's cup. Whoever finds it will receive a*
camel's load of corn. We are bound by that promise."
12:73 *The brothers said, "By Allah, you know certainly that we did not*
come to make mischief in the land and are not thieves."
12:74 *"What," said the Egyptians, "will be the penalty for this if you are*
found to be liars?"
12:75 *They said, "The penalty will be on the one in whose camel-pack it*
will be found, he will be given up to you in satisfaction for it. This is how
we punish the unjust."
12:76 *Joseph began to search their sacks before he came to the sack of his*
brother [Benjamin]. From the sack of his brother he drew out the cup.
We planned this for Joseph. By the King's law, he had no power to seize
his brother if Allah had not willed it. We uplift whomever we please, but
above every one else is the all-knowing.
12:77 *They said, "If he steals, a brother of his has stolen before," but Joseph*
kept his secret, and did not reveal it to them. He said, "You are in the
worse condition, and Allah knows what you allege."
12:78 *They said, "Oh, Prince, he has a very aged father, who will grieve*
him. Take one of us instead, for we see that you are a generous person."
12:79 *He said, "Allah forbids that we take someone other than him with*
whom our property was found, for then we should be acting unjustly."
12:80 *When they saw that Joseph was unyielding, they privately conferred.*
The eldest of them said [to Benjamin], "Do you not know that your father
took a pledge from you in Allah's name and how you failed in duty with
regard to Joseph? So I will not leave this land until my father permits me,
or Allah decides for me for of those who decide is He the best. Return to
your father and say, 'Oh, our father, your son has stolen. We bear witness
to what we know. We could not guard against the unforeseen. Ask for
yourself in the city where we have been and of the caravan with which we
have arrived. You will find we are telling the truth.'

12:83 *Jacob said, "No, you have arranged all this among yourselves.
Patience is most fitting for me, and Allah may bring them back to me
together for he is the knowing, the wise."*
12:84 *He turned away from them and said, "Oh, how I am grieved for Joseph!" and his eyes became white with grief for he bore a silent sorrow.*
12:85 *They said, "By Allah, will you never cease to think of Joseph until
you are at the point of death, or dead?"*
12:86 *He said, "I only plead my grief and my sorrow to Allah, but I know
from Allah what you do not know. Go, my sons, and seek tidings of Joseph
and his brother, and do not give up hope of Allah's mercy for only the
unbelievers despair of the mercy of Allah."*
12:88 *And when they came in to Joseph, they said, "Oh, Prince, distress has
reached us and our family, and we have poor merchandise, so give us full
measure, and be charitable to us for Allah will repay the almsgivers."*
12:89 *Joseph said, "Do you know what you did to Joseph and his brother
in your ignorance?"*
12:90 *They said, "Are you indeed Joseph?" He said, "I am Joseph, and this
is my brother. Allah has been gracious to us. For he who guards against
evil and is patient will be rewarded. Allah will not allow the reward of
the righteous to be lost!"*
12:91 *They said, "By Allah, now Allah has chosen you above us, and we
have indeed been sinners!"*
12:92 *He said, "No blame will be on you this day. Allah may forgive you
for He is the most merciful of those who show mercy. Go with this shirt
of mine, and lay it on my father's face, and he will recover his sight, and
come to me with all your family."*
12:94 *When the caravan departed from Egypt, their father said, "I surely
perceive the smell of Joseph. Do not think I am feeble."*
12:95 *They said, "By Allah, it is your old mistake." Then when the bearer
of good tidings came, he cast the shirt on his father's face, and Jacob's eye-
sight returned. Then he said, "Did I not tell you that I knew from Allah
what you did not know?"*
12:97 *They said, "Oh, Our father, ask pardon for our crimes for us for we
have truly been sinners."*
12:98 *He said, "I will ask your pardon of my Lord for He is forgiving and
merciful."*
12:99 *When they came to Joseph, he took his family to him, and said, "Enter Egypt in safety if Allah wills."*
12:100 *And he raised his parents onto the throne, and they fell down
bowing themselves unto him. Then he said, "Oh, my father, this is the
meaning of my dream of old. My Lord has now made it true, and He
has surely been gracious to me since He took me from the prison and
has brought you up out of the desert, even after Satan stirred up strife*

between me and my brothers. My Lord is gracious to whom He will for He is knowing and wise.

12:101 *"Oh, my Lord, you have given me some power and have taught me to interpret dreams. Maker of the heavens and of the earth, You are my guardian in this world and in the next. Cause me to die a Muslim, and join me with the just."*

12:102 *This is one of the secret stories, which We reveal to you. You were not with Joseph's brothers when they conceived their design and laid their plot. And though you try, the greater part of men will not believe you. You will not ask them for any reward for this message. It is simply a reminder for all mankind.*

Abraham

6:74 *Remember when Abraham said to his father Azar, "Do you take idols for gods? I see that you and your people are in manifest error." So did We show Abraham the kingdom of the heavens and of the earth that he might be a believer. When the night covered him, he beheld a star. He said, "This is my Lord," but when it set, he said, "I do not love gods that set."*

6:77 *When he saw the moon rising, he said "This is my Lord," but when the moon set, he said, "Unless my Lord guides me, I will go astray." When he saw the sun rise in splendor, he said, "This is my Lord. This is the greatest of all," but when it set, he said, "Oh, my people! I am free of your guilt of worshipping false gods. I turn myself wholly towards Him Who created the heavens and the earth. I am not one of the unbelievers."*

6:80 *His people argued with him. He said, "Have you come to dispute with me about Allah when He has guided me? I do not fear the gods you have set up besides Allah unless He wills it. My Lord has knowledge of all things. Will you not remember? How should I fear your gods when you do not fear worshiping your gods alongside Allah without permission? Then which of the two parties has more right to salvation? Can you answer that? Those who believe and do not confuse their belief with wrong doing; they will have safety because they are rightly guided." This was the argument that We gave to Abraham to use against his people. We raise whom We desire to grades of wisdom. The Lord is wise and knowing.*

6:84 *We gave him Isaac and Jacob and guided both aright, and before them, We guided Noah. Among the descendants of Abraham are David and Solomon and Job and Joseph and Moses and Aaron. This is how We reward the righteous. And Zacharias, John, Jesus, and Elias were all righteous. And so were Ishmael, Elisha, Jonas, and Lot. We favored these above all nations. And from among their fathers and offspring and brethren, We chose them and guided them into the straight path. This is Allah's guidance. He gives guidance to whomever He chooses from his servants. But if they revere other gods along with Him, all their works would be in vain.*

Lord, Make This Land [Mecca] Secure

14:35 *Abraham said, "Oh, Lord, make this land [Mecca] secure, and save me and my children from serving idols. "Oh, my Lord, the unbelievers have led many men astray, but whoever follows me, he truly will be my brother, and to whosoever disobeys me, You are forgiving and merciful.*
14:37 *"Oh, our Lord, I have settled some of my offspring in a barren valley, near Your holy house [the Kabah], Oh, our Lord, so they may keep regular prayer. So fill the hearts of men to yearn toward them, and supply them with fruits that they may be thankful.*
14:38 *"Oh, our Lord, You truly know what we hide and what we reveal. Nothing on earth or in heaven is hidden from Allah. Praise be to Allah who has given me, in my old age, Ishmael and Isaac. My Lord is the hearer of prayer. Lord, make of me and my posterity those who observe regular prayer. Oh, our Lord, grant my petition. Oh, our Lord, forgive me and my parents and the believers on the day when an account will be taken."*

We Drowned Those Who Rejected Our Signs

7:59 *We sent Noah to his people, and he said, "Oh, my people, worship Allah. You have no other god but Him. I fear for you the punishment of a dreadful day."*
7:60 *The chiefs of his people said, "We clearly see that you are in error."*
7:61 *He said, "There is no error in me, my people, I am a messenger from the Lord of the worlds. I bring to you the messages of my Lord and offer you good advice for I know from Allah what you do not know. Do you wonder why a warning comes to you from your Lord through a man among you? It is so you will guard against evil and receive His mercy."*
7:64 *But they rejected him, so We saved him and those who were with him in the ark, and We drowned those who rejected Our signs for they were a blind people.*

Moses

I Punish Those I Desire

7:103 *After them We sent Moses with Our signs to Pharaoh and his nobles, but they rejected them. See what was the end of those who made mischief! And Moses said, "Oh, Pharaoh, I am a messenger from the Lord of the worlds. I have no right to speak anything but the truth about Allah. Now I come to you with clear proof of my mission from your Lord, so let the Children of Israel leave with me."*
7:106 *Pharaoh said, "If you have come with a sign, let me see it if you are telling the truth."*

7:107 *So Moses threw down his rod, and it was clearly a serpent. Then he drew his hand from his bosom, and it was clearly white [with leprosy] to the onlookers.*
7:109 *The nobles of Pharaoh's people said, "This is a knowing sorcerer. He plans to expel you from your land. What do you advise be done?"*
7:111 *They said, "Put him and his brother off awhile, and send the collectors to your cities so they can bring every skilled sorcerer to you."*
7:113 *And the sorcerers came to Pharaoh. They said, "We will surely be rewarded if we win."*
7:114 *He said, "Yes, and you will certainly be brought nearest to me."*
7:115 *They said, "Oh, Moses! Will you throw down your rod first, or will we throw down ours?"*
7:116 *Moses said, "Throw yours down." And when they had thrown them down, they bewitched the people's eyes, and frightened them with a great feat of magic. Then We spoke to Moses, "Throw down your rod," and it devoured the lies they told. So the truth was established, and all that they had done proved in vain. They were vanquished on the spot and were made to look small.*
7:120 *And the magicians fell down prostrate in adoration saying, "We believe in the Lord of the worlds, the Lord of Moses and Aaron."*
7:123 *Pharaoh said, "Do you believe in him before I give you permission? This is surely a trick you have devised in my city in order to drive out its people, but you will soon see what will happen.*
7:124 *I will cut off your hands and feet on opposite sides then will crucify you altogether."*
7:125 *They said, "We return to our Lord, and you [the Pharaoh] will take revenge on us because we believed the signs of our Lord when they came to us. Lord, give us your constancy and patience that we may die as Muslims."*
7:127 *The elders of Pharaoh's people said, "Will you leave Moses and his people to spread corruption in our land and forsake you and your gods?" He said, "We will slay their male children and spare their females. Then they will submit."*
7:128 *Moses said to his people, "Ask for help from Allah, and patiently wait for the earth is Allah's, and He will give it as an inheritance to whomever He pleases. And the righteous will inherit Paradise."*
7:129 *They said, "We were persecuted before you came to us and since you have been with us." Moses said, "It may be that your Lord will destroy your enemy and make you rulers in the land so He will see how you act."*
7:130 *We have already punished Pharaoh's people with years of droughts and scarcity of food that they might learn. When good fell to them they said, "This is due to us, " but if evil came to them, they said it was due to*

the evil omens of Moses and his people. In truth, their evil omens were from Allah, but most of them do not know.
7:132 *They said to Moses, "Whatever sign you bring to bewitch us, we will not believe in you." So We sent them the flood, the locusts, the lice, the frogs, and the blood. All were clear signs, but they were an arrogant and sinful people. Each time any plague fell on them, they said, "Oh, Moses, pray for us to your Lord because you have a promise from Him. If you remove the plague, we will truly believe you, and we will let the Children of Israel leave with you."*
7:135 *But every time We removed a plague from them, they broke their promise when the time Allah granted them was over. Therefore, We took vengeance on them. We drowned them in the sea because they rejected Our signs and did not take warning from them. And We gave to the people who were considered weak the lands in the east and the west with Our blessings. The promise of the Lord was fulfilled for the Children of Israel because of their patience and constancy, and We destroyed the great works and the buildings of Pharaoh and his people.*
7:138 *And We took the Children of Israel across the sea, and they discovered people who worshipped idols. They said, "Oh, Moses, make us a god like the gods they have." He said, "You are an ignorant people. As for these people, their practices will be destroyed. What they are doing is in vain. Should I seek a god other than Allah for you when it was Allah who favored you above all other nations?"*
7:141 *And remember when We rescued you from Pharaoh's people, who punished you with dreadful suffering, slaughtering your male children and sparing your daughters? That was a great trial from your Lord. We appointed a term with Moses of thirty nights of solitude, which We completed with ten other nights so that his whole time with his Lord amounted to forty nights. And Moses said to his brother Aaron before he went up, "Take my place among my people, do right, and do not follow the way of sinners."*
7:143 *When Moses came at Our set time and his Lord spoke with him, he said, "Oh, Lord, show yourself to me so I may look upon you." Allah said, "You cannot bear to see me, but look up on the mountain, and if it remains firm in its place, then you will see Me." And when Allah manifested Himself to the mountain it turned it to dust, and Moses fell down senseless. And when he recovered he said, "Glory be to You! I turn to you to repent, and I am the first of the believers."*
7:144 *Allah said, "Oh, Moses, I have chosen you above all men. Take My words and make them known. Be one of the grateful." And We wrote on the tablets for him about laws concerning all matters, both commanding and explaining all things. We said, "Take a firm hold of these, and command your people to take the right path, which is written here. Soon*

I will show you the homes of the wicked. I will turn away from the arrogant. If they see every sign, they will not believe them. If they see the true path, they will not take it, but if they see the path of error, they will take it. They rejected Our signs and failed to take the warning. Those who reject Our signs and the coming of Judgment Day will be rewarded for what they have done."

7:148 *During his absence, the people of Moses chose for worship a calf made of their gold ornaments and believed they heard it make a comforting sound. They did not see that it could not speak to them nor lead them. They worshiped it and became wrongdoers. They repented when they saw their error and said, "If Our Lord does not show mercy and forgive us, we will perish."*

7:150 *When Moses returned to his people, angry and grieved, he said, "You have done evil in my place during my absence. Do you wish to hasten the judgment of Allah? He threw down the tablets and seized his brother by the head dragging him to him. Moses said, "Son of my mother, the people judged me weak and almost killed me. Do not make my enemies rejoice over me or place me among the wrong doers." Moses said, "Oh, Lord, forgive me and my brother, let us enter into Your mercy for You are the most merciful of the merciful."*

7:152 *Those who took the calf as a god will receive the wrath of the Lord and humiliation in this present life. This is how We repay those who deceive Allah. But for those who have done evil, then afterwards repent and believe, the Lord will be forgiving and merciful.*

7:154 *And when the anger of Moses was calmed, he took up the tablets. In their writing was guidance and mercy for those who fear their Lord. And Moses chose seventy of his men for Our meeting. When the earth trembled, he said, "Oh, my Lord, if it had been your will, You could have destroyed them and me before this time. Will You destroy us for the deeds of the foolish ones among us? It is Your trial alone. With it, You will mislead whom You wish and guide whom You wish to the right path. You are our protector. Forgive us and have mercy on us because You are the best of those who forgive.*

7:156 *Ordain for us what is good in this world and in the world to come because we have turned to You." Allah said, "I punish those I desire, but My mercy embraces all things, and ordain mercy for those who do right, and pay the poor tax, and believe in Our signs.*

We Made a Curse to Follow Them

28:1 *TA. SIN. MIM. These are the signs that make the Book clear. We will tell you portions of the story of Moses and Pharaoh in truth for the teaching of the believers.*

28:4 *Now Pharaoh lifted himself in the land and divided his people into classes. He persecuted the lowest class by slaying their male children, but He let their females live. He was an evil tyrant.*

28:5 *We desired to show favor to those who were oppressed in the land, to make them spiritual leaders, to make them heirs, and to give them the land. We desired to punish Pharaoh and Haman and their warriors with a scourge that they feared.*
28:7 *We inspired the mother of Moses saying, "Suckle your child, and if you fear for him, launch him into the river, and do not fear, nor grieve, for We will bring him to you and make him one of the messengers."*
28:8 *Then the Pharaoh's family took him up from the river though, he was to be an enemy and a sorrow to them, for Pharaoh, Haman, and their hosts. Pharaoh's wife said, "He is a joy to me and you. Do not kill him. He will be useful to us, or we may adopt him as a son." But they did not know what they were doing.*
28:10 *The heart of Moses's mother became empty, and she nearly claimed him back as her son, but We strengthened her heart so that she might be a believer. She said to his sister, "Follow him," and she watched him from afar so they did not know it.*
28:12 *And We caused him [the baby Moses] to refuse the nurses' breasts, until his sister came and said, "Should I show you a family of a house that will rear him for you and will be careful of him?" So We restored him to his mother, so she would be comforted and might not grieve and might know that the promise of Allah was true. But most men do not know. And when he had reached maturity and had become a man, We bestowed wisdom and knowledge on him. In this way We reward the righteous.*
28:15 *He entered the city unnoticed, and he found two men fighting. One was of his own race, the other was of his enemies' race. The Jew asked Moses for his help against their enemy, and Moses struck the Egyptian with his fist and killed him. He [Moses] said, "This is a work of Satan, for he is an enemy, a manifest misleader."*
28:16 *He said, "Oh, my Lord, I have wronged my soul; forgive me." So Allah forgave him, for He is forgiving and merciful.*
28:17 *He said, "Lord, because you showed me this grace, I will never again help the wicked."*
28:18 *Moses was in the city at noon, fearful and vigilant. When the man he had helped the day before cried out to him again for help, Moses said to him, "You are plainly a quarrelsome man." And when Moses decided to lay hands on the man who was an enemy to the Jews, the man said to him, "Oh, Moses, will you kill me as you killed that man yesterday? You desire only to become a tyrant in this land and not to become a peacemaker."*
28:20 *But a man came running up from the farthest end of the city. He said, "Oh, Moses, the chiefs consult together to slay you, so leave. I counsel you as a friend."*

28:21 *So he left in fear and vigilance. He prayed, "Oh, Lord, deliver me
from the unjust people." When he turned towards Midian, he said, "Maybe my Lord will guide me in an even path."*
28:23 *When he arrived at the water of Midian, he found a company
of men watering their flocks, and he found beside them two women
keeping back their flocks. He said, "What is the matter?" They said "We
cannot water our flocks until the shepherds have driven off their flocks.
Our father is very old."*
28:24 *So Moses watered their flocks for them then retired to the shade and
said, "Oh, my Lord, I am in need of any good [a wife] you will send me."*
28:25 *One of the two women came back to him, walking bashfully. She
said, "My father calls you so he may reward you for watering our flocks
for us." When Moses came to him and had told him his story, the old man
said, "Do not fear. You have escaped from an unjust people."*
28:26 *One of the two women said, "Oh, my father, hire him for the best
man you can hire is strong and trustworthy."*
28:27 *He said to Moses, "I intend to marry you to one of my two daughters
if you will be my hired servant for eight years, and if you fulfill ten, it will
be of your own free will for I do not wish to make it hard for you. You will
find me, if Allah wills, one of the righteous."*
28:28 *Moses said, "This will be an agreement between me and you. Whichever of the two terms I fulfill, there will be no injustice to me. Allah is
witness of what we say."*
28:29 *So when Moses had fulfilled the term and was traveling with his
family, he saw a fire on the mountain side. He said to his family, "Wait
here for I see a fire. I may bring you tidings from it or a brand from the
fire to warm you."*
28:30 *When he came up to the fire, a voice cried to him from the right
side of the valley from a tree in the sacred hollow: "Oh, Moses, I am
Allah, the Lord of the worlds. Throw down now your staff." When he
saw it move as though it were a serpent, Moses retreated and fled and
did not return. "Oh, Moses, draw near and do not fear, for you are in
safety," cried the voice.*
28:32 *Put your hand into the bosom of your robe, and it will come out
white [like a leper's], but unharmed, and draw your hand close to your
side to guard against fear. These will be two signs from your Lord to Pharaoh and his nobles for they are a sinful people."*
28:33 *Moses said, "Oh, my Lord, I have killed one of them, and I fear that
they will kill me, and my brother Aaron is more eloquent in speech than
I am. Send him with me as a helper and to make good my cause for I fear
they will accuse me of falsehoods."*
28:35 *He said, "We will strengthen your arm with your brother, and We
will give you both authority, and they will not equal you in Our signs.
You two and those who follow you will win the day."*

28:36 *When Moses came to them with Our clear signs they said, "This is nothing but a magical device. We never heard the like among our fathers of old." And Moses said, "My Lord knows best who brings guidance from Him and who will be repaid in Paradise. It is certain that the wicked will not prosper."*
28:38 *Pharaoh said, "Oh, nobles, you have no other god that I know of but me, so Haman, kindle a fire for me to bake bricks of clay, and build me a tower that I may climb up to the god of Moses for I think he is a liar."*
28:39 *He and his hosts were unjustly arrogant in the land. They thought that they would not have to return to Us. So We seized him and his hosts and cast them into the sea. See what was the end of the wrongful doers? And We made them leaders who call to the Fire of Hell, and on Judgment Day, they will not be helped. We made a curse to follow them in this world, and on Judgment Day they will be among the despised.*
28:43 *We gave the book of the Law to Moses for man's enlightening, guidance, and mercy after We destroyed the former generations so they would be mindful.*
28:44 *And you were not on the western slope of Sinai when We revealed the commandments to Moses, nor were you one of the witnesses. But We raised up generations after Moses and lengthened their days. Nor did you dwell among the Midians [a city on the Red Sea] reciting Our signs, but We kept sending messengers to them. And you were not on the slope of Sinai when We called to Moses, but it is of the mercy of your Lord that you warn people who have never had a warner come to them, so they may be mindful. If We had not sent you and had a disaster happened as a result of their own deeds, they might say, "Oh, our Lord, why have you not sent a messenger to us? Then we would have followed your signs and have been of the believers."*

The Plots of the Unbelievers Only End in Failure

40:23 *We had sent Moses of old with Our signs and with clear authority to Pharaoh, and Haman, and Karun, and they said, "Sorcerer, impostor."*
40:25 *When he brought the truth to them from Us, they said, "Slay the sons of those who believe as he does, and spare their females," but the plots of the unbelievers only end in failure.*
40:26 *Pharaoh said, "Leave me alone to kill Moses, and let him call on his Lord. I fear that he will change your religion or cause mischief in the land."*
40:27 *Moses said, "I take refuge with my Lord and your Lord from every arrogant one who does not believe in the Day of Reckoning."*
40:28 *And a believer from the Pharaoh's family, who had hidden his faith said, "Will you kill a man because he says, 'My Lord is god,' when he has already come to you with clear signs from your Lord? If he is a liar, the burden of the lie is on him, but if he is a man of truth, part of what he*

*warns will fall upon you. Allah does not guide wrongdoers and liars. Oh,
my people, today the kingdom is yours; you are the eminent of the earth,
but who shall defend us from the vengeance of Allah if it should come to
us?" Pharaoh said, "I only show you what I think, and I will only guide
you in a right way."*
40:30 *Then the man who believed said, "Oh, my people, I truly fear for
you the like of the day of disaster of the people of old. A plight like that
of the people of Noah and Ad [an ancient people of southern Arabia]
and Thamud [the people of a ruined Nabatean city near Medina] and
of those after them. Yet Allah never wants injustice for his servants. And,
Oh, my people, I indeed fear for you the day of summoning, the day when
you will turn your back and flee. You will not have a protector in Allah.
Whomever Allah leads astray, there will be no guide for him."*
40:34 *Joseph came to you with clear signs, and you continued to doubt the
message which he gave to you until when he died, you said, "Allah will
not send a messenger after him." This is how Allah misleads the doubters
and wrong doers. They who dispute the signs of Allah without authority
having reached them are greatly hated by Allah and the believers. So Allah seals up every arrogant, disdainful heart.*
40:36 *And Pharaoh said, "Oh, Haman, build a tower for me so I can reach
the roads—the roads of the heavens—and may mount to the god of Moses, for I think he is a liar." So the Pharaoh made his evil deed to seem
fair to himself, and he turned away from the path of truth, but the plot of
Pharaoh ended only in his ruin.*
40:38 *The believer said, "Oh, my people, follow me; I will lead you to the
right course. Oh, my people, this present life is only a passing joy, but the
life to come is the life that will last. Whoever has committed evil will be
paid back in like, while he who does things that are right, whether male
or female, and is a believer will enter the Garden. They will be given
abundance without measure. And, Oh, my people, how strange that I
call you to salvation, while you call me to the Fire. You invite me to deny
Allah and to join with Him gods of whom I know nothing, but I invite
you to the mighty, the forgiving. No doubt you call me to one who has
no claim in this world or the Hereafter and that we will return to Allah. The wrongdoers will be the companions of the Fire. Soon you will
remember what I say to you. I entrust my affair to Allah, who watches
over His servants."*

Sparingly to Whom He Pleases

28:76 *Now Korah [a wealthy opponent of Moses] was of the people of Moses, but he rebelled against them for We had given him such treasure
that its keys would have burdened a company of strong men. When his
people said to him, "Do not brag, for Allah does not love a braggart.
Seek to attain Paradise by means of what Allah has given you. Do not*

neglect your part in this world, but be kind as Allah has been kind to you, and do not sin for Allah does not love sinners." Korah said, "I have been given this only because of the knowledge I have." Did he not know that Allah had destroyed generations before him that were mightier than he in strength and had amassed more wealth? The guilty will not be asked about their crimes.

28:79 *And Korah went forth to his people in his worldly glitter. Those who desire the present life said, "Oh, that we had the like of that which has been bestowed on Korah. He is possessed of great good fortune." But those to whom knowledge had been given said, "Woe to you. The reward of Allah in the hereafter is best for him who believes and works righteousness, and none will win it but those who have patiently endured."*

28:81 *We caused the earth to swallow him [Korah] and his palace, and he had no one to help him against Allah, nor could he defend himself. In the morning, those who had coveted his position said, "Allah gives abundantly to whom he will and sparingly to whom He pleases. If Allah had not been gracious to us, He could have caused the earth to swallow us. The ungrateful can never prosper."*

David and Solomon

34:10 *Of old, We bestowed grace on David, "Oh, hills and birds, sing His praise with Us." And We made the iron soft for him. "Make coats of mail [armor] and measure the links and do what is right because I see all that you do." And We made the wind serve Solomon. The morning course was a month's journey, and the evening's course was a month's journey. We made a fountain of molten brass flow for him, and there were jinn who worked in front of him with permission from his Lord; and if any of them turn from Our command, We will cause them to taste the torment of the Fire. They worked for him as he wished making fortresses, images, large basins for watering camels, and cooking pots built into the ground. "Give thanks, House of David. Few of My servants are that thankful."*

34:14 *When We decreed the death of Solomon, nothing showed his death to them but a little worm of the earth that gnawed the staff which supported his corpse [Solomon died standing, supported by his staff. Until a worm ate the staff and the corpse fell down, the jinns did not know he was dead and continued to work.]. And when it fell down, the jinn knew clearly that if they had known the unknown, they would not have continued in despised work.*

34:15 *There was a sign for Saba [an ancient kingdom of southern Arabia] in their homeland—two gardens, one on the right hand and one on the left. "Eat of your Lord's supplies, and give thanks to Him. A fair land and a gracious Lord." But they turned away, so We sent upon them the flood. In exchange for their gardens, We gave them two gardens of*

bitter fruit and tamarisk and a few jujube trees. This was the reward
We gave them because of their ingratitude, but who do We repay like this
except the ungrateful?
34:18 *And We placed between them and the towns We had blessed, towns*
that were easy to see, and We fixed easy stages for the journey, "Travel
to them both safely by night and day." But they said, "Oh, Lord, make
the distance between our journeys longer, and they wronged themselves
in that, so We made them an example and scattered them abroad. Here
there are signs for everyone who is patient and grateful. Satan's calcula-
tions were true concerning them because they all followed him except a
group of the faithful. Yet he had no power over them except that We could
test the man who believes in life to come from the one who doubts it, for
the Lord watches all things.

We Seal up the Hearts of the Transgressors

10:71 *Tell them the history of Noah when he said to his people, "Oh, my*
people, if my stay and my reminding you of the signs of Allah are grievous
to you, I still trust Allah. So choose a course of action—you and your false
gods. Do not let your plans be uncertain to you. Then come to some deci-
sion about me, and do not delay. If you turn your backs on me, I ask no
reward from you. My reward is with Allah alone, and I am commanded
to submit to Allah's will." But they treated him as a liar, and We rescued
him and those with him in the ark, and We made them to inherit the
earth while We drowned those who rejected Our signs. See what was the
end of those who were warned?
10:74 *Then after him, We sent messengers to their peoples, and they*
brought them clear signs, but they would not believe in what they had
denied earlier. So We seal up the hearts of the transgressors. After them
We sent Moses and Aaron with Our signs to Pharaoh and his nobles, but
they were arrogant and a guilty people. When the truth came to them
from Us, they said, "This is clear sorcery."
10:77 *Moses said, "What do you say of the truth when it has come to you,*
'Is this sorcery?' but sorcerers will not prosper."
10:78 *They said, "Have you come to us to turn us away from the faith of*
our fathers so that you and your brother will have greatness in this land?
We are not going to believe in you."
10:79 *Pharaoh said, "Fetch me every skilled magician." When the magi-*
cians arrived, Moses said to them, "Cast down what you have to cast."
10:81 *And when they had cast them down, Moses said, "What you have*
brought is sorcery, and Allah will render them vain. Allah does not up-
hold the work of mischief-makers. Allah will verify the truth by his words,
though the guilty may be averse to it." And none believed in Moses except
some of the children of his people because they feared that Pharaoh and

his nobles would persecute them. Pharaoh was a tyrant in the land and one who committed excesses.
10:84 *And Moses said, "Oh, my people, if you believe in Allah, put your trust in Him and submit."*
10:85 *They said, "In Allah we put our trust. Oh, our Lord, do not make us subject to the persecution of unjust people, and deliver us by Your mercy from the unbelieving people."*
10:87 *Then We revealed to Moses and to his brother this message: "Provide houses for your people in Egypt, and in your houses, places of worship and proclaim good tidings to the believers."*
10:88 *And Moses said, "Oh, our Lord, You have given the Pharaoh and his nobles splendor and riches in this present life. Oh, our Lord, they do lead people astray from Your way. Oh, our Lord, destroy their riches, and harden their hearts so they do not believe until they have see the painful doom."*
10:89 *Allah said, "Your prayer is heard, Moses and Aaron. Keep to the straight path, and do not follow the path of those who have no knowledge."*
10:90 *We led the Children of Israel through the sea, and, due to spite and tyranny, Pharaoh and his hosts followed them until they drowned. Pharaoh said, "I believe there is no god but He in whom the Children of Israel believe, and I submit to Him."*
10:91 *"Yes now, but just a little while before you were rebellious and one of the wrongdoers. But this day We will rescue you and your body so that you may be a sign to those who will come after you, but truly, most men disregard Our signs."*
10:93 *We settled the Children of Israel in a beautiful home and provided them with good things, but they fell into disagreements when the knowledge (the Law) came to them. The Lord will decide between them on Resurrection Day concerning their differences.*

Noah

11:25 *We sent Noah to his people, and he said, "I come to you a with a clear warning that you worship no one but Allah. I fear you will receive the punishment of a grievous day." Then the chiefs of the unbelievers among Noah's people said, "You are only a mortal like ourselves, and we see that your only followers are the dullest among us who are quick to judge. We do not see in you anything that excels above our own abilities. No, we think you are a liar."*
11:28 *Noah said: "Oh, my people, see if I have a clear revelation from my Lord and whether He has sent mercy to me, which has been made unclear to you. Can we force you to accept it if you are against it? Oh, my people, I do not ask for riches: my reward is of Allah alone, and I will not drive*

away those who believe because they will meet their Lord, but I see that you are an ignorant people. Oh, my people, who would help me against Allah if I were to drive them away? Will you not consider? I do not tell you that I have the treasures of Allah, nor do I say, 'I know the things unseen,' nor do I say, 'I am an angel,' nor do I say of those you hold with scorn, 'Allah will not bestow good things on them.' Allah knows best what is in their minds for then I would be one of the unjust."

11:32 *They said: "Oh, Noah, you have already disputed with us and lengthened the disputes. Bring what you threaten to us if you are telling the truth."*

11:33 *He said, "Only Allah will bring it to you at His sole pleasure, and you will not escape. No, my advice will be of no profit to you if Allah desires to mislead you. He is your Lord, and to Him you will return."*

11:35 *Do they say, "This Koran is his own invention?" Say: If I have invented it, my guilt will be on me, but I am clear of that guilt.*

11:36 *It was revealed to Noah: "None of your people will believe, except the ones who already believed, so do not be grieved at their doings. Build the Ark under Our eyes and after Our revelation, and do not plead with Me for those who are unjust, for they are to be drowned."*

11:38 *So he built the Ark, and whenever the chiefs of his people passed by, they laughed at him. He said, "If you laugh at us, we truly will laugh at you, even as you laugh at us." In the end you will know who will receive a punishment that will shame him, and who will receive a lasting doom.*

11:40 *Then our sentence came to pass, and the earth's surface gushed water. We said, "Carry two of every kind into it—male and female, and your family, except those who are doomed, and the true believers." But only a few believed with him.*

11:41 *He said, "Embark on the Ark. In the name of Allah, be its sailing and its anchoring. For my Lord is right-forgiving and merciful." The Ark moved on with them amid waves like mountains, and Noah called to his son—for he had stayed behind—"Leave with us, Oh, my child, and do not be with the unbelievers." He said, "I will go to a mountain that will secure me from the water." Noah said, "No one will be secure from the decree of Allah this day except him on whom He will have mercy." And the waves passed between them, and he was drowned.*

11:44 *And it was said, "Oh, earth, swallow your water. Oh, clouds, stop the rain." and the water subsided, and the decree was fulfilled. The Ark rested upon Al-Djoudi, and a voice said, "Away with the tribe of the wicked."*

11:45 *Noah called on his Lord and said, "Oh, Lord, surely my son is of my family, and your promise is true, and you are the most just of judges."*

11:46 *Allah said, "Oh, Noah, he is not of your family because he was a wrongdoer. Do not ask of Me that which you do not know. I warn you so that you will not become one of the ignorant.*

> 11:47 *He said, "Oh, my Lord, I do seek refuge in You for fear that I will ask a question of which I have no knowledge. Unless You forgive me and have mercy on me, I will be one of the lost."*
> 11:48 *It was said to him, "Oh, Noah, descend with peace from Us and with blessings on you and on the people who will be born from those with you. As for other people, We will let them enjoy the things in this world, but afterwards, We will send them a grievous punishment."*
> 11:49 *This is one of the secret stories that We reveal to you. No one knew the story before this. Be patient, for the end is for those who fear Allah.*

Mohammed is the final prophet and the Koran is pure and perfect, whereas the Jewish and Christian scripture have been corrupted. Jews and Christians must submit to Islam. The Koran continues and perfects the Scriptures.

> 16:43 *The messengers we sent before you [Mohammed] were but men to whom We sent Our revelation. If you do not know this, ask someone who knows [the Jews]. We sent them with clear proof and scriptures. We have shown you the message so that you can explain to mankind what has been revealed for them, and perhaps, they may reflect.*

> 11:15 *We will repay those who desire this present life and its fineries for their deeds there. They will have nothing less than what they earned. These are the ones for whom there is nothing in the next world but the Fire. Their plans are all in vain, and their deeds are fruitless. Can they be counted equal with those who rest on clear proofs from their Lord and to whom a messenger—who is from Allah, teaches the Koran, and who is preceded by the Book of Moses—has been sent as a guide and a mercy? These believe in it, but those who do not believe in it will find their appointed place in the Fire. So have no doubts about the Book, the truth from your Lord. But most men do not believe.*

Allah Does Not Guide the Wicked

> 28:48 *Yet when the truth came to them [the Meccans] from Us they said, "Why is he not given what was given to Moses?" Did they not reject what was given to Moses? They said, "Two works of sorcery [the Torah and the Koran] that helped each other, and we disbelieve them both."*
> 28:49 *Say: Then bring a Book from Allah that will be a better guide than this so I may follow it if you speak the truth. If they do not answer you, then know that they are following their own lusts. Who is more widely astray than he who follows his own desires without guidance from Allah? Allah does not guide the wicked. And now We have caused our word to reach them so they may be warned. Those [some of the Jews] to whom We gave the Scriptures before do believe in it [the Koran]. When it is recited*

to them they say, "We believe in it for it is the truth from Our Lord. We were Muslims before it came."
28:54 *They will receive their reward twice because they suffered with patience, repelled evil with good, and gave to charity out of that which We provided them.*

It is Islam that defines the Jews and Christians.

29:46 *Do not dispute with the followers of the Book [the Jews] except in the best way and unless it is they who have dealt wrongfully with you. Say: We believe in what has been sent down to us and has been sent down to you. Our Allah and your god are one, and to Him are we submitted.*

41:45 *It is true that long ago We gave the Torah [the first five books of the Old Testament] to Moses, and arguments arose from that. If word had not come before from Allah, then there certainly would have been a judgment between them because they had great doubts and questions about it.*

45:16 *Long ago we gave to the Children of Israel the Torah and the wisdom and the gift of prophecy, and We provided them with the good things. We favored them over all nations. We gave them clear commandments, but after they received knowledge, they began to differ amongst themselves because of envy. Your Lord will judge between them on the Day of Reckoning concerning these issues which separated them.*

Be as Apes, Despised and Loathed.

7:159 *And among the people of Moses there is a certain number who guide others with truth and establish justice. And We divided them into twelve tribes, or nations, and We inspired Moses when the people asked for drink, saying, "Strike the rock with thy staff," and from there gushed twelve springs, and each tribe knew its own place for water. We gave them clouds to shade them, and sent manna [food from heaven] and the quails to them. "Eat the good things We have provided you." They did no harm to Us, but they did injure themselves [when they stored the manna instead of trusting that more would be furnished the next day].*
7:161 *When it was said to them, "Live in this town and eat wherever you wish and speak with humility and enter the gate in humility. We will forgive you wrongs, and We will give more to those who do good." But those who did wrong among them changed that word [the Jews made a pun and changed hittat, absolution, to habbat, corn] into another that had been told to them, so We sent them a plague for their wrong doings.*
7:163 *Ask them about the town that stood by the sea, how the Jews broke the Sabbath. Their fish came to them on their Sabbath day appearing on the surface of the water. But during the work week there were no fish to catch. So We made a trial of them for they were evildoers. And when*

some of them said, "Why do you preach to those whom Allah is about to destroy or chastise with awful doom?" They said, "To do our duty for the Lord so that they may be able to ward off evil."

7:165 *When they disregarded the warnings that had been given to them [not to work on the Sabbath], We rescued those who had forbidden wrongdoing, and We punished the wrongdoers for their transgressions. But when they persisted in what they had been forbidden, We said to them, "Be as apes, despised and loathed." [The Jews were changed into apes.]*

16:116 *Do not say while describing something, "This is lawful, and this is forbidden," in order to invent a lie against Allah. Those who invent lies against Allah will never prosper. Such lies may bring a momentary pleasure, but they will certainly have a painful punishment. The things which We have mentioned to you before are also forbidden to the Jews. We did them no injustice; they were unjust to themselves. Your Lord is forgiving and merciful toward those who do wrong in ignorance but who later repent and make amends.*

11:110 *We gave Moses the Torah, but differences arose there. If your Lord had not decreed a delay in judgment, it would have been judged between them [Jews] then, but your people also have grave doubts about the Koran.*

He Would Use Others to Punish the Jews

7:167 *Then the Lord declared that until Resurrection Day, He would use others to punish the Jews, for the Lord is quick to punish, and most surely is He forgiving and merciful. And We sent them out on the land as separate nations. Some of them were righteous and some were not. We have tried them with prosperity and adversity in order that they might return to Us.*

7:169 *After them came an evil generation. They inherited the Scriptures [the Torah], but they chose the pleasures of this world saying, "Everything will be forgiven us." If similar vanities came to them again, they would seize them again. But did they not accept a promise through the Scripture that they would not speak anything of Allah but the truth? And they have studied what is in the Book [Koran], but the home in the hereafter is for those who fear Allah. Do you not understand? And for those who keep the Scriptures and keep regular prayer, We will not waste the reward of the righteous. When We shook the mountain over them, as if it were a covering, and they thought it was going to fall on them, We said "Hold fast to what We have given you, and remember what is in it so you may guard against evil."*

6:19 *Say: What thing is weightiest in testimony? Say: Allah is witness between me and you, and this Koran has been inspired in me so that I can warn you and all whomever it reaches. Do you really bear witness that there are other gods besides Allah? Say: I do not bear witness. Say: He is the only god, and I am innocent of worshiping others besides Him. Those to whom We have given the Scriptures [the Jews] know him [Mohammed] as they do their own children, but those who have lost their own souls will not believe.*

Are They Waiting to See If The Angels Come to Them?

6:156 *Lest you should say, "The Scriptures were sent down only to two sects [Jews and Christians] before us, but we were unaware of what they read." Or lest you should say, "If the Book had only been sent down to us, we would have followed the guidance better than they did." But now has come a clear proof from your Lord, and a guidance and a mercy. Who could do more wrong than to reject Allah's signs and turn away from them? We will reward those who turn away from Our signs with a dreadful penalty because they have turned aside.*

6:158 *Are they waiting to see if the angels come to them, or the Lord Himself, or that some of the signs of the Lord should come to pass? On the day when some of the Lord's signs will come, it will do no good for those who are not already believers, nor if they did no good works in virtue of its faith. Say: Wait. We wait also.*

6:159 *As to those who split their religion into sects, you have no concern with them. Their affair is with Allah only. Hereafter, He will tell them what they have done. He who does good works will receive a tenfold reward, but he who does an ill deed will receive like punishment, and they will not be treated unjustly. Say: As for me, my Lord has guided me to the right path: a true religion and the creed of Abraham, the true in faith, who was no unbeliever.*

6:162 *Say: Truly, my prayers and my worship and my life and my death are all for Allah, Lord of the worlds. He has no partner. This I am commanded, and I am the first of the Muslims. Say: Shall I seek any Lord other than Allah when He is Lord of all things? Each soul earns only on its own account, and no bearer of burdens shall bear the burdens of another. At last you will return to your Lord, and He will tell you how you disputed with Him. It is He who made you the inheritors of the earth; He raised some of you in rank above others that he may prove you by the gifts He has given you. The Lord is swift to punish, but He is also gracious and merciful.*

The Koran mentions a Jew who converted to Islam.

46:4 *What are you thinking when you worship other gods? Show me which part of earth or heaven they created. Bring me their revelations if you are telling the truth. And who is more mistaken than he who calls on gods who will have no answers until the Resurrection? And on Judgment*

Day he will become enemies with them [his false gods] and deny that he worshipped them.
46:7 *And when We clearly reveal the truth to the unbelievers, they say it is surely magic and sorcery. Or they say "He has invented it." Say: If I have invented it, then you will obtain not one blessing for me from Allah. He knows what is between me and you, and He is forgiving and merciful.*
46:9 *I am not Allah's first messenger, nor do I know what He will do with me and you. I follow what is revealed to me through inspiration, and my charge is to warn you [the Meccans]. What do you think? This Scripture is from Allah, and you reject it, and a witness [a Jew, Bin Salama] from the Children of Israel testifies that he has seen earlier scripture like it and believes it, while you proudly show scorn. Surely, Allah does not guide the unjust.*
46:11 *But the unbelievers say, "If the believers' scriptures were true, we would have had them first." And they refuse the scriptures; they say they are a legend, a lie.*
46:12 *Before this Book [the Koran] was the book of Moses, a rule and a mercy. This book confirms in Arabic the warning to the unjust and the good tidings to the just.*

I272 Mohammed continued to preach Islam and condemn the old Arabic religions. There were those of the Quraysh who defended their culture and religion and argued with him. Mohammed called them mockers and cursed one of them, "Oh Allah, blind him and kill his son." The Koran records the Meccan's resistance as plots and schemes.

6:124 *So We have placed wicked ringleaders in every city to scheme there, but they only plot against themselves, and they do not realize it. And when a sign comes to them they say, "We will not believe until we receive one like those that Allah's messengers received." Allah knows best where to place His message. The unbelievers will be disgraced when they receive their punishment for their scheming.*
6:125 *For those whom Allah intends to guide, He will open their hearts to Islam. But for those whom He intends to mislead, He will make their hearts closed and hard, as though they had to climb up to the heavens. Thus does Allah penalize the unbelievers. And this is the right way of your Lord. We have detailed Our signs for those who will listen and see. They shall have an abode of peace with their Lord. He will be their protecting friend because of their works.*
6:128 *One day He will gather them all together and say, "Oh, jinns, you took away a great part of mankind." And their friends among men will say, "Oh, Lord, some of us profited by others, but we have arrived at our appointed term, which You had set for us." He will say, "The Fire is your home where you will abide forever, as long as Allah wills." The Lord is*

wise and knowing. So We let the wrongdoers turn to each other because of their works.

6:130 *Oh, race of jinn and mankind, were there not messengers among you giving you my warning of the meeting of this your day? They shall say, "We testify against ourselves." This world's life deceived them, and they will testify against themselves that they were unbelievers.*

6:131 *The messengers were sent because the Lord would not destroy the unbelievers' cities until they were warned of their negligence.*

Will You Fear Any besides Allah?

16:45 *Are the people who plan evil actions sure that Allah will not cause the earth to swallow them or that punishment might not catch up to them from an unknown source? Or will Allah seize them while they are on a journey leaving them with no escape. Or might He cause them to waste away? Your Lord is Compassionate and Merciful.*

16:48 *Do they not consider that Allah has created their very shadows that move to the right and the left, bowing to Allah in the most humble manner? All creatures in the heavens and the earth bow down only to Allah. The angels bow too because none are arrogant before their Lord. They all fear Allah, high above them, and they do everything they are commanded.*

16:51 *Allah has said, "Do not worship two gods. There is only one Allah. Fear Me, and Me only. You should be afraid. Everything in the heavens and the earth belong to Him, and to Him constant obedience is due. Will you fear any besides Allah?*

They Worship Only as Their Fathers Worshipped before Them

11:103 *Here is a true sign for him who fears the punishment of the hereafter. That is a day on which mankind will be gathered together; that will be a day that is witnessed by all creatures. We only delay it until an appointed time. When that day comes, no one will speak a word but by permission of Allah. Of those gathered, some will be miserable and others blessed. The wretched ones will be in the Fire, and there will be sighing and moaning for them. They will abide there as long as the heavens and earth will last unless your Lord pleases otherwise. Your Lord does what He chooses.*

11:108 *As for the blessed ones—their place will be in the Garden. They will abide there as long as the heavens and the earth will last, a gift that will never end. Do not have doubts, therefore, concerning what these men worship. They worship only as their fathers worshipped before them. We will surely pay them back their portion with nothing lacking.*

They Plotted Mighty Plots

14:42 *Do not think that Allah is unaware of the deeds of the wicked. He only gives them relief until the day when all eyes will stare up with terror. They will run forward in fear with their heads raised, their gaze riveted, and their hearts vacant. Warn men of the day when the punishment will overtake them and when the evildoers will say, "Oh, our Lord, give us relief for just a while longer. Then we will answer Your call and follow Your messengers." Did you [the unbelievers] not once swear that there would be no end for you?*

14:45 *Yet you dwell in the homes of those who wronged their own souls [the ruined cities of Ad, Thamud and others], and We made it clear to you how We dealt with them, and We held them up to you as examples. They plotted mighty plots, but Allah knew their plots, though their plots were powerful enough to move the mountains.*

14:47 *Do not think that Allah will fail his promise to his messengers. Allah is mighty and vengeful. On the day when the earth will be changed into another earth, and so will the heavens, men will come to Allah, the one, the victorious. You will see the wicked on that day linked together in chains, their garments of tar pitch, and faces covered with Fire that Allah may reward every soul as it deserves. Allah is prompt to reckon.*

14:50 *This is a message for mankind so that they may be warned and know that He is the only god, and men of understanding should take heed.*

It Was a Plot of Yours by Night and by Day

34:22 *Say: Call upon your gods, beside Allah. They do not possess the weight of an atom in the heavens or earth nor do they have any share in either, nor is any of them a helper to Allah. No one can intercede for Allah unless He permits it. Until the time when fear is removed from their hearts, they will say, "What does your Lord say?" They will say, "The truth, and He is the high, the great."*

34:24 *Say: Who gives you sustenance from the heavens and the earth? Say: Allah. And either we or you have guidance, or we are in grave error. Say: You will not be asked what our faults are nor will we be questioned about your actions. Say: Our Lord will bring us together. He will judge between us in justice for He is the judge and the knowing.*

34:27 *Say: Show me those you have idolized besides Him. You cannot. He is Allah, the exalted in power and the wise. We have sent you [Mohammed] to mankind to bring good tidings and to warn them, but most men do not understand. And they say, "When will this promise come to pass if you are telling the truth?" Say: Yours is the promise of a day, which you cannot retard for an hour, nor hasten.*

34:31 *The unbelievers say, "We will not believe in this Koran nor in the Books which came before it." If you could see when the wrongdoers will stand before their Lord, blaming each other. Those who were despised will say to those who were proud, "If it were not for you, we would have been believers." Then the proud ones will say to the weak, "Was it we who kept you away from the guidance once it reached you? No, but you are guilty."*

34:33 *And the weak will say to the proud ones, "No, but it was a plot of yours by night and by day. You ordered us to disbelieve in Allah and praise others besides Him." And they will proclaim their repentance after they have seen the punishment. We will put yokes on the necks of the unbelievers. They will be rewarded for what they have done. We have never sent a warner to any city without the wealthy ones saying, "We do not believe the message you have sent." They said, "We are more abundant in riches and in children; we cannot be among the punished."*

34:36 *Say: My Lord can be liberal or sparing in his giving, but most men will not acknowledge it. It is not your riches nor your children that will bring you near to Us. Only those who believe and do good will have a double reward for what they have done, and they will dwell securely in the mansions of Paradise. Those who strive to invalidate Our signs, will be brought to doom.*

Then Plot against Me. Do Not Delay.

7:189 *It is Allah Who created you from a single person [Adam] and Who brought forth his wife that he might dwell with her. When they are united, she carries a light burden, which goes unnoticed until it becomes heavy. Then they cry to Allah saying, "If You give us a goodly child we vow we will be forever grateful."*

7:190 *Yet when Allah gives them a goodly child, they praise idols for what Allah has given to them. Allah is exalted above the idols they prefer to Him. Do they truly venerate others who create nothing, while they themselves were created by Him? These others can give no aid nor can they help themselves. If you call them to guidance, they will not obey. It is the same whether you call them or keep silent.*

7:194 *Those you call on besides Allah are His servants like you are. Call on them then, and let them answer you if you are truthful. Do they have feet to walk with? Do they have hands to hold with? Do they have eyes to see with? Do they have ears to hear with? Say: Call on these god-partners of yours. Then plot against me. Do not delay. My Lord is Allah who revealed the Scripture. He befriends the good. Whoever you call on besides Allah is not able to help you nor can they help themselves. If you call them to guidance, they will not hear you. You see them look towards you, but they do not see. Keep to forgiveness, command what is right, and turn away from the ignorant. And if a suggestion from Satan afflicts you, seek refuge with Allah. He hears and knows all things. Those who guard against evil when thoughts from Satan assault them remember Allah's guidance, and they see clearly. Their brethren plunge them deeper in error and do not cease in their efforts.*

7:203 *If you do not bring a revelation, they [the Meccans] say, "Why do you not have one?" Say: I only follow that which is inspired by my Lord These are clear proofs from your Lord and guidance and mercy for those who have faith. And when the Koran is read, listen to it with attention and hold your peace that mercy may be shown to you. Remember the Lord humbly within yourself in a low voice in the mornings and the evenings [prayer]. Do not be one of the neglectful ones. Those who are with the Lord are not too proud to serve Him. They celebrate His praises and prostrate themselves before Him.*

There Is No God but Allah

28:69 *Your Lord knows what their hearts conceal and what they reveal. He is Allah. There is no god but Allah. All praise is due to Him in this life and the hereafter. He is the supreme power, and to Him you will be brought back.*

28:71 *Say: What would you think if Allah should enshroud you with a long night until the day of resurrection? Who besides Allah could bring you light? Do you not hear? Say: Have you thought if Allah should make a perpetual day for you until the day of resurrection? Who besides Allah could bring you the night in which to take your rest? Do you not see? Out of His mercy He has made for you the night so you can rest, and the day so you can see what you need of His bounteous supplies and so you may be grateful.*

28:74 *One day Allah will call to them and say, "Where are the gods you invented?" We will bring up a witness from every nation and say, "Bring your proofs." Then they will know that the truth is with Allah alone, and the gods of their own devising will desert them.*

The Meccans keep saying that if Mohammed were right about the Judgment Day, then let them see it, now.

I Will Fill Hell with Jinns and Men Together

32:4 *It is Allah Who created the heavens and the earth and everything in between in six days before ascending His throne. You have no one besides Allah to protect you. Will you not think about this? He governs all things in the heavens and on earth. At the end of this world, all things will return to Him on a day that will seem to last a thousand years.*

32:6 *This is He Who knows all things—seen and unseen. He is mighty and merciful and has created all good things. He began creating man from clay then made his seed from a worthless fluid. He shaped him and breathed his Spirit into him and gave him the senses of sight, sound, and understanding. Small thanks do you give.*

32:10 *And they say, "What? When we have been buried in the ground, shall we really be resurrected?" Yes, but they deny that they will meet their Lord. Say: The angel of death has been put in charge of you and will take your lives. You will be returned to your Lord. If you could only see when the wicked shall hang their heads before their Lord, and say, "Lord, We have seen and heard. Return us to life. We will act righteously because now we are convinced."*

32:13 *If We had wished, We could have given guidance to every soul. My word will come true: "I will fill Hell with jinns and men together. So taste the evil of your deeds. You forgot that you would have a meeting on Judgment Day. We will forget you. Taste the eternal punishment because of your actions.*

32:15 *Only they believe in Our signs, who, when they are recited to them, fall down in adoration and celebrate the praises of their Lord, and they are not scornful. They shun their beds to pray to their Lord in fear and hope, and spend charitably from what We have given them.*

32:17 *No soul knows the hidden delights that are reserved for the righteous. There is a reward for their good deeds. Is the man who believes no better than the man who does not believe? They are not the same. As a reward for their behavior there are Gardens of repose waiting for those who believe and do good works.*

32:20 *The wicked will live in the Fire. Whenever they try to leave, they shall be forced back, and it will be said to them, "Taste the torment of the Fire, that you used to deny." Certainly, We will cause them to taste the lesser penalty in this life before tasting the supreme penalty so that they may repent and return. And who is more wrong than he who is reminded of the signs of his Lord and who then turns away from them? We will certainly punish the guilty.*

If You Are Telling the Truth, Then Resurrect Our Fathers.

45:18 *We have now put you on the right path, so follow it, and do not follow the base desires of those who do not know. They cannot help you against Allah. Truly, the wicked are patrons to each other, but Allah is the patron of the righteous. These are obvious proofs for mankind and a guidance and a mercy to those whose faith is strong.*

45:21 *Do the wicked believe that We will treat them as We do those who believe and do good deeds so that their lives and deaths are equal? They have poor judgment. Allah created the heavens and the earth with truth so that every soul may be repaid for what it has earned and so none of them are wronged.*

45:23 *What do you think of a person who has made a god of his passions? Allah has purposely allowed him to go astray and has sealed his ears and his heart and has placed a veil over his eyes. Who will guide him after Allah has rejected him? Will you not accept this warning?*

45:24 *And they say, "There is only this present life. We live and we die, and nothing but time can destroy us. They have no knowledge of this, only speculation. When Our clear signs are recited to them, their only argument is to say, "If you are telling the truth, then resurrect our fathers." Say: Allah gives you life and then causes you to die. He will reassemble you on the Day of Resurrection, there is no doubt about this. However, most men do not know this.*

45:27 *The kingdom of the heavens and the earth belong to Allah. The liars will perish in the Hour of Judgment, and you will see every nation kneeling, each nation called to its record. It will be said to them, "Today you will be repaid for what you have done; our record speaks only the truth about you. We have written down everything that you have done." For those who have believed and have acted righteously, their Lord will admit into His mercy. This is the ultimate victory.*

45:31 *But it will be said to those who have rejected Allah, "Were Our revelations never recited to you? But you arrogantly scorned them and so became a guilty people." When it was said, "The promise of Allah is true, and there is no doubt that the Hour is coming," you said, "We do not know what the hour is. We think it is only speculation, and we are not convinced." And the evil consequences of their actions will appear to them, and they will be surrounded by that which they used to mock. And it will be said to them, "Today We will forget you like you forgot your meeting with us, and your home will be the Fire, and no one will be there to help you. This is because you treated Allah's signs as a joke, and the life of this world deceived you." Therefore, on that day there will be no escape from it; and they will not be able to make amends.*

45:36 *Praise be to Allah, Lord of the heavens and the earth, the Lord of the worlds! To Him belongs the greatness in the heavens and the earth because He is mighty and wise.*

And if Mohammed were actually a prophet, why not show them something other than words. Why not do a miracle?

Allah Is the Master of All Plotting

13:27 *The unbelievers say: Why does his Lord not send a sign down to him? Say: Allah will truly mislead whom he chooses and will guide to Himself those who turn to Him. They believe and their hearts find rest in remembering Allah. Without a doubt all hearts find rest in the remembrance of Allah. Those who believe and do what is right will be blessed and find joy in the end.*

13:30 *Therefore, We have sent you to a nation before which other nations have passed away so that you may recite Our revelations to them. Nevertheless they deny the merciful Allah. Say: He is my Lord; there is no god but Him. I put my trust in Him, and to Him I will return.*

13:31 *If there were a Koran that could move mountains, tear the earth apart, or make the dead speak, this would be it! Allah is in command of all things! Do the believers not know that if it had been Allah's will, He could have guided all the people? Disaster will never cease to afflict the unbelievers for their wrongful deeds or to come into their homes until Allah's will is fulfilled. Allah will not fail to keep His promise.*

13:32 *Many messengers who came before you were mocked. For a long time We allowed the unbelievers to go unpunished, but finally We punished them. Then how terrible was Our punishment!*

13:33 *Who is it that watches over every soul and knows all its actions? And yet they worship gods other than Allah. Say: Then name them! Would you inform Him of something on the earth that is unknown to Him? Or are these merely meaningless words? Certainly, their lies seem to make sense to the unbelievers because they are kept from the right path. No one can help those whom Allah has sent astray. They will receive punishment in this life, but what is worse is their punishment in the life to come, and they will have no protector against Allah.*

13:35 *Paradise is promised to those who fear Allah. It is a land watered by flowing rivers where food is plentiful and shade is perpetual. This is the reward for those who fear Allah. But the end of the unbelievers is the Fire. And those to whom We have given the Scriptures [Jews] rejoice in what has been revealed to you, although some groups among you deny a part of it. Say: I am commanded to worship Allah alone and not to regard any as His equal. I call on Him, and to Him I will return. Therefore, We have revealed this judgment of authority in Arabic. If you were to follow their desires after having received this knowledge, then you would find neither a guardian nor a defender in Allah.*

13:38 *Messengers were sent before you and were given wives and children, but none of them was able to perform a miracle without the permission of Allah. For every time period there is a Book revealed. Allah will destroy and build up what He pleases for He is the source of revelation.*

13:40 *Whether We allow you to see the fulfillment of part of our threats or We cause you to die before it takes place, your part is only to spread the message while it is Our part to give out the punishment. Do they not recognize that We take control of their lands and invade its diminishing borders? When Allah makes a decree, nothing can be done to change it, and He is quick at His reckoning. Those who lived before them devised plots as well, but Allah is the master of all plotting. He knows every soul. The unbelievers will come to know for whom the heavenly home is destined. The unbelievers will say, "You are not a messenger of Allah." Say: Allah and whoever has knowledge of the Scriptures is a sufficient witness between you and me.*

If Judgment Day were to come, then the Meccans asked Mohammed to tell Allah to bring it here this day and prove Mohammed was a true prophet.

Those That Came before Them Also Plotted

16:19 *Allah knows what you hide and what you admit doing. The false gods you pray to besides Allah have created nothing and were themselves created. They are dead, lifeless, and they do not know when they will be resurrected. Your Allah is the only god. The arrogant do not believe in the afterlife; their hearts refuse to know. Truly Allah knows what they hide and what they admit. He does not love the arrogant.*

16:24 *When it is said to them, "What has your Lord revealed?" They say, "Ancient myths."*

16:25 *Let them bear their full burdens on Judgment Day along with some of the burdens of the ignorant whom they have led astray.*

16:26 *Those that came before them also plotted, but Allah destroyed the foundations of their buildings so that their roofs fell upon them, and they had no idea where their punishment came from.*

16:27 *On Judgment Day Allah will disgrace them and say, "Where are my equals for whose sake you opposed my guidance?" The knowledgeable will say, "Today the unbelievers are covered in shame and misery. The angels caused them to die while they are doing wrong." The wicked will then try to submit saying, "We did not knowingly do evil." The angels will say, however, "Allah knows what you have done, so enter the gates of Hell to dwell there forever. Evil is the home of the arrogant."*

16:30 *And it will be said to the righteous, "What has your Lord revealed?" They will reply, "All that is good." There is a good reward in this life for those who do good, and the home of the afterlife is even better. The home of the righteous is indeed excellent: they will enter eternal Gardens with underground rivers, where they will have everything they wish for. This is how Allah rewards the righteous, those whom the angels cause to die when they are doing good. The angels will say, "Peace be to you. Enter the Garden because of what you used to do [doing good]."*

16:33 *Are the wicked waiting until the angels come, or the Judgment Day? Earlier generations did the same. Allah was not unjust to them; they were unjust to themselves. The evil consequences of their actions caught up to them, and the thing that they mocked surrounded them.*

16:35 *The idolaters say, "If Allah wished it, we would not have worshipped any except Him, neither ourselves nor our fathers. We would not have forbidden anything without His order." The earlier generations said the same thing. Do Allah's messengers have any duty other than to deliver his Word? It is true that We have sent a messenger to every nation saying, "Serve Allah and shun false gods. Some were guided by Allah, but He will not guide those he confuses. So travel through the land and see what became of the unbelievers."*

16:37 *If you are worried about their guidance, Allah does not guide those who lead others astray, and they do not have anyone to help them. They swear by Allah that He will not resurrect them after they die. It is a binding promise for Him. Allah will clarify their confusion. Those who do not believe are liars. If We intend something, all We have to do is say, "Be," and it is.*

16:41 *Those who are oppressed because of their faith and have to flee from their homes [Mecca], We will certainly give them a fine home in this world. Their reward in the afterlife will be even greater. These are the people who are patient and who put their trust in Allah.*

This Is Nothing but Pure Sorcery

11:7 *He made the heavens and the earth in six days, and His throne extends over the waters so that He might judge which of you excels in your actions. If you say, "You will be raised again after death," the unbelievers will certainly exclaim, "This is nothing but pure sorcery."*

11:8 *If We defer their penalties to some definite time, they will ask, "Why hold it back?" On the day it comes to them, there will be no one to turn it away from them, and the penalty they scoffed at will enclose them in on every side.*

11:9 *If We cause man to taste Our mercy and then deprive him of it, he becomes despairing, and ungrateful. If We grant him grace after some misfortune befalls him, he will say, "The evils are passed away from me," and he becomes joyous and boastful, but not those who endure with patience and do the things that are right. They will have forgiveness and a great reward.*

Why Are the Signs Not Sent Down to Him from His Lord?

29:44 *Allah created the heavens and the earth in truth. This is a sign to those who believe.*

29:47 *So it is that We have sent down the Book [Koran] to you [Mohammed]. Those [the Jews] to whom We have given the Book of the law believe in it, and some other Arabians there believe in it. None, save the unbelievers, reject our signs.*

29:48 *You [Mohammed] were not a reader of the Scripture before this book came, nor did you write one with your right hand. Then the critics could have treated it as a vain thing and doubted it. But it is a clear sign in the hearts of those whom knowledge has reached. None but the unjust reject Our signs. They say, "Why are the signs not sent down to him from his Lord?" Say: The signs are in the power of Allah alone. I am only a plain warner. Is it not enough for them that We have revealed to you the Book to be recited to them? This is a mercy and a warning to those who believe. Say: Allah is witness enough between me and you. He knows all that is in the heavens and the earth. Those who believe in the falsehood and reject Allah—these will be the lost ones.*

29:53 *They will challenge you to hasten the punishment. If there had not been a season fixed for it, the punishment would have already come upon them. It will come on them suddenly when they are not looking for it. They will ask you to hasten the punishment, but Hell will encompass the unbelievers. One day the punishment shall wrap around them, both from above them and from below them, and Allah will say, "Taste your own doings."*

29:56 *Oh, My servants who believe, My earth is vast; therefore, serve Me. Every soul will have a taste of death. Then to Us you will return. Those who believe and serve righteousness, We will house in Gardens with palaces, beneath which the rivers flow. They will abide there forever. How good the reward of the workers, those who patiently endure and put their trust in their Lord.*

He Could Seal up Your Heart

42:13 *He has prescribed the same faith to you as that which He commanded to Noah, which We have revealed to you, and which We commanded unto Abraham and Moses and Jesus saying, "Observe this faith, and do not let yourselves be divided." The way is hard for those who worship gods other than Allah. Allah chooses for Himself whoever He wills and guides to Himself those who turn to Him.*

42:14 *When the knowledge came to them, then they became divided out of jealousy among themselves, and if a decree from the Lord had not gone out about an appointed term, a judgment would have already been made between them. Those who have inherited the Book [Christians] after them are in doubt about it.*

42:15 *For this reason, call them [Christians] to the faith and stand steadfast as you have been commanded and do not follow their desires. Say: I believe in the Book that Allah has sent down. I am commanded to decide justly between you. Allah is your Lord and our Lord. We have our works and you have your works. There will be no strife between us. Allah will make us all one, and to Him shall we return.*

42:16 *Their Lord will condemn the disputes of those who argue about Allah after they have acknowledged Him, and they will receive a terrible wrath and severe punishment. It is Allah who has sent down the Book [the Koran] with truth and the law. What will convince you that the Hour may be at hand? Those who do not believe in it wish to speed its coming, but those who do believe in it are afraid because they know it to be the truth. Those who dispute the coming of the Hour are in great error.*

42:19 *Allah is gracious to His servants. He gives sustenance to those He chooses. He is strong and mighty.*

42:20 *Whoever desires the harvest of the hereafter, We will give him an increase in his harvest. Whoever chooses the harvest of this world, We will also give him an increase, but he will not have a portion in the life to come. Do they have false gods besides Allah who have established a religion that is not sanctioned by Allah? Had it not been for a decreed respite until the Judgment Day, the matter would have been decided between them. The wrongdoers will have a painful torment. On that day, you will see the wrongdoers in fear because of their own works and the burden that will fall on them, but those who believe and do good things will dwell in the meadows of Paradise, and they will have what they desire from their Lord. This is the greatest grace. This is the bounty Allah gives to His servants who believe and do the right things. Say: For this I ask no wage of you, save the love of my kin [other Muslims]. And whoever earns the merit of a good deed, We will have his good increased for Allah is forgiving and grateful.*

42:24 *Will they say he [Mohammed] has forged a lie against Allah? If Allah pleased, He could seal up your heart, but Allah will wipe out the lie and will confirm the truth by His words for He knows the secrets of all men. He is the One Who accepts repentance from his servants and forgives sins and knows what you do. He listens to those who believe and do the things that are right and increases His bounties to them. As for the unbelievers, they will have a terrible punishment.*

Taste the Punishment of Eternity

10:45 *One day, He will gather them all together. It will seem as if they had waited but an hour of the day. They shall recognize one another. Those who denied the meeting with Allah and were not guided aright will perish! Whether We show you some of what We promised or take your soul, all return to Us. Then shall Allah bear witness to what they have done.*

10:47 *Every people was sent a messenger, and when their messenger comes on Judgment Day, a rightful decision will take place between them, and they will not be wronged. Yet they say, "When will this promise be fulfilled, if you tell us the truth?" Say: I have no power over any harm or profit to myself except as Allah desires. Every people has a term. When their term is reached, they can not delay or advance it an hour.*

10:50 *Say: Tell me. If Allah's punishment comes to you by night or by day, what portion of it would the sinner desire to hasten? When it comes to pass, will you believe it? Yes, you will believe it then. Yet did you wish to hurry its coming? Then it will be said to the unjust, "Taste the punishment of eternity. You receive what you have earned." They ask you, "Is this true?" Say: Yes, this is the truth, and you will not escape it. If every soul that has sinned possessed all that is on earth, it would surely offer it as ransom. They will feel regret when they have seen the punishment, and there will be a rightful decision between them, and they will not be dealt with unjustly. So it is that all that is in the heavens and the earth is Allah's. Is not then the promise of Allah true? Yet most of them do not know. He gives life and causes death, and to Him you will return.*

[Mohammed] Is Not Mad

7:179 *We have created many of the jinn and men for Hell. They have hearts with which they cannot understand, eyes with which they cannot see, and ears with which they cannot hear. They are like cattle—no, even worse, for they are neglectful.*

7:180 *The most beautiful names belong to Allah. So call Him by them, and avoid those who use His name profanely for they will suffer for what they do.*

7:181 *Among those whom We have created are a people who guide others with truth and do justice. As for those who reject Our signs as lies, We draw them to destruction in ways they will not see. They have been granted a delay, but My scheme is certain. Have they not considered that their companion [Mohammed] is not mad? He is only a plain warner. Have they not considered the kingdoms of heaven and of the earth and all the things that Allah created? Do they not see that their own term may be drawing near? What message will they believe after this? If you are rejected from the guidance of Allah, you will have no other guide. He leaves them to wander blindly in distraction.*

7:187 *They will ask you [Mohammed] about the fixed time of the final Hour. Say: That knowledge is only with my Lord. He alone will reveal it at its proper time. It weighs heavily on jinns and men. It will suddenly come to you. Say: The knowledge of it is only with Allah. Most men do not know.*

7:188 *Say: I have no power over any good or harm to myself except as Allah wills. If I had knowledge of his secrets, I would multiply the good, and evil would not touch me. I am only a warner, a bearer of glad tidings to those who believe.*

The Scoffers Were Destroyed

6:1 *Praise be to Allah, Who created heaven and earth, as well as darkness and light. Yet the unbelievers have other gods.*

6:2 *He created you from clay and decreed the term of your life, and He has a set time for the Resurrection, and still you have doubts. And He is Allah in the heavens and on the earth. He knows your secrets and what you reveal, and He knows what you have earned through deeds.*

6:4 *And never did Allah reveal a single sign to them, but they [the Meccans] turned away from it. And now they reject the truth when they hear it, but soon they will learn about the truth that they once mocked. Do they not see how many generations We have destroyed before them? We had made them more powerful than you [the Meccans]. We sent rains in abundance and gave fertile rivers to flow beneath their feet, yet We destroyed them because of their sins and raised another generation. And if We had sent a Message down to you [Mohammed] on parchment so they could have touched it with their hands, the unbelievers would have said, "This is only magic."*

6:8 *They say, "Why has an angel not been sent down to him?" If We had sent down an angel, their judgment would have condemned the unbelievers suddenly, and no time would have been granted to them to repent. If We had made him an angel, We would have sent him as a man, and We would have caused confusion in a matter in which they are already confused. Messengers before you were mocked, but the scoffers were destroyed by the thing they mocked.*

6:11 *Say: Travel through the land and see the consequences of those who rejected the truth. Say: Who possesses the heavens and the earth? Say: Allah. He had prescribed mercy for Himself as a law. Without a doubt He will gather you together on Resurrection Day. Those who have lost their souls will not believe this. To Him belongs whatever dwells in the night or in the day. He hears and knows.*

6:14 *Say: Should I choose other than Allah for my protector, creator of the heavens and of the earth, He who feeds, but is never fed? Say: I am commanded to be the first who submits himself to Allah. You should not be of the unbelievers. Say: I fear if I should I rebel against my Lord the terror of a dreadful day. On that day, if anyone avoids punishment, it will be due to the mercy of Allah, and this will be a triumph. If Allah touches you with trouble, none can remove it but He, and if He touches you with good fortune, no one can ruin it because He has power over all things. He is supreme above his servants, and He is wise and knows.*

And after Judgment Day comes Paradise and Hell.

Sheets of Fire Will Cover Them

7:35 *Oh, children of Adam, if messengers come to you from among yourselves relating My signs to you, then those who refrain from evil and mend their ways will have no fear or grieving. But they who reject Our signs and scorn them will be companions of the Fire and will abide there forever.*

7:37 *Who does greater wrong than one who invents a lie against Allah or rejects His signs? To them shall a portion here below be assigned in accordance with the Book of our decrees until the time when our messengers arrive to take their souls and say, "Where are they whom you used to call beside Allah?" They will say, "They are gone from us." And they will testify against themselves that they were unbelievers.*

7:38 *He shall say, "Enter into the company of those who passed before you into the Fire, the generations of jinn and men. Every time a fresh generation enters, it will curse its sister peoples until all have followed each other into the Fire, and the last comers will say to the former, 'Oh, our Lord, these are the ones who led us astray. Give them a double torment of Fire.'" He will say, "You all will have double," but you do not understand this.*

7:39 *And the former of them will say to the latter, "You have no advantage over us, so taste the punishment that you earned." There will be no openings at the gates of heaven for those who have rejected Our signs and scorned them nor will they enter Paradise until the camel passes through the eye of the needle. This is Our reward to the guilty. They will make their bed in Hell, and sheets of Fire will cover them. This is how we will reward the evildoers.*

7:42 *But as for those who believe and do good works, no burden do We place on any soul but that which it can bear. They are the rightful owners of the Garden and will dwell there forever. And We will remove whatever ill feeling is in their bosoms. Rivers will roll beneath them, and they will say, "Praise to Allah who guided us here. We would never have been guided if it had not been for Allah. The messengers of the Lord truly brought us the truth." And they will hear the cry, "This is Paradise. You inherit it for your righteous deeds." And the dwellers of Paradise shall cry to the dwellers of the Fire, "We have found the promise of our Lord to be true. Have you also found what your Lord promised you to be true?" They shall answer, "Yes," and a herald shall proclaim between them, "The curse of Allah is on the evil doers."*

7:45 *Whoever would turn men from the path of Allah and seek to make it crooked, they were those who did not believe in the life to come. Between them is a veil, and on the Heights are men [men whose good and bad deeds balance each other] who know all by their markings [the men of Hell will have blackened faces and those of Paradise will have white shining faces], and they shall cry to the inmates of Paradise, "Peace be to you," but they will not enter, though they will hope. And when their eyes are turned towards the inmates of the Fire, they shall say, "Oh, our Lord, do not send us to the place of the wrongdoers." And the men on the Heights will cry to those whom they will know by their markings [darkened faces], "How did you profit from your wealth and your pride?" [Turning to the blessed, the men on the Heights say:] "Are not these the men to whom you swore Allah would show no mercy? Enter Paradise. You will have no fear, nor grief."*

7:50 *The dwellers of the Fire will cry to the dwellers of Paradise, "Pour some of the water on us or anything that Allah gives you." They shall say, "Allah forbids these things to unbelievers." For those who made their religion a sport and pastime and who were deceived by the life of the world, this will be the day We forget them as they forgot the meeting of this day*

and as they did deny Our signs. We have brought them the Book, which We explained in detail as a guide and a mercy to all who believe.
7:53 *Are they waiting for its fulfillment [the Koran's promises of rewards and punishments]? On this day those who disregarded it will say, "The Messengers of our Lord did bring the truth. Do we have any intercessor to intercede for us, or could we return to life on earth? Then we could act differently than we have acted." But they have lost their souls, and the gods of their own devising have fled from them.*

The Koran records the actual quotes of Mohammed's opponents.

41:26 *The unbelievers say, "Do not listen to this Koran. Instead speak during its reading so that you might gain the upper hand." But We will certainly give the unbelievers a taste of a terrible punishment, and We will repay them for their evil deeds. The reward of Allah's enemies is the Fire. The Fire will be their immortal home, a fitting reward for rejecting Our signs. And the unbelievers will say, "Lord, show us those jinn and men who misled us. We will crush them under our feet so that they become the lowest of all."*
41:30 *And for those who say, "Our Lord is Allah," and who continue down the right path, the angels will descend upon them saying, "Do not be afraid, or grieve, but instead receive the good news of the Garden of Bliss, which you are promised. We are your guardians in this life and in the hereafter. There you will have everything your souls desire, and there you will have everything you pray for. A gift from the forgiving and the merciful!"*

34:3 *The unbelievers say, "The Hour will never come on us." Say: By my Lord, it will surely come on you. He knows the unseen, and not the smallest atom in heaven or earth escapes him nor anything smaller or larger, but it is clearly in the book [of deeds]."*
34:4 *Allah will reward those who believe and do good things with a pardon and rich reward for them. For those who strive against Our signs, there will be a penalty, a painful doom of wrath. And those to whom knowledge has been given will see that what has been sent from the Lord is the truth, and that it leads to the path of the mighty, the praised.*
34:7 *The unbelievers say, "Should we show you a man who will tell you that when you are scattered in dust with the most complete disintegration, you will be created anew? He has invented a lie about Allah, or is a jinn [a creature made of fire who can help or hurt humans] in him?" No, those who do not believe in the next life are doomed by their mistakes. Do they not consider what is before them and behind them in heaven and earth? If We desired, We could cause the earth to swallow them up or cause the sky to fall on them. There is a Sign in this for every servant who returns to Allah.*

But Mohammed continued to insist that his Allah was true and that on a terrible day, all the non-believers would be eternally punished.

Whoever Rejects the Signs of Allah Are the Losers

> 39:53 *Say: Oh, My servants who have transgressed against your own soul*
> *[become apostates] do not despair of Allah's mercy for Allah forgives all*
> *sins. He is forgiving and merciful. Return to your Lord, and submit your-*
> *self to Him before the punishment comes to you. After that you will not*
> *be helped. Follow the most excellent guidance that has been sent down to*
> *you from your Lord before the punishment comes to you suddenly, while*
> *you are not even looking for it, unless a soul should say, "Oh misery, I*
> *failed in my duty towards Allah and was among those who mocked."*
> 39:57 *Or say: If only Allah had guided me, I would surely have been one of*
> *those who feared Him.*
> 39:58 *Or say when he sees the punishment: "If only I could have a sec-*
> *ond chance, then I would be of the righteous." No, My signs had already*
> *come to you, and you rejected them, and you were proud and one of the*
> *unbelievers. On Judgment Day, you will see those who have lied to Al-*
> *lah—their faces will be blackened. Is there not a home in Hell for the*
> *arrogant? And Allah will deliver those who fear him into their safe re-*
> *treat. No evil will touch them nor will they grieve.*
> 39:62 *Allah is the creator of all things, and He is the guardian of all things.*
> *He holds the keys to heaven and earth. Whoever rejects the signs of Al-*
> *lah are the losers. Say: Do you order me to worship other than Allah, you*
> *fools? It has been revealed to you and to those before you that if you wor-*
> *ship others besides Allah, your work in life will be in vain, and you will be*
> *of those who lose. No, rather worship Allah; be of the thankful.*
> 39:67 *They have honored Allah as they should for on the Resurrection*
> *Day the whole earth will be His handful, and the heavens will be folded*
> *together in his right hand. Praise be to Him. He is exalted above those*
> *they revere along with Him. There will be a blast on the trumpet, and all*
> *who are in the heavens and all who are in the earth will perish, except*
> *as Allah pleases. Then there will be another blast, and they will stand*
> *up waiting. And the earth will shine with the light of her Lord, and the*
> *Book shall be set down, and the prophets and witnesses will be brought*
> *up, and judgment will be given between them with justice, and they will*
> *not be wronged.*
> 39:70 *Every soul will be paid in full for its deeds, for He knows best what*
> *they do. And the unbelievers will be driven towards Hell in throngs. When*
> *they arrive, the gates will be opened, and its keepers will say, "Did mes-*
> *sengers not come to you from among yourselves reciting the signs of your*
> *Lord and warning you of the meeting with Him on this day of yours?"*
> *They will say, "Yes, the sentence of punishment on the unbelievers has*

been proved true." It will be said to them, "Enter the gates of Hell to dwell there forever." Evil is the abode of the arrogant.
39:73 *Those who keep their duty to their Lord will be driven in throngs to Paradise. When they arrive, its gates will be opened, and its keepers will say to them, "Peace be on you. Enter the Garden to abide there forever."*
39:74 *And they shall say, "Praise be to Allah, who has fulfilled His promise to us and has given us this earth as our heritage. We will dwell in Paradise wherever we please." So good is the reward of those who worked in virtue. And you will see the angels circling around the throne with praises of their Lord. Judgment will be given them in justice, and it will be said: "Glory be to Allah, the Lord of the worlds."*

30:1 *ALIF. LAM. MIM. The Greeks [the Byzantines who lost a battle to the Persians] have been defeated in a land near by, but even after their defeat, they will be victorious over their enemies within a few years. However, in the beginning and in the end, the decision is with Allah. On that day, the believers will rejoice with the help of Allah. He helps those whom He pleases. He is the mighty, the merciful. This is Allah's promise. Allah does not break his promises, but most people do not know.*
30:7 *They only know the outward appearance of the life of this world, but they are ignorant of the hereafter.*
30:8 *Do they not reflect within themselves that Allah did not create the heavens and the earth and everything in between except for a serious purpose and for a fixed duration? But truly, most men do not believe that they will meet their Lord.*

How Many Generations We Have Destroyed before Them?

32:23 *It is true that long ago We gave the Torah to Moses. Do not doubt Our meeting with him. We made it a guide for the Children of Israel. And We appointed leaders from among them to guide by our command after they proved to be steadfast and kept faith in Our signs. Your Lord will certainly judge between them on Judgment Day regarding their disagreements.*
32:26 *Does it not serve as a lesson to remember how many generations We have destroyed before them? They can walk among the ruined homes of the unbelievers. Do they not see that We send the rain to parched land and bring forth crops for them and their cattle? Can they not see it? They say, "If you are telling the truth, when will this judgment take place?"*
32:29 *Say: On the Day of Decision, the faith of those who disbelieve will not help them, and they will not get a reprieve. So turn away from them and wait. They are waiting too. [Wait for their punishment just as they wait for your downfall.]*

Mohammed continued to tell about older Arabian cultures that had refused to listen to their prophets. In every case, Allah smote them with a terrible scourge.

Both of You Come, Either Willingly or Unwillingly

41:3 ***The Book brings good news and a warning. Still, most of them will turn away and not hear. They say, "Our hearts are concealed under veils from your teachings. We are deaf and there is a barrier between us and you. Do what you wish. We will do as We wish."***

41:6 ***Say: I am only a man like you. It has been revealed to me that your Allah is the only god. Go straight to Him and ask His forgiveness. Woe to those who join gods with Allah, those who do not pay the poor tax, and those who do not believe in the afterlife. As for those who believe and do the right things, they will have a never ending reward.***

41:9 ***Say: Do you really deny Him Who created the world in two days, and do you believe He has equals with Him? He is the Lord of all the worlds. In four days He placed the towering, strong mountains upon the earth. He blessed it and placed food throughout to meet the needs of everyone. He then turned His attention to heaven which was a vapor, and said to it and the earth, "Both of you come, either willingly or unwillingly." They both said, "We will come willingly." So in two days He created the seven heavens, and He assigned to each heaven its mandate. He adorned the lower heaven with stars and left it guarded. That was the decree of the mighty, the all-knowing.***

41:13 ***But if they turn away, say to them, "I have warned you of a disaster like the scourge that punished Ad [Ad lay on an old trade route north of Mecca. It was abandoned in Mohammed's day] and Thamud [the people of a ruined Nabatean city near Medina]."***

41:14 ***When their messengers came from all directions saying, "Serve only Allah," they answered, "If our Lord had wished, He would have sent angels down to us, so we do not believe the message you carry."***

41:15 ***As for the people of Ad, they were unjustly arrogant throughout the land, and they said, "Who has more power than us?" Could they not see that Allah, Who created them, was more powerful than themselves? Still, they continued to reject Our signs! So we sent a furious wind against them during days of disaster so that We might make them taste the penalty of disgrace in this life. The penalty of the afterlife will be even more disgraceful. They will not be helped.***

41:17 ***We showed the people of Thamud [the people of a ruined Nabatean city near Medina] the right way, but they preferred blindness to guidance. So the scourge of humiliation overtook them because that was what they earned. However, We saved those who believed and acted righteously. On the day when the enemies of Allah are gathered to face the Fire, they will***

be marched together in groups. When they reach the Fire, their ears, eyes, and skin will bear witness against them for what they have done.
41:21 *They will say to their skins, "Why do you testify against us?" And their reply will be, "Allah, Who has given speech to all things, has made us speak. He created you originally, and you will be returned to Him. You did not try to hide yourselves so that your ears, eyes, and skins could testify against you. You thought that Allah was unaware of most of the things that you did. But this evil thought of yours [that there are other gods] has brought you to destruction, and now you are one of the lost."*
41:24 *And though they are resigned, the Fire will still be their home. If they ask for goodwill, they will not receive it. We have given them companions in this world who made their present and past seem good to them. They deserve the fate of the past generations of jinns and men. They are certainly losers.*

It Was Not Allah Who Wronged Them

30:9 *Have they not traveled through the land and seen what became of those who came before them? They were stronger than those today. They worked the land and were more numerous. Their messengers came to them with clear proof of Allah's sovereignty. It was not Allah who wronged them; they wronged themselves. Evil was the consequence of those who did evil. They treated our signs as lies, and made a mockery of them.*
30:11 *Allah began creation, then reproduced it, and to Him you shall be returned.*
30:12 *On the day when the hour arrives, the guilty will be speechless with despair; the false gods they joined with Allah will not help them. They will deny those whom they believed to be Allah's equal. On the day when the hour arrives, men will be sorted from one another; those who believed and did good deeds will enjoy themselves in a Garden of Delight, but those who called Our signs and the resurrection lies will be brought forth for punishment.*

He Does Not Love the Unbeliever

30:40 *Allah created you, fed you, will cause you to die, and then will resurrect you. Are there any of your false gods who can do any of these things? Praise be to Allah! He is exalted far above those whom you join with Him. Trouble has appeared on land and sea as a result of evil that men's hands have done so that it might make them taste the fruit of their labors, in the hope that they might turn to Allah. Say: Travel the land and see what came of those who came before you. Most of them worshiped others besides Allah.*
30:43 *Set your face toward the right religion before the day comes which no one can stop. On that day, men will be sorted into two groups. Unbelievers will be responsible for their disbelief. The righteous will prepare*

their couches of repose in Paradise. He will reward from his bounty those who believe and do good deeds. He does not love the unbeliever.

The Overwhelming Wrath of Allah

12:105 *How many signs in the heavens and on the earth do they pass by, yet they turn aside from them? And most of them do not believe in Allah, without also joining other gods with Him. Do they feel secure that the overwhelming wrath of Allah will not come upon them or that the Hour will not come upon them suddenly, while they are unaware? Say: This is my way. I call on Allah resting on a clear proof—I, and whoever follows me. Glory to Allah. I am not one of the unbelievers.*

12:109 *We have never sent any messengers but men, whom We did inspire, chosen out of the people of the cities. Have they not traveled through the land to see what has been the end of those who were before them? But the mansions of the next life shall be better for those who fear Allah. Do they not comprehend?*

12:110 *Respite will be granted until the last messengers have lost all hope and deemed that they were reckoned as liars. Our aid reached them, and We delivered whom We willed. Our vengeance was not averted from the wicked. Certainly in their histories is an example for men of understanding. It is not an invented tale, but a confirmation of previous scriptures, an explanation of all things, and guidance and mercy for people who believe.*

We Destroyed Them as We Raided Them at Night

7:3 *Follow what has been revealed to you by the Lord, and do not follow any protectors beside Him. How little you remember. How many cities have We destroyed? We destroyed them as We raided them at night or while they slept in the afternoon. When Our wrath reached them, they could only reply, "Yes, we were wrongdoers."*

7:6 *Yes, We will call those to account to whom Our message has been sent. We will also question the messengers. And We will tell them their story with knowledge, as We have not been absent from them.*

Did They Feel Safe from Allah's Strategy?

7:94 *Whenever We sent a prophet to any city, We afflicted its people with adversity and trouble so they would learn humility. Then We gave them good in the place of evil until they grew wealthy and said, "Our fathers, too, knew troubles and affluence." Then We called them into account when they were unaware.*

7:96 *If the people of these cities had believed in Us and feared Allah, We would have given them all sorts of blessings from heaven and earth. But they rejected the truth, and We took vengeance on them for their deeds. Did the people of those towns feel secure that Our wrath would not come to them at night, while they slumbered? Did the people of those towns feel secure that Our wrath would not come to them in broad day, while they were amusing themselves? Did they feel safe from Allah's strategy? No one can feel secure against the strategy of Allah except those who perish. Is it not clear to those who inherit this land from its ancient people that if We please, We can punish them for their sins and seal the hearts of the unbelievers?*

7:101 *We tell you stories of some of these towns. A messenger came to them with clear signs of his mission, but they would not believe what they had already rejected as a lie. This is how Allah seals up the hearts of the unbelievers*

I272 One day Mohammed stood with the angel, Gabriel, as the Quraysh performed the rituals of their religion. Among them were the leaders who defended their native culture and religion and opposed Mohammed. When the first leader passed by Gabriel, Gabriel threw a leaf in his face and blinded him. Gabriel then caused the second one to get dropsy which killed him. The third man Gabriel caused him to develop an infection which killed him. The fourth man was caused later to step on a thorn which killed him. Gabriel killed the last man who dared not to worship Allah with a brain disease.

MOHAMMED'S PROTECTOR AND WIFE BOTH DIE

I278 Mohammed's protector was his uncle, Abu Talib. When Abu Talib fell ill, some of the leaders of the Quraysh came to his bedside. They said to him, "You are one of our leaders and are near dying. Why don't you call Mohammed and let's see if we can't work out some solution to the pain and division in our tribe? Why doesn't he leave us alone, not bother us and we will not bother him? We will have our religion and he can have his."

I278 So Abu Talib called Mohammed to his side. "Nephew, these men have come so that you can give them something and they can give you something." Mohammed said, "If they will give me one word, they can rule the Persians and the Arabs. And they must accept Allah as their Lord and renounce their gods."

I278 The Quraysh said, "He will give us no agreement. Let Allah judge between us." And they left.

I278 Mohammed turned his attention to his dying uncle. He asked him to become a Muslim and then Mohammed could intercede for him on judgment day. His uncle told him, "The Quraysh would say that I only accept Islam because I fear death. But I should say it just to give you pleasure." He drifted off, but as he died, his lips moved. His brother put his head close to Abu Talib and listened. He then said, "Nephew, my brother said what you wished him to say." Mohammed's reply was, "I did not hear him." Mohammed left.

Abu Talib had taken the orphan Mohammed into his home and raised him. He took Mohammed on caravan trading missions to Syria and taught him how to be a businessman. Abu Talib was the clan chief who protected Mohammed's life when the rest of Mecca wanted to harm him. Abu Talib was Mohammed's life and security, but he was damned to Hell, he was not a Muslim and no amount of friendship could prevent that.

After Abu Talib's death, the pressure on Mohammed was greater. It reached the point where one of the Quraysh threw dust at Mohammed. This was the worst that happened.

The death of his wife had no political effect, but it was a blow to Mohammed. His wife was his chief confidant, and she consoled him.

MARRIAGE

M113 About three months after the death of Khadija Mohammed married Sauda, a widow and a Muslim.

M113 Abu Bakr had a daughter, Aisha, who was six years old. Soon after marrying Sauda Mohammed was betrothed to Aisha, who was to become his favorite wife. The consummation would not take place until she turned nine.

> M031, 5977 ***Aisha reported Mohammed having said: I saw you in a dream for three nights when an angel brought you to me in a silk cloth and he said: Here is your wife, and when I removed (the cloth) from your face, lo, it was yourself, so I said: If this is from Allah, let Him carry it out.***

POLITICAL BEGINNINGS

CHAPTER 6

24:52 It is such as obey Allah and His Apostle, and fear Allah and do right, that will win (in the end).

I279 With Abu Talib's death, Mohammed needed political allies. Mohammed went to the city of Taif, about fifty miles away, with one servant. In Taif he met with three brothers who were politically powerful. Mohammed called them to Islam and asked them to help him in his struggles with those who would defend their native religions.

I279 One brother said that if Mohammed were the representative of Allah, then the brother would go and rip off the covering of the Kabah, Allah's shrine.

I279 The second brother said, "Couldn't Allah have found someone better than Mohammed to be a prophet?"

I279 The third brother said, "Don't let me even speak to you. If you are the prophet of Allah as you say you are, then you are too important for me to speak with. And if you are not, then you are lying. And it is not right to speak with liars."

I280 Since they could not agree, Mohammed asked them to keep their meeting private. But Taif was a small town and within days everyone knew of Mohammed's presence. Taif was a very religious town in the old ways of the Arabs. Mohammed kept condemning them and their kind, until one day a mob gathered and drove him out of town, pelting him with stones.

I281 Half way back to Mecca, he spent the night. When he arose for his night prayer, the Koran says that jinns came to hear him pray.

> 46:29 ***We sent a company of jinn so that they might hear the Koran. When the reading was finished, they returned to their people with warnings. They said, "Oh, people! We have heard a scripture sent down since the days of Moses verifying previous scriptures, a guide to the truth and the straight path. Oh, people! Hear the Messenger of Allah and believe Him that He will forgive your faults and protect you from tormenting punishment."***
>
> 46:32 ***Those who do not respond to Allah's messenger cannot defeat His plan on earth, and he will have no protectors beside Him. Such men are in flagrant error. Have they not seen that Allah, who created the heavens***

> *and the earth and was not wearied by their creation, can give life to the dead? Yes, He has power over all things.*
> 46:34 *On the day the unbelievers are set before the Fire and are asked, "Is this not the truth?" they will say, "Yes, by Our Lord!" He will say, "Then taste the punishment because you did not believe." Then be patient, as the messengers had patience and firmness, and do not try to hasten their doom. When they see what has been promised them, it will be as if they had waited but one hour. Will any perish except those who have transgressed?*

The Koran speaks further about Satan.

> 7:8 *The weighing on that day will be just [a balance will be used to weigh the good and bad deeds of life], and those who weigh heavy in good deeds will be happy. And those who weigh light, their souls will suffer because they rejected Our signs.*
> 7:10 *And We have given mankind authority on earth and given you the means for a livelihood. How little are the thanks you give. We created you, then fashioned you, then said to the angels, "Fall prostrate to Adam, and they obeyed in worship, save Iblis. He refused to fall prostrate."*
> 7:12 *Allah said, "What prevented you from prostrating in worship when I asked?" Ilbis said, "I am nobler than Adam and You created me from fire, while You created him from clay."*
> 7:13 *Allah said, "Then go down from here. Paradise is no place for pride. Get out! You are of the degraded ones."*
> 7:14 *He said, "Give me a reprieve until the day when mankind will be raised from the dead."*
> 7:15 *Allah said, "You will be of the reprieved."*
> 7:16 *He [Satan] said, "Because you have thrown me out, I will lie in wait for them in your straight path. Then I will assault them from before and from behind, and from their right hand and from their left, and You will not find most of them to be thankful."*
> 7:18 *Allah said, "Get out of here, disgraced and banished! If any of them follow you, I will fill Hell with you all."*
> 7:19 *"Oh, Adam! You and your wife will dwell in Paradise and eat where you will, but do not come to this tree, or you will become one of the wrongdoers."*
> 7:20 *Then Satan whispered to them, telling them of their hidden and evil inclinations. He said, "Your Lord has forbidden you from this tree fearing that you might become angels or one of the immortals." And he swore to both of them, "I am a friend to you." So he used deceit to cause their fall, and when they had tasted of the tree, they knew their shame and began to hide themselves sewing together leaves of the garden for clothing. And*

their Lord called to them, "Did I not forbid you this tree, and did I not say to you, 'Satan is your open enemy'?"
7:23 *They said, "Oh, our Lord! We have wronged ourselves; if you will not forgive us and have mercy on us, we will surely be lost."*
7:24 *Allah said, "Get out. Your descendents will be enemies of each other. Earth will be home and your livelihood for a time. There you will live, there you will die, and from there you will be raised."*

PREACHING BACK IN MECCA

I282 When the fairs returned to Mecca, Mohammed went out to the crowd of visitors and told them he was the prophet of Allah and brought them the Koran. They should abandon their ancient religions and follow him.

If You Make Reprisals

16:93 *If Allah wished, He could make mankind one nation, but He causes some to err and some to be guided as he pleases. You will certainly be questioned about what you did.*
16:94 *Do not use your oaths to practice deceit between you or a foot that was firmly planted may slip, and you might have to taste the evil consequences of having kept men from the path of Allah. A terrible punishment would befall you. Do not exchange the covenant of Allah for a small price. What Allah gives is better for you if you only knew it.*
16:96 *The things you have are temporary while what Allah has is eternal. Truly, We will give to those who are patient a reward that corresponds with their best actions. Whoever does good, whether male or female, and believes, We will certainly give a happy life, and We will certainly give them their reward for the best of their actions.*
16:116 *Do not say while describing something, "This is lawful, and this is forbidden," in order to invent a lie against Allah. Those who invent lies against Allah will never prosper. Such lies may bring a momentary pleasure, but they will certainly have a painful punishment. The things which We have mentioned to you before are also forbidden to the Jews. We did them no injustice; they were unjust to themselves. Your Lord is forgiving and merciful toward those who do wrong in ignorance but who later repent and make amends.*
16:120 *Abraham was an example of someone who was obedient to Allah, upright, and who did not worship others besides Allah. He was grateful for Allah's favors. Allah had chosen him and guided him on the right path. We gave him good in this world. In the afterlife, he will be among the righteous.*
16:123 *We revealed to you this message, "Follow the ways of Abraham, the upright. He did not worship false gods alongside Allah.*

16:124 *The Sabbath was commanded only for those who disagreed about it. Allah will judge between them on Judgment Day about their differences.*
16:125 *Use your wisdom and beautiful preaching to call everyone to the way of your Lord. Reason with them in the best way that you can. Surely your Lord knows best who strays from His path and who follows the right way. If you make reprisals, then punish in the same manner in which you were afflicted. But if you show patience, it is the best for those who are patient. Be patient; your patience comes from Allah. Do not grieve for them, and do not be distressed because of their plots. Allah is with those who guard against evil and those who do good.*

Do You Equally Share Your Wealth with Any Slave You Own?

30:28 *He gave you a parable that relates to yourselves: Do you equally share your wealth with any slave you own? Would you fear your slave as you would fear a free man? This is how We explain Our signs to those who understand. No, you do not. The wicked, without knowledge, pursue their base desires. But who can guide those whom Allah has allowed to go astray? There will be no one to help them.*
30:30 *Set your resolve as a true convert to the religion that Allah has created, and for which He has created man. Allah's creation can not be changed. This is the right religion, but most people do not know. Turn to Him in repentance; observe your prayers; and do not be one of those who join other gods with Allah, those who split up their religion into sects, and where every division rejoices in its own tenets.*
30:33 *When men are touched by troubles, they turn to their Lord and pray to Him: but when He has given them a taste of His mercy, suddenly some of them begin to worship other gods, as if to show their ingratitude for the favors that We have shown them. Enjoy yourselves for a little while. In the end you will know how foolish you have been. Have We given them any evidence that says that there are other gods that may be worshiped along with Allah?*
30:36 *When We give men a taste of mercy they rejoice, but if evil comes to them as a result of their actions, they despair. Do they not see that Allah gives generously or sparingly to whomever He chooses? Truly, there are signs here for those who believe.*

They Were Always Easily Deceived

30:46 *Among His signs is that He sends the winds as heralds of glad tidings giving tastes of His mercy, and that ships may sail by His command, and that you may seek his favor, and that you may be grateful. Before you, We sent messengers to their own peoples, and they went to them with clear signs. Then, We punished those who were wicked, while it was Our pleasure to help the believers.*

30:48 *It is Allah Who sends the winds and raises the clouds and, as he wishes spreads them across the sky, or breaks them up, until you see the rain pouring down from their midst. When He lets it rain on those servants of his whom he pleases, they are filled with joy, even though before the rain came they had lost all hope. Look at the signs of Allah's mercy, how He gives life to the earth after it was parched. In the same way He will raise the dead to life. He has power over all things. However, if We were to send a wind that destroyed their crops, they would become ungrateful and would disbelieve.*
30:52 *You cannot make the dead to listen, or the deaf to hear the call when they turn their backs. Neither can you lead the blind from their errors. You cannot make any hear except those who believe in Our signs and submit to Allah. You were weak when Allah created you; then afterwards He gave you strength. After strength, with age comes weakness and gray hair. He creates what he pleases. He is the wise, the powerful.*
30:55 *On the day when the Hour arrives, the wicked will believe that they have waited only an hour. They were always easily deceived. But those with knowledge and faith will say, "The truth is you have waited by Allah's decree until the Judgment Day. This is the Judgment Day, but you did not know." On that day their excuses will not help the wicked, and they will not be asked again to make amends.*

He Could Have Made Mankind of One Nation

11:111 *And truly your Lord will repay everyone according to their deeds for He is well aware of what they do.*
11:112 *Continue on the right path as you have been commanded—you and those who have turned to Allah with you—and do no wrong. He knows what you do. Do not depend on the evildoers for fear that the Fire will seize you. You have no protector beside Allah, and you will not be helped against Him. Observe prayer at early morning, at the close of the day, and at the approach of night, for good deeds drive away evil deeds. This is a warning for the mindful. Be patient, for Allah will not let the reward of the righteous perish.*
11:116 *Why were there not men with virtue, who were not corrupt, in the generations before you except the few whom we saved from harm? The evildoers enjoyed the selfish pleasures of earthly life, and became sinners. Your Lord would not destroy cities unjustly while its people were doing right.*
11:118 *If the Lord pleased, He could have made mankind of one nation, but only those to whom your Lord has granted His mercy will cease to differ. For this He created them, for the word of your Lord will be fulfilled: "I will completely fill Hell with jinn and men together."*

11:120 *All that We relate to you of the stories of these messengers is to make your heart firm. The truth has reached you through them, and this is the truth, a warning, and a reminder to those who believe.*
11:121 *To those who do not believe say, "Do whatever you can. We will do our part. Wait. We too will wait."*
11:123 *To Allah belong the secrets of the heavens and earth, and all things return to Him, so worship Him and put your trust in Him. Your Lord is not unmindful of your doings.*

Allah Misleads Whom He Will

14:3 *Those who love their life in this world, above the life that is to come, and stray from Allah on a crooked path, they are badly in error. We have only sent a messenger who speaks the language of his own people [Arabic] so that he might speak clearly to them. But Allah misleads whom He will and guides whom He will. He is mighty and wise.*

14:31 *Tell My servants who have believed that they should observe regular prayer and charitably spend out of what We have given them, in secret and openly before the day comes when there will be no bargaining nor friendship.*

28:83 *As to the hereafter, We will give it to those who do not seek to exalt themselves in the land or to do wrong. There is a happy end for those who fear Allah. Whoever does good will have a reward better than the deed, and whoever does evil will be rewarded only to the extent of their deeds.*

There Is a Slave Who Belongs to Several Partners

39:29 *Allah sets forth a parable: "There is a slave who belongs to several partners and another slave owned by one man. Are the two in like circumstances?" No, Praise be to Allah. But most of them do not know.*
39:30 *You [Mohammed] truly will die, and they will die too. Then, on Judgment Day, you will argue with one another in the presence of your Lord.*

Some He Justly Left in The Error of Their Ways

7:26 *Oh, children of Adam, We have sent clothing to cover your shame, and splendid garments, but the clothing that guards against evil is piety. This is one of the signs of Allah that man may remember. Oh, children of Adam, do not let Satan seduce you in the same way that he caused your parents to leave the Garden, stripping them of their robes of innocence so they would know their shame. He and his tribe watch you from a place where you cannot see them. They are the guardians of those who do not believe. And when they commit some shameful deed [ancient religious practices], they say, "We found our fathers doing it, and Allah has commanded it." Say: Allah never commands what is shameful. Do you say things of Allah that you do not know?*

7:29 *Say: My Lord has commanded what is right. Turn your faces towards Him at every time and place of worship, and call upon Him being sincere in your obedience to Him. As he created you, so you will return to Him. He has guided some, and some He justly left in the error of their ways because they have taken Satan as their supporter instead of Allah and think that they were guided aright.*

7:31 *Oh, children of Adam, wear your goodly apparel when you go to the mosque. Eat and drink, but do not be excessive for Allah does not love the excessive. Say: Who has forbidden the beautiful gifts of Allah that He has provided for His servants and the healthful food which He has provided for sustenance? Say: These are for the believers in this present life and will be theirs the Day of the Resurrection. We make Our signs plain for people of knowledge.*

7:33 *Say: Truly my Lord has forbidden only indecencies, whether open or secret; sin; wrongful oppression; and unjust violence. My Lord has forbidden making other gods besides Allah when He has not sent down authority and forbidden you to say things about Allah that you do not know. Every nation has a set term, and when their term is reached, they cannot put it off nor advance it an hour.*

Allah Does Not Love Those Who Exceed the Limits

7:54 *Your Lord is Allah who created the heavens and earth in six days then mounted the throne. He throws the veil of night over the day, each seeking the other in haste. He created the sun and the moon and the stars, all under His command. Is it not all His to create and govern? Blessed be Allah the Lord of the worlds.*

7:55 *Call on your Lord with humility and in secret for Allah does not love those who exceed the limits. Do not create disorder on the earth after it has been ordered. Call on Him with fear and longing desire. The mercy of Allah is near to those who do good.*

7:57 *It is He Who sends the winds as the heralds of His glad tidings, and when they carry a heavy cloud, We lead it to a dead, parched land and send down water upon it, by which We cause the growth of fruits of all kinds. And We will bring forth the dead. Perhaps you remember. In good land, plants spring forth abundantly by the will of its Lord, and in that which is bad, they spring forth scantily. So do We explain Our signs by various symbols for those who are thankful.*

We Could Have Elevated Him

7:172 *Remember when the Lord brought forth the children of Adam from their seed, their descendants, and made them testify against their own souls saying, "Am I not your Lord who cherishes you?" They said, "Yes,*

we so testify." Just in case you say on the day of Resurrection, "We were unaware of this." Or in case you say, "Our fathers before us may have taken false gods, but we are their seed after them. Will You destroy us for what wrongdoers did?"
7:174 *In this way We explain Our signs in detail that they might return to Allah. Tell them [the Jews] the story of the man to whom We gave Our signs but he passed them by, and Satan overtook him, and he went astray [A Jew converted to Islam and then renounced it.]. If it had been Our will, We could have elevated him, but he clung to the earth and followed his own desires. His likeness is that of a dog, which if you attack him hangs out his tongue, and if you leave him alone, hangs out his tongue. This is the parable of those who reject Our signs. Tell them this story so they may reflect on it. Evil is the story of those who reject Our signs and wrong their own souls.*

Are the Two Men Equal

16:73 *The others they worship besides Allah do not have the ability to provide anything in the heavens and the earth and have no power at all. Do not make likenesses of what you think Allah looks like. Allah knows and you do not.*
16:75 *Allah gives you a parable. One man is a slave to another; he has no power. Another man has received many favors from Allah, and he spends from his wealth secretly and openly. Are the two men equal? Praise be to Allah. However, most do not understand. Allah gives another parable of two men. One man is dumb with no power. He is a tiresome burden to his master; no good comes from anything he is directed to do. Is he equal to the man who commands justice and walks the right path?*
16:77 *The mysteries of the heavens and the earth belong to Allah. The decision of the Hour of Judgment is as fast as the blink of an eye or even quicker. Allah has power over all things. Allah has brought you from your mother's womb knowing nothing and has given you hearing, sight, intelligence, and emotions so that you may give thanks.*
16:79 *Do they not look at the birds poised in mid-air? Nothing holds them up except Allah. Truly there are signs here for people who believe.*

Who Does More Wrong Than He Who Invents a Lie Against Allah?

29:60 *How many animals are there that do not provide their own sustenance? Allah sustains them and you. He hears and knows all things. If you ask them who created the heavens and the earth and subjugated the sun and the moon, they would certainly say, "Allah." Then how are they turned away? Allah makes wide provisions to whichever of His servants He pleases, and He grants by strict measure to whomever He pleases. Allah knows all things. If you ask them who sends rain from heavens and revives the earth after its death, they will certainly answer, "Allah." Say:*

Praise be to Allah. Yet most of them do not understand. This present life is no other than a pastime and a game, but truly the hereafter is life indeed. If they only realized this.

29:63 *If you ask them who sends rain from heavens and revives the earth after its death, they will certainly answer, "Allah." Say: Praise be to Allah. Yet most of them do not understand. This present life is no other than a pastime and a game, but truly the hereafter is life indeed. If they only realized this.*

29:65 *When they embark on ships, they call upon Allah, vowing sincere devotion to Him. When He brings them safely to land, they give a share of their worship to others. They become ungrateful for what We have given them, so that they may enjoy worldly things, but they will soon know their error.*

29:67 *Do they not see that We have made a secure sanctuary [Mecca] while men are being ravaged all around them? Will they then believe in false gods and reject the bounty of Allah? Who does more wrong than he who invents a lie against Allah or denies the truth when it comes to him? Is there not a home in Hell for the unbelievers?*

29:69 *As for those who make efforts for Us, We will surely guide them in Our ways for Allah is with those who do right.*

There Is No Changing the Words of Allah

10:57 *Oh, men, a warning has come to you from your Lord and a medicine for what is in your hearts and a guidance and a mercy for those who believe. Say: In this, let them rejoice through the grace of Allah and His mercy. It is better than what they hoard.*

10:59 *Say: Have you considered what Allah has sent you for sustenance? You have forbidden some things and made some unlawful. Say: Has Allah permitted this, or do you invent things to attribute to Allah?" What will happen to those on the day of Resurrection who invented a lie about Allah? Allah is generous to man, but most of them are ungrateful.*

10:61 *Whatever business you are in, or whatever you read from the Koran, or whatever you do, We will be witnesses over you. Not the weight of an atom on earth or in heaven is concealed from the Lord. But the least and the greatest of these things are recorded clearly in the book [the book of life's deeds].*

10:62 *The friends of Allah will have no fear, nor shall they be put to grief. Those who believe and fear Allah will receive good tidings in this life, and in the next. There is no changing the words of Allah. This is the great triumph. And do not let their [the Meccans] speech grieve you for all power belongs to Allah. He is the hearer and the knower.*

10:66 *Surely, whatever is in the heavens and the earth belongs to Allah. What do they follow who worship others beside Allah? They follow only*

guesses, and they are but liars. He has appointed the night so you can rest, and the day to make things visible. These are signs for those who hear.
10:68 *They [Christians] say, "Allah has begotten a son. Glory be to Him. He is the self-sufficient. His is all that is in the heavens and the earth." You have no authority for that claim. Do you say things of Allah that you do not know? Say: They who devise a lie against Allah will not prosper. A portion of the world for a time will be theirs. Then they return to Us. Then We will make them taste the severest torment because they were unbelievers.*

35:32 *We have given the Scriptures as an inheritance to those We have chosen. Some of them wrong their own souls, some stay midway between good and evil, and others are foremost in goodness by permission of Allah. This is the highest grace.*

41:46 *Whoever does good, does so for themselves. Whoever does evil, does so for themselves. Your Lord does not act unfairly with his servants.*

45:14 *Tell the believers to forgive those who do not hope for the days of Allah. It is up to Him to reward men according to their actions. Whoever does good, does so for their own soul, and whoever does wrong, does so against themselves. In the end, you will be brought back to your Lord.*

Mohammed spoke of the greatness of Allah to the Meccans and the visitors.

16:1 *The doom of Allah is coming. Do not rush toward it. Glory to Him! Let Him be exalted high above the false gods whom others worship!*
16:2 *At His command the angels descended with His revelation to those servants He chose saying, "Warn them that there is no god except Allah. Fear me."*
16:3 *He has created the heavens and the earth for just reasons. He is far superior to the equals that they ascribe to Him. He has created man from a drop of sperm. Later this same man is His sworn enemy. He has created cattle for you. They give you warm clothes, many benefits, and you eat them. You feel pride and sense their beauty as you drive them home in the evening and as you lead them to the pasture in the morning. They carry your burdens to lands otherwise inaccessible except through great hardship. Your Lord is most kind, most merciful. He has created horses, mules, and donkeys for you to ride and display. He has created other things which you are unaware of. Allah's way is the right way. The other paths are not straight. If He had wished, then He could have guided all of you.*
16:10 *He sends the rain from the sky. It provides drink and nourishes the plants which feed your livestock. With rain He produces for you corn, olives, dates, grapes, and every kind of fruit. Truly there is a sign here for those who think. He has made the night and the day, and the sun and the*

moon your servants. He rules the stars. Truly, there are signs here for sensible people. Think of all of the things of varied colors which He has made upon the earth. Truly there are signs here for people who pay attention.
16:14 *He has made the sea your servant so that you may eat the fresh food that it provides and the enjoy the materials that you use for adornment [pearls and coral]. You see the ships that slice through the waves so that you may seek Allah's bounty and be thankful. He has placed the mountains firmly upon the earth, and the rivers and roads so you can find your way, and landmarks and stars that you can guide by. Is the Creator like those who cannot create? Will you remember this? You cannot count the number of Allah's favors. Allah is certainly forgiving and merciful.*

Those Who Have More Do Not Give an Equal Share to Their Slaves

16:65 *Allah sends rain down from the clouds and with it gives life to the earth. Truly there is a sign here for people who will listen. In cattle there is a lesson to you. We give you pure milk; it is easy and tasty for those who drink it. From the fruit of the date-palm and the grapevine, you obtain things to drink and eat. Truly, there is a sign here for people who are wise.*
16:68 *Your Lord taught the bee to make hives in the mountains, in trees, and in buildings. They feed on fruits and submissively follow Allah's path. Honey comes from their bellies which is therapeutic for mankind. Truly, there is a sign here for people who reflect.*
16:70 *Allah creates you and causes you to die, and some of you will be brought back to the worst part of life so that after attaining knowledge, they do not know anything. Allah is knowing and Powerful.*
16:71 *Allah has given more of His gifts of material things to some rather than others. In the same manner, those who have more do not give an equal share to their slaves so that they would share equally. Would they then deny the favors of Allah?*
16:72 *Allah has given you wives from among your own people and sons and grandsons from your wives. He has given you many good things. Do they believe in lies and deny the grace of Allah? The others they worship besides Allah do not have the ability to provide anything in the heavens and the earth and have no power at all. Do not make likenesses of what you think Allah looks like. Allah knows and you do not.*
16:75 *Allah gives you a parable. One man is a slave to another; he has no power. Another man has received many favors from Allah, and he spends from his wealth secretly and openly. Are the two men equal? Praise be to Allah. However, most do not understand. Allah gives another parable of two men. One man is dumb with no power. He is a tiresome burden to his master; no good comes from anything he is directed to do. Is he equal to the man who commands justice and walks the right path?*

16:77 *The mysteries of the heavens and the earth belong to Allah. The decision of the Hour of Judgment is as fast as the blink of an eye or even quicker. Allah has power over all things. Allah has brought you from your mother's womb knowing nothing and has given you hearing, sight, intelligence, and emotions so that you may give thanks.*
16:79 *Do they not look at the birds poised in mid-air? Nothing holds them up except Allah. Truly there are signs here for people who believe.*
16:80 *Allah has given you houses to live in and has given you the hides of animals so you may make tents, which you may carry with you on journeys. And He has given you their wool, fur, and hair, which you make useful and comfortable things from.*
16:81 *Allah has given you shelter from the sun and has given you mountain retreats and garments that ward off the cold and armor that protects against violence. He does this to complete his favor to you so that you may submit to His Will.*

He Knows What They Conceal

11:3 *If you ask your Lord for a pardon, then turn to Him, He will give you goodly enjoyments until an appointed time, and He will bestow His favors on everyone who deserves them, but if you turn away, then I fear you will see the penalty of the great day. You will return to Allah. He has Power over all things.*
11:5 *Surely they fold up their hearts to hide their thoughts from Him, but even when they cover themselves in their garments, He knows what they conceal and what they make public. He knows what is in the secrets of their hearts.*
11:6 *There is no moving beast on earth that does not depend on Allah for nourishment. He knows its resting place and its home. All has been clearly recorded. He made the heavens and the earth in six days, and His throne extends over the waters so that He might judge which of you excels in your actions.*

Allah Does What He Pleases

14:18 *A parable of those who do not believe in their Lord is that their works are like ashes, which the wind blows hard and scatters on a stormy day. They will have no gain from what they earn. This is the great error. Do you not see that Allah created the heavens and the earth with truth? If He wished, He could remove you and cause a new creation to arise. This is not difficult for Allah.*
14:21 *They will all come before Allah together, and the weak will say to those who were arrogant, "We were your followers. Can you save us from any part of Allah's wrath?" They will say, "If Allah had guided us, we surely would have guided you. It is all the same now, whether we rage or bear these torments with patience. We have no place to hide."*

14:22 *When the decision has been judged, Satan will say, "Allah gave you a promise of truth. I, too, made you a promise, but I deceived you. I had no power over you, but I called and you answered me, so blame yourselves not me. I cannot help you nor can you help me, though you joined me with Allah, I never believed that I was His equal. The evildoers will have a grievous torment."*

14:23 *But those who have believed and done good works will be brought into the Gardens, underneath which the rivers flow. They will abide there forever with the permission of their Lord. Their greeting there will be: Peace.*

14:24 *Do you not see how Allah gives you a parable of a good word being like a good tree that has roots firmly fixed and branches that reach into heaven? It yields its fruit in every season by the will of its Lord. Allah gives these parables to men so they may reflect. And the parable of an evil word is that of a bad tree. It is torn from the earth by the root. It has no stability.*

14:27 *Allah will give strength to those who believe in His word, which stands firm in this life and in the hereafter, but the wicked will He cause to err. Allah does what He pleases.*

14:28 *Have you not seen those who repay the goodness of Allah with ungratefulness and lead their people into the abode of Hell? They will be burned there in the Flame. They set up equals with Allah to mislead man from His way. Say: Enjoy yourself now because you are surely headed into the Fire.*

14:32 *It is Allah who created the heavens and the earth and sends down water from the clouds, which bring forth fruits to feed you. He has made the ships your subjects so they may sail through the sea by His command, and He has put the rivers to your service. He has subjected the sun and the moon to you in their constant courses, and He has subjected the day and the night to you. Everything that you ask of Him, He gives to you. If you would add up the favors of Allah, you would not be able to count them. Surely man is unjust and ungrateful.*

He Does Not Like Ingratitude from His Servants

39:1 *The revelation of this Book is sent down from Allah, the mighty, the wise. We have revealed the Book to you in truth, so serve Allah with sincere devotion.*

39:3 *Does Allah not deserve your sincere worship? But those who take protectors other than Allah say, "We only serve them that they may bring us nearer to Allah." Allah will judge between them and the faithful concerning where they differ. Allah does not guide the false and the ungrateful.*

39:4 *If Allah had desired to have a son, He would have chosen what He pleased out of his own creation. Glory be to Him. He is Allah, the one, the absolute. He created the heavens and the earth. He makes night overlap*

the day and day overlap the night, and He controls the sun and the moon so that each speeds to an appointed goal. He is mighty and gracious. He created you all from a single being, and then He created a mate. He sent down to you four pairs of cattle [cows, goats, sheep and camels]. He created you in the wombs of your mothers, creation upon creation in triple darkness. This is Allah, your Lord. His is the kingdom. There is no god but Allah. How then are you so turned away from Him?
39:7 *If you render Him no thanks, Allah is rich without you, but He does not like ingratitude from His servants. If you are thankful, He will be pleased with you. No one will bear the burden of another; they will only bear their own. In the end you will return to your Lord, and He will tell you what you did in this life for He knows the very secrets of your hearts.*

29:41 *The likeness for those who take protectors other than Allah is the likeness of the spider who builds a house. The frailest of all houses, surely, is the house of the spider, but they do not know this. Allah truly knows whatever they call on beside Him. He is mighty and wise. These are the examples We set forth for men, and none understand them except the wise.*

Ungrateful Ones Reject Our Signs

31:26 *To Allah belongs all things in the heavens and the earth for Allah is the absolute and praiseworthy. If all the trees that are upon the earth were to become pens, and the sea, with seven more seas to increase it, were ink, His words would not be exhausted for Allah is mighty and wise. Your creation and your resurrection are only those of a single soul. Allah hears and sees all things. Do you not see that Allah causes the night to enter into the day and he merges the day into the night and that He has subjected the sun and the moon to His laws, each running its course to an appointed term? Allah is aware of all that you do. This is because Allah is the truth, and whatever you call upon besides Him is false. Allah is the most high and the most great.*
31:31 *Do you not see how the ships speed on in the sea through the grace of Allah that He may show you of His wonders? Surely there are signs in this for the patient, grateful ones. When the waves cover them like dark shadows, they call upon Allah with sincere devotion, but when He delivers them safely to land, some of them falter between belief and unbelief. Yet, the deceitful and ungrateful ones reject Our signs. Oh, mankind, do your duty to your Lord, and fear the day when a father will not be able to help his son, nor will a son be able to help his father. The promise of Allah is the very truth. Do not let this present life deceive you nor let the deceiver deceive you concerning Allah.*
31:34 *The knowledge of the Hour is with Allah. He sends down the rain, and He knows what is in the wombs, but no one knows what he will earn*

tomorrow, nor does he know in what land he will die, but Allah is the knower and the aware.

He Gives Sparingly to Whomever He Desires

42:1 *HA. MIM. AIN. SIN. KAF. Allah sends inspiration to you as He did to those before you. He is mighty and wise. All that is in the heavens and all that is in the earth is His. He is the High, the Great.*
42:5 *The heavens are almost split apart while the angels celebrate praise of their Lord and ask forgiveness for those on earth. Allah is indulgent and merciful. But those who take protectors besides Him—Allah watches them, but you have no charge over them.*
42:7 *So We have revealed to you an Arabic Koran so that you may warn the mother-city [Mecca] and all around it, and warn them of that day of the gathering, of which there is no doubt, when some will be in Paradise and some in the Flame.*
42:8 *If Allah had desired, He could have made them one people and of one creed, but He brings whom He will into His mercy. As for the evildoers, they will have no friend or helper. Have they taken other patrons than Him? Allah is the protecting friend. He gives life to the dead, and He is mighty over all things.*
42:10 *Whatever your differences may be, the decision rests with Allah. This is Allah, my Lord. I trust in Him and turn to Him. He is the Creator of the heavens and of the earth, and He gave you mates from among yourselves and mates for cattle, too. This is how He multiplies you. There is nothing else like Him. He is the hearer and the seer. He holds the keys of the heavens and of the earth. He gives open-handedly or He gives sparingly to whomever He desires. He knows all things.*

Nowhere on Earth Where You Can Escape Allah

42:27 *If Allah were to enlarge His provision to His servants, they would surely exceed their bounds on the earth, but He sends down what He pleases in due measure for He is well-acquainted with His servants. He is the One who sends down the rain after men have despaired and spreads His mercy far and wide. He is the protector, worthy of all praise.*
42:29 *Among His signs is the creation of the heavens and of the earth and the living creatures He has scattered through them. He has the power to gather them all together when He wills. Whatever misfortune befalls you, it is because of what you have done, and yet He forgives many things.*
42:31 *There is nowhere on earth where you can escape Allah. You have no guardian or helper beside Allah. Among His signs are the ships in the sea like mountains. If He wishes, He can still the wind so they lie motionless on the back of the waves. These are the signs for those who are patient and grateful. Or, He can cause them to perish for the evil the sailors have earned, but He forgives much.*

42:35 *Those who argue about Our signs should know that there will be no escape for them. Whatever you receive is but a passing comfort for this life. What is better with Allah and more enduring for those who believe and put their trust in their Lord is to avoid greater crimes and shameful deeds, and when they are angered, forgive.*

42:38 *Those who listen to their Lord and observe regular prayer are those whose affairs are guided by mutual counsel, who spend from what We have given them, and who, when a wrong is done them, defend themselves. Let the punishment for evil be equal to the evil, but he who forgives and is reconciled will be rewarded by Allah himself for He does not love those who act unjustly.*

42:41 *Whoever defends himself after being wronged will bear no blame against him. The blame is only against those who unjustly wrong others and rebel on earth disregarding justice. These will have a grievous punishment. Whoever bears wrongs and is patient and forgiving shows courage in their acts.*

42:44 *Whomever Allah sends astray will no longer have a protector. And you will see the wrongdoers when they see the doom saying, "Is there any way to return?" And you will see them brought before the Fire made humble by disgrace, and looking with stealthy glances. The believers will say, "Truly, they are losers who have lost themselves and their families on Resurrection Day. Now the wrongdoers will be in lasting torment." They have no protectors other than Allah, and there is no road for him whom Allah causes to err.*

42:47 *Listen to your Lord before the day comes when you cannot turn back. You will have no refuge on that day, nor will you be able to deny your sins.*

42:48 *If they turn aside from your [Mohammed's] message, We have not sent you to guard over them. Your duty is only to deliver the message. When we cause man to taste Our gifts of mercy, he will rejoice in it, but if evil afflicts him for deeds he has done, then man is ungrateful.*

42:49 *To Allah belongs the kingdom of the heavens and of the earth. He creates what He will, and He gives daughters and sons to whom He will, or He gives them children of both sexes, and He makes barren whom He will for He is wise and powerful.*

They Commit Unrighteous Excesses on the Earth

10:22 *It is Allah Who enables them to travel by land and sea, so they board ships which sail with favorable wind, and they rejoice. Then a strong wind overtakes them, and waves come on from every side, and they think that they are lost. They cry to Allah, professing sincere faith to Him only saying, "If you rescue us from this, then we will be of the thankful." But when We rescue them, they commit unrighteous excesses on the earth. Oh, men, your rebellion is against yourselves, an enjoyment of the life of this world. Soon you will return to Us, and We will tell you what you have done.*

34:1 *Praise be to Allah, to whom all things on heaven and earth belong, and to Him be praise in the next world for He is wise and all-informed. He knows what comes down to earth and what goes out from it and what comes down from heaven and what goes up to it. He is merciful and forgiving.*

35:1 *Praise be to Allah, creator of the heavens and of the earth, who made the angels as messengers with pairs of wings, two, three, and four. He increases in creation what He pleases for He has power over all things. No one can withhold the mercy that Allah grants to man, and no one can release that which Allah withholds. He is mighty and wise.*

He Could Blot You Out and Bring a New Generation

35:9 *It is Allah who sends the winds so they raise the clouds. Then We lead the clouds to a land that is in a drought to revive the earth. This will be like the resurrection.*
35:10 *If anyone seeks power, all power belongs to Allah. Good words ascend to Him and the righteous deed He exalts, but those who plot evil deeds await a terrible penalty, and their plots will be rendered in vain.*
35:11 *Allah created you from dust and from a sperm drop. Then He made you two sexes, and no female bears or brings forth without His knowledge. No man lives a long life or is cut off from long life but it is an ordained decree. All this is easy for Allah.*
35:12 *Nor are the two seas alike. One is fresh, sweet, and pleasant to drink, and the other is salt and bitter. Yet from each we eat fresh fish and take ornaments to wear, and you see the ships plough the waves to seek the bounty of Allah, so you may be grateful.*
35:13 *He makes the night pass into the day and the day to pass into the night. He has subjected the sun and the moon to His service so that each runs its course for an appointed term. This is Allah your Lord. His is the kingdom. Any gods you call on beside Him have not the least power. If you invoke them, they will not hear your prayer, and if they heard, they could not grant you. On Judgment Day they will reject your partnership with them, and none can inform you like the One who is aware.*
35:15 *Oh, men, it is you who need Allah, but Allah is free of needs and worthy of praise. If it were His will, He could blot you out and bring a new generation. This would not be difficult for Allah.*
35:18 *A burdened soul cannot bear the burden of another, and if the soul that is weighed down calls out for help with its burden, none of it can be carried by another, even if he is kin. Warn only those who fear their Lord in secret and keep prayer. Whoever purifies himself does so only for himself, and Allah is the goal.*

35:19 *The blind and the seeing are not alike, nor the darkness and light, nor the shade and the sun, nor are the living and the dead alike. Allah can cause anyone to hear, but you cannot make those who are in their graves hear. You can only warn.*

35:24 *We have sent you [Mohammed] out with the truth as a bearer of glad tidings and as a warner. Among people there have always been those who warn. And if they reject you, so were the messengers before you rejected. They also brought clear proofs of their mission and the Psalms and the Scriptures [Gospels] giving light. Then I punished the unbelievers and how great was My wrath.*

35:27 *Have you not seen that Allah sends water down from the heavens and produces various colors? In the mountains are traces of white and red and various hues, and others intensely black. And men, reptiles, and animals are also various hues. Those servants who possess knowledge fear Allah. Allah is mighty and often forgiving.*

35:29 *Those who read the Scripture of Allah, keep regular prayer, and spend what We have bestowed on them publicly and privately, and hope for a gain that will not perish, Allah will pay them their reward, and He will give them more out of His bounty for He is grateful and responsive. The Scripture We have revealed to you is the truth, verifying what was revealed before for Allah sees and observes His servants.*

Severe in His Vengeance

13:1 *ELIF. LAM. MIM. RA. These are the verses of the Book; that which has been sent down to you from your Lord is true, although most people do not believe it.*

13:2 *It is Allah who raised the heavens with invisible pillars, ascended to His throne, and ruled the sun and moon, each pursuing its course for an appointed time. He commands all things making His signs clear so that you may have strong faith in meeting your Lord. It was He who laid out the earth and placed the mountains and rivers on it. He made all plants, with their male and female parts, and caused the night to end the day. Certainly these are signs for those reflect on them.*

13:4 *And on the earth there are tracts of land beside each other with vineyards and cornfields and palm trees. These plants are all nurtured by the same water, yet some taste better than others. Surely there are signs in this for those who consider them.*

13:5 *If anything should make you wonder, it is those who say, "When we are dust, will we then be raised in a new creation?" It is these who do not believe in their Lord, who have chains around their necks, and who are prisoners of the Fire, where they will live forever. They urge you to advance the cause of evil rather than good, despite the fact that many who have come before them have received punishment. Allah is forgiving of His people despite their sins, yet also severe in His vengeance. And the unbeliever says "Why has his Lord not sent a sign down to him?" But You are only to give warning, and each people has its own leader.*

13:8 *Allah knows what every female womb bears and of each and every change that occurs within. With Him everything is measured. He knows both the unseen and the visible. He is the great, the most high. Whether you speak in secret or freely, whether you hide yourself in the darkness or walk about in the daylight, it is the same to Him. Each person has angels all around him who guard him by Allah's command. Allah will not change a people's condition until they change the condition of their hearts. And if Allah wants to punish a people, there is nothing they can do to stop it, and without Him they have no defender. It is He who causes the lightening to flash, rousing both fear and hope, and brings together heavy clouds. The thunder sings His praises, as well as the angels, in awe of Him. He sends thunderbolts to destroy whomever he wishes while the unbelievers dispute about Allah. His wrath is strong.*

13:14 *True prayer is to Him alone. Those who pray to any other besides Him will receive no response. It is like one who reaches out his hands to bring water to the mouth and never reaches it. The prayers of the unbelievers are futile. All beings in heaven and earth will bow before Allah, either willingly or by force, as do their own shadows in the morning and at night.*

13:16 *Say: Who is the Lord of the heavens and of the earth? Say: It is Allah. Say: Then why do you take gods other than Him who have no power to harm or do good to themselves? Say: Are the blind equal to those who can see, or is dark equal to light? Have their gods made a creation such as His so that the two creations seem the same to them? Say: Allah is the creator of all things and the conqueror of all. He sends down rain from the skies that fills the rivers to overflowing so that the flood carries swelling foam, like that which is made from ore when it is smelt to make jewelry and tools. It is in this way that Allah portrays that which is true and that which is false. The scum is washed away, and that which is useful remains. Allah, therefore, speaks in parables.*

39:49 *When trouble befalls a man he cries to Us. Afterwards, when We have given him a favor, he says, "Allah gave this to me because of certain knowledge I have." No, it is a test, but most of them did not know. Generations before them said the same, but their deeds did not profit them. The evils they earned overtook them. And whoever will do wrong among this generation, their own misdeeds will overtake them, as well. They will not escape Allah. Do they know that Allah gives generously to those He will and that He is sparing to whom He will? These are signs to those who believe.*

I283 One of the chiefs of a visiting tribe was taken with the power of Mohammed. He said, "By Allah, if I could take this man from the Quraysh,

I could eat up the Arabs with him." He asked Mohammed, "If I give allegiance to you and Allah gives you victory over your enemies, will we have authority over you?" Mohammed replied that Allah gave authority where he pleased. The chief said back, "So we protect you with our arms and lives and you will reap the benefit! Thanks, but no thanks."

I285 Mohammed approached one visitor and the visitor said, "Perhaps you have something like what I have." He handed Mohammed a scroll of Luqman[1]. Mohammed said, "This is fine, but I have something better, a Koran which Allah has revealed to me." The visitor said Mohammed's Koran was a fine saying, but he did not join.

The Koran speaks of Luqman.

> 31:12 ***We bestowed wisdom upon Luqman [a wise man] saying, "Be thankful to Allah." Whoever is thankful profits his own soul, and whoever is thankless, Allah requires no praise; Allah is self-sufficient, but is worthy of all praise. And remember what Luqman said to his son by way of warning, "Oh my son, do not worship others with Allah for false worship is the greatest sin."***
> 31:14 ***We have commanded man to be good concerning his parents. His mother carried him with pain upon pain, and it took two years before he was weaned. Be grateful to Me and to your parents. Your journey ends with Me. But if they [your parents] strive with you to join with Me things of which you have no knowledge, do not obey them. Be kind to those with whom you keep company in this world, but follow the path of those who turn to me. In the end, you will return to me, and then I will tell you of your doings.***
> 31:16 ***"Oh, my son [Luqman's son], if it were but the weight of a grain of mustard seed and hidden in a rock or in the heavens or in the earth, Allah would bring everything to light, for Allah is subtle and informed of all. Oh, my son, observe regular prayer, command the right and forbid the wrong, and be patient with whatever befalls you. These acts of duty require courage. Do not turn your cheek in scorn to other men, nor walk with disrespect on the earth for Allah does not love the arrogant or boastful. Let your pace be medium and lower your voice for the least pleasing of voice is surely the voice of a braying ass."***

THE BEGINNING OF POWER AND JIHAD IN MEDINA

Medina was about a ten-day journey from Mecca, but since ancient times the Medinans had come to Mecca for the fairs. Medina was half Jewish and half Arabian, and there was an ongoing tension between the two.

---

1. Luqman was a philosopher and a writer of wisdom mentioned in the Koran.

The Jews worked as farmers and craftsmen and were literate. They were the wealthy class, but their power was slowly waning. In times past the Arabs had raided and stolen from the Jews who retaliated by saying that one day a prophet would come and lead them to victory over the Arabs. In spite of the tensions, the Arab tribe of Khazraj were allies with them.

I286 So when the members of the Khazraj met Mohammed, they said among themselves, "This is the prophet the Jews spoke of. Let us join ranks with him before the Jews do." They became Muslims, and their tribe was rancorous and divided. They hoped that Islam could unite them, and soon every house in Medina had heard of Islam.

I289 The next year when the Medinan Muslims returned to Mecca, they took an oath to Mohammed. They returned to Medina, and soon many of Medinans submitted to Islam.

I294 At the next fair in Mecca, many of the new Muslims from Medina showed up. During the early part of the night about seventy of them left the caravan to meet with Mohammed. He recited the Koran and said, "I invite your allegiance on the basis that you protect me as you would your children." The Medinans gave their oath. After the oath, one of them asked about their now severed ties to the Jews of Medina. If they helped Mohammed with arms and they were successful would he go back to Mecca? Mohammed smiled and said, "No, blood is blood, and blood not to be paid for is blood not to be paid for." Blood revenge and its obligation were common to them. "I will war against them that war against you and be at peace with those at peace with you."

I299 One of the Medinans said to those who made the pledge, "Do you realize to what your are committing yourselves in pledging your support to this man? It is war against all. If you think that if you lose your property and your best are killed, and then you would give him up, then quit now. But if you think that you will be loyal to your oath if you lose your property and your best are killed, then take him, for it will profit you now and in Paradise." They asked what they would receive for their oath, Mohammed promised them Paradise. They all shook hands on the deal.

I301 In the morning the leaders of the Quraysh came to the caravan. They had heard that the Medinans had come to invite Mohammed to Medina and had pledged themselves to war against the Quraysh. The Quraysh wanted no part of war with the Medinans. Those Medinans in the caravan who were not Muslims were puzzled by all of this since they had no idea about the pledge in the night.

The Koran is very clear that the proper relationship between humanity and Allah is fear.

Fear Your Lord

39:8 *When trouble touches a man, he cries to his Lord and repents, yet no sooner does He grant a favor than he forgets what he cried for and praises other gods than Allah and misleads others from Allah's path. Say: Enjoy your ungratefulness for a little while for surely you will be a companion to the Fire.*

39:9 *Is he equal to an unbeliever who worships devoutly in the hours of the night, prostrate or standing in devotion, mindful of the life to come, and hoping for the mercy of his Lord? Say: Are those who know equal with those who do not know? Only men of understanding will take the warning.*

39:10 *Say: Oh, My servants who believe, fear your Lord. For those who do good in this world, good awaits. Allah's earth is spacious. Those who are patient will be rewarded in full measure.*

39:11 *Say: I am commanded that I serve Allah with sincere devotion. I am commanded to be the first of those who submit. Say: If I should disobey my Lord, I fear the penalty of a grievous day. Say: I serve Allah being sincere in my obedience.*

39:15 *Worship what you will besides Him. Say: The losers will be those who will lose their own souls and their families on the day of resurrection. Surely, this is a clear loss. They will be covered by Fire from above and below. With this Allah stirs fear in His servants, so fear Me, My servants.*

6:50 *Say: I do not say that I have the treasures of Allah nor do I know the unseen. I do not say to you that I am an angel, but I only follow what is revealed to me. Say: Are the blind and the seeing equal? Will you reflect on this? Warn those who fear they will be brought to judgment before their Lord. They shall have no patron or intercessor but Him to guard against evil.*

6:52 *Do not send away those who cry to their Lord morning and evening seeking His favor. You [Mohammed] are not accountable for them nor they for you, but if you should drive them away you will be wrong. And We have tried some of them in comparison to others so that they say, "Are these the ones who are favored by Allah? Is it not Allah who best knows the grateful?*

BACK IN MEDINA

I304 Back in Medina the Muslims now practiced their new religion openly. But most of the Arabs still practiced their ancient tribal religions. The Muslims would desecrate the old shrines and ritual objects. They would even break into houses and steal the ritual objects and throw them into the latrines. On one occasion they killed a dog and tied the dog's body to the ritual object and thew it into the latrine.

THE OPENING WORDS OF WAR

I313 Up to now the main tension in the division in the Quraysh tribe over the new religion had been resolved by words. Curses and insults had been exchanged. Mohammed condemned the ancient religion and customs on an almost daily basis. The Quraysh had mocked Mohammed and abused lower class converts. What blood had been drawn had been in the equivalent of a brawl. Dust had been thrown, but no real violence. No one had died.

IMMIGRATION

I314 The Muslim Medinans had pledged Mohammed support in war and to help the Muslims from Mecca. The Muslims in Mecca left and went to Medina. The Muslims from both Mecca and Medina were about to be tested.

> 29:1 ***ELIF. LAM. MIM. Do men think that they will be left alone when they say, "We believe," and that they will not be tested? We tested those who lived before them, so Allah will surely know who is sincere and who is false. Do the ones who work evil think that they will escape Us? Their judgment is evil.***
>
> 29:5 ***Whoever hopes to meet Allah, the set time will surely come. He hears and knows. Whoever makes efforts for the faith makes them for his own good only. Allah is independent of His creatures. As for those who believe and do good works, We will blot out all evil from them, and We will reward them according to their best actions.***
>
> 29:8 ***We have commanded that men show kindness to their parents, but if they try to make you worship others besides Me, do not obey them. You will all return to Me, and I will tell you what you did. And those who believe and do the things that are right, We will admit them to the company of the righteous.***
>
> 29:10 ***Some men say, "We believe in Allah," yet when they meet with sufferings in the cause of Allah, they regard trouble from man as if it were the wrath of Allah. If help comes from Allah, they are sure to say, "We were on your side!" Does Allah not know what is in the hearts of His creatures? Yes, and Allah knows those who believe, and He well knows the hypocrites.***

THE KORAN OF MEDINA

POLITICAL POWER

CHAPTER 7

8:46 Obey Allah and His messenger, and do not argue with one another for fear that you will lose courage and strength. Be patient for Allah is with the patient.

I324-326 All of the Muslims, except for Mohammed, Ali and Abu Bakr, had left for Medina. The Quraysh saw that Mohammed had new allies outside of Mecca and their influence. They feared that Mohammed would join them and they knew that his oath of allegiance included war with the Quraysh and Mecca. So the Quraysh assembled as a council in order to figure out what to do. In the end the Quraysh let them go. The Quraysh wanted the their problem to go away.

> 8:30 *Remember the unbelievers who plotted against you and sought to have you taken prisoner or to have you killed or banished. They made plans, as did Allah, but Allah is the best plotter of all.*
> 8:31 *When Our revelations are told to them they say, "We have heard them before, and if we wanted to, we could say the same kinds of things. They are nothing but the fables of old." And then they said, "Allah! If this is indeed the truth sent down from You, then send down a shower of stones upon our heads or some other terrible punishment." But Allah would not punish them while you were there with them. He would not punish them if they asked to be forgiven. Nevertheless, Allah would be justified in punishing them because they have prevented the believers from entering the Sacred Mosque, even though they have no right to guard it. The Allah-fearing are its only guardians although most of them do not realize it. Their prayers at the Sacred House are nothing more significant than whistling or clapping hands to Allah. "Taste your punishment for your disbelief."*
> 8:36 *The unbelievers spend their wealth with the intent to turn others away from Allah's path. In this way they drain their wealth, but they will regret it, and they will be conquered in the end. The unbelievers will be driven into Hell. Allah will divide the bad from the good. He will take the wicked, pile them on top of one another, and cast them into Hell; truly they are the losers.*

I336-337 In Medina Mohammed set to work building the first mosque. There were now two groups of Muslims in Medina, the Quraysh Immigrants from Mecca and the Helpers from Medina.

THE COVENANT

I341 Mohammed wrote up a charter or covenant for a basis of law and government. The religion of Islam now had a political system. Islam now had power over those outside the mosque. All Muslims, whether from Mecca, Medina or anywhere else, were part of a community, ***umma,*** that excluded others. There was one set of ethics for the Muslims and another set for the non-Muslims. Duality was established as a fundamental principle of Islamic ethics.

I341 Muslims should oppose any who would sow discord among other Muslims. A Muslim should not kill another Muslim, nor should he help a non-Muslim against a Muslim. Muslims are friends to each other, to the exclusion of non-Muslims. Muslims shall avenge blood shed of another Muslim in jihad. A non-believer shall not intervene against a Muslim.

I342 The Jews who align themselves with Mohammed are to be treated fairly. Jews are to help pay for war if they are fighting with the Muslims as allies. No Jew may go to war without the permission of Mohammed, except for revenge killings. Jews must help Muslims if they are attacked. All trouble and controversy must be judged by Mohammed. No Meccans are to be aided.

MARRIAGE

M177 About seven months after arriving in Medina Mohammed, aged fifty-three, consummated his marriage with Aisha, now age nine. She moved out of her father's house into what was to become a compound of apartments adjoining the mosque. She was allowed to bring her dolls into the harem due to her age.

> M008,3311 ***Aisha reported that Mohammed married her when she was seven years old, and he was taken to his house as a bride when she was nine, and her dolls were with her; and when he (Mohammed) died she was eighteen years old.***

THE HYPOCRITES

CHAPTER 8

47:33 Believers! Obey Allah and the messenger, and do not let your effort be in vain.

THE HYPOCRITES

I351 Before Mohammed arrived, the Arabs who practiced their ancient religions were content with their religion and tolerant of others. Many Arabs became Muslims due to a pressure to join Islam. But in secret they were hypocrites who allied themselves with the Jews because they thought Mohammed was deluded.

I365 The Koran gives an analogy about the hypocrites:

> 2:8 ***And some of the people [the Jews] say, "We believe in Allah and the Day," although they do not really believe. They wish to deceive Allah and His believers, but they fool no one but themselves although they do not know it. Their hearts are diseased, and Allah has increased their suffering. They will suffer an excruciating doom because of their lies.***
> 2:11 ***And when they are told, "Do not make evil in the earth," they say, "We are only trying to make peace." But they truly are the evil-doers even though they do not realize it. When it is said to them, "Believe as others have believed," they say, "Should we believe as the fools believe?" They are the fools, if only they knew it! And when they meet with the faithful they say, "We believe too." But when they are alone with their fellow devils [Jews and Christians] they say, "Really, we are with you. We were only mocking them." Allah will throw their mockery back on them and leave them to wander alone in their blindness.***

I355 One of the Medinans became a Muslim and later began to doubt the truth of Mohammed and said, "If this man is right, we are worse than donkeys." His best friend had converted and told Mohammed of his friend's doubts. Allegiance to Islam comes before family, nation, or friend. When Mohammed confronted him about his remarks and doubts, he denied it. The Koran's comments:

> 9:74 ***They swear by Allah that they said nothing wrong, yet they spoke blasphemy, and some Muslims became unbelievers. They planned what they could not carry out [a plan against Mohammed], and only***

disapproved of it because Allah and His Messenger had enriched them by His bounty [the resistance to Mohammed decreased when the money from the spoils of war came into the Medinan economy]. If they repent, it will be better for them, but if they fall back into their sin, Allah will afflict them with a painful doom in this world and the next. On earth, they will have neither friend nor protector.

1356 Ironically, the friend who reported the doubts to Mohammed later turned against him, killed two Muslims during battle, and fled to Mecca. Mohammed ordered him killed, but he escaped. Again the Koran says:

3:86 *How will Allah guide the people who fall into disbelief after having been believers and having acknowledged the messenger as true and after having received clear signs? Allah does not guide those that do evil. As for these, they will receive Allah's curse, as well as the curse of His angels and of all mankind, and they will live under it forever. Their punishment will not be lightened nor will they be forgiven except for those who repent and change their ways. Allah is forgiving and merciful.*

1357 Mohammed used to say about one of the hypocrites that he had the same face as Satan. The man used to sit and listen to Mohammed and then take back to the hypocrites what he said. He said of Mohammed, "Mohammed is all ears. If anyone tells him anything, he will believe it." The Koran speaks of him and other hypocrites:

9:61 *There are some of them who injure the Messenger and say, "He is only a hearer." Say: He is a hearer of good for you. He believes in Allah and believes in the faithful. He is a mercy to those of you who believe, but those who injure the Messenger of Allah will suffer a painful doom. They swear to you by Allah to please you, but Allah and His Messenger are worthier, so they should please Him if they are believers.*
9:63 *Do they not know that whoever opposes Allah and His Messenger will abide in the Fire of Hell, where they will remain forever? This is the great shame.*
9:64 *The hypocrites are afraid that a sura [chapter] would be sent down about them telling plainly what is in their hearts. Say: Go on mocking, but Allah will bring to light all that you fear.*

1358 One of the hypocrites excused his criticism by saying that he was only talking and jesting. No criticism was too small to be unnoticed.

9:65 *If you ask them, they will surely say, "We were only talking idly and jesting." Say: Do you mock Allah, His signs, and His Messenger? Make no excuse. You have rejected faith after you accepted it. If we forgive some of you, we will punish others because they are evildoers. Hypocritical men and women have an understanding with one another. They command what is evil, forbid what is just, and do not pay the poor tax. They have forgotten Allah, and He has forgotten them. The hypocrites are the rebellious wrongdoers. Allah promises the hypocritical men and women and the unbelievers the Fire of Hell, and they will abide there; it is enough for them. Allah has cursed them, and an eternal torment will be theirs.*

1365 The hypocrites change their faces depending upon who they are with. When they are with the Muslims, they believe. But when they are with the evil ones (the Jews) they say they are with the Jews. It is the Jews who order them to deny the truth and contradict Mohammed.

2:16 *It is these who have bought error at the price of guidance. Their purchase is profitless, and they have lost the right direction. They are like the ones who lit a fire, and when it shed its light all around them, Allah took it away and left them in total darkness where they were unable to see. Deaf, dumb and blind, they will never turn back to the right path.*
2:19 *Or like the ones who, standing beneath a storm cloud dark with thunder and lightning, put their fingers in their ears to keep out the sound, fearing death. Allah surrounds the unbelievers. The lightning nearly takes their sight away. Each time the lightning flashes on them, they walk around, but when the darkness comes, they stand still. If Allah willed it, He could destroy their hearing and sight because Allah has power over everything.*

The Koran argues against the hypocrites.

57:12 *The day will come when you will see true believers, men and women, with their light stretching out before them and on their right hands, and they will hear it said to them, "Good news comes to you today of Gardens watering by flowing rivers where you will live forever." This is the ultimate victory!*
57:13 *On that day the hypocritical men and women will say to the believers, "Wait for us so that we kindle our lights from yours," but they will say to them, "Go back and find your own light!" A wall with a gate will be in between them, and those receiving mercy will be on the inside, and those on the outside in front of it will receive the torment of Hell. They will cry out to them and say, "Were we not with you?" and they will reply, "Yes, but you allowed yourselves to be led into temptation, you hesitated, and you doubted. Your lowly desires deceived you until Allah's punishment arrived. The deceiver tricked you about Allah. No ransom will be accepted from you today or from the faithless. The Fire will be your home for that is the proper place for you, and a wretched doom it is!*

4:150 *Those who deny Allah and His Messenger and those who seek to separate Allah from His messengers saying, "We believe in some, but reject others," therefore seeking a middle ground, these are truly unbelievers. And for the unbelievers We have prepared a disgraceful punishment. But those who believe in Allah and His messengers and make no distinction between them, they will be rewarded by Him. Allah is forgiving and merciful!*

They Will Be Seized and Murdered

33:60 *If the hypocrites, the men with diseased hearts and the troublemakers in Medina, do not desist, We will raise you up against them and they will not remain in the city much longer. They will be cursed, and wherever they are found, they will be seized and murdered. It was Allah's same practice with those who came before them, and you will find no change in Allah's ways.*

33:63 *When the people ask you about the Hour of Doom, say: Knowledge of it is Allah's alone. And who can tell whether the Hour is not nearly upon us? Truly, Allah has cursed the unbelievers and has prepared the Fire for them, where they will live forever with no friend or helper to be found! On the day their faces are rolling in the Fire they will cry out, "If only we had obeyed Allah and His Messenger!" And they will say, "Our Lord! Truly we obeyed our chiefs and great men, but they led us astray from Your path. Our Lord! Give them a double punishment, and curse them with a heavy curse."*

33:69 *Believers! Do not be like those who disrespected Moses. Allah cleared him of the insults they spoke of him [There were complaints about Mohammed's distribution of the spoils of war], and he was highly exalted in Allah's sight. Believers! Fear Allah and speak only the truth so that He may guide your works and forgive your sins. And whoever obeys Allah and His Messenger will be greatly blessed.*

33:72 *We gave Our trust to the heavens, the earth, and the mountains, but they refused the responsibility and were afraid to take it. And although man has undertaken it, he has proven unjust, foolish! Therefore, Allah will punish the hypocritical men and women. But as for the believing men and women, Allah will show them mercy, for Allah is forgiving and merciful!*

The Hypocrites Do Not Understand

63:1 *When the hypocrites come to you, they say, "We testify that you are truly Allah's Messenger." Allah knows that you are indeed the one He sent. Allah testifies that the hypocrites are surely lying. They use their faith to conceal their true intention: to lead others away from Allah's path. What they do is evil. This is because they believed and then denied the faith. Therefore, their hearts have been hardened and they lack understanding.*

63:4 *When you see them, their appearances are pleasing to you. When they speak, you listen to their words. They are like pieces of wood leaning against a wall! Every shout they hear they think is against them. They are your enemies; beware of them. Allah will destroy them! How wicked they are!*
63:5 *And when they are told, "Come, Allah's Messenger will plead for your forgiveness," they turn their faces away and leave with arrogance. It will be the same for them whether you ask for their forgiveness or not; Allah will never forgive them for Allah does not give guidance to the wicked.*
63:7 *They are the ones who say, "Do not give anything to those who follow Allah's Messenger, and they will be forced to leave him." The treasures of the heavens and earth are Allah's, but the hypocrites do not understand. They say, "If we return to Medina, the strong will surely drive the weak from it." Strength is with Allah and His Messenger and the believers, but the hypocrites do not understand it.*
63:9 *Believers! Do not let your wealth or your children cause you to forget about Allah. Those who forget will suffer great loss. Give to Allah's cause [jihad] from that which We have given you before death comes to you and you say, "My Lord! Will you not grant me more time so that I may give to charity and do good works?"*
63:11 *But Allah will grant no soul more time when its appointed time has arrived! And Allah knows all that you do.*

So He Caused Hypocrisy to Take Its Turn in Their Hearts

9:75 *There are some of them who made this agreement with Allah, "If He gives us of His bounties, we will surely give regular charity and surely be of the righteous." Yet when He gave them out of His bounty, they hoarded it and turned their backs on their promise and withdrew. So He caused hypocrisy to take its turn in their hearts until the day when they will meet Him, because they broke their promise to Allah, and they lied again and again. Do they not know that Allah knows their secret thoughts and private talks, and that Allah knows all things unseen?*
9:79 *They who slander such of the faithful as give charity freely, and those who find nothing to give but the fruits of their labor, and scoff at them, Allah will scoff at them, and there is a grievous torment in store for them. Whether you ask forgiveness for them, Mohammed, or do not ask for it, it will be the same. If you ask forgiveness for them seventy times, Allah will by no means forgive them. This is because they have rejected Allah and His Messenger. Allah does not guide ungodly people.*

Not all Muslims in Mecca left for Medina. They were to have the same fate as the hypocrites.

4:97 *When the angels take the souls of the unbelievers back [Muslims in Mecca who did not immigrate with Mohammed and reverted to their*

native religions. These unbelievers fought against Mohammed at Badr], they will ask, "What have you been doing?" The unbelievers will reply, "We were weak and oppressed in the earth." The angels will say, "Was Allah's earth not big enough for you to flee and seek asylum in?" It will be these who will have Hell as their home and a terrible journey to it.
4:98 *As for the men, women, and children who were too weak to escape and were not shown the way, Allah will forgive them, for Allah is forgiving and gracious.*

2:205 *When they turn their backs to you, they hurry to do evil throughout the land, laying waste to crops and cattle, but Allah does not love evil. And when it is said to them, "Fear Allah," arrogance leads them to sin. Hell will be enough for them, an evil dwelling-place.*

They Follow What Angers Allah

47:20 *The believers say, "Why is a sura not sent down for us?" But when an authoritative sura [chapter of the Koran] is sent to them and it mentions war, you see those with diseased hearts look at you as if they are on the verge of death! It would be better for them to be obedient and to speak proper words. And if they are indeed called to war and they remain true to Allah, it will be best for them. But if you were not ready, and rejected the faith, you would be sure to cause evil in the land and cut off your ties with your family! These are the ones whom Allah has cursed, making them deaf and blinding their eyes! Will they not then earnestly seek to contemplate the Koran, or have they locked up their hearts? Those who go back to being unbelievers after they have clearly received Allah's guidance are deceived by Satan and given false hope. This is because those who hate what Allah has revealed say, "We will obey part of what you have commanded," but Allah knows what they say in secret. What will they do when the angels come to take away their souls when they die, slashing their faces and backs? This is because they follow what angers Allah and hate anything that pleases Him; therefore, He will make their efforts useless.*
47:29 *Do those with diseased hearts think that Allah will not bring their malice to light? If We willed it, We could have shown them to you so that you would have surely recognized them by their appearance, but you will certainly recognize them by the tone of their words. Allah knows everything that you do.*
47:31 *And We will certainly put you to the test until We recognize the brave and perseverant among you, and We will try your purported record.*
47:32 *The unbelievers who turn others away from Allah's path and do not obey the messenger after they have clearly received his guidance will in no manner bring injury to Allah. He will bring all their actions to nothing.*

3:88 *But the ones who repent after having been believers and increase in their disbelief, their repentance will never be accepted. These are the ones who have gone too far astray.*
3:91 *As for those unbelievers who die rejecting the faith, were all the gold in the world offered as their ransom, it would not be accepted. A terrible punishment awaits them, and they will have no one to help them.*
3:92 *You will not be truly righteous until you have given what you truly love to charity; for whatever you give, it is known to Allah.*

There Is Nothing Good in Most of Their Secret Conversations

4:105 *Truly, We have sent the Scriptures down to you with the truth so that you might judge between people according to what Allah has taught you. Do not side with the traitors, and ask Allah's forgiveness. Allah is always forgiving and merciful. Neither should you take the side of those who deceive their own souls. Allah does not love the deceitful and sinful.*
4:108 *They try to hide themselves from people, but they cannot hide themselves from Allah. He is with them at night when their words displease Him, and Allah knows all that they do. Yes, you may plead in their favor in this world, but who will plead in their favor with Allah on the Day of Resurrection, or who will defend them?*
4:110 *Those who do evil or those who have betrayed their own souls and then ask Allah's forgiveness will find Allah forgiving and merciful. Anyone who commits a sin, sins against his own soul. Allah is all-knowing and wise!*
4:112 *Anyone who commits an offense or a crime and blames an innocent person, will bear the guilt of defamation and blatant sin.*
4:113 *If it had not been for Allah's grace and mercy, a group of them [hypocrites] would have certainly plotted to mislead you. They have only succeeded in leading themselves astray, and they cannot harm you. Allah has sent His Scripture and wisdom to you and has taught you things you did not know before. Allah's grace toward you has been great. There is nothing good in most of their secret conversations except that which commands charity, goodness, and peace among the people. Whoever does this to please Allah, We will give them a rich reward.*
4:115 *Anyone who opposes the Messenger after having received Our guidance and follows a path other than that of the true believer will be left to their own devices. We will lead them into Hell, an evil home.*

He Will Deceive Them

4:138 *Warn the hypocrites that torturous punishment awaits them. The hypocrites take unbelievers as friends rather than believers. Do they look for honor at their hands? Truly all honor belongs to Allah.*
4:140 *He has already sent down to you in the Book that when you hear Allah's revelations rejected and mocked by unbelievers you should not sit*

and listen to them until they talk about something else, for if you stayed you would become like them. Truly Allah will gather all the hypocrites and unbelievers together in Hell. These are the ones who watch you closely, and if you are successful they say, "Did not we stand with you?" And if the unbelievers are successful they say, "Did we not gain power over you, and did we not defend you from the believers?" Allah will judge between the two of you on the Day of Resurrection, and Allah will not allow the unbelievers to be victorious over the believers.

4:142 *The hypocrites wish to deceive Allah, but He will deceive them. When they stand for prayer, they rise slowly so as to be seen by others, and they hardly remember Allah. They go back and forth being neither a part of one group or the other. You will not be able to guide anyone Allah leads astray.*

4:145 *The hypocrites will be thrown into the lowest abyss of the Fire, and there will be no one to help them. Except for those who ask for forgiveness and change their ways, who hold tightly to Allah and are sincere in their dedication to Allah, they will be counted with the believers, and Allah will give the believers a great reward. Why should Allah inflict punishment on you if you are grateful and believe? Allah will reward you for your works, for He knows all things.*

4:148 *Allah does not love harsh words to be spoken in public, unless by someone who has been wronged. Allah is all-hearing and all-knowing. Whether you do good in public or in private, whether you pardon a wrong, truly Allah is forgiving and all-powerful!*

Believers! Fear Allah

59:11 *Have you not noticed the hypocrites? They say to fellow unbelievers among the People of the Book [Jews] "If you are driven out, we will surely go with you. And we will never follow the orders of anyone who is against you. If you are attacked, we will certainly come to your aid." But Allah witnesses that they are truly liars. No! If the People of the Book were driven out, the hypocrites would not go with them. If they [Jews] were attacked, they would not come to their aid, or if they did come, they would surely flee and they would not be helped. They are so devoid of understanding that they fear you more than they fear Allah!*

59:14 *They will not fight you in a group unless they are fortified in their cities and behind walls. The disputes among them are many. You think of them as a unified group, but their hearts are divided. They are a people devoid of understanding. They act like those who preceded them, who also tasted the consequences of their own actions. A painful punishment awaits them.*

59:16 *The hypocrites are like Satan when he says to someone, "Be an unbeliever." And when he has become an unbeliever he says, "I do not share in your guilt. Truly, I fear Allah, the Lord of the worlds." Therefore, the end of both will be in the Fire, where they will live forever. That is the reward for the evil-doers.*

59:18 *Believers! Fear Allah, and let every soul be careful of what it sends on to tomorrow. Fear Allah, for Allah knows all that you do. Do not be like those who have forgotten Allah, and Allah has caused them to forget their own souls. Such people are evil-doers. The prisoners of the Fire and the heirs of the Garden are not equals; the heirs of the Garden will be alone in their victory.*

This Secret Talk Is Only the Work of Satan

58:8 *Have you not noticed those who, although they have been forbidden to talk in secret, talk privately together, plotting wickedness, hostility, and insubordination towards the Messenger? And when they see you, they greet you not as Allah greets you [Instead of "Peace be upon you" the unbelievers said, "A plague be upon you." This is a pun, since the two phrases sound almost identical in Arabic], and they say among themselves, "Why should Allah punish us for what we say?" Hell is sufficient punishment for them. They will be burned in its Fire, a wretched home.*

58:9 *Believers, when you speak privately together, do not speak with wickedness, hostility, and insubordination towards the Messenger, but rather with goodness and fear of Allah. Yes, fear Allah to whom you will all be gathered. This secret talk is only the work of Satan so that he causes the believers anguish. But he can only harm them with Allah's permission. Let the faithful put their trust in Allah.*

We Will Punish Them Twice

9:101 *Of the Arabs of the desert round about you, some are hypocrites, and of the people of Medina, some are stubborn in hypocrisy. You do not know them, Mohammed. We know them, and We will punish them twice. Then they will be given a great doom.*

9:102 *Others have acknowledged their faults; they mixed a right action with one that is wrong. Allah may turn to them in mercy, for Allah is forgiving and merciful. Take charity from their wealth [some of the Muslims who did not go on the Tabuk campaign were taxed a third of their wealth.] so that you may cleanse and purify them. Pray for them for your prayers will be a relief to them, for Allah hears and knows. Do they not know that Allah accepts repentance from His servants, that He accepts offerings, and that Allah is constant and merciful?*

9:105 *Say: Work so Allah can behold your work and so will His Messenger and the faithful. You will be brought before Him who knows the seen and the unseen. He will tell you the truth of all your works. Others await the decision of Allah, whether He will punish them, or whether He will forgive them, but Allah is knowing, wise.*

Allah Will Turn Their Hearts Away

9:124 *Whenever a sura [chapter] is sent down, there are some of them who say, "Whose faith has it increased?" It will increase the faith of those who believe, and they will rejoice.*
9:125 *But as for those in whose hearts is a disease, it will add doubt to their doubt, and they shall die unbelievers. Do they not see that they are tested once or twice every year? Yet they do not turn in repentance nor are they warned. Whenever a sura is revealed, they look at one another and say, "Does anyone see you?" Then they turn aside. Allah will turn their hearts away because they are a people who do not understand.*
9:128 *Now a Messenger has come to you from among yourselves. He is full of concern for you that you will fall into distress. He is compassionate and merciful to the faithful. If they turn away say, "Allah is sufficient for me. There is no god but Allah, and in Him I put my trust. He is the Lord of the glorious throne."*

THE JEWS

CHAPTER 9

9:63 Do they not know that whoever opposes Allah and His Messenger will abide in the Fire of Hell, where they will remain forever? This is the great shame.

When Mohammed came to Medina about half the town were Jews. There were three tribes of Jews and two tribes of Arabs. Almost none of the Jews had Hebrew names. They were Arabs to some degree. At the same time many of the Arabs' religious practice had elements of Judaism. The Jews were farmers and tradesmen and lived in their own fortified quarters. In general they were better educated and more prosperous than the Arabs.

Before Mohammed arrived, there had been bad blood and killing among the tribes. The last battle had been fought by the two Arab tribes, but each of the Jewish tribes had joined the battle with their particular Arab allies. In addition to that tension between the two Arab tribes, there was a tension between the Jews and the Arabs. The division of the Jews and fighting on different sides was condemned by Mohammed. The Torah preached that the Jews should be unified, and they failed in this.

All of these quarrelsome tribal relationships were one reason that Mohammed was invited to Medina. But the result was further polarization, not unity. The new split was between Islam and those Arabs and their Jewish partners who resisted Islam.

I351 About this time, the leaders of the Jews spoke out against Mohammed. The rabbis began to ask him difficult questions. Doubts and questions about his doctrine were about Allah. Doubts about Allah were evil. However, two of the Jewish Arabs joined with Mohammed as Muslims. They believed him when he said that he was the Jewish prophet that came to fulfill the Torah.

THE REAL TORAH IS IN THE KORAN

Mohammed said repeatedly that the Jews and Christians corrupted their sacred texts in order to conceal the fact that he was prophesied in their scriptures. The stories in the Koran are similar to those of the Jew's scriptures, but they make different points. In the Koran, all of the stories found in Jewish scripture indicated that Allah destroyed those cultures that did not listen to their messengers. According to Mohammed, the scriptures of the Jews have been changed to hide the fact that Islam is the true religion.

I364 But the Jews did not believe that Mohammed was a prophet. As a result, they are in error and cursed by Allah. And by denying his prophethood they conspired against him and Islam.

I367 Mohammed is the final prophet. His coming was in the original Torah. Allah has blessed the Jews and protected them and now they refuse to believe the final and ideal prophet. The Jews are not ignorant, but deceitful. The Jews know the truth of Mohammed and cover the truth and hide the truth with lies.

> 2:40 ***Children of Israel! Remember the favor I have given you, and keep your covenant with Me. I will keep My covenant with you. Fear My power. Believe in what I reveal [the Koran], which confirms your Scriptures, and do not be the first to disbelieve it. Do not part with My revelations for a petty price. Fear Me alone. Do not mix up the truth with lies or knowingly hide the truth [Mohammed said the Jews hid their scriptures that foretold Mohammed would be the final prophet]. Be committed to your prayers, give to charity regularly, and bow down with those who bow down. Would you instruct others to be righteous and forget to attend to your own duties? You read the Scriptures! Do you not have sense? Seek guidance with patience and prayer; this is indeed a hard duty, but not for the humble who remember that they will have to meet their Lord and will return to Him.***

> 2:6 ***As for the unbelievers, whether you warn them or not, they will not believe. Their hearts and ears are sealed up by Allah, and their eyes are covered as well. There will be a dreadful doom awaiting them.***

I367 The Koran repeats the many favors that Allah has done for the Jews—they were the chosen people, delivered from slavery under the pharaoh, given the sacred Torah and all they have ever done is to sin. They have been forgiven many times by Allah, and still, they are as hard as rocks and refuse to believe Mohammed. They have perverted the Torah after understanding it.

> 2:75 ***Can you believers then hope that the Jews will believe you even though they heard the Word of Allah and purposefully altered it [Mohammed said the Jews hid their scriptures that foretold Mohammed would be the final prophet] after they understood its meaning? And when they are among the believers they say, "We believe too," but when they are alone with one another they say, "Will you tell them what Allah has revealed***

to you so that they can argue with you about it in the presence of your Lord?" Do you not have any sense? Do they not realize that Allah knows what they hide as well as what they reveal?
2:78 *There are illiterate people among them who do not know the Scriptures but only lies and unclear conjectures. Wretchedness will come to those who write their own scriptures and then claim, "This is from Allah," so that they can sell it for a pitiful price. They will have a mournful fate because of what they have written and for what they have earned by their actions.*
2:80 *And they say, "The Fire will not touch us except for a few days." Say: Did you receive such a promise from Allah because Allah will not break his promise, or do you merely speak of Allah what you do not know? Surely those who do evil and become surrounded by sin will be prisoners of the Fire where they will live forever. Those who believe and do good deeds are the rightful owners of the Garden where they will live forever.*

1369 The Jews' sins are so great that Allah has changed them into apes. Still they will not learn and refuse to admit that Mohammed is their prophet. They know full well the truth and hide and confuse others. Even when they say to Mohammed they believe, they conceal their resistance.

2:63 *And remember, Children of Israel, when We made a covenant with you and raised Mount Sinai before you saying, "Hold tightly to what We have revealed to you and keep it in mind so that you may guard against evil." But then you turned away, and if it had not been for Allah's grace and mercy, you surely would have been among the lost. And you know those among you who sinned on the Sabbath. We said to them, "You will be transformed into despised apes." So we used them as a warning to their people and to the following generations, as well as a lesson for the Allah-fearing.*

They Reject What Has since Been Sent Down

2:87 *We gave Moses the Scriptures and sent other messengers after him. We gave Jesus, the son of Mary, clear signs and fortified him with the Holy Spirit [the angel Gabriel, not the Spirit of the Trinity]. So whenever a messenger is sent that does not conform to your desires, will you become insolent and either deny him or kill him?*
2:88 *They say, "Our hearts are hardened." But Allah has cursed them for their unbelief. Their faith is weak. And when the Scriptures came from Allah, confirming what they already had, they refused to believe in it, although they had long prayed for victory over the unbelievers. Therefore, Allah's curse is on those without faith! They have sold themselves for a vile price by not believing what Allah has sent down, begrudging Him the right to send it to whichever messenger He pleases. They have brought*

relentless wrath upon themselves. Disgraceful punishment awaits the unbelievers.
2:91 *When they are told, "Believe in what Allah has sent down," they say, "We believe in what was sent down to us." They reject what has since been sent down even though it is true and confirms their own scriptures. Say: Then why did you kill the messengers of Allah in the past if you are truly believers?*

I370 The Jews have understood the truth of Mohammed and then changed their scriptures to avoid admitting that Mohammed is right.

5:59 *Say: Oh, people of the Book [Jews and Christians], do you not reject us only because we believe in Allah, in what He has sent down to us, in what He has sent before us, and because most of you are wrongdoers? Say: Can I tell you of retribution worse than this that awaits them with Allah? It is for those who incurred the curse of Allah and His anger; those whom He changed into apes [Jews] and swine [Christians]; those who worship evil are in a worse place, and have gone far astray from the right path.*
5:61 *When they presented themselves to you, they said, "We believe," but they came as unbelievers to you, and as unbelievers they left. Allah well knew what they concealed. You will see many of them striving with one another to hurry sin, to exceed limits, and to eat unlawful things. What they do is evil. Why do their doctors and rabbis not forbid them from the habit of uttering wickedness and eating unlawful food? Certainly, their works are evil.*
5:64 *The Jews say, "The hand of Allah is chained up." Their own hands will be chained up [on the Last Day, the Jews will have their right hand chained to their necks], and they will be cursed for what they say. No, both His hands are outstretched. He bestows His gifts at His own pleasure. That which has been sent down to you from your Lord will surely increase the rebellion and unbelief of many of them. We have put animosity and hatred between them that will last until Resurrection Day. Every time they kindle a fire for war, Allah will extinguish it. Their aim will be to assist mischief on the earth, but Allah does not love those who assist mischief.*
5:65 *If only the people of the Scriptures [Jews and Christians] will believe and guard against evil, we will surely take their sins away from them and will bring them into Gardens of delight. If they will observe the Law and the Gospel and what was sent down to them from their Lord, they will surely be nourished from above them and from beneath their feet. Some of them are on the right course, but many of them do evil.*
5:67 *Oh, Messenger, deliver what has been sent down to you from your Lord. If you do not, you will not have delivered His message. Allah will*

protect you from evil men, for Allah does not guide unbelievers. Say: Oh, people of the Book [Jews and Christians], you have no ground to stand on until you observe the Law and the Gospel and that which was sent down to you from your Lord. The Book [the Koran] that was sent down from your Lord will certainly increase the rebellion and unbelief of many of them, but do not be grieved for the unbelievers.

5:69 *Those who believe and those who are Jews, Sabers [unknown, but perhaps a sect of Christians in Iraq], and Christians–whoever believes in Allah and in the last day–does what is right. They will have no fear, nor will they be put to grief.*

5:70 *We made the covenant of old with the Children of Israel, and We sent messengers to them. Whenever there was a messenger with news that they did not desire, they became rebellious, and some of them they treated as liars, and some they killed. They thought no harm would come of it, so they became blind and deaf. Then Allah turned to them in mercy. Then again many of them became blind and deaf, but Allah sees what they do.*

You Will Find The Jews and the Polytheists To Be the Most Passionately Hostile

5:77 *Say: Oh, people of the Book, do not step out of the bounds of truth in your religion, and do not follow the desires of those who have gone wrong and led many astray. They have themselves gone astray from the even way.*

5:78 *Those among the Children of Israel who disbelieved were cursed by the tongue of David and of Jesus, Son of Mary, because they were rebellious and persisted in excesses. They did not restrain one another from the iniquity they committed. Their actions were detestable.*

5:82 *You will find the Jews and the polytheists to be the most passionately hostile to those who believe. You will find the Christians to be the nearest in affection to those who believe. This is because they are devoted men of learning, and they are not arrogant. When they hear what has been revealed to the Messenger, you will see their eyes overflow with tears because they recognize the truth saying, "Oh, our Lord, we believe. Write us down with the witnesses. Why should we not believe in Allah and in the truth that has come down to us? Why should we not hope that our Lord will bring us into Paradise with the just?"*

5:85 *Therefore, Allah has rewarded them for their words with Gardens with rivers flowing beneath; they will abide there forever. This is the reward of the good, but they who do not believe and treat Our signs as lies will be the companions of Hellfire.*

2:174 *Those [the Jews] who conceal any part of the Scriptures which Allah has revealed in order to gain a small profit shall ingest nothing but Fire in their stomachs. Allah will not speak to them on the Day of Resurrection, and they will pay a painful penalty. They are the ones who buy error at the price of guidance and torture at the price of forgiveness; how intently they seek the Fire!*

MOHAMMED TRULY FOLLOWS THE RELIGION OF ABRAHAM

I381 Christians and Jews argued with Mohammed that if he wished to have salvation, then he would have to convert. But Mohammed is the one who truly follows the religion of Abraham. Mohammed is the true Jew with the true Torah.

> 2:135 *They say, "Become a Christian or a Jew, and you will be rightly guided to salvation." Say: No! We follow the religion of Abraham, the upright, and he was no idol worshipper. Say: We believe in Allah and in that which has been revealed to us, and to Abraham, Ishmael, Isaac, Jacob, and the tribes, and in that given to Moses and Jesus and all other messengers by our Lord. We make no distinction between any of them, and we bow down to Allah.*
> 2:137 *If they believe as you do, they will be on the right path, but if they turn against it, they are only cutting themselves off from you, and Allah will be a more than adequate defender against them. He is all-hearing and all-knowing. We take on Allah's own dye. And who has a better dye than Allah? It is Him we worship.*
> 2:139 *Say: Will you [the Jews] argue with us about Allah, knowing that He is both your Lord and ours? We are responsible for our actions as you are for yours, and we are devoted to Him alone. Will you say, "Truly Abraham, Ishmael, Isaac, Jacob, and the tribes, were all either Jews or Christians"? Say: Do you know best, or does Allah? Who is more evil than one who receives a testimony from Allah and hides it? Allah is never unaware of what you do. Those are a people who have passed away. They have received what they deserved and you will receive what you deserve. You will not be asked to answer for what they did.*

I383 Mohammed entered a Jewish school and called the Jews to Islam. One asked him, "What is your religion, Mohammed?"

"The religion of Abraham."

"But Abraham was a Jew."

"Then let the Torah judge between us." He meant the Torah of the Koran.

> 3:66 *Abraham was neither a Jew nor a Christian, but a righteous man, a Muslim, not an idol worshipper. Doubtless the ones who follow Abraham are the closest to him, along with this messenger and the believers. Allah is protector of the faithful. Some of the People of the Book try to*

lead you astray, but they only mislead themselves, although they may not realize it.

3:70 *People of the Book [Jews and Christians]! Why do you reject Allah's revelations when you have witnessed their truth? People of the Book! Why do you cover up the truth with lies when you know that you hide the truth?*

I397 Three Jews came to Mohammed and said, "Do you not allege that you follow the religion of Abraham and believe in the Torah which we have and testify that it is the truth from Allah?" He replied, "Certainly, but you have sinned and broken the covenant contained therein and concealed what you were ordered to make plain to men. I disassociate myself from your sin [the Jew's altering the part of the Torah that prophesied the coming of Ahmed (a variation of the name Mohammed)]".

I399 Jews came to Mohammed and said, "Is it true that what you have brought to us is from Allah? For our part we cannot see that it is arranged as the Torah is." He replied, "You know quite well that it is from Allah. You will find it written in the Torah which you have." By this he meant the real Torah that they concealed.

AN OMINOUS CHANGE

I381 In Mecca Mohammed spoke well of the Jews, who were very few. In Medina there were many Jews and his relations were tense. Up to now Mohammed had lead prayer in the direction of Jerusalem. Now the ***kiblah***, direction of prayer, was changed to the Kabah in Mecca. Some of the Jews came to him and asked why he had changed the direction of prayer. After all, he said that he followed the religion of Abraham. The Koran responded:

2:142 *The foolish ones will say, "What makes them turn from the kiblah [the direction they faced during Islamic prayer]?" Say: Both the east and the west belong to Allah. He will guide whom He likes to the right path. We have made you [Muslims] the best of nations so that you can be witnesses over the world and so that the messenger may be a witness for you. We appointed the former kiblah towards Jerusalem and now Mecca so that We could identify the messenger's true followers and those who would turn their backs on him. It was truly a hard test, but not for those whom Allah guided. It was not Allah's purpose that your faith should be in vain, for Allah is full of pity and merciful toward mankind. We have seen you [Mohammed] turn your face to every part of Heaven for guidance, and now We will have you turn to a kiblah that pleases you. So turn your face towards the direction of the sacred Mosque, and wherever the believers are, they will turn their faces toward it. The People of the Book know that this is the truth from their Lord, and Allah is not unaware of what they do. Even if you were to give the People of the Book [Jews] every sign, they would not accept your kiblah, nor would you accept theirs. None of them will accept the kiblah of the others. If you should follow their way after receiving the knowledge you possess, then you will certainly be a part of the unrighteous.*

2:146 *Those to whom we gave the Scriptures know Our messenger as they do their own sons [Jews who were secretly convinced of the truth of Mohammed], although some of them knowingly conceal the truth. This is the truth from your Lord; therefore, do not doubt it at all.*

2:177 *Righteousness is not determined by whether you face the east or the west. The one who is righteous believes in Allah, the Last Day, the angels, the Scripture, and the messengers; he gives his wealth for love of Allah to his family, to orphans, to the needy, to the wayfaring traveler, to the beggar, and for the ransom of slaves. The righteous one observes his prayers and pays the poor tax. The righteous one keeps his promises and stands firm in the face of suffering and hardship and war. These are the true believers, the Allah-fearing.*

I382 Mohammed summoned the Jews to Islam and made it attractive and warned them of Allah's punishment and vengeance. The Jews said that they would follow the religion of their fathers. The Koran:

2:168 *All people! Eat that which is lawful and wholesome in the earth and do not follow Satan's footsteps for he is your declared enemy. He commands you to commit evil and shameful acts and urges you say words about Allah when you know nothing. When it is said to them, "Follow what Allah has revealed," they say, "No, we follow the practices of our ancestors." What? Even though their ancestors were ignorant and without guidance? The unbelievers can be compared to animals who only respond to a shout or a cry. They are deaf, dumb, and blind, understanding nothing.*

Since Islam is the successor to Judaism, Allah was the successor to Jehovah. It was actually Allah who had been the deity of the Jews and the Jews had deliberately hidden this fact by corrupted scriptures. For this the Jews will be cursed.

2:159 *Those who conceal the clear signs and guidance [Mohammed said that the Jews corrupted the Scriptures that predicted his prophecy] that We have sent down after We have made them clear in the Scriptures for mankind, will receive Allah's curse and the curse of those who damn them. But for those who repent, change their ways, and proclaim the truth, I will relent. I am relenting and merciful. Those who reject Me and die unbelievers will receive the curse of Allah and of the angels and of mankind. They will remain under the curse forever with no lightening of their punishment and no reprieve. Your Allah is the one god. There is no god but Him. He is compassionate and merciful.*

Remember My Favor That I Gave You

2:47 *Children of Israel! Remember My favor that I gave you, lifting you up above all other nations. And fear the day when no soul will stand up for another, nor will any intervention be accepted from them nor will any ransom be taken; nor will they be helped.*

2:49 *And remember when We rescued you from Pharaoh's people? They subjected you to severe torment, killing your sons and only letting your daughters live. That was a great trial from your Lord. We parted the sea for you, saving you and drowned Pharaoh's people in front of your very eyes. And when We made a treaty with Moses for forty nights, in his absence you worshipped the calf and committed a terrible sin. Nevertheless, We forgave you so that you might be grateful.*

2:54 *And remember We gave Moses the Scripture and the ability to know right from wrong so that you would be guided to the right path. Then Moses said, "My people! You have wronged yourselves by worshipping the calf. Therefore, turn to your Creator and kill the wrong-doers among you. That will please your Creator and He will show you mercy. Surely He is relenting and merciful."*

2:55 *And when you said, "Moses! We will not believe in you until we see Allah manifest before us," a lightning bolt struck you while you looked on. We then brought you back to life so that you could have the chance to be grateful. We sent a cloud to give you shade and sent down manna and quails to you saying, "Eat of the good things We have provided for you." The Jews did Us no harm [the Jews stored up the manna and quails]; they only harmed themselves. And when We said, "Enter this city and eat from its plenty whatever you wish. Enter its gates humbly, asking forgiveness, and We will forgive your sins and reward the righteous." But the evil-doers changed the words We told them into something else, so We sent down Our wrath upon them for their sin.*

2:60 *And remember when Moses asked for water for his people We said, "Strike the rock with your staff." Then twelve fountains gushed out so that each tribe knew its drinking place. We said, "Eat and drink what Allah has provided, and do not act corrupt or cause evil on the earth." When you said, "Moses! We are tired of eating only one kind of food [manna and quails]. Ask your Lord to give us the many kinds of produce grown in the soil like herbs, cucumbers, corn, lentils, and onions." He said, "What! Would you give up that which is superior for what is inferior? Return to the city, and you will find what you want there." They were filled with shame and wretchedness. The wrath of Allah came down upon them because they rejected Allah's signs and killed his messengers without cause. That occurred because of their disobedience and sin.*

2:62 *Truly, those who believe in the Koran, along with Christians, Jews, and Sabians [perhaps the Christians of Iraq], and whoever believes in Allah and the Day and is righteous will be rewarded by their Lord. They should have no fears or regrets.*

Then Your Hearts Were Hardened like Rocks

2:67 *When Moses said to his people, "Allah has commanded that you sacrifice a cow," they said, "Are you mocking us?" Moses then said, "Allah forbid that I should become like these ignorant fools!"*

2:68 *They said, "Call on your Lord to instruct us on what kind of cow we should use." He said, "Your Lord says the cow should not be too young or too old, but in between. Do as you are commanded."*

2:69 *They said, "Call on your Lord to tell us what color she should be." He replied, "Your Lord says it should be a fawn-colored cow with a pure and rich tone that gives pleasure to those who see it."*

2:70 *They said, "Call on your Lord to tell the exact kind of cow it should be, because they all look alike to us. We wish for guidance if it is Allah's will."*

2:71 *Moses answered, "Your Lord says it should be a cow not used to plough the earth or water the field, healthy and without imperfections." They said, "Now you have told us the truth." So they sacrificed the cow, although they did not care to do it.*

2:72 *Remember when you killed a man and then fought among yourselves about it, and Allah brought to light what you tried to hide. We said, "Strike the corpse with a part of the sacrificed cow." It is in this manner that Allah shows you His signs so that you will understand. Then your hearts were hardened like rocks, or even worse, for there are some rocks from which rivers gush forth; some are split in two and water comes out of them, and others fall down from fear of Allah. Allah is not at all unaware of your actions.*

2:83 *And remember when We made a covenant with the Children of Israel saying, "Worship Allah alone. Be good to your parents, your families, to orphans, and to those in need. Encourage others to be righteous, pray regularly, and give to charity." But then you all turned your backs on the promise, except a few, and paid no attention.*

2:84 *And when We made a covenant with you We said, "You shall not shed the blood of your people or turn them out of your cities." You agreed to this and were yourselves witnesses. Then after this you began killing your people and driving them out from your homes, backing one another up against them with sin and hatred. If they had come to you as captives, you would have liberated them, even though their banishment was illegal. [Two Jewish tribes of Medina went to war against a third Jewish tribe] Do you believe in one part of the Scriptures and deny the rest? What is the reward for those of you who act in this way except disgrace in this life and cruel torment of the Day of Resurrection? For Allah is never unaware of what you do. These are the people who purchase the life of this world at the price of the life to come; their torment will not be alleviated nor will they be helped.*

Allah Is the Enemy of the Unbelievers

2:92 *Moses came to you with clear signs, but when he was away you [the Jews] worshipped the calf and were wicked. And remember when We made a covenant with you and raised the towering height of Mount Sinai above you saying, "Hold tightly to what We have given you and obey Our commandments." You replied, "We hear but we rebel." And because of your unbelief, the worship of the calf was made to sink into your hearts. Say: Your faith bids you to do evil if you are in fact believers. Say: If Allah's Paradise is only for you and no others, then wish for death if you are telling the truth!*

2:95 *But they will never wish themselves dead because they know what they have done; Allah knows the sinners. In fact, you will see they love this life more than others, more than the idol worshippers. Each would love to see a thousand years, but even if this were so, they would never be able to escape their doom; Allah sees all they do.*

2:97 *Say: Whoever is an enemy of Gabriel—he who revealed Allah's revelation to you [Mohammed] confirming previous scriptures as guidance and good news for believers—whoever is Allah's enemy and the enemy of His angels and messengers, of Gabriel or Michael, will find Allah is the enemy of the unbelievers.*

2:99 *We have sent clear signs down to you, and only the perverse will deny them. What! Is not it true that every time they make a covenant some of them break it? The majority of them are unbelievers. And when Allah sent a messenger to them, confirming the scriptures they already had, many of them flung the Scripture of Allah behind their backs as if they knew nothing!*

2:104 *Listen, believers! Do not say to the messenger, "Raina," ['Listen to us'] but say: "Unsurna," ['Regard us respectfully']. [This was a pun used by the Jews of Medina. 'Raina' conveys a sense of 'Our Evil One'] Take notice; painful punishment awaits the unbelievers. Those who disbelieve among the People of the Book [Jews and Christians] and the pagans wish that no good should be sent down to you from your Lord; but Allah will choose whom He pleases to receive His mercy. Allah is boundless in His grace.*

A Donkey Who Is Made to Carry a Load of Books

62:5 *Those to whom the Torah [the first five books of the Old Testament] was given and do not follow it can be compared to a donkey who is made to carry a load of books but is unable to understand them. Those who reject Allah's revelations are a sorry example. Allah does not guide those who do wrong.*

62:6 *Say: You Jews! If you believe that you are Allah's favorite people, set apart, then wish that you will die if you are telling the truth! But they will never wish to die because of their previous actions that have been sent on before them. Allah knows the evil-doers.*

62:8 *Say: The death from which you flee will certainly find you, and then you will return to the knower of things done in secret and in the open, and He will tell you everything you have ever done.*

Those Who Invent Lies about Allah after This Are Surely Evil-Doers

3:93 *All food was permissible for the Children of Israel, except that which Israel itself forbade, before the Law was sent down. Say: Bring the Law and read it if what you say is true. Those who invent lies about Allah after this are surely evil-doers. Say: Allah speaks the truth. Therefore, follow the religion of Abraham, the righteous. He was not one of the idolaters.*

3:96 *The first house of worship ever built for mankind was at Mecca, a sacred site, a guiding light for all the nations. In it are clear signs and the place where Abraham prayed; whoever enters there is safe. Pilgrimage to the House is a duty to Allah for everyone who is able to make the trip. And as for the unbelievers, certainly Allah has no need for them.*

3:98 *Say: People of the Book! Why do you reject Allah's revelations? Allah sees all that you do. Say: People of the Book! Why do you deter believers from Allah's path seeking to make it crooked when you yourselves were witnesses to Allah's covenant? Allah is never unaware of what you do.*

3:99 *Believers! If you were to listen to some of the People of the Book, they would make you unbelievers after you have already believed! But how could you deny the faith when Allah's clear signs are given to you and the messenger is there among you? Those who hold firmly to Allah will be shown the right path.*

They Threw Them behind Their Backs and Sold Them for a Meager Price

3:181 *Allah has heard those who have said, "Truly Allah is poor and we are rich." [The Jews of Medina said this when asked for money by Mohammed.] We will certainly record their words as well as their unjust murders of the messengers. We will say to them, "Now taste the torment of the Fire. This is what you get for the wrong that you have done. Allah will never treat His servant unjustly."*

3:183 *To those [the Jews] who say, "Truly, Allah has commanded that we are not to believe a messenger until he presents a sacrifice and it is consumed by Fire from heaven," say: messengers came before me with clear signs and even performed the very miracle you describe. Why then did you [the Jews] kill them if what you say is true? If they treat you like a liar, then surely messengers before you have been treated as such even though they came with clear signs, with Psalms, and with the illuminating Scriptures.*

3:185 *Every soul will taste death, and you will only receive your rewards on the Day of Resurrection. Whoever escapes the Fire and is led into Paradise will have attained the ultimate goal for the life of this world is but a vain comfort.*

3:186 *You will undoubtedly be tested concerning your wealth and your soul, and you will certainly hear things that will try you from those who received the Scriptures before you and from the idolaters. But if you stand firm and fear Allah, this is all that is necessary for your life's affairs.*

3:187 *When Allah entered into a covenant with those to whom the Scripture had been given He said, "Make these Scriptures known to mankind and do not hide them," but they threw them behind their backs and sold them for a meager price! [Mohammed said that the original Torah predicted his coming. The Jews corrupted their scriptures to conceal his prophecy.] Their exchange was evil. Do not think that those who exult in their sins and love to be praised for what they have not done will escape their punishment. A painful punishment is waiting for them.*

We Destroy Your Faces and Twist Your Heads around Backwards

4:44 *Have you not thought about those [Jews] to whom a part of the Scripture was given? They buy error for themselves and wish to see you go astray from the right path. But Allah knows your enemies best. Allah is sufficient as your protector, and Allah is sufficient as your helper. Some among the Jews take words out of the context of the Scriptures and say, "We have heard, and we disobey. We hear as one who does not hear. Look at us!" in this way twisting the phrase and defiling the faith. But if they said, "We hear and obey. Hear us and look at us!" it would be better for them and more righteous. But Allah has cursed them for their disbelief; only a few of them have faith!*

4:47 *To those of you [Jews and Christians] to whom the Scriptures were given: Believe in what We have sent down confirming the Scriptures you already possess before We destroy your faces and twist your heads around backwards, or curse you as We did those [the Jews] who broke the Sabbath for Allah's commandments will be carried out.*

They Consumed Other's Wealth by Cheating

4:153 ***The People of the Book [Jews] demand that you cause a book to be sent down to them from heaven, but they demanded a harder thing from Moses. They said to him, "Show Allah to us plainly." And they were killed by a bolt of lightening for their wicked presumption. They worshipped the calf after they had received clear signs, but We forgave them of that and gave Moses indisputable authority.***

4:154 ***And We lifted Mount Sinai over them when We made the covenant with them and said, "Enter the gates in humility, and do not break the Sabbath," and We received their solemn vow. But they broke the covenant, rejected Allah's signs, and unjustly killed the messengers, and they said, "Our hearts are hardened." It is Allah who has hardened their hearts because of their disbelief, so only a few are believers.***

4:156 ***They rejected the faith and have spoken slanderously of Mary. They said, "We killed the Messiah, Jesus the son of Mary, Allah's messenger." But they did not kill him or crucify him, although it appeared so to them [the person crucified was not Jesus, but someone else]. And those who argued about it were in doubt concerning him. They had no clear knowledge about him and only went with opinion. They did not really kill him, but Allah lifted him up to Himself. Allah is mighty and wise!***

4:160 ***Because of the wickedness of certain Jews, and because they turn many away from Allah's path, We have made certain wholesome foods unlawful for them because time and again they have hindered people from Allah's path. They have taken usury, even though they were forbidden to do so, and they consumed other's wealth by cheating. We have prepared painful torment for the unbelievers. But the learned among them, and those who deeply believe in what has been sent down to you and in what was sent down before you, and those who attend their prayers, and pay the poor tax, and believe in Allah and the Last Day, these will be given a great reward.***

4:163 ***We have sent Our signs to you as We did to Noah and the messengers who came after him, and as We sent signs to Abraham, Ishmael, Isaac, Jacob and the tribes, and to Jesus, Job, Jonah, Aaron, and Solomon, and to David, to whom We gave the Psalms. Some of the messengers We have told you about before, but there are also some about whom We have not yet spoken, and Allah spoke directly to Moses. We sent messengers who brought good news as well as warnings so that after the coming of these messengers, mankind would have no excuse against Allah. Allah is mighty and wise! And Allah is His own witness that what He has sent down to you is His own knowledge, as are the angels. But Allah is a sufficient witness!***

4:167 ***Those who do not believe and who lead others away from Allah's path have certainly strayed very far from the path themselves. Allah will*** *not forgive the unbelievers and those who do wrong, nor will He forgive them or guide them to any path except the path to Hell, where they will live forever. And that is easy for Allah. People! The Messenger has come to you with truth from your Lord. If you believe, it will be better for you. But if you do not believe, know that all that is in the heavens and earth belongs to Allah. Allah is all-knowing and wise!*

With Whom Allah Is Angry

58:14 *Have you not taken notice of those who befriend the people with whom Allah is angry? They are neither a part of your group or theirs, and they knowingly swear a lie. Allah has prepared a dreadful punishment for them, for their actions are evil. A humiliating punishment awaits those [Jews who pretend to be Muslims] who use their faith as a disguise and turn others away from Allah's path. Neither their wealth or their children will protect them from Allah. They will be prisoners of the Fire, where they will live forever.*

58:18 *On the day Allah will raise them all to life, they will swear to Him as they swear to you now, thinking that their words will help them. Are they not the liars? Satan has possessed them and caused them to forget their praise of Allah. They are of Satan's company. Truly, will it not be Satan's company who will be the losers? Those who oppose Allah and His Messenger will be laid low. Allah has declared, "Surely I will be victorious, along with My messengers." Truly Allah is strong and mighty.*

58:22 *You will find no one who is a believer in Allah and the Last Day loving those who oppose Allah and His Messenger, even if it is their fathers, sons, brothers, or closest relations. Allah has engraved the faith on their hearts and with His own spirit He has strengthened them. He will lead them into the Gardens beneath which rivers flow, to live forever. Allah is very pleased with them, as they are with Him. This is Allah's company. And truly, will it not be Allah's company who will be victorious?*

THE CHRISTIANS

CHAPTER 10

33:21 You have an excellent example in Allah's Messenger for those of you who put your hope in Allah and the Last Day and who praise Allah continually.

1404 While some Christians were in Medina, they argued religion with Mohammed. They held forth with the doctrine of the Trinity and the divinity of Christ. Mohammed later laid out the Islamic doctrine of the Christian doctrine. The Koran tells in detail the real story of Jesus, who is just another of Allah's prophets, and that the Trinity of the Christians is Allah, Jesus and Mary.

1406 No one has power except through Allah. Allah gave the prophet Jesus the power of raising the dead, healing the sick, making birds of clay and having them fly away. Allah gave Jesus these signs as a mark of his being a prophet. But Allah did not give the powers of appointing kings, the ability to change night to day. These lacks of power show that Jesus was a man, not part of a Trinity. If he were part of God, then all powers would have been in his command. Then he would not have to have been under the dominion of kings.

> 3:20 ***If they argue with you, then say: I have surrendered myself entirely to Allah, as have my followers. Say to the People of the Book and to the ignorant: "Do you surrender to Allah?" If they become Muslims, then they will be guided to the right path, but if they reject it, then your job is only to warn them. Allah watches over all His servants.***
> 3:21 ***Warn those who do not believe in Allah's revelations, and who unjustly kill the messengers and those who teach justice, of the excruciating punishment they will receive. Their works will be meaningless in this world and in the world to come, and they will have no one to help them!***
> 3:23 ***Consider those who have received part of the Scriptures. When they are called to accept the Book of Allah, some of them turn away and are opposed to it. This is because they say, "We will only have to endure the Fire for a few days." They have created their own lies regarding their religion. How will they react when We gather them together on the assured day, and every soul will receive what it has earned, and they will not be dealt with unjustly?***

> 3:26 *Say: Allah! Lord of heaven and earth, you give power to whom you choose and take it away from whom you chose. You lift up whom you choose, and You bring down whom you choose. All that is good lies within your hand. You have power to do all things. You cause the night to turn into day, and the day to turn into night. You bring the living out of the dead, and the dead out of the living, and You give generously to whom you please.*

1407-8 Christ spoke in the cradle and then spoke to men as a grown man. Speaking from the cradle is a sign of his being a prophet. Christ's prophethood was confirmed by making clay birds fly. By Allah Christ healed the blind, the lepers, and raised the dead.

> 5:109 *One day Allah will assemble the messengers and say, "What response did you receive from mankind?" They will say, "We have no knowledge. You are the knower of secrets." Then Allah will say, "Oh Jesus, Son of Mary, remember my favor to you and your mother when I strengthened you with the Holy Spirit [Gabriel] so that you would speak to men alike in childhood and when grown. I taught you the Scripture, wisdom, the Torah, and the Gospel, and you created the figure of a bird with clay, by my permission, and breathed into it. With My permission it became a bird. You also healed the blind and the leper, with My permission. With My permission you raised the dead. I restrained the Children of Israel from harming you when you went to them with clear signs, and the unbelievers said, "This is nothing but plain sorcery."*
> 5:111 *When I revealed to the disciples, "Believe in Me and the One I sent," they said, "We believe and bear witness to You that we are Muslims."*

1408 Christ only comes through Allah. Christ's signs of being a prophet come only from Allah. Jesus enjoins others to worship Allah, not him. But people refused to hear him, the Disciples came forth to help him with his mission. The Disciples were servants of Allah and were Muslims just like Christ.

> 3:44 *This is one of the secret revelations revealed to you, Mohammed. You were not there when they cast their lots to see who would have guardianship of Mary, nor were you there when they argued about her. And remember when the angels said to Mary, "Allah brings you good news of His Word. His name will be Messiah, Jesus, Son of Mary, worthy of honor in this world and the world to come, one who is near to Allah. He will speak to the people when in the cradle and as a man. He will live a righteous life." She said, "My Lord! How can I have a son when no man has ever touched me?" He said, "It will be so. Allah creates what He will, and when He decrees a plan, all He must do is say, 'Be' and it is!" Allah will teach him the Scriptures and Wisdom, the Law, and the Gospel. He*

will be sent out as a messenger to the Children of Israel saying, "I have come to you with a sign from your Lord. I will make a figure of a bird out of clay and then, by Allah's will, I will breathe life into it. By Allah's permission I cause the blind to see, heal the lepers, and bring the dead back to life. I will tell you what you should eat and what you should store up in your houses. This will be a sign for those who truly believe. I have come to fulfill the Law which came before me and to give you permission to do certain things which were once unlawful. I come to you with a sign from your Lord, so fear Allah and obey me. Allah is my Lord and yours, so worship Him. That is the right path."

3:52 *When Jesus saw that they did not believe, he said, "Who will be my helpers for Allah?" The disciples replied, "We will be Allah's helpers! We believe in Allah and witness our submission to Him. Lord! We believe in what you have revealed and we follow Your messenger; therefore, record us as Your witnesses."*

I409 Christ was not crucified. When the Jews plotted against Christ, they found Allah to be the best plotter. Allah took Jesus up directly to him and will refute those who say he was crucified and was resurrected. On the final day, the Day of Resurrection, those who follow Christ but do not believe in his divinity will be blessed. Those who insist that Christ is God, part of the Trinity, and reject true faith will be punished in Hell.

3:54 *So the Jews plotted and Allah plotted, but Allah is the best of plotters. And Allah said, "Jesus! I am going to end your life on earth and lift you up to Me. [Jesus did not die on the cross. He was taken to Allah. He will return to kill the anti-Christ and then die a natural death.] I will send the unbelievers away from you and lift up those who believe above all others until the Day of Resurrection. Then all will return to Me and I will judge their disputes. As for the unbelievers, they will be punished with excruciating agony in this world and the world to come. They will have no one to help them. As for the believers who do good works, He will fully reward them. Allah does not love those who do wrong. These signs and this wise warning We bring to you."*

3:59 *Truly, Jesus is like Adam [neither had a father] in Allah's sight. He created him from the dust and said to him, "Be!" and he was.*

Although the Koran says less about Christians than Jews, it does address them.

The Messiah, Jesus, The Son of Mary, Is Only Allah's Messenger

4:171 *People of the Book [Christians]! Do not overstep the boundaries of your religion and speak only what is true about Allah. The Messiah, Jesus, the son of Mary, is only Allah's messenger and his Word which he sent into Mary was a spirit from Him. Therefore, believe in Allah and His messengers and do not say, "Trinity." Hold back and it will be better for you. Allah is only one god. Far be it from Allah to have a son! All in the heavens and earth are His. Allah is the sufficient as a protector. The Messiah does not condescend to be Allah's servant, nor do His favored angels. Those who disdain service to Him, and are filled with arrogance, Allah will gather them all together before Him.*

61:6 *And remember when Jesus, son of Mary, said, "Children of Israel! I am Allah's messenger sent to confirm the Law which was already revealed to you and to bring good news of a messenger who will come after me whose name will be Ahmad." [Ahmad was one of Mohammed's names. This quote of Jesus is not found in any Christian scriptures.] Yet when he [Mohammed] came to them with clear signs, they said, "This is merely sorcery!" And who is more evil than the one who, when called to submit to Islam, makes up a lie about Allah? Allah does not guide the evil-doers! They wish to put out Allah's light with their mouths, but as much as the unbelievers hate it, Allah will perfect His light.*
61:9 *It is He who has sent forth His messenger with guidance and the true religion so that, though the idolaters hate it, He will make His religion victorious over all the others.*

We Gave the Revelations Found in the Gospels

57:26 *And We sent Noah and Abraham and placed messengers among their descendents and gave them the Scriptures. Some of them followed the right path, but many were evil-doers. After them we sent other messengers, and after them came Jesus, son of Mary. To him We gave the revelations found in the Gospels and placed compassion and mercy in his followers' hearts. But as for the monastic lifestyle, that was their idea. The only command We gave them was to please Allah, but they failed in this. We only gave the true believers their reward for many of them were corrupt.*
57:28 *Believers! Fear Allah and trust in His messenger. He will give you a double portion of His mercy and will give you a light in which to walk. He will forgive you, for Allah is forgiving and merciful*
57:29 *The People of the Book [Jews and Christians] must realize that they have no say in Allah's grace [as to who is a prophet]. The gift of grace lies in His hands alone, and He gives it to whom He pleases, for Allah is full of boundless grace.*

Let the People of the Gospel Judge According to What Allah Has Sent Down

5:46 *We caused Jesus, the son of Mary, to follow in the footsteps of the messengers, confirming what was revealed in the Torah. We gave him the*

Gospel, with its guidance and light, confirming what was revealed in the Torah, a guidance and warning to those who fear Allah.
5:47 *Let the people of the Gospel judge according to what Allah has sent down to them, and whoever will not judge by what Allah has sent down, they are evildoers. We sent down the Book of the Koran with truth confirming the previous Scriptures and guarding it in safety. Judge between them by what Allah has sent down, and do not follow their desires away from the truth which has come to you. For every one of you, We appointed a law and a way. If Allah had pleased, He would have made you a single nation, but His plan is to test you by what He has given to each. So strive, as if in a race, to do good deeds. To Allah you will all return, and He will let you know the subjects of your disputes.*

Unlike Any I Have Inflicted on Any Other Creature

5:112 *Remember when the disciples said, "Oh Jesus, Son of Mary, is your Lord able to send down a table to us spread with food from heaven?" He said, "Fear Allah if you are believers." They said, "We desire to eat from it, to satisfy hearts, to know that you have spoken the truth to us, and to be witnesses to the miracle." Jesus, Son of Mary, said, "Oh Allah, our Lord, send down a table spread with food from heaven that it will become a recurring festival from the first of us and to the last of us, and a sign from You, and do nourish us, for You are the best provider." Allah said, "I will send it down to you, but whoever among you disbelieves after that, I will surely inflict a punishment on him unlike any I have inflicted on any other creature."*
5:116 *And when Allah says, "Oh Jesus, Son of Mary, did you say to mankind, 'Take me and my mother as two gods, beside Allah?'" He will say, "Glory be unto You. It is not for me to say what I had no right to say. If I had said that, You would have known it. You know what is in my heart. I do not know what is in Your heart. You know all that is hidden." "I only said what You commanded me to say, 'Worship Allah, my Lord and your Lord,' and I was a witness of their actions while I was among them. When You caused me to die, You watched them, and You are witness of all things. If You punish them, they are Your servants, and if You forgive them, You are mighty and wise."*
5:119 *Allah will say, "This day the truth will profit the truthful. They will have Gardens beneath which the rivers flow, and they will remain there forever." Allah is well-pleased with them and they with Him. This shall be the great bliss. Allah's is the sovereignty of the heavens and of the earth and of all that they contain. He is able to do all things.*

The Koran often uses the term People of the Book. At the time of Mohammed there were no books in Arabic. The written Arabic was used mostly for business. Since both Christianity and Judaism used religious texts this was distinctive. The term People of the Book can refer to either Jews, Christians, or both Jews and Christians. While in Medina Mohammed spoke of Allah's problems with the People of the Book.

The Jews and Christians Will Never Be Satisfied

2:109 *Many of the People of the Book wish to turn you back into unbelievers because of their jealousy, even after they have clearly seen the truth. Forgive them and endure them until Allah shows His will to you. Truly Allah has power over all things. Attend to your prayers and pay the zakat [the poor tax]. You will be rewarded by Allah for whatever good you do. Allah sees all you do.*

2:111 *And they say, "Only Jews and Christians will enter Paradise." Those are their vain wishes. Say: Show your proof if you are telling the truth. But those who submit to Allah and do good deeds will be rewarded by their Lord. They will have nothing to dread or regret. The Jews say the Christians are wrong, and the Christians say the Jews are wrong, although they both read the Scriptures. The ignorant say they are both wrong. On the Day of Resurrection Allah will judge their disagreements.*

2:114 *Who is more evil than the people who wish to destroy Allah's mosques and forbid that His name be spoken in them [the Meccans prohibited the Muslim entry into the Kabah]? They should instead be entering into them with fear. They will meet with shame in this world and an awful torment in the world to come. The east and the west belong to Allah; therefore, wherever you go Allah is there. He is omniscient and all-knowing.*

2:116 *They say, "Allah has produced a son." All glory is to Him! All in the heavens and earth belong to Him, and will obey Him, the one and only creator of the heavens and earth. When He makes a decree, He only has to say to it, "Be!" and it is. And the ignorant ask, "Why does Allah not speak to us or give us some sign?" The same question was asked by those who came before them, and their hearts are the same. Certainly we have made the signs clear for those who have unshakable faith.*

2:119 *We have sent you to bring the truth and to warn the people. You will not have to answer for the prisoners of Hell. The Jews and Christians will never be satisfied with you unless you follow their religion. Say: Allah's guidance is the only true guidance. If you were to follow their wishes, despite your knowledge, there would be no one to help you or shield you from Allah's wrath. Those to whom we have given these Scriptures, and read them as they should be read, truly believe in what they say. Those who do not believe what they say will certainly meet with eternal damnation.*

2:122 *Children of Israel! Remember the favor that I have done for you and that I lifted you up above all other nations. Dread the day when no soul will stand for another, ransom will be taken from no soul, no intervention will be of any use to it, and the soul will be given no help.*

To Jesus, Son of Mary, We Gave Clear Signs

2:252 *These are Allah's signs, which we tell you in truth, as you are one of the messengers. Of these messengers We have raised some up above others. To some Allah has spoken directly, and others he has raised to a high status. To Jesus, son of Mary, We gave clear signs and the strength of the Holy Spirit [the angel Gabriel]. If it was Allah's will, those who came after him would not have fought with each other after receiving clear signs, but they chose to argue. So some believed and some disbelieved, and if Allah had willed it they would not have fought with each other, but Allah is doing what He intended.*

5:18 *The Jews and Christians say, "We are sons of Allah and his beloved." Say: Then why does He punish you for your sins? No, you are only a part of the men He has created. He forgives whom He pleases and chastises whom He pleases, and with Allah is the sovereignty of the heavens and of the earth and of all that is between them. All things return to Him.*
5:19 *Oh, people of the Scriptures [Jews and Christians], Our Messenger has been sent to you again to clear up the reason for the break in His messengers [The reason there have been no prophets since Jesus, six hundred years] for fear you will say, "We have had no bearer of good tidings, nor any warner." So now a bearer of good tidings and a warner has reached you. Allah is almighty.*

As Soon as Their Skins Are Burnt Away

4:53 *Should those who would fail to give even a penny to their fellow man have a share in the kingdom? Do they envy the people for what they have received from Allah's bounty? We gave the Scriptures and wisdom to the children of Abraham, and a grand kingdom. Some of them believe in His Messenger while others turn away from him. The flames of Hell are sufficient punishment for them! Those who reject Our revelations We will cast into the Fire. As soon as their skins are burnt away, We will give them new skins so that they will truly experience the torment. Truly Allah is mighty and wise!*
4:57 *But as for those who believe and do good works, We will lead them into the Gardens, watered by flowing rivers, where they will live forever; there they will be married to pure spouses, and We will lead them into the cool shade.*

3:64 *Say: People of the Book [Christians and Jews]! Let us settle upon an agreement: We will worship no one except Allah, we will set up no one as His equal, and none of us will take one from among us as a lord besides Allah. If they reject your proposal say, "Bear witness then that we are Muslims."*
3:65 *People of the Book! Why do you argue about Abraham [whether Abraham was a Jew or Christian] when the Law and the Gospel were*

not sent down until after him? Do you not understand? Listen, you are the ones who have argued about things of which you have some knowledge [arguments about Moses and Jesus], so then why do you argue about things of which you have no knowledge? Allah has knowledge, but you do not.

Either by Choice or by Force

3:72 *Some of the People of the Book say to each other, "Believe in what has been sent down to the believers in the morning. Then at the end of the day, deny it so they themselves might turn away from their religion." Believe in no one unless he is a follower of your religion. Say: Allah's guidance is the only true guidance! Do not believe that anyone will receive a revelation like that which was sent to you or think that they will ever argue with you in the presence of your Lord. Say: Surely grace is given by the hand of Allah. He gives it to whom He pleases. Allah is generous and wise. Allah specially selects to bestow His mercy on whom He chooses. Allah is the Lord of boundless grace.*

3:75 *Among the People of the Book [Jews and Christians] are some whom you can trust with a pile of gold, and they will pay it all back, but there are others among them who cannot be trusted with a single silver coin, for they will not pay it back unless you firmly demand it. This is because they say, "We are not bound to keep our word to the ignorant pagans," and they knowingly tells lies about Allah. But those who are true to the faith and guard against evil, surely Allah loves those who fear Him.*

3:77 *Those who sell their covenant with Allah and their oaths for a meager price will have no part in the world to come. Allah will not deign to speak to them or even glance in their direction on the Day of Resurrection, nor will He forgive them. They will have a painful end. And there are some of them who distort their words when quoting Scripture so you will think what they say is truly from the Scriptures, but what they say is not found in the Scriptures at all. They claim, "This is from Allah," when it is not from Him, and they consciously speak lies against Allah.*

3:79 *It is not possible that any human to whom Allah has given the Scriptures and wisdom and a position as His messenger should say, "Worship me rather than Allah." Instead he should say, "Be faithful servants of Allah for you have educated others in the Scriptures and have studied them intensely." Allah would not command you to worship the angels and messengers as your gods. Why would He encourage you to become unbelievers after you have already become Muslims? When Allah made a covenant with the messengers He said, "I give you the Scriptures and wisdom, and later a messenger will come to you who will confirm what you have been given. Believe in him and help him. Do you agree and accept the terms of My covenant with you?" They said, "We agree." And He said, "Then all of you be witnesses to this, as will I." If anyone turns back after promising this, they are perverse sinners. Do they look for a religion other than that of Allah when every creature in the heavens and in the earth have shown submission to Him, either by choice or by force? And all will return to Him.*

OTHER RELIGIONS

CHAPTER 11

4:69 Those who obey Allah and His Messenger will live with the messengers and the saints and the martyrs and the righteous. What wonderful company!

The Koran condemns all religions that were not Islam.

2:21 *People! Serve your Lord, who has made you and those who came before you, so that you can defend yourselves against evil. Your Lord has made the earth your resting-place and the sky your covering and has sent down rain to nourish the fruits that you eat. Therefore, do not deliberately worship gods other than Allah.*
2:23 *If you doubt what We have revealed to Our slave [Mohammed], then write a sura comparable to it and call your gods other than Allah to help you if what you say is true. But if you fail, and you certainly will, then fear the fire prepared for the unbelievers, which is fueled by people and stones [ritual objects of the old Arabian religions].*
2:25 *Give the good news to those who believe and do good works. They will live in gardens with flowing rivers [Paradise], and when fed fruits from there, they will say, "This is what we ate before," and they will be given fruit just like it. They will live there forever, married to chaste spouses.*
2:26 *Allah is not ashamed to compare a gnat with a larger creature. Those who believe know it is the truth from their Lord, but the unbelievers ask, "What does Allah mean by making such a comparison?" By this He causes many to stray while He also guides many by it, but he only causes the evil-doers to go astray. The losers break Allah's covenant after accepting it and tear apart what He has put together and bring about corruption on the earth.*
2:28 *How can you not believe in Allah when you were dead and He gave you life? He can cause you to die and then bring you back to life, and again you will return to Him. It is He who created all that is on the earth for you, and then he turned to the heaven and made them seven heavens. He is all-knowing.*

They Will Never Come Out of the Fire

2:164 *Surely in the creation of the heavens and the earth; in the changing from day to night; in the ships that navigate the waters with useful cargo; in the rain which Allah sends down from the skies and revives the*

dead earth, spreading life to all its creatures; and in the changing of the winds and clouds driven between the heaven and earth there are clear signs here for those who understand them.
2:165 *And yet there are some who worship idols giving them the love that is due Allah. But those who believe have a stronger love for Allah. If only the evil-doers had known that they will see their doom, that all power belongs to Allah, and that He is severe in His punishment. On the day when the leaders [those opposing Mohammed] renounce their followers and face their punishment, all their bonds will be broken.*
2:167 *The followers will say, "If we only had one last chance, we would renounce them as they have renounced us." In that way Allah will show them their regrettable actions, and they will never come out of the Fire.*

5:36 *As to the unbelievers, if they had twice the riches of the earth to be their ransom from torment on the Resurrection Day, it would not be accepted from them. Theirs would be a grievous penalty. Their wish would be to get out of the Fire, but they will never get out. A lasting doom will be theirs.*

Those Who Worship Gods other than Allah Have Strayed into Grievous Error

4:116 *Allah will not forgive those who worship idols, but He will forgive those He pleases for all other sins. Those who worship gods other than Allah have strayed into grievous error. Rather than calling on Him, they call upon female gods, and they pray to nothing but Satan, the rebel. Allah has cursed Satan because he said, "I will tempt a number of your servants and lead them astray and will arouse vain desires in them and command them to slit the ears of the cattle [a religious ritual for sacrificial animals]. I will command them to spoil Allah's creation [tattoos, scarification, piercing, etc.]." Whoever chooses Satan as a protector rather than Allah is ruined and beyond forgiveness.*
4:120 *Satan makes promises and stirs up vain desires within them, but he makes promises only to trick them. These will make their home in Hell, and they will not be able to escape it.*
4:122 *But those who believe and do good works, We will lead them into the Gardens beneath which rivers flow, where they will live forever. This is Allah's promise, and whose words hold more truth than His? This will not be according to your desires, nor to the desires of the People of the Book [Jews and Christians]. Those who do evil will be paid back with evil and will find no one but Allah to protect or help them. As for the believers who do good works, whether man or woman, they will enter Paradise, and they will not be treated unjustly in the least.*
4:125 *And whose religion is better than those who submit themselves to Allah, do good, and follow the faith of Abraham, the righteous? For Allah*

Himself took Abraham as a friend. All that is in the heavens and earth belongs to Allah; Allah surrounds all things.

The unbelievers, the Christians, Jews and pagans will burn forever in the fire of Hell.

98:1 *The unbelievers among the People of the Book [Jews and Christians] and the idolaters did not turn away from their unbelief until the proof came to them in a messenger from Allah reading holy pages containing true scriptures. The People of the Book did not become divided until after the clear proof had come to them.*
98:5 *And they were commanded nothing more than to serve Allah, worshipping none other than Him, being pure in their faith, being steadfast in their prayers, and paying the zakat [the poor tax]. For this is the true religion.*
98:6 *The unbelievers among the People of the Book and the idolaters will burn for eternity in the Fire of Hell. Of all the created beings, they are the most despicable. As for those who believe and do good works, they are the most noble of all created beings.*
98:8 *Their reward is with their Lord, in the Gardens of Paradise, beneath which are flowing rivers. They will live forever. Allah takes pleasure in them, and they take pleasure in Him. In this way those who fear Allah will be rewarded.*

The Lowest of Creatures in Allah's Sight

8:52 *They are like Pharaoh's people and the ones before them who treated their Lord's revelations as lies. Therefore, Allah will punish them for their sins. Allah is strong and severe in His vengeance. Allah will never change the blessings He has given a people until they change what is in their own hearts. Allah is all-hearing, all-knowing.*
8:54 *In the same way as the Pharaoh's people and those before them, they denied their Lord's revelations. Therefore, We destroyed them for their sins, and We drowned Pharaoh's people for they were all evil-doers. The lowest of creatures in Allah's sight are those who deny Him, those who repetitively break their treaties and do not fear Allah. If you capture them in war, separate the leaders from the followers so that the followers may be warned.*

Their Religion Will Never Be Accepted from Them

3:84 *Say: We believe in Allah and in what has been sent down to us; and in what has been sent down to Abraham, and Ishmael, to Isaac and Jacob and the tribes; and in the Scriptures given to Moses, Jesus, and the messengers from their Lord. We make no distinction among them, and to Him we submit as Muslims. Those who follow a religion other than*

Islam, their religion will never be accepted from them, and in the world to come they will undoubtedly be among the lost.

Punished Them with a Harsh Punishment

65:8 *How many cities have turned away from the command of their Lord and His messengers! Therefore, We judged them severely and punished them with a harsh punishment. They tasted the evil consequences of their own behavior, and the consequences of their behavior were ruinous.*
65:10 *Allah has prepared a severe punishment for them. Those who are wise fear Allah for He has sent down a reminder: a Messenger who gives you clear signs from Allah so that he may bring those who believe and do good works out of the darkness and into the light. Those who believe in Allah and do good works, Allah will lead into the Gardens beneath which rivers flow, where they will live forever. Allah has given them rich provisions.*
65:12 *It is Allah who created seven heavens and as many earths. The divine command is sent down through all of them so that you will know that Allah has power over all things and that Allah comprehends all things with His knowledge.*

33:56 *Truly, Allah and His angels bless the Messenger! Believers, bless him and greet him with all the respect he is due.*
33:57 *Truly, those who speak evil of Allah and His Messenger will have Allah's curse upon them in this world and the world to come. He has prepared a torturous punishment for them. And those who speak evil of believing men and women, when they have done nothing to deserve it, will carry the guilt and a clear sin.*

Those Who Oppose Allah and His Messenger Will Be Laid Low

58:5 *Those who oppose Allah and His Messenger will be laid low, just as those who came before them. And now that We have sent down clear signs, the unbelievers will receive a humiliating punishment. On the day Allah raises all of them to life, He will tell them of what they did. Allah has recorded it even though they do not remember it, and Allah witnesses all things.*
58:7 *Do you not realize that Allah knows all that is in the heavens and the earth? If three people are speaking in secret together, He is the fourth; if there are five, He is the sixth. Whether there are fewer or more, He is with them wherever they may be. Then, on Resurrection Day, He will tell them everything they have done, for Allah knows all things.*

Allah Guides Whom He Pleases

22:1 *People, fear your Lord, for the earthquake of the Hour of will truly be a dreadful thing.*

22:2 *On that day, every nursing mother will abandon her infant, every woman who is pregnant will abort her burden, and you will see people staggering around as if they are drunk, even though they are not. Allah's wrath will be powerful upon them.*

22:3 *Among the people there are those who [Abu Jahl], in ignorance, argue about Allah and follow every rebellious devil. It is decreed that whoever takes him as a friend will be led astray, and they will be led to the torment of the Fire.*

22:5 *You people, if you are in doubt about the resurrection, remember how We created you from the dust, then from sperm, then from clots of blood, and then from pieces of flesh, both shaped and shapeless so that We may prove Our power to you. We cause you to remain in the womb for an appointed period; then We bring you forth as infants so that you may grow to maturity. There are some of you who die young, and others who live to be so old that they forget all they ever knew. And you have seen the earth parched and lifeless, but as soon as We send down rain, life begins to stir and swell bringing forth every kind of luxuriant herb.*

22:7 *And undoubtedly the hour will come when Allah will raise all of those who are in the grave to life. And among the people there are some who argue about Allah without knowledge, guidance, or the illuminating scriptures. They turn away in contempt and lead others away from Allah's path. They will be disgraced in this world, and on the resurrection day they will be made to taste the torment of the Fire. And We will say to them, "This is what your misdeeds have earned you, for Allah is not unfair to His servants."*

22:11 *And there are some who say they serve Allah, yet they stand on the periphery of faith. If they are blessed with good fortune, they are satisfied with it, but when trials come upon them, they turn away in infidelity giving up this world and the world to come. That is a clear loss. They call upon gods that can neither harm them nor help them. This is a grievous sin. They call upon him who would rather harm them than help them. Truly evil is both the master and the friend.*

22:14 *But Allah will lead those who believe and do good works into Gardens watered by flowing rivers. Allah completes all that He plans.*

22:15 *If anyone thinks that Allah will not make His Messenger victorious in this world and the world to come, let them tie a rope to the ceiling of his house and hang himself with it. Then let him see if that course of action remedies his anger. We have sent down the Koran containing clear signs. Allah guides whom He pleases.*

They Will Be Beaten with Iron Rods

22:18 *Do you not see how all that is in the heavens and earth adore Allah, the sun, moon, and stars, the mountains, trees, and beasts, along with many of the people? But a great number of them are deserving of punishment. And those whom Allah disgraces will have no one to honor them. Allah does all that He pleases.*

22:19 *These two, the believers and the unbelievers, argue with each other about their Lord, but for the unbelievers, clothing of Fire has been made for them. Boiling water will be poured on their heads. It will scald their insides and their skin as well. They will be beaten with iron rods. Every time they, in their torment, attempt to escape from the Fire, they will be dragged back into it, and they will be told, "Taste the torture of the burning."*

22:23 *But Allah will lead those who believe and do good works into the Gardens, beneath which are flowing rivers. They will be adorned with gold bracelets and pearls and clothed in silk garments. They were guided by the righteous words. They were guided to the glorious path.*

22:25 *But the unbelievers who lead others away from Allah's path and keep them from entering the Holy Mosque [the Kabah], which We have given to all mankind—both natives and visitors, and those who sinfully seek to profane it—We will make them taste a painful punishment.*

Denial on the Unbelievers' Faces

22:70 *Do you not realize that Allah knows all that is contained within the heavens and earth? Truly all is recorded in the Book; this is easy for Allah. Nevertheless, they worship others besides Allah who have not been warranted, and about whom they know nothing. Those who commit this sin will have no one to help them.*

22:72 *When Our clear signs are recited to them, you will plainly see the denial on the unbelievers' faces. They can barely prevent themselves from attacking those who recite the signs to them. Say to them, "Shall I tell you of something much worse than these signs? It is the Fire of Hell, which Allah has promised for the unbelievers. What a wretched home it is."*

22:73 *People, here is a parable, listen to it: Those on whom you call besides Allah are unable even to create a fly, even though they combine their power to try. And if the fly were to carry a speck of dust away from them, they would be unable to bring it back. Weak are both the called-upon and the caller. They do not give Allah the praise He is due, for Allah is strong, mighty.*

22:75 *Allah selects His messengers from among angels and men. Truly, Allah is all-hearing and all-seeing. He knows what is in front of them and what is behind them, and all things will return to Allah. Believers, bow down and prostrate yourselves, and worship your Lord. Do good works so that you will prosper.*

Throughout history Allah has punished all cultures and civilizations who did not do what their prophets said.

64:1 *All that is in the heavens and in the earth give praise to Allah. The entire kingdom and the all glory are His. He has power over all things.*
64:2 *It was He who created you, and although some of you are unbelievers and others believers, He sees everything you do. He created the heavens and the earth to reveal the truth. He created you and gave you your beautiful shape. All will return to Him.*
64:4 *He knows everything that is in the heavens and earth. He knows all that you hide and all that you make known. Allah knows all your deepest secrets.*
64:5 *Have you not heard of what happened to the unbelievers who came before you? They experienced the evil consequences of their actions, and a terrible punishment still awaits them. This is because when messengers came to them with clear signs they said, "Will simple humans be our guides?" So they rejected the message and turned away. Allah does not need them. Allah is self-sufficient and worthy of praise.*
64:7 *The unbelievers think that they will not be raised to life on the Day of Judgment. Say: Yes, you will be raised by my Lord, and you will be informed of everything you have ever done! That is easy for Allah. Therefore, believe in Allah and His messenger and in the light which we have sent down to you. Allah knows all your actions.*
64:9 *That day when He will gather you all together for a Day of Assembly, that will be a day of cheating. The believers will cheat the unbelievers out of their place in Paradise. Those who believe in Allah and do what is right, He will take away all their sins and lead them into the Gardens watered by flowing rivers, where they will live forever. This is the ultimate reward. But the unbelievers, those who reject Our revelations, will be prisoners of the Fire, where they will live forever. A torturous end!*

Allah Brought Utter Destruction to Them

47:10 *Have they not traveled through the land and seen the final consequences of those who came before them? Allah brought utter destruction to them, and a similar end waits for the unbelievers. This is because Allah protects those who believe. The unbelievers have no protector.*
47:12 *Truly, Allah will lead those who believe and do good works to the Garden beneath which rivers flow, while the unbelievers enjoy the pleasures of this world and eat their fill like the beasts of the field. And the Fire will be their final destination! And how many cities, which were stronger than your own city which drove you out, have We decimated, and they had no one to help them. Are those who follow the clear path sent down by their Lord equals to those who think their evil deeds are acceptable and those who follow their own cravings?*
47:15 *A description of the Paradise which Allah promised to those who fear Him: in it are flowing rivers of pure water and rivers of milk that never turn sour; rivers of wine, delectable to those who drink it and*

rivers of clear honey. In it there are all kinds of fruit, with forgiveness from their Lord. Are these to be measured against the ones who will live in the Fire for eternity, and who are made to drink boiling water that will tear their insides?

47:16 *Among them are some who will in fact listen to you, but when they leave you they go to those with knowledge and ask, "What is it that he said just now?" These are the ones whose hearts have been hardened by Allah and who follow their own desires. Those who follow the right path, however, will receive His increased guidance and He will teach them what to fear.*

47:18 *Do the unbelievers wait for the Hour of Doom to suddenly come and take them unaware? Its signs have already come, and when it is actually upon them, how then will they be warned? Therefore, know that there is no god except Allah, and ask forgiveness for your sins and for the sins of the men and women who believe. Allah knows the places you go as well as your place of rest.*

How Terrible Was My Rejection of Them

22:42 *And if they reject you, remember that so did the people of Noah, and of Ad and Thamud [ancient Arabic cities], and the people of Abraham and Lot, and those who lived in Midian [a city on the Red Sea] have also denied their messengers. Moses, too, was rejected. I endured the unbelievers for a long while; then I seized them, and how terrible was My rejection of them.*

22:45 *How many cities, which were full of sin, have we destroyed? Many wells lie neglected and castles abandoned. Have they not traveled through the land, or do they not have hearts with which to understand or ears to hear? It is not that their eyes are blind, but their hearts within their breasts are blind. They ask you to bring the punishment quickly. Allah will not fail to keep His promise. Truly, one day in Allah's sight is like a thousand years in your eyes. And how many nations have I endured, while they were full of wickedness? In the end I punished them, and to Me all will return.*

22:49 *Say: People, I have only been sent to give you a clear warning. Those who believe and do good works will be forgiven and will be richly provided for; but those try to refute Our signs will be the prisoners of the Fire.*

The Koran gives proof of Allah.

2:258 *Have you not remembered the one [Nimrod] who argued with Abraham about his Lord because Allah had given him power? Abraham said, "My Lord is the one who gives life and causes death." The other said, "I too have the power of life and death." "Allah causes the sun to rise in the east," Abraham said, "You make it rise in the west, then." The unbeliever was bewildered. Allah does not guide those who do evil.*

2:259 *Or remember the man [Esdras doubted that Jerusalem could be restored after its destruction by Nebuchadrezzar] who passed by a ruined and abandoned city and said, "How will Allah ever bring life to this city now that it is dead?" So then Allah caused him to die, and one hundred years later raised him back to life. "How long have you waited?" Allah asked him. He said, "A day, or part of a day." Allah said, "No, you have been gone a hundred years, but look at your food and drink which show no signs of having aged, and look at your donkey. And so We may use you as an example for mankind, see how We fix your bones and cover them with flesh." And when he [Esdras] realized what had happened to him he said, "I now know that Allah has the power to do all things."*

3:189 *All that is in the heavens and the earth belongs to Allah. Allah holds power over everything. In the creation of the heavens and the earth and in the changing of day to night, there are clear signs for those who are wise. Those who remember Allah when they stand, sit, and lie down, and reflect upon the creation of the heavens and earth say, "Lord! You have not made this creation in vain. All glory to You! Keep us from the torture of the Fire. My Lord! Surely those whom you cast into the Fire will be eternally shamed. The evil-doers will have no one to help them."*
3:193 *Lord! We have heard the voice of the one calling us to the true faith saying, "Believe in your Lord," and we have obeyed him. Lord! Forgive us of our sins and cleanse us of our evil deeds and cause us to die with the righteous. Lord! Give us that which Your messengers promised us, and keep us from shame on the Day of Resurrection. Truly, You never break your promise."*

Allah gave encouragement to Mohammed in his labors.

33:1 *Messenger! Fear Allah and do not listen to the unbelievers and hypocrites. Truly Allah is all-knowing and wise. Follow that which is revealed to you from your Lord, for Allah knows all that you do, and trust in Allah. Allah is sufficient as your protector.*
33:6 *The Messenger is more closely related to the believers than they are to themselves, and his wives are like their mothers. Allah decrees that those who are related by blood are closer to each other than other believers, and are closer than those who have fled their country [left Mecca to come to Medina] for Islam, but showing kindness to fellow believers is decreed by Allah.*
33:7 *Remember that We entered into a covenant with you [Mohammed], as we did the with the other messengers, with Noah, Abraham, Moses, and Jesus, son of Mary. We made a strict covenant with them so that He might question the loyal about their sincerity. But He has prepared a dreadful punishment for the unbelievers.*

33:45 *Messenger! We have sent you to witness, to bring good news and to warn. You will summon others to Allah, by His permission, and guide them like a light-giving lamp. Therefore, announce to the believers that great blessings from Allah await them, and do not listen to the unbelievers and hypocrites. Ignore their talk. Put your trust in Allah for Allah is sufficient as your protector.*

Allah changes His revelations when needed.

2:106 *Whatever of Our revelations We repeal or cause to be forgotten, We will replace with something superior or comparable. [There are as many as 225 verses of the Koran that are altered by later verses. This is called abrogation.] Do you not know that Allah has power over all things? Do you not know that Allah reigns sovereign over the heavens and earth and besides Him you have no protector or helper?*

Allah Is Cruel in His Retribution

3:7 *It is He who has revealed the Scriptures to you. Some of its verses are clear and basic in their meaning. These are the foundation of the Book, and others are metaphorical. Those whose hearts have a tendency to err follow the metaphorical verses seeking to cause arguments when they attempt to interpret them. Only Allah knows their meaning. And those who are firmly grounded in knowledge say, "We believe in it. All of it comes from our Lord," but only those who possess understanding will listen. Our Lord! Do not let our hearts go astray after You have guided us to what is right, and grant us Your mercy for You are the most generous giver. Lord! Surely You will gather all of mankind together on the assured day. Allah will not fail to keep His promise. As for the unbelievers, neither their wealth or their children keep Allah's wrath from them, and they will be fuel for the Fire like Pharaoh's people and those who came before them who rejected Our revelations. Allah destroyed them for their sins. Allah is cruel in his retribution.*

2:1 *ELIF. LAM. MIM. This Scripture is not to be doubted. It is a guide for those who fear Allah; who believe in the unseen [Allah and Judgment Day] and are dedicated to prayer; who give from what We have given to them for the cause; who believe in what has been sent down to you [Mohammed] and in what has been sent down before you; and who have complete faith in the life to come. These are the ones who are on the right path from their Lord. These will certainly be triumphant.*
2:6 *As for the unbelievers, whether you warn them or not, they will not believe. Their hearts and ears are sealed up by Allah, and their eyes are covered as well. There will be a dreadful doom awaiting them.*

The Koran teaches more about the world of the jinns and magic.

> 2:102 *They followed what the evil ones read against the kingdom of Solomon. It was not Solomon who was an unbeliever, but the evil ones teaching people sorcery and that which was revealed in Babylon to the angels Harut and Marut [The angels Harut and Marut were sent down from heaven to be tempted. They sinned and will be punished on Judgment Day. Until then they teach magic]. But neither of them instructed the people without first saying, "Truly we are only sent to tempt you; therefore, do not become disbelievers." And from the two angels they learned how to create animosity between husbands and wives, although they cannot cause harm unless it is Allah's will, and they learned what would harm them and what did not benefit them. And surely they know that those who bought into the sorcery would have no part in the life to come! And the price for which they sold their souls was vile; if they had only known! If they had kept their faith and guarded against evil, their reward from Allah would certainly have been better, if they had only realized!*

PREACHING

Mohammed began to preach the religion of Islam to the Medinans just as he had the Meccans.

> 2:151 *We have sent a messenger to you of your own people who will reveal Our signs to you and purify you, who will teach you the Scriptures and the wisdom, and who will teach you new knowledge. Therefore, remember Me and I will remember you. Give Me thanks and do not reject Me.*
> 2:153 *Believers, seek help with patience and prayer for Allah is with the patient. Do not say that those who are killed for Allah's cause are dead. No, they are alive even though you do not see them.*
> 2:155 *We will certainly test you with fear and hunger, with loss of wealth and lives and crops. Give good news to those who persevere who, when faced with misfortune, say, "We belong to Allah, and to Him we will surely return." It is these who will receive Allah's blessings and mercy, and they are guided to the right path.*
> 2:158 *The two hills of Safa and Marwat [these hills in Mecca were used in pagan rituals] are among Allah's signs. It is not a sin if while visiting the sacred House [the Kabah] you walk around them, as is the pagan custom. One who does good of his own accord will be rewarded. Allah is responsive and aware of all things.*
> 2:256 *There should be no coercion in religion. The truth stands out clearly from error. Whoever renounces idolatry and believes in Allah will take hold of a strong handle that will not be broken. Allah hears and knows all. Allah is the protector of the faithful, leading them from out*

of the darkness and into the light. As for those who do not believe, their protectors are false idols who lead them from the light and into the darkness. They are prisoners of the Fire and will live there forever.

Allah Only Forbids You to Make Friends

60:8 *Allah does not forbid you to deal with kindness and fairness towards those who have not made war upon you on account of your religion, or who have driven you forth from your homes. Allah loves those who act with fairness. Allah only forbids you to make friends of those who, on account of your religion, have warred against you, have driven you out of your homes, and have helped those who drove you out. Whoever makes friends of them are unjust.*

2:201 *There are some people who say, "Our Lord, give us riches in this world," but those people will have no place in the world to come. But there are others who say, "Lord, give us good in this world and in the world to come, and protect us from the anguish of the Fire." These will receive what they have earned, and Allah's reckoning is swift.*
2:203 *Give praise to Allah on the chosen days. Whoever leaves on the second day, or stays on longer, will not be blamed if he truly fears Allah. Fear Allah then, and know that you will be gathered to Him. There are some people whose talk about this world will overwhelm you, and they call Allah to witness what is in their hearts, yet these are the most violent of your enemies.*

Allah Does Not Guide Those Who Disbelieve

2:263 *Kind words and forgiveness are better than charity coupled with an insult. Allah is self-sufficient and gracious.*
2:264 *Believers! Do not taint your charity by reminding others of your generosity or by taunting them, like those who spend their wealth to show off and do not believe in Allah or the Last Day. Such people are like rocks barely covered with soil: when the rain falls they are left bare. No good will come of their deeds. Allah does not guide those who disbelieve. Those who give away their wealth with the aim to please Allah are like a garden on a hillside where the rain is plentiful and the yield is doubled, and if there is no rain, then the dew is sufficient. Allah sees all you do.*
2:266 *Would any of you like to have his garden of palms and vines, watered by flowing rivers, to be destroyed by a fiery wind when he is in his old age with dependant children? It is in this way that Allah makes His revelations known to you so that you will reflect.*
2:267 *Believers! To charity give of your wealth [pay the poor tax], which you have earned lawfully, and from that which We have given you from the earth. Do not give worthless things that you yourself would not even want. Know that Allah is self-sufficient, and worthy of praise.*

2:268 *Satan threatens to take away all that you have earned and commands you to perform vulgar acts, but Allah promises you His forgiveness and riches. Allah is generous and all-knowing. He gives wisdom to whom He pleases, and one who receives the gift of wisdom is truly rich; nevertheless, only those who understand keep this in mind. Whatever you give to charity or whatever oath you make, it is known to Allah. The evil-doers have no one to help them. It is good to do charitable works publicly, but it is better to give to charity in private, and it will do away with some of your sins. Allah knows what you do.*

2:272 *It is not your job to set them on the right path, but Allah will guide whom He pleases. Whatever good you do will come back to you, given that you only give to please Allah. All the good you do will come back to you in full; you will not be wronged.*

2:274 *Those who give to charity both day and night, and in secret and in public, will be rewarded by their Lord. They will not have anything to fear or regret.*

2:275 *Those who live on lending others money at a high rate of interest will rise before Allah like one whom Satan has touched and made mad because they claim that their practices are no different from trading. Allah allows trading, but has forbidden usury [excessive interest on a loan]. One who is admonished by his Lord and changes his ways can keep what he has earned. His case is for Allah to judge. But those who go back to their old ways will be prisoners of the Fire, where they will live forever.*

We Hear and Obey Our Lord

2:284 *Everything in the heavens and earth belongs to Allah. Whether you proclaim your thoughts or conceal them, Allah will judge you for them. He will forgive whom He pleases and punish whom He pleases. Allah has power over everything.*

2:285 *The messenger believes in what has been shown to him by his Lord, and the believers do too. They all believe in Allah, His angels, His Scriptures, and His messengers. We treat His messengers equally, and they say, "We hear and obey our Lord. We ask for Your forgiveness Lord. We will return to You."*

64:14 *Believers! You certainly have enemies among your wives and children, so beware of them! If you forgive and bear with them, then Allah too will be forgiving and merciful. Your riches and your children are only a source of temptation! But with Allah is the great reward! Therefore, keep your duty to Allah and fear Him with all your might. Listen, obey, and give to charity for the benefit of your soul. Those who keep themselves from greediness will truly prosper. If you give to Allah a generous*

loan, He will pay you back twice and forgive you for Allah is gracious and long-suffering.
64:18 *He is the knower of the unknown and the known. He is mighty and wise!*

The Vilest Creatures in Allah's Sight

8:21 *The vilest creatures in Allah's sight are the ones who are deaf, dumb, and without sense. If Allah had recognized any potential in them, He would have given them the ability to hear. Even if He makes them hear, they would still turn their backs and deny the faith. Believers! Answer the call of Allah and His messenger which gives you life. Know that Allah comes between a person and his own heart and that you all will be gathered to Him. Protect yourselves from sinning because it will not only be the unbelievers who will face temptation. Allah is severe in His punishment.*
8:27 *Believers! Do not betray the trust of Allah and His messenger or knowingly betray His secrets. And know that your children and your wealth are merely temptations and that Allah's reward is immense. Believers! If you fear Allah, He will give you wisdom to discern right from wrong, He will cleanse you of evil and forgive your sins. Allah is the Lord of boundless grace.*

3:18 *Allah bears witness that there are no gods except Him, as do the angels and those who possess wisdom. There is no god except Him, maintaining His creation with justice. He is mighty and wise! In Allah's eyes, Islam is the only true religion. The People of the Book [Christians and Jews] argued among themselves, out of jealousy for one another, only after the knowledge had been sent down to them. For those who reject Allah's revelations, Allah will be quick in His judgment of them.*
3:29 *Say: Whether you hide what is in your hearts or make it widely known, Allah knows all. He knows all that is in the heavens and earth. Allah has control over all things. The day will undoubtedly arrive when every soul will be judged for the good it has done. As for its evil deeds, it will wish they were far removed from him. For Allah warned you to fear Him, and Allah shows compassion to those who serve Him.*
3:31 *Say: If you love Allah, then follow me. Allah will love you and forgive you of your sins. Allah is forgiving and merciful. Say: Obey Allah and His messenger, but if they reject it, then truly, Allah does not love those who reject the faith.*

Fear Allah as He Deserves to Be Feared

3:101 *Believers! Fear Allah as He deserves to be feared! When death finds you, die as true Muslims.*
3:103 *Hold firmly to Allah's rope [the Koran] and do not be divided among you. And remember Allah's goodness to you, how when you were enemies*

He joined your hearts together in love so that through His grace you became like brothers. And when you were on the brink of the pit of Fire, He saved you. It is in this way that Allah makes His signs clear to you so you will find the right path. Let there be a group formed from among you who calls for goodness, commands justice, and forbids what is wrong. These are the ones who will be victorious.

3:161 *No messenger would steal from his followers [Mohammed was accused of not fairly distributing the war booty] for anyone who steals must present what they have stolen on the Day of Resurrection. Then every soul will receive that which it has earned. No one will be treated unjustly. Can one who wishes to please Allah be compared to one who has drawn His wrath and whose home is in Hell? A wretched home!*
3:163 *There are many levels of Allah's rewards, and Allah is aware of all that they do. Allah has certainly shown His grace to the believers by sending them a messenger of their own to give them His revelations, to cleanse them, and to impart the knowledge of the Scriptures and wisdom to them for before they were sinning grievously.*

We Have Sent Down Iron with Its Strength for War

57:16 *Has not the time come for those who believe to submit to Allah's warning and to the truth He has sent down? This is so they will not be like those who came before and to whom the Scriptures were given, whose lives were prolonged but their hearts hardened, and many of them were evil-doers. Know that Allah gives life to the earth after it is dead. Now We have made Our signs clear to you so that you will understand.*
57:18 *Those who give to charity, whether they are men or women, and those who loan generously to Allah, will be paid back double what they have given. They will receive a noble reward.*
57:19 *Those who believe in Allah and His messenger are truthful ones who will testify [against the unbelievers] before the presence of their Lord. They will receive their reward and their light, but those who deny Allah will be the prisoners of Hell.*
57:20 *Know that the life of this world is only a game and an amusement, a show and vain boasting among you! The quest for more wealth and more children can be compared to the plants which spring up after the rain. Their growth makes the man rejoice, but soon they will whither and turn yellow becoming dry and crumbling away. In the world to come, either a terrible punishment or forgiveness and reward awaits you. The life of this world is only a fleeting joy.*
57:21 *Therefore, urge one another on in seeking forgiveness from your Lord and in earning admittance into a Paradise as vast as the heavens and earth prepared for those who believe in Allah and His messengers.*

That is the grace of Allah, and He gives it to whom He pleases. Allah's grace is boundless.

57:22 *Every disaster that happens to the earth, or to yourselves, was preordained before We caused it to occur. Truly that is easy for Allah so that you will not grieve over good things that have passed you by or be overly joyous at the good you have received. Allah does not love the boastful, the arrogant, nor those who are selfish with their wealth and urge others to be the same. And those who turn away from Allah's path should know that Allah is self-sufficient, praiseworthy.*

57:25 *We have sent Our messengers with clear signs, and We have caused the Scriptures and the balance of justice to come down through them. We have sent down iron with its strength for war as well as its many other uses for mankind so that Allah would know those who would help Him and His messengers, although unseen. Allah is powerful and mighty.*

Allah Is Always Watching You

4:1 *People! Fear your Lord who created you from one soul, and from that soul created its spouse, and from them He spread the earth with innumerable men and women. Fear Allah in whose name you claim your rights to one another and show reverence to the mother who gave birth to you. Allah is always watching you!*

4:39 *And what do they have to fear if they believe in Allah and the Last Day and they give to charity from that which Allah has given them? Allah is aware of all they do. Truly Allah will not be unjust even as much as the weight of an mustard seed. He will doubly reward you for your good deeds and gives from Himself a great reward.*

4:41 *How will it be for them when We produce a witness from every nation and bring you [Mohammed] forth to testify against them? On that day, the unbelievers and those who disobeyed the Messenger will wish they could sink into the earth for they cannot hide a single thing from Allah.*

He Could Destroy You All

4:131 *All that is in the heavens and the earth belongs to Allah! We command you, as We have already commanded those to whom the Scriptures were given before you, to fear Allah. But if you deny Him, know that all that in the heavens and earth belongs to Allah. Allah is self-sufficient and praiseworthy. All that is in the heavens and the earth belongs to Allah. Allah is a sufficient protector. If it were His will, He could destroy you all and create others to take your place. Allah has the power to do this.*

4:134 *If anyone desires the reward of this world, let them know that with Allah is the reward of this world and the world to come, for Allah sees and hears all things.*

4:135 *Believers! Stand up for justice when you bear witness before Allah, even if it is against yourself, your parents, or your family. Whether they are rich or poor, Allah is closer to the both of them than you are. Therefore, do not follow your passion, as it will cause you fall away from the truth. If you alter your testimony or refuse to give it, Allah is certainly well aware of what you do.*
4:136 *Believers! Believe in Allah and His Messenger and in the Scriptures which were sent down to His Messenger and in the Scriptures He sent down before him. Those who deny Allah, His angels, His Scriptures, His messengers, and the Last Day have gone far astray. Those who are believers, then deny the faith, then believe again and deny again and go on in increasing disbelief, Allah will not forgive them or guide them on the right path.*
4:173 *But for those who believe and do good works, Allah will give them their reward and more from His bounty. But as for those who are arrogant and boastful, He will severely punish, and they will have no one to help or protect them besides Allah. People! You have received proof from your Lord and a clear light has been sent down to you. Those who believe in Allah and hold tightly to Him, these He will allow to enter into His mercy and grace, and He will guide them.*

33:41 *Believers! Remember Allah always, and praise Him in the morning and in the evening. He blesses you and His angels intercede for you so He may lead you out of the darkness and in the light, and He is merciful to the believers. Their greeting on the day they meet Him will be, "Peace!" And He has prepared a great reward for them.*

22:17 *As for the believers, and the Jews, the Sabians [unclear, possibly Christians of Iraq], the Christians, the Magians [Zoroasterianism], and the idolaters, truly Allah will judge them on Resurrection Day, for Allah witnesses all things.*

Between Us a Hatred and Hostility Has Sprung up Forever

60:2 *If they have the upper hand of you, they will prove your enemies. They will stretch out their hands and tongues to hurt you and will desire that you reject the truth. Neither your kindred nor your children will be of profit to you on the Last Day. He will sever the connections between you. Allah sees your actions.*
60:4 *There is a good example in Abraham of those who followed him when they said to their people, "We are clear of you and of what you worship besides Allah. We renounce you, and between us a hatred and hostility has sprung up forever until you believe in Allah alone." Do not imitate the language of Abraham to his father, "I will pray for your forgiveness, but I will obtain nothing for you from Allah." Oh, our Lord, in You we trust, to You we repent, and to You we will return at last.*

60:5 *Oh, our Lord, do not make us a trial for those who disbelieve, but forgive us, Lord, for you are the mighty and wise. There is in them a good example for all who hope in Allah and in the Last Day. If any turn away, Allah is truly rich and praiseworthy. Allah will, perhaps, establish good will between yourselves and those whom you take to be your enemies. Allah is powerful, gracious, and merciful.*

Allah Did Not Wrong Them

9:69 *You act like those who lived before you who were mightier than you in strength and more abundant in wealth and children. They enjoyed their portion, so you enjoy your portion as they who were before you enjoyed theirs, and you talk like they talk. Their works are fruitless in this world and in the hereafter. These are the lost ones.*

9:70 *Has the story not reached them of those before them—of the people of Noah, and of Ad, and of Thamud [cities of the Arabs], and of the people of Abraham, and of the inhabitants of Midian [a town on the Red Sea], and of the overthrown cities? [All of these were destroyed by Allah because they did not listen to their messengers.] Their messengers came to them with clear proofs of their mission. Allah did not wrong them, but they wronged themselves.*

9:71 *The faithful of both sexes are mutual friends. They command what is just and forbid what is evil. They observe regular prayer, contribute regularly to charity, and they obey Allah and His Messenger. Allah will show His mercy to these. Allah is mighty and wise. Allah promised the faithful, both men and women, Gardens beneath which the rivers flow in which they shall abide, and blessed mansions in the Gardens. The best, though, will be Allah's good pleasure in them. This is the supreme triumph.*

To Pray for the Forgiveness of Unbelievers

9:112 *Those who turn to Allah and those who serve, who praise, who fast, who bow down, who prostrate themselves, who command what is just and forbid what is evil, and keep to the bounds of Allah—they do rejoice. So give these good tidings to the faithful.*

9:113 *It is not for the Messenger or the faithful to pray for the forgiveness of unbelievers, even though they be of kin, after it has become clear to them that that they are people of Hellfire. Abraham prayed for his father's forgiveness because of a promise he had made to him, but when it was shown to him that he was an enemy to Allah, he cut himself off from his father for Abraham was tenderhearted and long-suffering.*

9:115 *Allah will not mislead people after He has guided them aright until He makes clear to them that which they ought to dread. Allah knows all things. Allah's is the kingdom of the heavens and of the earth. He gives life, and He takes it. You have no patron or helper except Allah.*

5:7 *Remember the favor of Allah upon you, and His promise with which He has bound you when you said, "We have heard and will obey." Fear Allah for He knows the very secrets of your hearts.*
5:8 *Oh, believers, stand up as witnesses for Allah by righteousness, and do not let the ill will of others, make you act unjustly. Be just; this is next to piety. Fear Allah for Allah is aware of all you do. Allah has promised to those who believe and do things that are right that they will have His pardon and a great reward. Those who disbelieve and reject Our signs as lies—these will be mated with Hellfire.*
5:11 *Oh, believers, remember Allah's favor on you. When certain folks were determined to stretch out their hands against you, He kept them from you. Fear Allah then and let the faithful trust Allah.*

5:49 *So judge between them by what Allah has sent down, and do not follow their low desires, but be aware of them for fear that they corrupt you from any of those laws which Allah has sent down to you. If they turn away, then know that Allah desires to punish them for some of their crimes, for truly most men are rebellious. Do they desire the judgments of the age of pagan ignorance? [All civilization, culture, and history before Islam is the age of ignorance.] What better judge can there be than Allah for those who believe firmly?*

They Are a People Who Do Not Understand

5:55 *Your protectors are Allah and His Messenger and those who believe, who observe regular prayer and regular charity, and who bow in worship. And whoever takes Allah, His Messenger, and those who believe for friends, they truly are the people of Allah and must be triumphant. Oh, you who believe, do not take those who have received the Scriptures [Jews and Christians] before you, who have scoffed and jested at your religion, or who are unbelievers for your friends. Fear Allah if you are true believers. When you call to prayer, they make it a mockery and a joke. This is because they are a people who do not understand.*

5:101 *Oh, believers, do not ask us of things which, if they were told, might only pain you. If you ask about such things when the Koran is being revealed, they will be declared to you. Allah will pardon you for this for He is forgiving and gracious. Some before you asked questions concerning such things, and afterwards they quickly lost faith.*
5:103 *Allah did not ordain superstitions like those of the she-camel let loose to free pasture, or idol sacrifices for twin births in animals, or stallion camels freed from work [these are all customs of the ancient Arabian religions]. The unbelievers have invented this blaspheme against Allah, and most of them do not understand.*

5:104 *When it was said to them, "Accept what Allah has revealed and His messengers" they said, "Our fathers' faith is sufficient for us." Even though their fathers knew nothing and had no guidance?*

The Koran extols the virtues and qualities of Allah.

2:255 *Allah! There is no god but Him, the living-one, the everlasting. He is not overtaken by slumber or sleep. All things in heaven and earth belong to Him. Who can intervene with Him except as He permits it? He knows what was before mankind and what is after them. They can only understand what He chooses for them to understand. His throne encompasses the heavens and the earth, and the preservation of them both does not tire Him. He is the most high, the great.*

There Is No God but Him

64:11 *Nothing misfortunate occurs unless Allah wills it. Whoever believes in Allah, He will guide his heart. Allah knows all things. So obey Allah and His messenger. But if you turn your backs to them, Our messenger is not to blame, for his duty is only to deliver Our warning clearly. Allah! There is no god but Him! Let the faithful put their trust in Allah.*

62:1 *All that is in the heavens and earth sings the praises of Allah, the supreme Lord, the holy, the mighty, and the wise.*
62:2 *He sent to the people of Mecca a messenger from among their own to reveal His revelations to them, to make them pure, and to teach the Scriptures and wisdom, although before now they were clearly in error as well as the others among them who have not yet accepted the faith. He is the mighty and the wise! That is the grace of Allah; He gives it to whom He pleases. His grace is boundless.*

Those Who Reject Allah's Revelations Will Receive Severe Punishment

3:1 *ELIF. LAM. MIM. There is no god except Him, the living, the eternal. He has sent down to you the Scriptures with the truth, which confirm the scriptures which came before it. And He has already sent down the Law of Moses and the Gospel of Jesus to guide mankind and to show them the difference between good and evil.*
3:4 *Those who reject Allah's revelations will receive severe punishment. Allah is mighty, Lord of revenge. Nothing in the earth or in heaven is hidden to Him. It is He who forms you in your mothers' wombs according to His pleasure. There is no god except Him, the mighty, the wise!*

That You Should Not Believe in Allah

57:1 *All that is in the heavens and earth gives praise to Allah for He is mighty and wise.*
57:2 *The heavens and the earth are His kingdom. He controls life and death, and He holds powers over everything! He is the first and the last, the seen and the unseen. He knows all things!*

57:4 *It was He who in six days created the heavens and the earth and then ascended to His throne. He knows everything that enters the earth and everything that leaves it, and all that is sent down from heaven and all that rises up to it. Wherever you are, Allah is there, and He sees all your actions.*
57:5 *He is the absolute ruler of the heavens and the earth, and all things will return to Allah. He causes the night to turn into day, and the day to turn into night. He knows the deepest secrets of your heart.*
57:7 *Believe in Allah and His messenger, and give charitably of the inheritance which He has given you for those of you who believe and give generously will be greatly rewarded. What reason do you have that you should not believe in Allah when His messenger has called you to believe in your Lord, and He has already made a covenant with you if you are true believers? It is He who sends clear signs down to His messenger so he may lead you out of the darkness and into the light, for Allah is kind and merciful to you.*

Allah Will Not Forgive Those Who Worship Other Gods besides Him

4:48 *Allah will not forgive those who worship other gods besides Him, but for other sins, He will forgive whom He pleases. Those who serve gods other than Allah have committed a terrible sin.*
4:87 *Allah! There is no god except Him. He will undoubtedly gather you all together on the Day of Resurrection. And whose words have more truth than Allah's?*

59:1 *Let everything that is in the heavens and earth praise Allah! He is mighty and wise!*
59:21 *If this Koran had been sent up on a mountain, you would have seen it humble itself and break apart in fear of Allah. We sent down these allegories so that people will reflect upon them. He is Allah, and there is no other god except Him. He knows that which is seen and unseen. He is compassionate and merciful. He is Allah, and there is no god other than Him. He is the king, the holy, the giver of peace, the faithful, the guardian, the mighty, the supreme, the exalted one! Praise be to Allah apart from all idols!*
59:24 *He is Allah, the Creator, the Maker, the Evolver! The most excellent names are ascribed to Him. Let everything that is in the heavens and earth praise Allah! He is mighty and wise!*

Their Works Are Like a Mirage of Water in the Desert

24:34 *We have sent clear signs down to you and shown you the people who came before you as an example and a warning for those who fear Allah.*
24:35 *Allah is the light of the heavens and the earth. His light is like an alcove in which there is a lamp encased in glass, and this glass glistens like a star. The lamp is lit from the oil of a blessed tree, which is neither an olive*

of the east nor the west. Its oil would give light even if it was not touched by fire. It is light upon light. Allah will guide whom He pleases to His light, and Allah sends down such parables for mankind, for Allah knows all things. His light is found in the mosques which Allah has permitted to be built so that His name will be remembered inside them, where He is praised in the morning and in the evening. To those who cannot be diverted by business from remembering Allah, who regularly attend their prayers and pay the poor tax, who fear the day when hearts will pound and eyes will roll, and who pray that Allah will reward them for their good works and give to them of His bounty, Allah gives generously.
24:39 *But as for the unbelievers, their works are like a mirage of water in the desert to a thirsty traveler. When they finally reach it, they find it to be nothing; all they find is Allah who will pay them back all they are due. Allah is quick to settle His accounts. Or they are like the depths of a deep, dark ocean, covered by waves riding upon waves, above which there are clouds, darkness upon darkness. When someone reaches his hand out in front of himself, it can barely be seen. Truly those to whom Allah does not give light will find no light at all.*

The Heavens and Earth Sing Allah's Praises

24:41 *Have you not seen how everything in the heavens and earth sings Allah's praises? Even the birds praise Him as they spread their wings. He notices the prayer and praise of every creature, and Allah knows all they do. And the kingdom of the heavens and earth belong to Allah, and to Allah will it all return. Have you not seen how Allah gathers the clouds together and then piles them atop one another? Then He causes the rain to fall; then He sends down clouds like mountains filled with hail which He causes to fall on whom He pleases and turns it away from whom he pleases. The bright flash of His lightening is nearly blinding.*
24:44 *Allah causes the day to turn into night. Surely this is a lesson for those who possess understanding. Allah created every animal from water. Some of them crawl upon their bellies, and others walk upon two legs, while some walk upon four feet. Allah has created what He pleased. Yes, Allah has power over all things. We have sent down clear signs. And Allah guides whom He will to the right path.*
24:47 *There are those who say, "We believe in Allah and His Messenger and we obey." But just as soon as this is said, they turn their backs. These are not the believers. And when they are summoned before Allah and His Messenger so that He may judge them, some of them refuse to come. But if truth had been on their side, they would have come to Him obediently. Are their hearts diseased or do they have doubt? Are they afraid that Allah and His Messenger will judge them unjustly? No, they are the unjust.*
24:51 *But when Allah and His Messenger call the true believers to judge between them, their response is, "We have heard, and we obey." These are*

the ones who will be successful. Those who obey Allah and His Messenger and who dread and fear Allah will be the winners. And they have sworn by Allah, a most solemn oath, that if they are given the order, they would certainly march forth. Say to them, "Do not swear. It is worth more to show your obedience. Truly, Allah is well aware of all you do."
24:54 *Say: Obey Allah and the Messenger. But if you turn away, He is still responsible for fulfilling His duty as you are bound to fulfilling yours. If you are obedient, then you will guided on the right path. The sole duty of the Messenger is to warn you clearly.*
24:55 *Allah has promised those who believe and do good works that they will be leaders in the land as He did with those who came before them, and He will establish their religion which He has chosen for them and will exchange their feelings of fear for security. They will worship Him and no others besides Him. Those who do not believe in Him after this are truly wicked. Observe your prayers, pay the poor tax, and obey the Messenger so that you may receive mercy. Never think that the unbelievers can thwart Allah's plan on earth. Their destination will be the Fire, a wretched home.*

Allah Is Benevolent

22:61 *So it will be. Allah causes the night to turn into day, and the day to turn into night. Allah is all-hearing and all-seeing. So it will be, for Allah is the truth, and all those they call upon besides Him are false. Truly, Allah is the highest and the greatest.*
22:63 *Do you not recognize how Allah sends water down from heaven, and the next day the earth is covered in green? Surely Allah is benevolent and all-knowing. All that is contained in the heavens and earth belong to Him. Assuredly He is rich and worthy of praise. Do you not see how Allah has made all that is in the earth, and the ships that travel the seas, subject to His control? And He holds the heavens from falling on the earth, which it will only do with His permission. Surely Allah is compassionate and merciful to mankind. It is He who gave you life, and He will also cause you to die; then He will bring you back to life again. Truly people are ungrateful creatures.*
22:67 *For every people We have appointed a ritual which they are to observe. Therefore, do not allow them to argue with you about the matter, but send them to your Lord for you are surely on the right path. But if they argue with you say, "Allah knows best what you do." If they continue to argue say, "Allah will judge between you concerning your differences on the Resurrection Day."*
22:70 *Do you not realize that Allah knows all that is contained within the heavens and earth? Truly all is recorded in the Book; this is easy for Allah.*

Nevertheless, they worship others besides Allah who have not been warranted, and about whom they know nothing. Those who commit this sin will have no one to help them.

JIHAD, WAR AGAINST ALL

CHAPTER 12

4:42 On that day, the unbelievers and those who disobeyed the Messenger will wish they could sink into the earth for they cannot hide a single thing from Allah.

In Mecca, Mohammed had divided the community into Islam and those of the native Arabic religions. In Mecca he adopted all the classical Jewish stories to prove his prophesy and spoke well of the Jews. But there were almost no Jews living in Mecca, and therefore, no one to differ with him.

In Medina half of the population were Jews, who let Mohammed know that they disagreed with him. So in Medina, Mohammed argued with Jews as well as the non-Muslim Arabs. Even though there were very few in the town who were Christian, Mohammed argued against them as well. All non-Muslims were verbally attacked in Medina.

I415 It was thirteen years after he started preaching and one to two years after going to Medina that Mohammed prepared for war as commanded by Allah. He would fight his enemies, those who were not Muslims.

THE FIRST RAIDS

I416-423 Mohammed sent forth his fighters on seven armed raids to find the trade caravans headed to Mecca.

JIHAD—THE FIRST KILLING

I423-4 Mohammed sent Abdullah out with eight men. A caravan of the Quraysh passed by the Muslims as they overlooked the road from a rise. The caravan was loaded with leather and raisins. When the Quraysh saw them they were scared because they had slept not too far from here, but one of the Muslims had a shaved head. Now a shaved head was a mark of pilgrim so the Quraysh felt better. They were safe. They were also in a sacred month when weapons were not carried.

I425 The Muslims took council. They were in a dilemma. If they attacked the caravan now, they would be killing in a sacred month. Luckily, the sacred month ended today and tomorrow there would be no taboo about killing. But there was another problem. By tonight they would be in the sacred area of Mecca. In the sanctified area, there could never be any killing. They hesitated and talked about what to do. They decided to go ahead and kill as many as possible today and take their goods.

I425 Islam drew first blood against the Quraysh of Mecca. They attacked the unarmed men. Amr was killed by an arrow. He was the first man to be killed in jihad. One man escaped and they captured two prisoners. They took their camels with their goods and headed back to Mohammed in Medina. On the way they talked about how Mohammed would get one fifth of the stolen goods, spoils.

I425 When they got back, Mohammed said that he did not order them to attack in the sacred month. So he held the caravan and the two prisoners in suspense and refused to do anything with the goods or prisoners. The prisoners said, "Mohammed has violated the sacred month, shed blood therein, stolen goods and taken prisoners." But the Koran said:

> 2:216 ***You are commanded to fight although you dislike it. You may hate something that is good for you, and love something that is bad for you. Allah knows and you do not. When they ask you about fighting in the holy month, say: Fighting at this time is a serious offense, but it is worse in Allah's eyes to deny others the path to Him, to disbelieve in Him, and to drive His worshippers out of the Sacred Mosque. Idolatry is a greater sin than murder. They will not stop fighting you until you turn away from your religion. But any of you who renounce your faith and die an unbeliever, will have your works count for nothing in this world and the world to come. These people will be prisoners of the Fire, where they will live forever.***

I426 To resist the doctrine of Islam and to try and persuade Muslims to drop their faith is worse than killing. Before Islam, the rule of justice in Arabia was a killing for a killing, but now to resist Islam was worse than murder. Those who argue against Islam and resist Islam can be killed as a sacred act. The spoils were distributed and a ransom set for the prisoners. The men who had killed and stolen were now concerned as to whether they would get their take of the spoils. So once again the Koran spoke:

> 2:218 ***Those that have embraced the Faith, and those that have fled their land and fought for the cause of Allah, may hope for Allah's mercy. Allah is forgiving and merciful.***

I426 As Muslims who had been exiled and fought they were blessed by Allah. They received their spoils and Mohammed took his one fifth of the spoils of war.

You (Quraysh) count war in the holy month a grave matter
But graver is your opposition to Mohammed and your unbelief.
Though you defame us for killing Amr
Our lances drank Amr's blood
We lit the flame of war. —*Abu Bakr, the first caliph*

THE BATTLE THAT CHANGED THE WORLD

CHAPTER 13

64:12 So obey Allah and His messenger. But if you turn your backs to them, Our messenger is not to blame, for his duty is only to deliver Our warning clearly. Allah! There is no god but Him! Let the faithful put their trust in Allah.

FIGHTING IN ALLAH'S CAUSE—BADR

I428 Mohammed heard that Abu Sufyan was coming with a large caravan of thirty to forty Quraysh from Syria. Mohammed called the Muslims together and said, "Go out and attack it, perhaps Allah will give us the prey."

I428 As the caravan approached Medina, Abu Sufyan became worried and questioned every rider on the road about Mohammed. Then he heard intelligence that indeed Mohammed was going to attack. He sent out a fast rider to Mecca for aid.

I433 Mohammed and his men headed out of Medina for what was to prove to be one of the most important battles in all of history, a battle that would change the world forever.

I435 Mohammed was cheered. He said, "I see the enemy dead on the ground." They headed towards Badr where they camped near there for the night. He sent several scouts to the well at Badr and the scouts found two slaves with water camels. They felt sure they were from the Quraysh caravan and brought back them back to Mohammed. Two of Mohammed's men questioned them as Mohammed was nearby praying. The men replied that they were from the Quraysh. Mohammed's men began to beat them and torture the slaves as Mohammed prayed.

I436 Mohammed told his men that the slaves told them the truth until they started to beat and torture them. Then the slaves had lied but it had been the lie that they wanted to hear. Mohammed asked the men how many of the Quraysh there were and who were the leaders of the Quraysh. When they told him he was delighted and told his warriors that Mecca had sent their best men to be slaughtered.

I439-440 Both armies had an idea of the location of the other. Mohammed went ahead to chose a place to camp and set up for battle on the morrow.

I440-444 The Quraysh marched forth at daybreak. The battle started.

I445 Some arrows flew and one Muslim was killed. Mohammed addressed his army. "By Allah, every man who is slain this day by fighting with courage and advancing, not retreating, will enter Paradise." One of his men had been eating dates said, "You mean that there is nothing between me and Paradise except being killed by the Quraysh?" He flung the dates to the side, picked up his sword and set out to fight. He got his wish and was killed later.

I445 One of Mohammed's men asked what makes Allah laugh? Mohammed answered, "When he plunges into the midst of the enemy without armor." The man removed his coat of mail, picked up his sword and made ready to attack.

I445 Now the two armies started to close ranks and move forward. Mohammed had said that his warriors were not to start until he gave the order. Now he took a handful of pebbles and threw them at the Quraysh and said, "Curse those faces." The Muslims advanced. The battle had begun.

I451 As the battle wound down, Mohammed issued orders for the fighters to be on the look out for Abu Jahl, the enemy of Allah, among the slain. He was found still fighting in a thicket. A Muslim made for him and cut off his lower leg. Another Muslim passed by him as Abu Jahl lay dying and put his foot on his neck. The Muslim said, "Has Allah put you to shame, enemy of Allah?" Abu Jahl gasped, "How has He shamed me? Am I any more remarkable than any other you have killed?" The Muslim cut off his head.

I452 He took the head back to Mohammed and said, "Here is the head of the enemy of Allah" and threw it at Mohammed's feet. The Prophet said, "Praise be to Allah."

I455 As the bodies were dragged to a well, one of the Muslims saw the body of his father thrown in. He said, "My father was a virtuous, wise, kind, and cultured man. I had hoped he would become a Muslim. He died an unbeliever." His abode is hellfire forever. Before Islam killing of kin and tribal brothers had been forbidden since the dawn of time. After Islam brother would kill brother and sons would kill their fathers. Fighting in Allah's cause—jihad.

I454 The bodies of the Quraysh were thrown into a well. The Apostle of Allah leaned over the well and shouted at the bodies, "Oh people of the well, have you found what Allah promised to be true?" The Muslims were puzzled by his question. Mohammed explained that the dead could hear him.

I456 Now it was time to take the property from the dead who could no longer claim what had been theirs. It was now the spoils of jihad and the profit of Islam. Mohammed divided it equally among all who were there. He took one fifth for himself.

> 8:1 ***When they ask you about the spoils of war say: The spoils belong to Allah and His messenger. [This sura was written after the Battle of Badr.] Therefore, fear Allah and settle your arguments. Obey Allah and His messenger if you are truly believers.***

I459 Off they set for Medina with the spoils of war and the prisoners to be ransomed. Except for one prisoner, who had spoken against Mohammed. He was brought in front of the Prophet to be killed and before the sword struck, he asked, "Who will care for my family?"

M230 The Prophet replied, "Hell!" After he fell dead, Mohammed said, "Unbeliever in Allah and his Prophet and his Book! I give thanks to Allah who has killed you and made my eyes satisfied."

I476 After the battle of Badr there came about an entire sura of the Koran. The eighth chapter is called War Treasure or Booty and also the Spoils of War. The idea of the battle of Badr was Mohammed's. Many of the Muslims had no desire to go to war. The armed Muslims wanted to attack the caravan, not the army.

I477 The Muslims were not alone. No, Allah sent a thousand angels to help kill those who worshiped in the ancient ways and rituals. To resist Mohammed was a death sentence from Allah. When a Muslim meets a non-Muslim in war, they should never turn their backs, except as a tactical maneuver. A Muslim fighting in Allah's cause must face the enemy. To not do so brings on the wrath of Allah and the judgment of Hell.

> 8:2 ***The true believers are the ones whose hearts tremble with fear at the mention of Allah and whose faith grows stronger when His revelations are revealed to them and in Him they put their trust. True believers are dedicated to their prayers and give generously from that which We have given them. These are truly the believers. They will be raised up and receive forgiveness from their Lord, and they will receive generous provisions.***
>
> 8:5 ***Remember how your Lord commanded you to leave your homes to fight for the truth, but some of the believers were opposed to it? They disputed the truth after you had revealed it, as if they were being led to certain death before their eyes.***

8:7 *And when Allah promised that you would defeat one of the two groups of enemies, you wished to attack the group that was defenseless. [Mohammed had started out to attack a large, unarmed Meccan caravan. But a thousand-man army from Mecca arrived to protect the caravan.] But Allah wished to justify the truth of His words and to cut the unbelievers down so that the truth would triumph and the lies would be shown false, much to the opposition of the guilty.*

8:9 *Remember when you begged your Lord for help and He said, "I will send the ranks of a thousand angels to your aid?" Allah gave this as a message of good news to bring them hope for victory only comes from Allah. Allah is mighty and wise.*

8:11 *Remember when sleep overcame you, a sign of His reassurance? He sent down rain from the heavens to make you clean and to rid you of the grime of Satan, to strengthen your hearts and steady your feet. [The rain before the battle muddied the ground and hindered the Meccan cavalry.]*

8:12 *Then your Lord spoke to His angels and said, "I will be with you. Give strength to the believers. I will send terror into the unbelievers' hearts, cut off their heads and even the tips of their fingers!" This was because they opposed Allah and His messenger. Ones who oppose Allah and His messenger will be severely punished by Allah. We said, "This is for you! Taste it and know that the unbelievers will receive the torment of the Fire."*

8:15 *Believers! When you meet the unbelievers marching into battle, do not turn your back to them to retreat. Anyone who turns his back on them, unless it is for a tactical advantage or to join another company, will incur Allah's wrath and Hell will be his home, truly a tortuous end. It was not you, but Allah, that killed them. It was not you whose blows destroyed them, but Allah destroyed them so that He might give the believers a gift from Himself. Allah is all-hearing and all-knowing. Therefore, Allah will certainly thwart the plans of the unbelievers.*

8:19 *Meccans! If you sought a judgment, it has now come to you. If you cease in your persecution of the believers, it will be better for you, but if you continue in your war against the faithful, so will We continue to help them. Your vast forces will be no match for Us for Allah stands with the faithful.*

1478 When Mohammed speaks, a Muslim has only one choice. Listen and obey.

8:20 *Believers! Be obedient to Allah and His messenger, and do not turn your backs now that you know the truth. Do not be like the ones who say, "We hear," but do not obey.*

1480 If those who practice the old religions will submit to Islam then all will be forgiven. Only submission to Islam will save the unbeliever.

> 8:38 *Tell the unbelievers that if they change their ways, then they would be forgiven for their past. If, however, they continue to sin, let them remember the fate of those who came before them. Fight against them until they stop persecuting you, and Allah's religion reigns sovereign over all others. If they cease, Allah knows all they do, but if they turn their backs, know that Allah is your protector—an excellent helper.*

1481 After war and victory there is the spoils of war. One fifth is to go to the Apostle, Allah's prophet.

> 8:41 *Know that a fifth of all your spoils of war [the traditional cut for the leader was a fourth] belong to Allah, to His messenger, to the messenger's family, the orphans, and needy travelers. Sincerely believe in Allah and in what was sent down to you through His messenger on the day of victory when the two armies met. Allah is powerful over all things.*

The Koran shows how Allah helped the Muslims destroy the unbelievers.

> 8:42 *Remember when you were camped on the near side of the valley and the unbelievers were on the far side with the caravan below you? If you had made an agreement to meet in battle [against the caravan], you surely would have failed, but you went into battle [against the unbelievers army], nevertheless, so that Allah could accomplish his goal that those who were destined to die would die and so those who were meant to live would live. Allah hears and knows all.*
> 8:43 *Allah showed your enemies to you in a dream as an army few in number. If He had shown you a large army, you certainly would have been frightened and you would have had arguments among yourselves. But Allah spared you this for He knows your deepest secrets. And when you met them in battle, He made them appear to you as fewer in number than in reality so that Allah might carry out what had to be done. All things return to Allah.*

1482 In war (jihad) remember Allah all the time and you will prevail. Obey Mohammed, don't argue with him or each other. Don't quit, don't lose morale. Allah will see that you prevail. And when the unbelievers are slain, their troubles have just begun. Allah will use his angels to torture them forever.

> 8:45 *Believers! When you confront their army stand fast and pray to Allah without ceasing so that you will be victorious. Obey Allah and His messenger, and do not argue with one another for fear that you will lose courage and strength. Be patient for Allah is with the patient. Do not be like the Meccans who left home bragging and full of vainglory. They prevent others from following Allah's path, but Allah knows all that they do.*

8:48 *Satan made their sinful acts seem acceptable to them, and he said, "No one will defeat you this day, and I will be there to help you." When the two armies came within sight of one another, however, he quickly fled saying, "I am finished with you for I can see things which you cannot [the angels were helping to kill the unbelievers]. I fear Allah for Allah's punishment is severe."*
8:49 *The hypocrites [Muslims who were weak in their faith] and those with diseased hearts said, "Their religion has misled the Muslims." But those who have faith in Allah will discover that Allah is mighty and wise. If only you could witness the angels carrying off the unbelievers' souls! They slash their faces and backs saying, "Taste the torment of the Fire!"*

I483-4 Mohammed is to encourage war and lead the believers to war. With Allah 20 Muslims can kill and vanquish 200 of the non-Muslims. And 100 Muslims can destroy 1000 of the non-Muslims. The unbelievers are ignorant and easily defeated by jihad. Take no prisoners until Islam has made all submit. Forget the ransom and the money, submission of the non-believers is all that matters.

8:65 *Messenger! Call the faithful to fight. If there are among you twenty who will stand fast, they will overcome two hundred; and if there are a hundred of you, they will overcome a thousand unbelievers for they lack understanding. Allah has now lessened your burden because He knows that there is weakness in you. If there are among you a hundred men who will stand fast, they will overcome two hundred; and if there are a thousand among you, they will, by the permission of Allah, overcome two thousand. Allah is with the steadfast.*
8:67 *A prophet should not take prisoners of war until he has fought and slaughtered in the land. You desire the bounty of the world, but Allah desires the bounty for you of the world to come. Allah is mighty and wise. If there had not been a prior command from Allah, you would have been punished severely for what you had taken. But now enjoy the spoils you have taken, which are lawful and good, but fear Allah. Allah is forgiving and merciful.*

THE RAID ON THE TRIBE OF B. SULAYM

I540-543, T1365 Seven days after Mohammed returned from Badr, there were four more armed raids, but no contact with the enemy, the unbelievers.

I484 Mohammed was now a political force unlike any ever seen in history. The fusion of religion and politics with a universal mandate created a historic force that is permanent. There will be no peace until all the world is Islam. The spoils of war will provide the wealth of Islam. The awe of Mohammed is the fear of Allah.

> B1,7,331 *The Prophet said, "I have been given five things which were not given to anyone else before me.*
>
> 1. *Allah made me victorious by awe, by His frightening my enemies for a distance of one month's journey.*
> 2. *The earth has been made for me and for my followers a place for praying and to perform my rituals, therefore anyone of my followers can pray wherever the time of a prayer is due.*
> 3. *The spoils of war has been made Halal (lawful) for me yet it was not lawful for anyone else before me.*
> 4. *I have been given the right of intercession on the Day of Resurrection.*
> 5. *Every Prophet used to be sent to his nation but only I have been sent to all mankind.*

Mohammed left Mecca as a preacher and prophet. He entered Medina with about 150 Muslim converts. After a year in Medina there were about 250-300 Muslims and most of them were very poor. After the battle of Badr, a new Islam emerged. Mohammed rode out of Medina as a politician and general. Islam became an armed political force with a religious motivation, jihad.

JIHAD AND THE KORAN

CHAPTER 14

4:115 Anyone who opposes the Messenger after having received Our guidance and follows a path other than that of the true believer will be left to their own devices. We will lead them into Hell, an evil home.

The Koran uses the term "fighting in Allah's cause" for jihad.

2:190 *And fight for Allah's cause [jihad] against those who fight you, but do not be the first to attack. Allah does not love the aggressors.*
2:191 *Kill them wherever you find them, and drive them out of whatever place from which they have driven you out for persecution [the Meccans made Mohammed leave] is worse than murder. But do not fight them inside the Holy Mosque unless they attack you there; if they do, then kill them. That is the reward for the unbelievers, but if they give up their ways, Allah is forgiving and merciful.*
2:193 *Fight them until you are no longer persecuted and the religion of Allah reigns absolute, but if they give up, then only fight the evil-doers. The defilement of a sacred month and sacred things are subject to the laws of retaliation. If anyone attacks you, attack him in the same way. Fear Allah and know that He is with those who believe.*
2:195 *Spend your wealth generously for Allah's cause [jihad] and do not use your own hands to contribute to your destruction. Do good, for surely Allah loves those that do good.*

Fight for Allah's Cause

2:244 *Fight for Allah's cause [jihad] and remember that He hears and knows everything.*
2:245 *Who will lend Allah a generous loan, which He will pay back multiple times? Allah gives generously and takes away, and you will return to Him.*
2:246 *Have you not considered what the leaders of the Children of Israel said to one of their messengers when Moses died? They said, "Appoint a king for us, and we will fight for the cause of Allah." He said, "What if you decline to fight when ordered to do so?" They said, "Why would we not fight for Allah when we and our children have been driven out of our homes?" But in the end, when they were ordered to fight all but a few refused. Allah knows the evil-doers.*

2:261 *Those who give their wealth for Allah's cause are like the grain of corn that grows seven ears with each ear having one hundred kernels. Allah will multiply the wealth of those He pleases. Allah is caring and all-knowing. Those who give their wealth for Allah's cause [jihad] and do not follow their gifts with guilt-inducing comments or insults will be rewarded by their Lord. They will have nothing about which to fear or grieve.*

2:273 *Charity is for those who have fought for Allah's cause and are now unable to work the land or travel to trade. The ignorant will think that they are wealthy because they are so modest, but you can tell them by their appearance. They do not beg people unrelentingly. Whatever charity you give will be known to Allah. Allah has placed His curse on usury and His blessing on charitable giving. Allah has no love for the ungrateful and sinful.*

Give Us Victory over the Unbelievers

2:286 *Allah does not give a soul more than it can withstand. It shall be rewarded for whatever good or evil it has done. Lord, do not punish us if we forget or make a mistake. Lord, do not give us a burden such as that which was given to those who came before us. Lord, do not give us more than we are able to withstand. Forgive us and forget our sins, and show us mercy. Only You are our protector, and give us victory over the unbelievers.*

8:26 *Remember when there were only a few of you and you were despised throughout the nation, always afraid that your enemies would destroy you; it was then He sheltered you. He strengthened you with His help and gave you good things to eat so that you would be thankful.*

Do Not Let the Unbelievers Think That They Will Escape Us

8:59 *Do not let the unbelievers think that they will escape Us. They have no power to escape. Gather against them all of your armed forces and cavalry so that you may strike terror into the hearts of the enemies of Allah and your enemy, and others besides them whom you do not know but whom Allah knows. All that you give for Allah's cause [jihad] will be repaid. You will be treated with fairness.*

8:61 *And if they are of a mind to make peace, then make peace too, and put your trust in Allah for He is all-hearing and all-knowing. But if they plan to betray you, surely Allah is sufficient for you. It is He who has strengthened you with His help and with the believers, giving them affection for one another. If you had given them all the earth's wealth, you could not have bound them together, but Allah has bound them, for He is mighty and wise. Oh messenger! Allah's strength is sufficient for you and your followers.*

They Have Already Betrayed Allah

8:70 *Messenger! Tell the captives who are under your control, "If Allah finds good in your hearts [if the prisoners convert to Islam], He will give you something better than that which has been taken away from you, and He will show you forgiveness. Truly, Allah is forgiving and merciful." If, however, they plot to betray you, know that they have already betrayed Allah. He has therefore given you power over them. Allah is all-knowing and wise.*

8:72 *Truly, those who believe and have left their homes and have given of their wealth and lives for Allah's cause, and those who have taken them in and helped them, will be as close as family to each other. But those who believed but did not leave their homes, you are not beholden to them until they also go into exile. But if they seek your help on account of the faith, it is your duty to help them except those against whom you have a treaty. Allah knows all that you do.*

8:73 *The unbelievers give comfort and protection to each other, therefore, if you do not do the same for one another, there will be oppression in the land and widespread corruption.*

8:74 *Those who have believed and have left their homes and fought for Allah's cause [jihad], and those who have taken them in and given them help, they are the true believers. They will receive mercy and generous provisions. Those who have believed and left their homes to fight with you since then, they are also a part of your family. According to Allah those who are related to you by blood are the closest to you. Allah knows all things.*

Cut off Their Heads

47:1 *Those who deny Allah and prevent others from following Allah's path, He will make their plans fail. Those who believe and do good works, however, and believe in what Mohammed has revealed, as it is the truth sent down from their Lord, He will cleanse them of their sins and improve their circumstances.*

47:3 *This is because the unbelievers follow lies while the believers follow the truth sent down from their Lord. It is in this manner that Allah sets forth the rules of conduct for mankind.*

47:4 *When you encounter the unbelievers on the battlefield, cut off their heads until you have thoroughly defeated them and then take the prisoners and tie them up firmly. Afterward, either allow them to go free or let them pay you their ransom until the war is over. This you are commanded. If it had been Allah's will he would have taken out His vengeance upon them, but He has commanded this so that He may test you by using these others. As for those who are killed for Allah's cause [jihad], He will not let their sacrifice be in vain. He will lead them into Paradise, of which He has told them.*

47:7 *Believers! If you help Allah's cause [jihad], Allah will help you and make you stand firm. But as for those who deny Allah, they will be destroyed. He will make their plans fail because they have rejected His revelations. He will thwart their tactics.*

Do Not Be Weak and Offer the Unbelievers Peace

47:33 *Believers! Obey Allah and the messenger, and do not let your effort be in vain. Those who do not believe and who prevent others from following Allah's path and then die as unbelievers will not receive Allah's forgiveness. Therefore, do not be weak and offer the unbelievers peace when you have the upper hand, for Allah is with you and will not begrudge you the reward of your deeds.*

47:34 *Those who do not believe and who prevent others from following Allah's path and then die as unbelievers will not receive Allah's forgiveness. Therefore, do not be weak and offer the unbelievers peace when you have the upper hand for Allah is with you and will not begrudge you the reward of your deeds.*

47:36 *Truly this present life is only for play and amusement, but if you believe and fear Him, He will give you your reward and will not ask you to give up your worldly wealth. But if He were to ask you for all of it and strongly urge you, you would become greedy, and this would reveal your hatred.*

47:38 *You are called upon to give to Allah's cause [jihad], but some of you are greedy. Whoever of you acts miserly does so only at the expense of his own soul. Truly, Allah has no use for you, but you have need for Him. If you turn your backs on Him, He will simply replace you with others who will not act like you!*

Stand Together in Battle Array like a Solid Wall

61:1 *All that is in the heavens and earth gives praise to Allah for He is mighty and wise.*

61:2 *Believers! Why do you say you do things that you never actually do? [At the battle of Uhud, some who had pledged courage fled and failed to fight.] It is most hateful in Allah's sight when you say one thing and yet do another.*

61:4 *Truly Allah loves those who fight for His cause and stand together in battle array like a solid wall.*

61:5 *Remember when Moses said to his people, "My People, why do you try to persecute me when you know that Allah has sent me to you?" So when they went astray, Allah allowed their hearts to wander for Allah will not guide evil-doers.*

Fight Valiantly for Allah's Cause

61:10 ***Believers! Should I show you a profitable exchange that will keep you from severe torment? Believe in Allah and His messenger and fight valiantly for Allah's cause [jihad] with both your wealth and your lives. It would be better for you, if you only knew it!***

61:12 ***He will forgive you of your sins and lead you into Gardens beneath which rivers flow. He will keep you in beautiful mansions in the Gardens of Eden. That is the ultimate triumph. And He will give you other blessings for which you long: help from Allah and a swift victory. Give the good news to the believers.***

61:14 ***Believers! Be Allah's helpers just as Jesus, son of Mary, said to his disciples, "Who will help me to do the work of Allah?" and they replied, "We are Allah's helpers." Some among the Children of Israel believed in him and others did not. But for those who believed, We gave them victory over their enemies.***

57:10 ***And for what reason should you not give to Allah's cause [jihad], when the heavens and earth are Allah's inheritance alone? Those of you who gave to the cause before the victory and fought will receive a greater reward than those who gave and fought after it. But Allah has promised a good reward to all of you. Allah knows all that you do. Who will loan generously to Allah? He will pay him back double what he is owed, and he will receive a noble reward.***

4:88 ***Why are you divided into two groups concerning the hypocrites when Allah Himself has turned away from them because of their evil deeds? Do you wish to guide those whom Allah has led astray? You will not be able to guide those whom Allah leads astray.***

Seize Them and Kill Them Wherever They Are

4:91 ***You will also find others who seek to gain your confidence as well as that of their own people. Every time they are thrown back into temptation, they fall into it deeply. If they do not keep away from you or offer you peace or withdraw their hostilities, then seize them and kill them wherever they are. We give you complete authority over them.***

When You Travel Abroad to Fight for Allah's Cause

4:94 ***Believers! When you travel abroad to fight for Allah's cause [jihad], be discerning, and do not say to everyone who greets you, "You are not a believer," only seeking the fleeting joys of this world [by killing the unbeliever and taking their property]. With Allah are abundant joys. You too were like them before Allah granted His grace to you. Therefore, be perceptive; Allah knows all that you do.***

4:95 ***Believers who stay at home in safety, other than those who are disabled, are not equal to those who fight with their wealth and their lives*** *for Allah's cause [jihad]. Allah has ranked those who fight earnestly with their wealth and lives above those who stay at home. Allah has promised good things to all, but those who fight for Him will receive a far greater reward than those who have not. They will be conferred ranks especially from Him, along with forgiveness and mercy, for Allah is forgiving and merciful.*

Do Not Relent in Pursuing the Enemy

4:100 *Those who leave their homes for Allah's cause [jihad] will find many places of refuge and provisions in the earth. Those who leave their homes flying to fight for Allah and His Messenger and die, their reward from Allah is assured. Allah is gracious and merciful!*

4:101 *When you go forth through the land for war, you will not be blamed if you cut your prayers short because you fear that the unbelievers are about to attack you for the unbelievers are your undoubted enemies.*

4:102 *And when you [Mohammed] are with the believers conducting prayer, let a group of them stand up with you, taking their weapons with them. After they have prostrated themselves, let them go back to the rear and allow another group to come up and pray with you, also allowing them to be armed. It would please the unbelievers if you failed to carry your weapons and luggage so that they could attack you all at once. You will not be blamed if you lay down your weapons when a heavy rain impedes you or when you are sick, but you must always be vigilant. Allah has prepared a disgraceful torment for the unbelievers.*

4:103 *And when you have finished your prayers, remember Allah when you are standing, sitting, and lying down. But when you are free from danger, attend to your prayers regularly for prayer at certain times is commanded for believers.*

4:104 *Do not relent in pursuing the enemy. If you are suffering, so are they, but you have hope from Allah while they have none. Allah is all-knowing and wise!*

59:9 *Those who remained in Medina in their homes and have embraced the faith take care of those who have fled seeking refuge. They are not jealous of what the refugees have received but give them preference above themselves, even though they are poor. Those who keep themselves from their own jealousies will be prosperous. And those who came after them in the faith say, "Lord! Forgive us as well as those who preceded us in the faith, and do not cause us to have ill-will toward the faithful. Our Lord! Truly you are kind and merciful."*

Allah Is Able to Make Them Victorious

22:39 *Those who have been attacked are given permission to fight because they have been persecuted, and surely Allah is able to make them victorious. There are some who have been driven out of their homes unjustly just because they said, "Allah is our Lord." If Allah had not repelled some men by using others [war], the monasteries, churches, synagogues, and mosques, in which Allah's name is praised, would have been destroyed. But surely Allah will help those who help Him in His cause. Allah is strong and mighty. Allah will surely help those who, once we establish them as leaders in the land, pray regularly and pay the poor tax and command what is right and forbid what is wrong. And the final outcome of all things is in Allah's hands.*

22:58 *Those who fled their homes for Allah's cause [jihad] and were killed or died as a result, surely Allah will provide for them generously, for Allah is the best provider. Allah will certainly lead them in with a pleasing welcome. Allah is all-knowing and gracious. So it will be. Whoever retaliates with the same force with which he was wronged and continues to be oppressed, Allah will help him. Allah is merciful and forgiving.*

Fight Valiantly for Allah's Cause

22:78 *Fight valiantly for Allah's cause [jihad] as it benefits you to do for Him. He has chosen you, and has not made hardships for you in the religion; it is the religion of your father Abraham. It was Allah who called you Muslims, both in previous scriptures and now, so that the Messenger may be a witness for you and that you may be his witness against mankind. Therefore, pray regularly, pay the poor tax, and hold firmly to Allah, for He is your protector. He is he best protector and the best helper.*

So Make War on Them

9:7 *How can unbelievers be allies with Allah and with His Messenger except those with whom you made an agreement at the Sacred Temple [the Kabah]? So long as they are true to you, be true to them, for Allah loves the righteous.*

9:8 *How can there be a treaty for the others, since if they prevailed against you, they would not respect your agreement? They will speak fair words from their mouths, but their hearts will be against you. Most of them are rebellious and wicked. They have made some gains with the signs of Allah, and they have hindered many from His way. Evil is what they do. They do not respect the ties of blood or faith regarding the believers. These are the wrongdoers. Yet if they turn to Allah, observe regular prayer, and practice regular charity, they are your brothers in religion. We explain Our signs in detail for those who understand.*

9:12 *If the unbelievers break their oaths and revile your religion after an alliance is made, then fight the leaders of unbelief, for their oaths are nothing to them, so they may be stopped. Will you not fight against those Meccans who have broken their oaths, plotted to expel your Messenger, and attacked you first? Do you fear them? Allah is more worthy of your fear, if you are believers. So make war on them. Allah will punish them by your hands. He will put them to shame and will give you victory over them. He will heal the hearts of the believers and will remove the wrath in their hearts. Allah gives mercy to whom He will. Allah is knowing and wise.*

9:16 *Do you think that you will be abandoned as if Allah did not yet know those among you who struggle and who have not taken anyone for friends beside Allah, His apostle, and the faithful? Allah is well aware of what you do.*

Strives Hard in Allah's Cause

9:19 *Do you compare him who gives drink to the pilgrims and who visits the Sacred Temple to him who believes in Allah and the Last Day and strives hard in Allah's cause? They are not equal in the sight of Allah, and He does not guide the unrighteous.*

9:20 *They who have believed, have fled their homes, and have striven with all their might with their property and their souls in the cause of Allah will have the highest rank with Him. These are the ones who are triumphant. Their Lord sends them tidings of mercy from Himself and of His good pleasure and Gardens in which lasting pleasure will be theirs. They will abide there forever. Allah's presence is the greatest reward of all.*

9:100 *As for those who led the way: the first of the Emigrants [those who left Mecca with Mohammed], the Helpers [the Medinans who helped the Muslims from Mecca], and those who have followed their noble conduct, Allah is well pleased with them, and they with Him. He has made them Gardens under whose trees the rivers flow to abide therein forever. This will be the mighty achievement.*

They Could Not Spend Anything in Allah's Cause

9:120 *The people of Medina and the Arabs of the desert around them had no cause to abandon Allah's Messenger or to prefer their own lives to his because anything they did or suffered was seen as a deed of righteousness. Whether they suffer thirst, fatigue, or hunger in the name of Allah, or take any steps that anger the unbelievers, or receive any damage from the enemy, it is all written down for them as a good work. Allah does not allow the reward of the righteous [those who die in jihad] to perish.*

9:121 *They could not spend anything in Allah's cause [jihad], small or great, nor cross any valley but it is written down in their credit. Allah may reward them with better than they have wrought.*

5:33 *The only reward for those who war against Allah and His messengers and strive to commit mischief on the earth is that they will be slain or crucified, have their alternate hands and feet cut off, or be banished from the land. This will be their disgrace in this world, and a great*

torment shall be theirs in the next except those who repent before you overpower them. Know that Allah is forgiving and merciful.
5:35 *Oh you who believe, fear Allah, and seek the means to be near Him. Strive earnestly on his path so that you may attain happiness.*

JIHAD, THE JEWS' EXILE

CHAPTER 15

61:11 Believe in Allah and His messenger and fight valiantly for Allah's cause [jihad] with both your wealth and your lives. It would be better for you, if you only knew it!

THE AFFAIR OF THE JEWS OF QAYNUQA

I545 There were three tribes of Jews in Medina. The Beni Qaynuqa were gold smiths and lived in a stronghold in their quarters. It is said by Mohammed that they broke the treaty that had been signed when Mohammed came to Medina. How they did this is unclear.

I545 Mohammed assembled the Jews in their market and said: "Oh Jews, be careful that Allah does not bring vengeance upon you like what happened to the Quraysh. Become Muslims. You know that I am the prophet that was sent you. You will find that in your scriptures."

I545 They replied: "Oh Mohammed you seem to think that we are your people. Don't fool yourself. You may have killed and beaten a few merchants of the Quraysh, but we are men of war and real men."

I545 The response of the Koran:

> 3:12 ***Say to the unbelievers, "Soon you will be defeated and thrown into Hell, a wretched home!" Truly, there has been a sign for you in the two armies which met in battle [at the battle of Badr, 300 Muslim defeated 1000 Meccans]. One army fought for Allah's cause, and the other army was a group of unbelievers, and the unbelievers saw with their own eyes that their enemy was twice its actual size. Allah gives help to whom He pleases. Certainly there is a lesson to be learned in this for those who recognize it.***

I546 Some time later Mohammed besieged the Jews in the their quarters. None of the other two Jewish tribes came to their support. Finally the Jews surrendered and expected to be slaughtered after their capture.

I546 But an Arab ally bound to them by a client relationship approached Mohammed and said, "Oh Mohammed deal kindly with my clients." Mohammed ignored him. The ally repeated the request and again Mohammed ignored him. The ally grabbed Mohammed by the robe and enraged Mohammed who said, "Let me go!" The ally said, "No, you must deal kindly with my clients. They have protected me and now you would kill them all? I fear these changes." The response by the Koran:

> 5:51 ***Oh, believers, do not take the Jews or Christians as friends. They are but one another's friends. If any one of you take them for his friends, he surely is one of them. Allah will not guide the evildoers.***
> 5:52 ***You will see those who have a diseased heart race towards them and say, "We fear in case a change of fortune befalls us." Perhaps Allah will bring about some victory or event of His own order. Then they will repent of the thoughts they secretly held in their hearts.***
> 5:53 ***Then the faithful will say, "Are these the men who swore their most solemn oath by Allah that they were surely with you?" Their deeds will be in vain, and they will come to ruin. Oh, you who believe, if any of you desert His religion, Allah will then raise up a people whom He will love and who will be loved by Him. They will be humble towards the faithful and haughty towards the unbelievers. They will strive hard for Allah's cause [jihad], and not fear the blame of any blamer. This is the grace of Allah. He gives to whom He pleases. Allah is all-embracing and all-knowing.***

Mohammed exiled the Jews and took all of their wealth and goods.

THE RAID TO AL QARADA

I547 Mohammed's victory at Badr and ongoing jihad caused the Quraysh to go a different route to Syria. They hired a new guide to take them over the new route. Mohammed had intelligence about their route and sent a party to raid them. They were carrying a great deal of silver when the caravan stopped at a watering hole. The Muslims surprised them and the Quraysh managed to escape but Mohammed's men were able to steal all the caravan's goods, including the silver. The stolen goods were delivered to Mohammed in Medina.

THE ASSASSINATION OF AL ASHRAF, THE JEW

I548 When Al Ashraf, a Jew of Medina, heard that two of his friends had been killed at Badr, he said that the grave was a better place than the earth with Mohammed. So the "enemy of Allah" composed some poems bewailing the loss of his friends and attacking Islam.

I551 When Mohammed heard of Al Ashraf's criticism of his politics, he said, "Who will rid me of Al Ashraf?" A Muslim said, "I will kill him for you." Days later Mohammed found out that his assassin was not doing anything, including eating or drinking. Mohammed summoned him and asked what was going on. The man replied that he had taken on a task that was too difficult for him to do. Mohammed said that it was a duty which he should try to do. The assassin said, "Oh Apostle of Allah, I will have to tell a lie." The Prophet said, "Say what you like, you are free in the matter."

I552 By the use of lies three Muslims were able to kill Al Ashraf. When they returned to Mohammed, he was praying. They told him that they had killed the enemy of Allah. Their attack terrorized all the Jews. There was no Jew in Medina who was not afraid.

KILL ANY JEW THAT FALLS INTO YOUR POWER

I554 The Apostle of Allah said, "Kill any Jew who falls into your power." Hearing this Muhayyisa fell upon a Jewish merchant who was a business associate and killed him. His brother was not a Muslim and asked him how he could kill a man who had been his friend and partner in many business deals. The Muslim said that if Mohammed had asked him to kill his brother he would have done it immediately. His brother said, "You mean that if Mohammed said to cut off my head you would do it?" "Yes," was the reply. The older brother then said, "By Allah, any religion which brings you to this is marvelous." And he decided then and there to become a Muslim.

JIHAD, A SETBACK

CHAPTER 16

4:14 But those who disobey Allah and His Messenger and go beyond His limits, will be led into the Fire to live forever, and it will be a humiliating torment!

THE BATTLE OF UHUD

I555 Back at Mecca those who had lost at the battle of Badr told others, "Men of Quraysh, Mohammed has killed your best men. Give us money so that we may take revenge." Money was raised, men were hired. An army was put together.

I558 So the Meccans camped near Medina, ready for war. Ready for revenge. The Muslims now needed a strategy. Many, including Mohammed, wanted to sit and let the Meccans attack Medina. The town itself could be used in a defensive way—walls and rooftops would give any defender a strong advantage. But blood ran hot with the Muslim warriors. They were not afraid to meet the Meccans on the field of combat, man to man. After Badr, they were invincible. Allah had said as much. They said, "Mohammed lead us to our enemies, don't let them think that we are weak and cowards." The arguments went on until Mohammed went in his house and came out in his armor.

I559 But now, seeing him in his armor, the hot bloods repented and said that they should never try to persuade Mohammed to do anything. They had been wrong. Mohammed said, "When a prophet puts on his armor, he should not take it off until there has been war." So he marched out with a 1000 men to meet the Meccans.

I560 When they saw the Meccans, Mohammed said, "Let there be no fighting until I give the word." What they saw made the Muslims' blood boil. The Meccans had put their camels and horses into the crops of the Muslims. Mohammed placed 50 archers to protect his rear and flank. They must not move but hold that ground. Mohammed put on a second coat of mail (armor).

I562 The morrow came and the battle was to begin. Now the Meccans had brought their women for the sole purpose to urge on the men. Men do not want to be cowards in front of women. The women began to beat their tambourines and chant poetry:

If you advance we will hug you
And place soft rugs beneath you
If you retreat we will leave you
Leave and no more love you.

I570 The Muslims fought without fear and the battle went against the Meccans who were cut off from their camp that had the spoils of war. The Muslim archers left their positions to get to the spoils. The battle might go to Islam, but the treasure would be theirs. This left the flank and rear open and the Meccan cavalry took advantage and charged the rear where Mohammed was. The battle suddenly went against the Muslims.

I571 The Muslims were put to flight and many were slain. Even Mohammed got hit in the face by a rock, broke a tooth and split his lip. He was incensed. The Meccans were all around and the Muslims had to protect him with their bodies.

I574 At one point the Meccans thought that they had killed the man who had brought them so much pain. But one Muslim recognized the prophet under his helmet and spread the news of his living. Mohammed fled the field. He was a heavy man, and wore two suits of armor. He almost could not climb the rocks and hill without help.

I583 The day went to the Meccans, the Quraysh. The Meccans did not press their advantage. They came to extract tribal justice and they killed about as many the Muslims had killed at Badr. They did not want to dominate Islam. Abu Sufyan, the Meccan leader, agreed through an emissary that they would meet in combat next year.

We have paid you back for Badr
And a war that follows a war is violent
I could not bear the loss of my friends
Nor my brother and his uncle and my first born.
I have slaked my vengeance and fulfilled my vow.
The slave who killed Hamza has cooled the burning in my breast
I shall thank the slave now free
Until my bones rot in the grave. —*Hind*

I586 The dead Muslims were buried in the battlefield. Mohammed said, "I testify that none who are wounded in jihad but what he will be raised by Allah with his bleeding wounds smelling like the finest perfume." When Mohammed heard the women weeping for their dead, but he wanted wailing for his uncle Hamza as well. So the women wailed for Hamza and Mohammed felt better.

I587 When Mohammed entered his house he handed his sword to his daughter and told her, "Wash the blood from this for by Allah it has served me well today." The next day he ordered all the fighters who had been at Uhud to marshal themselves and be ready to head out to pursue the enemy. This move was pure strategy to impress the enemy that he was still strong and not weakened by his losses. They went about eight miles from Medina and camped for three days before returning to Medina.

I589 Mohammed was the supreme master of the psychology of war. He sent an agent, who pretended to be a friend of the Meccans, to Abu Sufyan, the Meccan leader. Abu Sufyan was thinking about going back and finishing off the Muslims. But Mohammed's agent told Abu Sufyan that Mohammed was coming very soon with an army, the like of which had never been seen. They were in a state of total fury and would sweep into Hell all that were in front of them. Abu Sufyan, the merchant, left for Mecca and security. They had settled their score.

THE KORAN AND THE BATTLE OF UHUD

Since Allah had sent angels to the previous battle of Badr and the outnumbered Muslims triumphed, how could they fail at Uhud?

I593 Two of the clans of Muslims had doubts about the battle. But Allah was their friend and they did not doubt Islam and went on into the battle because of their belief in Allah and Mohammed.

> 3:121 ***Remember when you [Mohammed] left your home early in the morning to lead the believers to their battle stations [battle of Uhud]? Allah heard and knew all. When two of your brigades showed cowardice, Allah protected them both. Let the faithful put their trust in Allah. Allah made you victorious at Badr when you were the weaker army. Therefore, fear Allah and be grateful to Him. Then you said to the believers, "Is it not enough for you that your Lord helped you by sending down three thousand angels?" Yes! And if you stand firm and fear Allah and you are suddenly attacked by your enemies, Allah will send down five thousand angels to wreak havoc upon them.***
>
> 3:126 ***Allah intended this to be good news for you so your hearts will know peace. Victory comes from Allah alone, He is mighty and wise so that He might destroy a portion of the unbelievers, humiliate them, and keep them from their purpose. It is none of your concern whether He forgives them or punishes them for, truly, they are evil-doers. All that is in the heaven and earth belongs to Allah. He will forgive whom He pleases and punish whom He pleases. Allah is forgiving and merciful.***

I595 The reason for the loss was that the archers did not hold their ground, When they saw that the Meccans were cut off from their camp, they ran to get the spoils of war. Greed caused them to disobey Mohammed. So they should always obey Mohammed, he speaks for the Lord of all. Those who did not follow orders should ask for forgiveness. If they will see that it was their fault and be remorseful they can still get their reward of heaven.

> 3:131 ***Obey Allah and His messenger so that you may receive mercy. Urge each other on to earn forgiveness from your Lord, and the Paradise as wide as heaven and earth is prepared for the righteous. Those who give freely, whether they are prosperous or poor; who control their anger; who are forgiving (for Allah loves those who do good); who, when they have sinned or wronged themselves, go to Allah and implore His forgiveness for their sins (for who except Allah can forgive you of your sins?) and do not knowingly continue in their sinning; these will be rewarded with their Lord's forgiveness and with the Garden watered by flowing rivers where they will live forever. The reward is great for those who serve Him!***
> 3:137 ***There have been many religions that have come and gone before you. Travel the world and see what became of those who rejected the faith. The Koran is a clear statement for mankind: a guide and a warning to those who fear Allah. Therefore, do not lose heart or despair; if you are a true believer, you will be victorious.***

I597 The reason that Allah let the Meccans win was to test the Muslims. Now they will know their true selves. Are they fair weather friends of Mohammed or can they see their faults? If they obey Mohammed, then they can become true Muslims. A true Muslim never loses his morale, never falls into despair.

I596 If you have been wounded or suffered losses in the battle, don't forget that the non-Muslims have also suffered. Over the long view, fortunes go up and down. You must take the long view and believe in Mohammed and know that all will turn out well in the end. But those who died have the best reward. They are martyrs for Islam. Those who do wrong are the hypocrites, the pretenders.

> 3:140 ***If you have been wounded [Muslims lost the battle of Uhud], be certain that the same has already befallen your enemies. We bring misfortune to mankind in turns so that Allah can discern who are the true believers, and so that We may select martyrs from among you. Allah does not love those who do evil. It is also Allah's purpose to test the believers and to destroy the unbelievers.***

I596 The Muslims must realize that Allah will purify them through tests such as the one they have just had. Those of true faith will not be discouraged. The hypocrites will be exposed and deprived of all blessing. Do you think you will get to heaven before Allah has tested you? Allah must know who is really a believer. A Muslim warrior must be given a trial. Losing at Uhud is merely a trial. After the big victory at Badr, those who were not there wanted to be part of the winning army. They were anxious to be able to show off as warriors, but when the actual killing started, many were not as good as they thought they would be.

> 3:142 ***Did you think that you would be permitted into Paradise before Allah tested you to see who would fight for His cause [jihad] and endure until the end? You used to wish for death before you saw it, but now that you have seen it with your own eyes, you turn and run from it. Mohammed is only a messenger, and many messengers have come before him. If he died or was killed, would you turn your backs on the faith? But those who do in fact turn their backs will not hurt Allah in the least. And Allah will surely reward those who serve Him with gratitude.***
> 3:145 ***No soul will ever die unless it is Allah's will. The length of each life is predetermined according to the Scriptures. Those who wish to receive their reward in this world will receive it, and those who wish to receive their reward in the world to come will also receive it. And We will undoubtedly reward those who serve Us with gratitude.***

I597 The Muslims should not think that they are the first to experience failure. In history many have failed in jihad, but they never lost heart or weakened. The lesson of Uhud is to be firm and not get depressed over a small failure.

> 3:146 ***Many of the messengers have fought for Allah's cause [jihad] alongside large armies. They were never frightened by what they encountered on Allah's path, nor did they weaken or cringe with fear. Allah loves those who stand firm. Their only cry was this, "Lord! Forgive us of our sins and the things we have done that were against our duty; help us stand firm and make us victorious over the unbelievers." Therefore, Allah gave them their reward in this world, as well as an excellent reward in the world to come. Allah loves those who do good.***

I599 Do not think that the jihad is over. Soon Islam will bring terror to the unbelievers. After death, they will burn in Hell. The evil that will bring about their destruction is that they do not practice the religion of Islam.

> 3:149 ***Believers! If you follow the unbelievers, they will cause you to reject the faith and lead you to eternal damnation. But Allah is your protector and the best of helpers. We will strike terror into the hearts of the***

unbelievers because they worship others besides Allah, which He gave them no permission to do. Their home will be the Fire, a terrible resting place for the evil-doers.

1599 Your slaughter of the unbelievers went well and you were about to wipe the unbelievers off the face of the earth, thanks to Allah. But then you disobeyed Mohammed. Allah did not destroy you because he is merciful. But your greed is of this world and you wanted the spoils of war of this world. But you must desire what comes after death, not the wealth of this world. You must learn this lesson with the grace of Allah.

3:152 *Allah fulfilled His covenant with you [Mohammed] when He allowed you to destroy your enemies [at the battle of Badr]. And then later, when you [the Muslims at Uhud] lost your courage, arguments broke out among you [the Muslims disobeyed orders and broke ranks to run and get the exposed spoils of the Meccans] and you sinned after you had come so close to what you wanted [spoils of war]. Some of you wish for the desires of this world and some of you for the world to come. Therefore, He caused you to be defeated so that you might be tested. Now He has forgiven you for Allah shows grace to the believers.*
3:153 *Remember when you [at Uhud the Muslims broke and fled] ran up the hill in cowardice and paid no attention to anyone and the messenger was behind you calling you back to the battle? Allah rewarded you with trouble for the trouble you caused Him so that you would not grieve for the spoils you lost or for what happened to you. Allah knows all that you do.*

1601 After the battle some were at ease, but others were in a state of anxiety because they did not trust Allah. The hypocrites divorced themselves from the decision and blamed others for failure. If they had had their way then everyone would have been safe. But when Allah decrees your time has come, nothing can stay the hand of death. Death must come and it is better to die in jihad.

3:154 *Then, after the trouble Allah sent down upon you, He sent down calmness to wash over some of you. Some were overtaken by sleep, and others lay awake, stirred by their own passions, ignorantly thinking unjust thoughts about Allah. And they ask, "What do we gain by this affair?" Say: Truly the affair is entirely in Allah's hands. They hide in their hearts that which they do not want to tell you. They speak out saying, "If we had any say in this affair then none of us would have been killed here." Say: If you had stayed at home, those of you who were destined to be killed would have died regardless. This has taken place so that Allah might test your faith and see what is in your hearts. Allah knows the deepest secrets of every heart. Those of you who fled in cowardice on the day the two armies met in battle must have been tricked by Satan because of some evil you have done. But now Allah has forgiven you for Allah is forgiving and gracious.*

Those who die in jihad will be rewarded by Allah.

3:156 *Believers! Do not follow the unbelievers' example when they say about their brothers who have been killed in a foreign country or in battle, "If only they had stayed at home they would not have died or have been killed!" Allah will make them regret what they have said. Allah is the giver of both life and death; Allah knows all that you do.*
3:157 *The forgiveness and mercy they, who die or are killed for Allah's cause, will receive from Allah will be far better than anything they could have gained. If you die or are killed, then surely you will all be gathered before Allah.*

I602 But Mohammed must be gentle with the Muslims. So he will overlook their faults and will forgive them. He will still consult with them, but the final decision must lie with Allah and Mohammed.

3:158 *It was because of Allah's mercy that you spoke so gently to them. For if you had dealt with them severely or been hard-hearted, they would have turned away from you. Therefore, forgive them and ask Allah to forgive them and counsel them in the affair of war; and when you have resolved the matters, put your trust in Allah. Allah loves those who trust Him. If Allah is helping you, no one can defeat you. But if He leaves you, who will be there to help you when He is gone? Therefore, let the faithful put their trust in Allah.*

I603 The Muslim's loss was a test that was brought on by their decisions. The hypocrites were told to fight in jihad or at least defend the city. Their excuses are those of an unbeliever.

3:165 *And when disaster [battle of Uhud] befell you, although it brought destruction twice as great to the unbelievers, you said, "Why is this happening to us?" Say to them, "You have brought this upon yourselves for Allah controls all things. The destruction which befell you the day the two armies met in battle was Allah's will so He would recognize who were the true believers and who were the hypocrites." And when they were told, "Come and fight for Allah's cause [jihad] and drive your enemies back," they replied, "If we knew how to fight, then we would have followed you."*
3:168 *Some of them were closer to unbelief than faith that day. What they said with their mouths was not what was in their hearts, but Allah knew what they were hiding in their hearts. It was these who said, while sitting at home, of their brothers, "If only they had listened to us, then*

they would not have been killed." Say: Try to avert your death if what you say is true!

3:169 *Never believe that those who have been killed for Allah's cause [jihad] are dead. No, they are alive with their Lord and receive rich provisions. They rejoice in the bounty Allah gives them and are joyful for those left behind who have yet to join them that they will have nothing fear or regret. They are filled with joy for Allah's grace and blessings. Allah will not fail to reward the faithful.*

3:172 *As for those who answered the call of Allah and His messenger after they were defeated [battle of Uhud], those of them who do good works and fear Allah will be richly rewarded. They are the ones who when it was said to them, "Your enemies are gathering vast armies against you, so fear them," it only increased their faith and they said, "Allah's help is enough for us. He is the most excellent protector." It was in this manner that they earned Allah's grace and blessings, and no harm came to them. And they worked to please Allah for Allah is full of boundless grace.*

I606 The success that the unbelievers are experiencing is temporary. They will grow in their evil and they will be punished. Allah will not leave the believers in this state. But this trial will separate the weak from the strong. Those who have wealth should spend it on Allah's cause.

3:175 *It is only Satan who causes you to fear his followers [the leaders of the Meccans]. Do not fear them; fear Me if you are truly believers. Do not be distressed for those who turn away from the faith for Allah is not hurt by them. Allah will refuse them any part of the world to come. Severe torment awaits them. Those who trade their faith for unbelief will do no harm to Allah, and they will receive a painful punishment.*

3:178 *Do not let the unbelievers think that we lengthen their days for their own good. We give them time only hoping that they will commit more serious sins. They will receive a shameful punishment.*

There Are Those as Well Who Give Their Lives to Earn Allah's Approval

2:207 *There are those as well who give their lives to earn Allah's approval; Allah shows compassion to His servants.*

2:208 *Believers, enter into submission to Islam with all your heart and do not follow the path of Satan. He is your avowed enemy. If you backslide after receiving these clear signs, then recognize that Allah is mighty and wise.*

2:210 *Are they going to wait until Allah comes down to them in the shadows of the clouds with His angels? By that time they will have already been judged for all decisions go back to Allah. Ask the Children of Israel how many clear signs We have sent down to them. But anyone who alters*

Allah's gift [the Koran] after they have received it will see that He is severe in His punishment.

2:212 *The life of this world is full of temptations for the unbelievers, and they ridicule the faithful. But those who fear Allah will be above them on the Day of Resurrection. Allah gives generously to whom He pleases.*

2:213 *All the people of the world were once only one nation. Then Allah sent messengers to bring them good news and to warn them with the Scriptures and the truth so it would be the deciding factor in people's disputes. Only the People of the Book argued about the Scriptures after having received clear signs because of their hatred for one another. Allah guided the believers to the truth concerning their disputes. Allah will guide whom He pleases to the right path.*

2:214 *Did you think that you would enter Paradise without having to experience the same trials as those who came before you? Suffering and affliction came to them, and they were so upset that each messenger and his followers called out, "When will Allah help us?" Allah's help is always near.*

Until He Divides the Bad from the Good

3:179 *It is not Allah's will that the believers should remain in their present condition but only until He divides the bad from the good [reveals the hypocrites]. Neither is it Allah's will to reveal the secrets of the unknown, but Allah chooses those of His messengers whom pleases to know them. Therefore, believe in Allah and His messengers, and if you have faith and fear Allah, then you will receive a great reward.*

3:180 *Never let those who selfishly store up the wealth Allah has given them think that they are doing good. No! It will be bad for them. The wealth they have amassed will be a weight upon their shoulders on the Day of Resurrection. The heavens and the earth are Allah's inheritance, and Allah knows all that you do.*

Do Not Be Fooled by the Unbelievers' Good Fortune

3:195 *And their Lord heard them and said, "I will not keep any man or woman from receiving the reward of their work. You are created from one another." For those who fled their homes and were expelled from their country and those who were persecuted because of Me and have fought and died, I will wash away their sins and lead them into the Garden watered by flowing rivers. A reward from Allah and with Allah is the best of rewards." Do not be fooled by the unbelievers' good fortune [winning at the battle of Uhud].*

3:197 *It is only a fleeting comfort! [The victory of the Meccans at Uhud will be avenged.] Hell will be their home, a wretched bed. As for those who fear their Lord, they will live forever in the Garden watered by flowing rivers, and they will receive Allah's welcome reception. Allah's reward is surely better for those who are righteous.*

3:199 *There are some among the People of the Book [Christians and Jews] who believe in Allah and in what has been sent down to you and in what was sent down to them. They bow in humility to Allah and do not trade Allah's revelations for a meager price. These will be rewarded by their Lord. Allah is quick in His accounting.*

3:200 *Believers! Be patient and outlast all others in your endurance. Stand firm and fear Allah so that you may be victorious.*

ASSASSINATION AS JIHAD

M276 After Uhud, several tribes allied themselves under the leadership of Sufyan Ibn Khalid. Mohammed dispatched an assassin to kill him, for without his leadership the coalition would fall apart. So the assassin, Abdullah, joined his forces and waited until he was alone with him. He killed Sufyan and cut off his head and went back to Medina.

M276 Abdullah then went straight to Mohammed. Mohammed welcomed him and asked him how it went. Abdullah presented Mohammed with the head of his enemy. Mohammed was gratified and presented him with his walking stick. He said, "This is a token between you and me on the day of resurrection. Very few will have such to lean on in that day." Abdullah attached it to his sword scabbard.

JIHAD, THE JEWS SUBMIT

CHAPTER 17

58:20 Those who oppose Allah and His Messenger will be laid low. Allah has declared, "Surely I will be victorious, along with My messengers." Truly Allah is strong and mighty.

CLEANSING

I652 It had been four years since Mohammed came to Medina. Mohammed went to one of the two remaining Jewish tribes to ask for blood money for the two men his fighter had killed. At first they said yes, but as they talked about it they decided that this would be a good time to kill Mohammed. Here he was in their quarter of Medina sitting on a wall near a roof. Why not send a man up and drop a rock on this man who had been such a sorrow to them? Mohammed got word of the plot and left.

I653 This was as good a reason as any to deal with the Jews. The same Jews who insisted that he was not the prophet. He raised his army and went off to put their fortresses under siege. These Jews were farmers and they grew the finest dates in all of Arabia. So Mohammed cut and burned their date palms as they watched. They called out, "You have prohibited wanton destruction and blamed those who do that. Now you do what you forbid."

I653 Now the other Jewish tribe had assured them that they would come to their defense. But no Jew would stand with another Jew against Islam. With no help from their brothers, the besieged Jews cut a deal with the apostle of Allah. Spare their lives and let them go with what they could carry on their camels, except for their armor.

I654 When there was fighting in jihad, the fighter got four-fifths. But since there had been no fighting there was no reason to give four-fifths to the jihadists. All of the spoils went to Mohammed, not just one fifth.

I654 There were some new problems created—the burning of the date palms and all the money going to Mohammed. The Koran had the answers. It was Allah who wrecked his vengeance upon the Jews and gave Mohammed power over them. It was even Allah who caused the Jews to tear down their own houses.

> 59:2 *It was He who caused the People of the Book [the Jews] to leave their homes and go into the first exile. They did not think they would leave, and they thought that their fortresses could protect them from Allah. But Allah's wrath reached them from where they did not expect it and cast terror into their hearts, so that they destroyed their homes with their own hands, as well as by the hands of the believers. Take warning from this example, you who have the eyes to see it!*

I654 And the Jews were very fortunate that Allah let them go with a few worldly possessions. They got out alive, Allah did not slay them, but they will burn in Hell since they resisted Mohammed. Resist Islam and Allah will punish you. As far as the wanton destruction of the palm trees, that cannot be laid to Mohammed, it was the Jew's fault. They should have done what Allah wanted and then the Jews would not have suffered Allah's vengeance.

> 59:3 *And if Allah had not decreed their exile, surely He would have punished them in this world. And in the world to come they will receive the punishment of the Fire because they had disobeyed Allah and His Messenger. Whoever disobeys Allah, knows that Allah is truly severe in His punishment.*
> 59:5 *Allah gave you permission to cut down some palm trees and leave others intact so as to shame the wicked [the Jews]. After Allah gave the spoils to His Messenger, you made no move with horses or camels to capture them [the Jews], but Allah gives His messengers power over what He chooses. Allah is all-powerful.*

I654 As for all the spoils of war going to Mohammed, there was no actual fighting, hence no need to give spoils to fighters. Mohammed can do as he wishes.

> 59:7 *The spoils of war taken from the people in the cities and given by Allah to His Messenger belong to Allah, to His Messenger and to his family, to the orphans, to the poor, and to the wayfaring traveler so that it will not stay among those of you who are wealthy. Take what the Messenger has offered you, and refuse what he has forbidden you. And fear Allah, for Allah is severe in His punishment.*
> 59:8 *A part of the spoils of war also belong to the poor refugees: the Immigrants driven from their homes and possessions who seek Allah's grace and help Allah and His Messenger. These are the sincere believers.*

THE BATTLE OF THE TRENCH

I669 Some of the Jews who had been exiled from Medina decided that they needed to destroy Mohammed and to do that they needed allies. Since allies were to be found in Mecca, they went there and parlayed with the leaders of the Quraysh. But since this was a war of religion, the Quraysh wanted was proof of religious supremacy to Mohammed. So the leaders said to the Jews, "You are People of the Book and you know our disagreement. Who has the better religion, us or Mohammed?" The leaders of the Jews replied that the Quraysh had the better religion.

I669 Now the Koran could not pass up such an insult to Mohammed. So the Koran says:

> 4:49 ***Have you not seen those who praise themselves for their purity? But Allah purifies whom He pleases, and they will not be treated unjustly in the slightest degree. See how they make up lies about Allah! That in itself is a terrible sin. Have you not seen those [Jews allied with the Meccans] to whom part of the Scriptures were given? They believe in idols and sorcery, and they say of the unbelievers, "These are guided on a better path than the believers." It is on these whom Allah has laid His curse. Those who are cursed by Allah will have no one to help them.***
> 4:53 ***Should those who would fail to give even a penny to their fellow man have a share in the kingdom? Do they envy the people for what they have received from Allah's bounty? We gave the Scriptures and wisdom to the children of Abraham, and a grand kingdom. Some of them believe in His Messenger while others turn away from him. The flames of Hell are sufficient punishment for them! Those who reject Our revelations We will cast into the Fire. As soon as their skins are burnt away, We will give them new skins so that they will truly experience the torment. Truly Allah is mighty and wise!***

I669-670 So the Meccans entered into an alliance with the Jews. Another Arab tribe joined the alliance as well.

As Mohammed had many spies in Mecca, so it took no time until he knew of the coming fight and he set out to prepare for it. There was a Persian who suggested to Mohammed that he build a trench as a barrier against the Meccans and their allies. For eight days the Arabs worked at building a trench, or ditch, around the weak points of Medina. To help with morale Mohammed personally pitched in and did his turn at manual labor.

I671 There was a fair amount of slacking and leaving work. The labor problems even worked their way into the Koran:

> 24:62 ***Only those who believe in Allah and His Messenger are the true believers, and when they are gathered together, do not leave until they have sought his permission. Those who ask your permission are the ones who truly believe in Allah and His Messenger. And when they ask your***

permission to leave for personal reasons, give permission to whom you please, and ask Allah for His indulgence on their behalf, for Allah is indulgent, merciful.
24:63 *Do not address the Messenger in the same way you address one another. Allah knows which of you leave quietly from the assemblies, hiding behind others. And let those who disobey his commands beware, for fear that some terrible punishment will come upon them.*
24:64 *Surely all that is in the heavens and earth belongs to Allah. He knows your intentions well. And one day all will be assembled before Him, and He will inform them of what they have done, for Allah knows all things.*

I673 But the work was done just in time. The Quraysh and the other allies camped near the trench. Mohammed and his army camped on their side of the trench and sent the women and children to the forts.

I674 One of the exiled Jews approached the last tribe of Jews in Medina to be allies with the attacking Meccans. At first the Jews would not even talk to him. After all, if Mohammed won, they would be left with the consequences of dealing with a man who had driven the other two tribes of Jews from Medina. But in the end the Jews agreed to lend aid if the battle started to go against Mohammed.

I677-683 Mohammed was able to use his agents to sow discord among those allied against him. The trench defense frustrated the Meccans. The weather was bad and the allies were distrustful of each other. In terms of actual combat only a handful of men were killed over the twenty-day siege. The Meccans broke camp and went back home. It was a victory for Mohammed.

33:9 *Believers! Remember Allah's grace when your enemies attacked you [the Battle of the Ditch], and We set a mighty wind against them [the Meccans and their allies, the confederates, put Medina under siege], and warriors they could not see, but Allah sees clearly all that you do. [The confederates' poor planning, poor leadership, and bad weather caused them to fail]*
33:10 *When they attacked you from above and from below, your eyes went wild, your hearts leapt up into your throats, and you doubted Allah's strength. There were the believers tried, and they were severely shaken. The hypocrites and the diseased of heart said, "Allah and His Messenger promised us only to deceive us." A group of them said, "People of Medina! It is not safe for you here. Therefore, go back to your city." Then another group said, "Our homes have been left defenseless," although they were not, and they really only wanted to run away.*
33:14 *If the enemy had infiltrated the entire city, the disaffected would have been incited to rebel, and they surely would have done so, but they*

would have maintained control for only a short while. Before they had
pledged to Allah that they would never turn their backs and flee. A pledge
to Allah must be answered for. Say: Fleeing will not help you. If you are
running away from death or slaughter, even if you do escape, you will
only be left to enjoy this world for a short time. Say: Who will keep you
from Allah if it is His will to punish you or to show you mercy? Only Allah
is your guardian and a helper.
33:18 *Allah truly knows those among you who hinder others and say to*
their friends, "Come to our side," and who only fight a little and help you
only begrudgingly. When they are overtaken with fear, then they look to
you, rolling their eyes as if they were on the verge of death. But as soon as
they are safe again, they attack you with their harsh words, greedily de-
manding the best of the spoils of war. These are not believers. Therefore,
Allah will make their actions useless; that is easy for Allah.
33:20 *They thought that the confederate tribes would never depart, and if*
the confederates should attack again, they would rather be in the desert
among the Bedouin tribes asking for news about you! But if they were
there with you, they would hardly take part in the battle.
33:21 *You have an excellent example in Allah's Messenger for those of you*
who put your hope in Allah and the Last Day and who praise Allah con-
tinually. And when the believers saw the confederates they said, "This is
what Allah and His Messenger promised us, and Allah and His Messen-
ger spoke the truth," and this served to increase their faith and devotion.
33:23 *Some among the believers have been faithful in their covenant with*
Allah. Some of them have fulfilled their covenant with their deaths, and
some are waiting for death, and they have not wavered in their determi-
nation. Allah will reward the faithful for the faithfulness and will punish
the hypocrites if He pleases or show them mercy if He pleases. Allah is
forgiving and merciful.

JIHAD, THE JEWS AGAIN

CHAPTER 19

58:5 Those who oppose Allah and His Messenger will be laid low, just as those who came before them.

THE SOLUTION FOR THE JEWS

I684 That same day the angel Gabriel came to Mohammed at noon. He asked if Mohammed were through fighting. Gabriel and the angels were going to attack the last Jewish tribe in Medina. Gabriel said, "Allah commands you to go to the Jews. I am headed there now to shake their stronghold."

I684 So Mohammed called upon his troops and they headed to the forts of the Jews. Now the Jews of Medina lived in forts that were on the outskirts of Medina. Mohammed rode up to the forts and called out, "You brothers of apes, has Allah disgraced you and brought His vengeance upon you?"

I685-689 Mohammed put the Jews under siege for twenty-five days. Finally, the Jews offered to submit their fate to a Muslim, Abu, with whom they had had been an ally in the past. His judgment was simple. Kill all the men. Take their property and take the women and children as captives. Mohammed said, "You have given the judgment of Allah."

I690 The captives were taken into Medina. They dug trenches in the market place of Medina. It was a long day, but 800 Jews met their death that day. Mohammed and his twelve year old wife sat and watched the entire day and into the night. The Apostle of Allah had every male Jew killed.

I693 Mohammed took the property, wives and children of the Jews, and divided it up amongst the Muslims. Mohammed took his one fifth of the slaves and sent a Muslim with the female Jewish slaves to a nearby city where the women were sold for pleasure. Mohammed invested the money from the sale of the female slaves for horses and weapons.

I693 There was one last piece of spoils for Mohammed. The most beautiful Jewess was his slave for pleasure.

I696-7 In the battle of the Trench it was Allah who had won the day. Allah is what gives the Muslim his strength and will. No matter what the unbelievers do Allah will triumph. Allah totally approves of the killing of the Jews, enslaving the women and children. It was good to give the Jew's property to the Muslim warriors. After all, Allah wanted it done and helped to do it.

> 33:25 ***And Allah drove back the unbelievers in their wrath, and they gained nothing by it. Allah aided the believers in the war, for Allah is strong and mighty. He brought down some of the People of the Book [the Jews] out of their fortresses to aid the confederates and to strike terror into their hearts. Some you killed, and others you took captive. He made you heirs of their land, their homes, and their possessions, and even gave you another land on which you had never before set foot. Allah has power over everything. [800 male Jews were executed, their property taken, and women and children enslaved.]***

THE KILLING OF THE JEW, SALLAM

I714-6 A Jew named Sallam helped to plan and organize the confederation of the tribes that attacked Mohammed in the Battle of the Trench. Mohammed sent five Muslim men to assassinate Sallam. When the men had done their work, they returned to Mohammed and fell to arguing as to who actually killed Sallam. Mohammed demanded to see their swords. He examined them one by one and then pointed to the sword that had been the killing weapon. It had food on it still from the thrust to the stomach.

You are the best of people

> 3:105 ***Do not be like those people who are divided among themselves and argue with one another after they have received clear signs. They will receive a dreadful punishment on the Day when some faces will shine with light and other faces will be darkened with despair. Then those whose faces are darkened will be asked, "Why did you reject the faith after having been believers? Taste now the retribution for your unbelief!" But those whose faces are light will receive Allah's mercy and enjoy it forever. These are Allah's revelations, which We tell you in truth. Allah does not will injustice on mankind. All that is in the heavens and the earth belongs to Allah, and to Him all things will return.***
> 3:110 ***You are the best of people ever brought together for mankind commanding what is right and prohibiting what is evil. You believe in Allah. If the People of the Book [Jews] had believed, it certainly would have been better for them. While some of them are believers, most of them are evil-doers. If they attempt to harm you, it will only result in minor injuries. If they go to war with you, they will turn and run away, and they will have no one to help them. They will be covered with shame wherever they go unless they make a covenant with Allah or with men. They have***

> *brought Allah's wrath upon themselves, and they have been humiliated because of their disbelief and because they have unjustly killed His messengers. This is because they have rebelled and become sinners.*
> 3:113 *Yet not all of them are the same. There are some among the People of the Book who are righteous and who recite Allah's revelations throughout the night and worship Him. They believe in Allah and the Last Day, and command what is right and forbid what is wrong and urge each other on to do good works. These are the righteous people. They will not be denied their reward for whatever good they do for Allah knows those who do good.*
> 3:116 *As for the unbelievers, neither their wealth nor their children will keep them from the wrath of Allah. They will be prisoners of the Fire where they will live forever. What they spend in this world is like an icy wind that blows over the fields and destroys the crops of a people who are also evil-doers. It is not Allah who does them wrong, but it is they who wrong themselves.*

The stories about the Jewish prophets are fewer in Medina.

Adam and Ilbis

> 2:30 *And when your Lord said to the angels, "I am going to place on the earth someone who will rule as a deputy for Me," they said, "Will You place one on earth who will do evil and cause bloodshed when we praise and glorify Your holy name?" He said, "I know what you do not."*
> 2:31 *He taught Adam the names of all things and then placed them before the angels. He said, "Tell Me the names of these things if you are so wise." They said, "Praise be to You! We do know nothing except that which You have taught us. Only You are all-knowing and wise." Then He said, "Adam, inform them of their names." After Adam named them, He said, "Did I not tell you that I know the secrets of the heavens and earth? I know all that is brought to light and all that is hidden."*
> 2:34 *And when We said to the angels, "Bow down and worship Adam," they all bowed down except Iblis [Satan], who refused because he was too proud, and he became an unbeliever.*
> 2:35 *We said, "Adam, live with your wife in the Garden, and eat then whatever you want of the fruits there, but never come near this tree or you both will become sinners." But Satan caused them to slip, and thus their banishment from the Garden. We said, "Henceforth, you will be enemies with one another, and the earth will provide you with a dwelling place and food for a while." Then Adam learned words of prayer from his Lord, and his Lord showed him mercy. Truly He is Relenting, and Most Merciful. And We said, "All of you get down from here, and when my guidance is revealed to you, those who follow it will have nothing to fear*

or regret. But those who deny and reject Our guidance will be prisoners of the fire, where they will live forever.

Allah Sent a Raven That Scratched Upon the Ground

5:27 *Tell them the true story of the sons of Adam when they both offered a sacrifice to Allah, and one's was accepted, but the other's was not. The one said, "I will surely slay you." The other said, "Allah only accepts from those that fear Him. Even if you stretch your hand against me to slay me, I will not stretch my hand to slay you. Truly I fear Allah, the Lord of the worlds. I would rather that you would bear the punishment of a sin against me and your own sin and become a companion of the Fire, for that is the reward of the unjust."*

5:30 *His passion led him to slay his brother. So he slew him, and he became one of those who perish. Allah sent a raven that scratched upon the ground to show him how to hide his brother's naked corpse. He said, "Oh, woe is me. Am I not able to be like this raven to hide away my brother's corpse?" Then he was full of regrets.*

5:32 *For this reason, We have decreed to the Children of Israel that whoever kills anyone, unless it is manslaughter, or for spreading mischief in the land, it will be as though he had slain all mankind. Whoever saves a life, it will be as though he had saved all mankind. Certainly Our messengers came to them [the Jews] with the proofs of their mission, and even after this, most of them committed excesses in the land.*

Abraham

2:124 *Remember when Abraham was tested by his Lord with certain commandments which he fulfilled, He said, "I will make you a leader to the nations." Abraham asked, "And also of my descendants?" Allah answered, "My covenant does not include evil-doers." We made the Kabah [stone temple] at Mecca a pilgrimage for people and a place of security, saying, "Make the place where Abraham stood to pray a house of worship." And We commanded Abraham and Ishmael, "Purify My house [the Kabah] for those who go around it, those who meditate there and those who bow down and worship there."*

2:126 *Then Abraham prayed, "My Lord! Make this a secure land and supply those who believe in Allah and the Last Day with plenty." He answered, "As for the disbelievers, I will let them enjoy themselves for a while; then I will drive them into the torment of the Fire, surely an evil fate."*

2:127 *And when Abraham and Ishmael built the House, Abraham prayed, "Accept this service from us, Lord. You are all-hearing, all-knowing. Lord! Make us submissive to You, and make our descendants a Muslim nation bowing down to Your will. Show us how we should worship and look upon us with mercy. Only You are forgiving and*

merciful. Our Lord, send them a messenger of their own who will make Your revelations known to them, teach them the Scripture, and with wisdom purify them of their sins. For only You are the mighty and the wise." And who abandons the religion of Abraham but a fool? We chose him in this world, and in the world to come, he will be among the righteous.
2:131 *When his Lord said to him, "Surrender to Me!" He said, "I have surrendered myself to the Lord of the universe."*
2:132 *Abraham imparted the faith upon his children, as well as Jacob, saying, "My children! Allah has chosen you for the true faith; therefore, do not die without fully submitting to Him."*
2:133 *Were you there when Jacob was on the verge of death? When he said to his children, "What will you worship after I am gone?" They said, "We will worship your Allah, the god of your fathers Abraham, Ishmael and Isaac, the one true god; to Him we will surrender." That generation has passed away. They will receive what they have earned as you will for what you do. You will not be called upon to answer for their actions.*
2:260 *When Abraham said, "My Lord, show me how you will bring the dead back to life," He replied, "Do you not have faith?" He said, "Yes, but just to comfort my heart." So Allah replied, "Take four birds and draw them to you, cutting their bodies into pieces. Scatter them over the tops of the mountains and then call to them and they will quickly fly back to you. Know that Allah is mighty and wise."*

Mary, mother of Jesus

3:33 *Allah chose to lift up Adam and Noah, the descendants of Abraham, and the descendants of Imran [who include Mary and Jesus] above other nations. They were the descendants of one another. Allah is all-hearing and all-knowing.*
3:35 *Remember when Imran's wife said, "My Lord! I dedicate the child in my womb to you for Your service. Accept this of me for only you are all-hearing and all-knowing." And when the child was born she said, "My Lord! I have given birth to a female child!" But Allah knew best what she had delivered for a male is not like a female. "And I have named her Mary, and I have given her and her children to you to protect from Satan, the rejected one [Islam teaches that all new-borns are touched by Satan]."*
3:37 *So the Lord accepted her graciously and made her grow into a good child and gave Zacharias guardianship over her. And whenever Zacharias went to the sanctuary to visit her, he found her well supplied with food. "Mary," he said, " Where did all this food come from?" And she answered, "It is from Allah for Allah gives generously to whom He pleases."*
3:38 *Then Zacharias prayed to His Lord saying, "My Lord! Grant me good descendants for you hear all prayers." And while he stood praying in the*

sanctuary, angels came to him and said, "Allah brings you good news of the birth of John who will verify Allah's word. He will be noble, pure, and a messenger from among the righteous."
3:40 *He said, "Lord! How can I have a son when I am in my old age and my wife is infertile?" The angels replied, "It is Allah's will, and He does as He pleases."*
3:41 *Zacharias said, "Lord, give me a sign." And He replied, "For three days and nights you will be unable to speak to anyone, except through signing. Continually give praise to your Lord and worship Him in the morning and at night."*
3:42 *And then the angels said, "Mary! Allah has chosen you and purified you. He has lifted you up above all other women. Mary, obey your Lord. Bow down and pray with the worshippers."*

Moses

5:20 *Remember when Moses said to his people, "Oh, my people, remember the goodness of Allah towards you when He appointed messengers among you, made you kings, and gave you what He had never given before to any human beings. Oh, my people, enter the holy land, which Allah has prescribed for you. Do not turn back in shame for you may be overthrown to your ruin."*
5:22 *They said, "Oh, Moses, men of might live there, and we will not enter it until they are gone. If they leave, then we will enter."*
5:23 *Then two men who feared their Lord and to whom Allah had been gracious said, "Enter in by the gate, and when you enter there, you will overcome. If you are believers, put your trust in Allah."*
5:24 *They said, "Oh, Moses, we will never enter while they remain there. You and your Lord should go and fight. We will sit here and watch."*
5:25 *Moses said, "Oh, my Lord, I only have control of myself and my brother, so make a distinction between us and this ungodly people."*
5:26 *He [Allah] said, "This land will be forbidden to them for forty years. They will wander the earth bewildered, so do not grieve over these ungodly people."*

Saul

2:247 *Their messenger said to them, "Allah has made Saul king over you, but they said, "Why should he be made king when we are more deserving than he is, and he is not even wealthy?" He said, "Allah has shown preference to him over you and has made him grow in both wisdom and physical strength. Allah gives authority to whom He pleases; Allah is all-embracing and all-knowing." Their messenger also said, "The sign of his authority will be that the Ark of the Covenant will come to you. Peace from your Lord lies within, as well as relics [Moses' shoes and staff and fragments of the tablets of the law] from the House of Moses and Aaron that were left. It will be carried by angels. It is surely a sign for believers."*

2:249 *And when Saul set out with his army, he said, "Allah will put you to the test at a river. Those who drink from it will depart from me, but those who do not drink or only do so from the palm of their hand will continue on to fight." All but a few drank from the river. So when they crossed the river, those that remained with him said, "Certainly we have no chance against Goliath and his forces." But those of them who were sure they would meet their Lord said, "Many times a small group has vanquished a large army by Allah's grace. Allah is with the perseverant."*

2:250 *When they came upon Goliath and his forces, they said, "Our Lord, give us endurance, make our feet stand firm and help us against these unbelievers." And by Allah's will they defeated them. David killed Goliath, and Allah gave him power and wisdom and taught him His will. If Allah had not defeated one people with another, then the earth would have been in a state of chaos, but Allah is generous to mankind.*

The Koran's last words about the Jews:

5:12 *Allah did, of old, make a covenant with the children of Israel, and We appointed twelve leaders among them, and Allah said, "I will be with you if you observe regular prayer, practice regular charity, believe in My messengers and help them, and offer Allah goodly gifts. I will surely wipe away your sins, and I will bring you into Gardens beneath which the rivers flow. Whoever of you does not believe this has gone astray from the even path."*

5:13 *Because they [the Jews] broke their covenant, We have cursed them and have hardened their hearts. They changed the words of Scripture [Islam claims that the Jews removed the references to Mohammed's coming from their Scripture.] from their places and have forgotten part of what they were taught. You will always discover them in deceits, except for a few of them, but forgive them and overlook their misdeeds. Allah loves those who act generously.*

5:41 *Oh, Messenger, do not let those who hurry to disbelief grieve you. Whether it is those who say the words, "We believe," while their hearts do not believe, or, it is the Jews, who will listen to any lie but do not come to you. They change words from their contexts and say, "If you are given this, take it, if you are not given this, then beware of it." For whomever Allah would mislead, you will be no help for him against Allah. Those whose hearts Allah does not desire to cleanse will suffer disgrace in this world and a grievous punishment in the next.*

5:42 *They [the Jews] are fond of listening to lies or devouring anything forbidden. If they do come to you [Mohammed], judge between them,*

or refuse to interfere. If you withdraw from them, they cannot harm you in any way, but if you judge, then judge between them with equity. Allah loves those who deal equitably. Why would they make you their judge since they possess their own law, the Torah, which holds the commands of Allah, yet they have not obeyed it? These are not believers.
5:44 *We have sent down the Torah, which was a guidance and light. The messengers who professed Islam used the Torah to judge the Jews, the rabbis, and the doctors because they were required to be the keepers and the witnesses of the Book. Therefore, Oh Jews, do not fear men but fear Me, and do not sell my signs for a miserable price. Whoever will not judge by what Allah revealed are the unbelievers.*
5:45 *We ordained in the Book, "Life for life, and eye for eye, and nose for nose, and ear for ear, and tooth for tooth, and for wounds retaliation." Whoever will give up retaliation, it is an act of atonement for his sins. Whoever does not use the laws of Allah to judge is unjust.*

MORE OF THE KORAN AND JIHAD

CHAPTER 19

4:59 Believers! Obey Allah and obey His Messenger and those among you with authority. If you have a disagreement about anything, refer it to Allah and His Messenger if you believe in Allah and the Last Day. This is the best and fairest way to settle a dispute.

How Could You Not Fight for Allah's Cause?

4:60 *Have you not noticed those who act like they believe in that which*
has been revealed to you and that which was revealed before you? They
wish to seek the judgment of Satan, although they have been commanded
to deny him, and Satan wishes to lead them astray into grievous sin. And
when it is said to them, "Come and be judged by what Allah has revealed
and by His Messenger," you see them turn their heads in disgust. But how
would they act if some disaster came upon them because of what they
have done with their own hands? They would come to you, swearing
by Allah, "We wish nothing but goodwill and reconciliation." But Allah
knows the secrets of their hearts. Therefore, turn away from them and
warn them, speaking words that will pierce their souls.
4:64 *We have sent messengers only so that people will obey them by Allah's*
permission. If the people hurt themselves by their own error, and they
came to you to ask Allah's forgiveness, and you asked Allah's forgiveness
on their behalf, they would certainly have found Allah forgiving and
merciful. But no, I swear by your Lord, they will not believe until they
make you judge in all their disputes. Then they will have no doubt in the
fairness of your judgment and will entirely submit to you.
4:66 *If We had commanded them, "Lay down your lives," or "Abandon*
your homes," only a few of them would have obeyed. But if they had done
as they were commanded, it would have been better for them and it would
have strengthened their faith. We would have given them of Ourselves a
great reward and guided them to the right path.
4:69 *Those who obey Allah and His Messenger will live with the messen-*
gers and the saints and the martyrs and the righteous. What wonderful
company! This is the bounty of Allah, and Allah's infinite knowledge is
sufficient. Believers! Be cautious, and either march forward in groups
or advance all together. There are some among you who are sure to hang
back, and if a disaster came upon you, would say, "Allah has dealt with

us graciously because we were not in the battle." If, however, you were met with victory, they, as if there were no friendship between you, would say, "If only I had been with them! Surely I would have been greatly successful!"

4:74 *Let those who would sell the life of this world for the world to come fight for Allah's cause [jihad]. Whoever fights for Allah's cause, whether he is killed or is victorious, We will grant him a great reward. How could you not fight for Allah's cause? For the weak men, women, and children who plead, "Lord! Rescue us from this city of oppressors [Mecca]. Send us a protector from Your presence; send a defender from Your presence."*

4:76 *The believers fight for Allah's cause [jihad] and the unbelievers fight for Satan. Therefore, fight against the friends of Satan. Truly Satan's strategy is weak.*

4:77 *Look at those who were told, "Lay down your arms of war for a time, attend to your prayers, and pay the poor tax." When they were told to resume fighting, some of them feared their fellow man more than they should have feared Allah, and said, "Lord! Why have you commanded us to fight? Why could you not have given us a longer respite?" Say: The joys of this world are fleeting. The world to come will be better for those of you who fear Allah, and you will never be treated unfairly in the least. Wherever you are, death will find you, even if you lock yourselves in high towers! If something good happens to them they say, "This is from Allah," but if something evil happens to them they say, "It was the Messenger's fault." Say: Everything is from Allah! But what is wrong with these people that they fail to understand what is told to them?*

4:79 *Whatever good comes to you is from Allah, but whatever evil happens to you is from yourself. We have sent you to mankind as a Messenger, and Allah is sufficient as your witness. Those who obey the Messenger obey Allah. As for those who turn away from you, We have not sent you to watch over them.*

4:81 *They promise obedience to you, but when they leave you, they gather together at night and plan to do other than what you say. Allah writes down all they say. Therefore, leave them alone and put your trust in Allah. Allah is sufficient as your protector. Will they not study the Koran? Were it not from Allah, they surely would have found many contradictions in it. And when they hear any news, whether it is good or bad, they announce it to everyone. On the other hand, if they had told the Messenger or those in authority, the wise among them would have learned it from them. If it were not for Allah's grace and mercy, all but a few of you would have followed Satan!*

4:84 *Therefore, fight for Allah's cause [jihad]. Do not lay the burden on anyone but yourself, and stir up the faithful. It may be that Allah will restrain the unbelievers' fury. Allah is mightier and stronger in His punishment.*

4:85 *Those who mediate between people for a good cause will gain from it, but those who mediate for an evil cause will bear the consequences. Allah has power over all things.*

Oh, Messenger, Make War on the Unbelievers and Hypocrites

66:6 *Oh, believers, save yourselves and your families from the Fire whose fuel is men and stones [ritual objects made from stone], over which are set fierce and mighty angels. They do not resist Allah's commands, but do precisely what they are commanded. Oh, unbelievers, do not make excuses for yourselves this day. You are only being rewarded for your deeds.*

66:8 *Oh, believers, turn to Allah in true penitence. Maybe your Lord will cancel your evil deeds and will bring you into the Gardens beneath which the rivers flow on the day when Allah will not humiliate the Messenger or those who have shared his faith. Their light will run before them and on their right hands. They will say, "Lord perfect our light, and pardon us. You have power over all things."*

66:9 *Oh, Messenger, make war on the unbelievers and hypocrites, and be hard on them. Hell will be their home, and wretched is the passage to it.*

66:10 *Allah sets forth as an example to unbelievers the wife of Noah and the wife of Lot. They were under two of Our righteous servants yet they both deceived them, so their husbands did not help them at all against Allah. It was said to them, "Enter into the Fire with those who enter."*

66:11 *Allah also holds forth to those who believe the example of the wife of Pharaoh. She said, "Lord, build me a house with you in Paradise and deliver me from Pharaoh and his doings and deliver me from the wicked."*

66:12 *Mary, the daughter of Imran who guarded her chastity and into whose womb We breathed of Our spirit, accepted the words of her Lord and of His revelations. She was one of the obedient.*

Who Strive with Their Lives and Their Wealth on Allah's Cause

49:13 *Oh, men, We have created you of a male and a female, and We have divided you into nations and tribes that you might have knowledge one of another. Truly, the most honorable of you in the sight of Allah is he who is the most careful of his duty. Allah is knowing and wise.*

49:14 *The Arabs of the desert say, "We believe." [A tribe of desert Arabs came to Medina during a famine. They converted to Islam and received charity.] Say: You do not believe, but you only say, 'We profess Islam,' for the faith has not yet found its way into your hearts. If you obey Allah and His Messenger, He will not withhold any of the rewards of your actions. Allah is indulgent and merciful. The true believers are only those who believe in Allah and His Messenger without doubts and who strive with their lives and their wealth on Allah's cause [jihad]. These are the sincere.*

49:16 *Say: Will you teach Allah about your religion when He knows all that is in the heavens and on the earth? Yes, Allah has knowledge of all things.*

49:17 *They think they did you [Mohammed] a favor when they [the desert Arabs] submitted to Islam. Say: Do not talk to me about having embraced Islam. Allah does a favor for you when He guides you to the faith if you are truthful. Allah knows the secrets of the heavens and of the earth, and Allah sees what you do.*

THE RAID ON THE MUSTALIQ TRIBE

I725 When Mohammed heard that the Arab tribe, the Mustaliq, were opposed to him and were gathering against him, he set out with his army to attack them. He contacted them at a watering hole and combat started. Islam was victorious and the Mustaliq and their women, children, and goods were taken as spoils of war and distributed to the fighters.

I729 The captives of the tribe of Mustaliq were parceled out as spoils. There was a ransom price set upon their heads. If the ransom were not paid then the people were treated as spoils and slaves. Now one of them was a beautiful woman with a high price on her. She came to Mohammed and asked him to see if the price could be reduced. Mohammed had a better idea. He would pay the ransom for the beautiful woman and she would become his wife. Now in spite of the fact that she was already married, there was no problem. It was a deal. Mohammed paid the ransom and the beautiful woman became wife number seven.

I729 This marriage had a side effect. The captives were now related to Mohammed's wife. They were all released without ransom.

THE DEATH OF A POETESS

I996 There was a poetess who wrote a poem against Islam. Mohammed said, "Who will rid me of Marwan's daughter?" One of his followers heard him and on that very night he went to the woman's home to kill her.

M239 The assassin was able to do the work in the dark as the woman slept. Her other children lay in the room, but her babe lay on her breast. The stealthy assassin removed the child and drove the knife into her with such force that he pined her to the bed.

I996 In the morning he went to Mohammed and told him. Mohammed said, "You have helped Allah and his Apostle." When asked about the consequences, Mohammed said, "Two goats won't butt their heads together over this."

M239 Mohammed turned to the people in the mosque, he said, "If you wish to see a man who has assisted Allah and his Prophet, look here." Omar cried, "What, the blind Omeir!" "No," said Mohammed, "call him Omeir the Seeing."

I996 The poetess had five sons and the assassin went to them and said, "I killed Bint Marwan, Oh sons. Withstand me if you can; don't keep me waiting." Islam became powerful that day and many became Muslims when they saw the power of Islam.

MOHAMMED'S FAMILY LIFE

CHAPTER 20

48:13 We have prepared a blazing Fire for these unbelievers who do not believe in Allah and His Messenger.

Mohammed had many wives. The Koran goes into detail about his romances.

THE LIE

When Mohammed went on his missions to attack those who resisted Islam, he took one of his wives with him. Which one got to go was determined by lots. Mohammed took Aisha with him on this trip to fight in Allah's cause in attacking the Mustaliq tribe.

I731 Now there was a problem in taking one of Mohammed's wives on an expedition and that was privacy. By now the veil had been prescribed for his wives. So the wife was not supposed to be seen or heard. To accomplish this a light cloth-covered howdah was used. Basically this was a box with a seat that could be mounted on a camel's saddle. On the way back on the expedition Aisha had gone out in the morning to relieve herself. When she got back she discovered that she had lost a necklace and went back to find it. The tent had been struck and the men in charge loaded the howdah on the camel and off they went without Aisha.

I732 When Aisha got back the entire group had moved on. She returned on a camel lead by a young Muslim who had lagged behind the main body and brought her back to Medina.

I732 Tongues began to wag, imaginations worked overtime and gossip spread. Aisha fell ill and was bedridden for three weeks.

I734-5 Tempers flared and men offered to kill the gossips. Something had to be done. In the end the innocence or guilt of Aisha was determined by revelation in the Koran which to this day is the sharia (Islamic law) about adultery.

> 24:1 ***A sura [chapter] which We have sent down and ordained, and in which We give you clear signs so that you will take warning. The man and woman who commit adultery should each be beaten with a hundred lashes, and do not let your pity for them prevent you from obeying Allah. If you believe in Allah and the Last Day, then allow some of the believers***

to witness their punishment. An adulterer can only marry an adulteress or an unbeliever, and a adulteress cannot marry anyone other than an adulterer or an unbeliever. Such marriages are forbidden for believers.

24:4 *Those who make accusations against honorable women and are unable to produce four witnesses should be given eighty lashes. Thereafter, do not accept their testimony, for they are terrible sinners, except those who repent afterwards and live righteously. Allah is truly forgiving and merciful.*

24:6 *If a husband accuses his wife of adultery but he has no witnesses other than himself, his evidence can be accepted if he swears by Allah four times that he is telling the truth and then calls down Allah's curse upon him if he is lying. If, however, the wife swears by Allah four times that she is innocent and calls Allah's curse down upon herself if she is lying, then she should not be punished.*

24:10 *If it were not for Allah's grace and mercy towards you and that Allah is wise, this would not have been revealed to you.*

24:11 *Truly there is a group among you who spread that lie [During an armed raid, Aisha—Mohammed's favorite wife since their marriage when she was age six—accidentally spent a day alone with a young jihadist. Gossip about what might have happened consumed the Muslims], but do not think of it as a bad thing for you [Aisha was cleared of doubt of sexual infidelity by a revelation in the Koran] for it has proved to be advantageous for you. Every one of them will receive the punishment they have earned. Those who spread the gossip will receive a torturous punishment.*

24:12 *Why did the believing men and women, when they heard this, not think better of their own people and say, "This is an obvious lie"? Why did they not bring four witnesses? And because they could not find any witnesses, they are surely liars in Allah's sight.*

24:14 *If it were not for Allah's goodness towards you and His mercy in this world and the world to come, you would have been severely punished for the lie you spread. You [the Muslims] gossiped about things you knew nothing about. You may have thought it to be only a light matter, but it was a most serious one in Allah's sight. And why, when you heard it, did you not say, "It is not right for us to talk about this. Oh, Allah! This is a serious sin." Allah warns you never to repeat this if you are true believers. Allah makes His signs clear to you, for Allah is all-knowing, wise. Those who take pleasure in spreading foul rumors about the faithful will be severely punished in this world and the world to come. And Allah knows, while you do not.*

24:20 *If it were not for Allah's grace and mercy towards you, you would have been punished long ago, but know that Allah is kind and merciful.*

24:21 *Believers, do not follow in Satan's footsteps for those who do so will be commanded to commit shameful and evil acts. If it were not for Allah's grace, not one of you would be pure. And Allah purifies those He pleases, and Allah is all-hearing.*
24:22 *And do not allow those among you who are wealthy and have many possessions to swear that they will not give to their family, the poor, and those who have fled their homes for Allah's cause [jihad]. Instead, let them be forgiving and indulgent. Do you not want Allah to show you forgiveness? Allah is forgiving and merciful.*
24:23 *Truly, those who carelessly slander believing women will be cursed in this world and the world to come. Their own tongues, hands, and feet will one day testify against them concerning their own actions. On that day Allah will give them what they have earned, and they will know that Allah is the clear truth.*

Since there were not four witnesses, then there was no adultery and the gossips got eighty lashes.

1736 But the scandal did not end here. One of those who got flogged for gossip was a poet and propagandist for the Muslim cause. The young warrior who led Aisha's camel was in a poem written by the poet and was offended. So he took his sword and cut the poet badly. The poet and his friends managed to bind the young warrior and take him to Mohammed. Mohammed wanted this to all go away. He gave the wounded poet a nice home and a Christian slave girl of pleasure as compensation for the sword blow.

Islam was no longer poor, indeed, the money from jihad poured in. But Mohammed was a simple man and had no attraction to money. Hence, his household was poor and the wives complained.

33:28 *Messenger! Say to your wives, "If you desire a life of this world and all its glittering adornment, then come. [All of the money from the spoils of war was spent on support of the Muslims and jihad. Mohammed's wives complained about the lack of household money.] I will provide for you and release you with honor. If, however, you seek Allah and His Messenger and the world to come, then know that Allah has prepared a great reward for those of you who do good works.*
33:30 *Wives of the Messenger! If any of you are proven guilty of public indecency, then you will be doubly punished; that is easy for Allah. But those of you who obey Allah and His Messenger and do good works will be doubly rewarded. We have prepared honorable provisions for you.*
33:32 *Wives of the Messenger! You are not like any other women. If you fear Allah, then do not be too lax in your speech for fear that lecherous-hearted men will lust after you. Stay in your homes and do not go out in*

public dressed in your fine clothes as they did in the time of ignorance [all non-Islamic history, civilization and customs are of the time of ignorance], but pray regularly, pay the poor tax and obey Allah and His Messenger. It is Allah's desire to remove all that is unclean from you, People of His House, and to make you pure. And remember what is said to you in your homes of Allah's revelations and wisdom, for surely Allah knows all mysteries and is aware of all.

33:35 *Allah has prepared forgiveness and a great reward for the men and women who submit to Him and believe, who are devout, truthful, patient, humble, generous, and pure; who fast, are modest, and always remember Allah.*

33:50 *Messenger! We allow you your wives whose dowries you have paid, and the slave-girls Allah has granted you as spoils of war, and the daughters of your paternal and maternal uncles and aunts who fled with you to Medina, and any believing woman who gives herself to the Messenger, if the Messenger wishes to marry her. This is a privilege for you only, not for any other believer. We know what We have commanded the believers concerning wives and slave-girls. We give you this privilege so you will be free from blame. Allah is forgiving and merciful!*

33:51 *You may turn away any of them that you please, and take to your bed whomever you please, and you will not be blamed for desiring one you had previously set aside for a time. Therefore, it will be easier for you to comfort them and prevent their grief and to be content with what you give each of them. Allah knows what is in your hearts, and Allah is all-knowing and gracious.*

33:52 *It will be unlawful for you to marry more wives after this or to exchange them for other wives, even though you are attracted by their beauty, except slave-girls you own. [Mohammed had nine wives and several slave-girls.] And Allah watches over all things.*

MARY, THE COPTIC SLAVE OF PLEASURE

M425 Mohammed was given two Coptic (Egyptian Christian) slaves. One he gave to another Muslim but he kept Mary, fair of skin with curly hair. He did not move her into the harem, but set up an apartment in another part of Medina. Mary gave something in sex that none of his wives could—a child and it was a male child, Ibrahim. Mohammed doted on him.

M426 The harem was jealous. This non-Arab slave had given Mohammed his best gift. One of his wives, Hafsa, was away and Mohammed took Mary to Hafsa's apartment in the harem. Hafsa returned and there was a scene. The harem was incensed. A slave in one of their beds was an outrage and a scandal. The wives banded together and it was a house of anger and coldness.

M427 Mohammed withdrew and swore he would not see his wives for a month and lived with Mary. Omar and Abu Bakr were appalled as Mohammed, their son-in-law had abandoned their daughters for a slave. But at last Mohammed relented and said that Gabriel had spoken well of Hafsa and he wanted the whole affair to be over.

The Koran:

> 66:1 ***Why, Oh, Messenger, do you forbid yourself that which Allah has made lawful to you? Do you seek to please your wives? [Mohammed was fond of a Coptic (Egyptian Christian) slave named Mary. Hafsa found Mohammed in her room with Mary, a violation of Hafsa's domain. He told a jealous Hafsa that he would stop relations with Mary and then did not. But Hafsa was supposed to be quiet about this matter.] Allah is lenient and merciful. Allah has allowed you release from your oaths, and Allah is your master. He is knowing and wise.***
> 66:3 ***When the Messenger confided a fact to one of his wives, and when she divulged it, [Hafsa had told Aisha (Mohammed's favorite wife) about Mary and the harem became embroiled in jealousy.] Allah informed Mohammed of this, and he told her [Hafsa] part of it and withheld part. When Mohammed told her of it, she said, "Who told you this?" He said, "He who is knowing and wise told me."***
> 66:4 ***"If you both [Hafsa and Aisha] turn in repentance to Allah, your hearts are already inclined to this, but if you conspire against the Messenger, then know that Allah is his protector, and Gabriel, and every just man among the faithful, and the angels are his helpers besides. Perhaps, if he [Mohammed] divorced you all, Allah would give him better wives than you—Muslims, believers, submissive, devout, penitent, obedient, observant of fasting, widows, and virgins."***

M429 Ibrahim became a favorite of Mohammed. But when the child was fifteen months old, he fell sick. Mary and her slave sister attended the child during his illness. Mohammed was there at his death and wept mightily. Mohammed was to suffer the Arabic shame of having no living male children to succeed him.

MARRIAGE TO HIS DAUGHTER-IN-LAW

M290 Mohammed had an adopted son, Zeid, and went by his house. Zeid was not there and Mohammed went on in the house. He wound up seeing his daughter-in-law, Zeinab, in a thin dress, and her charms were evident. Mohammed was smitten and said, "Gracious Lord! Good Heavens! How thou dost turn the hearts of men!"

M290 Well, Zeinab, had turned the head of the future king of Arabia and she told her husband what Mohammed said. The step-son went to Mohammed and said that he would divorce Zeinab so he could have her. Mohammed said no. But Zeid went ahead and divorced her anyway. In Arabia a union between a man and his daughter-in-law was incest and forbidden. But while Mohammed was with Aisha, he had a revelation and said, "Who will go and congratulate Zeinab and tell her that Allah has blessed our marriage?" The maid went right off to tell her of the good news. So Mohammed added another wife.

> 33:4 *Allah has not given any man two hearts for one body, nor has He made your wives whom you divorce to be like your mothers, nor has He made your adopted sons like your real sons. [Previous to this verse, an Arab's adopted children were treated as blood children. This verse relates to verse 37 of this sura.] These are only words you speak with your mouths, but Allah speaks the truth and guides to the right path. Name your adopted sons after their real fathers; this is more just in Allah's sight. But if you do not know their fathers' names, call them your brothers in the faith and your friends. There will be no blame on you if you sin unintentionally, but that which you intend in your heart will be held against you. Allah is forgiving and merciful.*
>
> 33:36 *And it is not the place of a believer, either man or woman, to have a choice in his or her affairs when Allah and His Messenger have decided on a matter. Those who disobey Allah and His Messenger are clearly on the wrong path. And remember when you said to your adopted son [Zayd], the one who had received Allah's favor [converted to Islam], "Keep your wife to yourself and fear Allah," and you hid in your heart what Allah was to reveal, and you feared men [what people would say if he married his daughter-in-law], when it would have been right that you should fear Allah. And when Zayd divorced his wife, We gave her to you as your wife, so it would not be a sin for believers to marry the wives of their adopted sons, after they have divorced them. And Allah's will must be carried out.*
>
> 33:38 *The Messenger will not be blamed for anything that Allah has given him permission to do. This was Allah's way with the messengers who came before you, and Allah's commands are absolute. The messengers fulfilled Allah's mission and feared Him, and feared no one but Allah. Allah takes sufficient account. Mohammed is not the father of any man among you. He is Allah's Messenger and the last of the messengers. Allah knows all things.*

Since Zeid was adopted, he was not really a son, so there was no incest.

M292 It was about this time that the veil was imposed. The wives became mothers of the faithful and could not marry after Mohammed died.

> 33:55 ***There is no blame on the Messenger's wives if they speak unveiled with their fathers, sons, brothers, nephews on either their brother's or sister's side, their women, or their slave-girls. Women! Fear Allah, for Allah witnesses all things.***

THE TREATY OF AL HUDAYBIYA

CHAPTER 21

4:136 Believers! Believe in Allah and His Messenger and in the Scriptures which were sent down to His Messenger and in the Scriptures He sent down before him. Those who deny Allah, His angels, His Scriptures, His messengers, and the Last Day have gone far astray.

I740 Mohammed decided to make a pilgrimage to Mecca. A difficult problem was how to do this peacefully. The state of affairs between Mohammed and the Meccans had always condemnation and violence. He called for all to go, but the Bedouin Arabs from around Medina refused his call. So he headed out with 700 men and 70 sacrificial camels. He and the others wore the white garments of the pilgrims so that the Meccans would not suspect jihad.

I741 As they approached Mecca, he found out that the Quraysh had come out prepared for war and were blocking the way. So Mohammed took an alternate and difficult route to Mecca and try to avoid the armed Meccans.

I743 The Meccans were not going to let him enter, war or no war. They would not submit to Mohammed's wishes. They would not lose face with the other Arabs.

I747 The Meccans set a man out to parlay and make a treaty with Mohammed. Umar was furious that Mohammed would even make a treaty with non-Muslims. To make a treaty with non-Muslims was demeaning to Islam. But Mohammed told him that Allah would not make them the loser. They would win over the Quraysh. Be patient.

I747 So they drew up a treaty to the effect that there would be no war for ten years, there would be no hostilities, no one could convert to Islam without their guardians' permission. In turn the Muslims could come next year and stay for three days in Mecca, but they could not enter this year.

I748 Many of the Muslims were depressed. Mohammed had promised that they could enter Mecca. Now they could not. Before they left they sacrificed the camels and shaved their heads doing as much of the rituals they could without getting into Mecca.

I749 On the way back to Medina, Mohammed added to the Koran, the sura called Victory about this treaty. Those who held back [the desert Arabs, Bedouins] and did not come on the pilgrimage would not profit by getting any spoils of war. And there is more war in the future.

> 48:15 *Those who lagged behind will say, when you go to take the spoils of war, "Let us follow you." They wish to change the word [the rules of how to divide the spoils of war] of Allah. Say: You will not follow us. Allah has already declared this. They will say, "No, you are jealous of us." No, they understand little. Say to those desert Arabs who were left behind, "You will be called to fight against a people of mighty strength. You will fight until they submit. If you obey, Allah will give you a goodly reward, but if you turn back, as you turned back before, He will punish you with a grievous penalty.*

I750 This was a victory for Islam. The government of Mecca dealt with Mohammed as an independent political power. Many more Arabs were attracted to Islam with its new power.

I754 The treaty greatly enhanced the Islam's power. Part of the treaty was that those who had become Muslims without the permission of their guardians would be returned to the Quraysh. But some of the women wished to stay and not return. The Koran ruled that their dowries be returned and the women could stay.

> 48:1 *We have won a glorious victory for you [Mohammed]—a sign that Allah forgives earlier and later sins, and fulfills His goodness to you and guides you on the right way. May Allah help you. He is a mighty help.*
> 48:4 *It is Allah who sends down tranquility to the hearts of the faithful that they might add faith to their faith, for Allah's are the armies of the heavens and of the earth, and He is knowing and wise.*
> 48:5 *That He may bring the believing men and the believing women into Gardens, beneath whose trees the rivers flow, to dwell therein forever, and that He may cancel their evil deeds—this is the great bliss with Allah.*
> 48:6 *It is Allah who will punish the hypocritical men and the hypocritical women, and the unbelieving men and women who think evil thoughts of Allah. Theirs will be an evil turn of fortune. The wrath of Allah is on them, and He has cursed them and prepared Hell for them. Evil is the journey.*
> 48:7 *The armies of the heavens and of the earth are Allah's, and He is mighty and wise.*
> 48:8 *We have sent you [Mohammed] as a witness, an announcer of good tidings, and a warner that you [the Meccans] may believe in Allah and His Messenger and may assist Him, honor Him, and praise Him morning and evening.*

48:10 *In truth, those who swear loyalty to you really swear that loyalty to Allah. The hand of Allah was over their hands. Whoever breaks his oath harms his own soul, but whoever will be true to his oath to Allah, He will give him a great reward.*
48:11 *The desert Arabs [Bedouins] who did not accompany you into war will say, "Our flocks and our families kept us busy, so we ask you to pardon us." They speak with their tongues what is not in their hearts. Say: Who can have any power over Allah in your behalf, whether he intends that you have some loss or he intends that you have an advantage? Yes, Allah is acquainted with your doings. You [the desert Arabs] thought that the Messenger and the faithful could never come back to their families, and this seemed pleasing to your hearts, and you thought an evil thought, for you are a people lost in wickedness. We have prepared a blazing Fire for these unbelievers who do not believe in Allah and His Messenger. Allah's is the kingdom of the heavens and of the earth. He will forgive whom He will, and He will punish whom He will. Allah is gracious and merciful.*

Allah Promised That You Will Capture Rich Spoils of War

48:17 *It will be no crime on the part of the blind, the lame, or the sick if they do not go to the fight [participate in jihad], but whoever obeys Allah and His Messenger, He will bring him into the Gardens beneath which the rivers flow, but whoever turns back, He will punish him with a sore punishment.*
48:18 *Allah was well pleased when the believers swore loyalty to you under the tree. He knew what was in their hearts, and He sent down tranquility on them and rewarded them with a speedy victory and with the rich spoils of war they took, for Allah is mighty and wise.*
48:20 *Allah promised that you will capture rich spoils of war [this refers to the destruction of the Jews of Khaybar, who were made* dhimmis *who paid special taxes,* jizya, *and lacked civil liberties], and He withheld men's hands from you that it may be a sign to the faithful and that He might guide you along the right way. There are other spoils of war, over which you have not yet had power, but Allah has encompassed them for you, for Allah is potent over all things.*
48:22 *If the unbelievers fight against you, they will surely turn their backs. They will find neither protector nor helper. Such has been Allah's method before. You will not find a change in Allah's course. It was He who held their hands from you and your hands from them in the valley of Mecca [Mohammed signed the treaty of Hudaybiya with the Meccans that recognized him as a powerful, political leader]. After that He gave you the victory over them, for Allah saw what you did.*
48:25 *These [the Meccans] are the ones who disbelieved and kept you away from the Sacred Mosque [the Kabah] and prevented the offering from reaching the place of sacrifice [the Meccans would not let*

Mohammed enter Mecca and make ritual sacrifices]. The believers might have been injured by accident [Mohammed could not attack the Meccans since there were both unbelievers and believers among them]. Allah will give mercy to whom he pleases or an attack would have been ordered. Had the believers not been among with the unbelievers, We would have surely punished the unbelievers with a sore punishment.

48:26 *When the unbelievers had fostered rage in their hearts—the rage of ignorance—Allah sent down His peace on His Messenger and on the faithful. He made them stay close to the command of self-restraint [not to kill the unbelievers] for they were most worthy and deserving of it, and Allah knows all things.*

48:27 *Allah truly fulfilled the vision for His Messenger when He said, "You will surely enter the Sacred Mosque [the Kabah], if Allah pleases, in full security having your faces shaved and your hair cut. You will not fear for He knows what you do not know, and He has granted, beside this, a speedy victory." He has sent His Messenger with guidance and the religion of truth that He may proclaim it over every religion. Allah's testimony is enough for you.*

48:28 *Mohammed is the Messenger of Allah, and his comrades are strong against the unbelievers, but compassionate among themselves. You will see them bowing down, prostrating themselves, and imploring favors from Allah and His acceptance. The marks are on their faces from the traces of their prostrations [dust would be on the foreheads from bowing down to the earth]. This is their picture in the Torah and their picture in the Gospel. They are like the seed that puts forth its stalk. It strengthens, grows stout, and rises upon its stem rejoicing the husbandman. The unbelievers become enraged at them. To those who believe and do good work, Allah has promised forgiveness and a great reward.*

60:10 *Oh, believers, when believing women come to you as refugees, test them. Allah best knows their faith, but if you know them for believers, do not send them back to the unbeliever. They are not lawful wives for them, nor are the unbelievers lawful husbands for these women. Give the unbelievers back what they have spent for their dowers. It will not be a crime for you to marry them, provided you give them their dowers. Do not retain any right in the unbelieving women. Demand back what you have spent for their dowers, and let the unbelievers demand back what they have spent for their wives. This is the law of Allah, which He ordains among you. Allah is knowing and wise.*

60:11 *If any of your wives desert from you to the unbelievers and, likewise, if their wives desert them for you, take any dowry, then give to those whose wives have fled away what they have spent for their dowers. Fear Allah in whom you believe.*

60:12 *Oh, Messenger, when believing women come to you and pledge an oath of allegiance to you and ascribe no other gods as partners to Allah and that they will not steal, they will not commit adultery, they will not kill their children, they will not slander or lie, and that they will not disobey you in any just matter, then receive their allegiance and ask pardon for them from Allah. Allah is indulgent and merciful.*

Mohammed's position as a political leader changed the way that Muslims should act around him.

49:1 *Believers, do not enter upon any affair before Allah and His Messenger permit you, but fear Allah, for He hears and knows.*
49:2 *Oh, believers, do not raise your voices above the voice of the Messenger or speak loudly to him as you speak loudly one to another for fear that your works will come to nothing without your awareness. Those who lower their voices in the presence of the Messenger of Allah are those whose hearts Allah has inclined to piety. Forgiveness and a rich reward will be theirs.*
49:4 *Those who call out to you [Mohammed] while you are within your apartments have no perception of what is due to you. If they would only wait patiently until you come to them, it would be far better for them. Allah is indulgent and merciful.*
49:6 *Oh, Believers, if any wicked person comes to you with news, verify it at once for fear that, through ignorance, you will harm others, and then be sorry for what you have done.*
49:7 *Know that a messenger of Allah is among you. If he were to give way to your wishes, you would certainly fall into misfortune, but Allah has endeared the faith to you and has given it favor in your hearts and has made unbelief, wickedness, and rebellion hateful to you. These are those who pursue a right course—a grace and favor from Allah. He is knowing and wise.*

Do You Hesitate to Give to Charity Before You Meet with Him?

58:11 *Believers, when you are asked to make room in your assemblies, do so. Allah will make room for you in the world to come. And when you are told to rise, do so. Allah will raise up the believers and those among you who have knowledge. Allah is aware of all that you do.*
58:12 *Believers, when you speak privately with the Messenger, give to charity before you meet. This will be better for you and will purify you. But if you do not have the means to do so, Allah is forgiving and merciful. Do you hesitate to give to charity before you meet with him? If you do not do it (and Allah will forgive you), then at least observe your prayers and pay the poor tax, and obey Allah and His Messenger, for Allah is aware of all that you do.*

If You Should Speak to His Wives, Do So Behind a Curtain

> 33:53 *Believers! Do not enter the Messenger's house early for a meal unless you are given permission. When you are invited, enter, and when you have finished your meal, leave. Do not remain there hoping to start a conversation, for this would annoy the Messenger, and he would be ashamed to send you home, but Allah is not ashamed to tell you the truth. And if you should speak to his wives, do so behind a curtain. This will be purer for both their hearts and yours. And you should not cause Allah's Messenger any trouble nor ever marry any of his widows, for this would be a grievous sin in Allah's sight. Whether you do a thing in the open or in secret, truly Allah knows all things.*

And with power comes criticism:

> 9:58 *Some of them speak ill of you in regard to the distribution of the poor tax, yet if some is given to them, they are content, but if nothing is given to them, they are angry. If only they were content with what Allah and His Messenger had given them and would say, "Allah is sufficient for us. Allah will soon give us out of His bounty, and so will His Messenger. We turn our hopes to Allah."*

JIHAD, THE FIRST DHIMMIS

CHAPTER 22

4:80 Those who obey the Messenger, obey Allah. As for those who turn away from you, We have not sent you to watch over them.

KHAYBAR

I756 After the treaty of Al Hudaybiya, Mohammed stayed in Medina for about two months before he collected his army and marched to the forts of Khaybar, a community of wealthy Jewish farmers who lived in a village of separate forts about 100 miles from Medina.

I758 Mohammed seized the forts one at a time. Among the captives was a beautiful Jewess named Safiya. Mohammed took her for his sexual pleasure. One of his men had first chosen her for his own slave of pleasure, but Mohammed traded him two of her cousins for Safiya. Mohammed always got first choice of the spoils of war and the women.

I759 On the occasion of Khaybar, Mohammed put forth new orders about the sex with captive women. If the woman was pregnant, she was not to be used for sex until after the birth of the child. Nor were any women to be used for sex who were unclean with regards to the Muslim laws about menstruation.

I764 Mohammed knew that there was a large treasure hidden somewhere in Khaybar, so he brought forth the Jew who he thought knew the most about it and questioned him. The Jew denied any knowledge. Mohammed told one of his men, "Torture the Jew until you extract what he has." So the Jew was staked on the ground, and a small fire built on his chest to get him to talk. When the man was nearly dead and still would not talk, Mohammed had him released and taken to one of his men who had had a brother killed in the fight. This Muslim got the pleasure of cutting off the tortured Jew's head.

I764 At Khaybar Mohammed instituted the first dhimmis. After the best of the goods were taken from the Jews Mohammed left them to work the land. Since his men knew nothing about farming, and the Jews were skilled at it, they worked the land and gave Mohammed half of their profits.

I774 There were a total of 1,800 people who divided up the wealth taken from the beaten Jews of Khaybar. A cavalry man got three shares, a foot soldier got one share. Mohammed appointed eighteen chiefs to divide the loot. Mohammed received his one-fifth before it was distributed.

FADAK

1777 The Jews of Fadak panicked when they saw what Mohammed did at Khaybar. They would be next, so they surrendered to Mohammed without a fight. Since there was no battle Mohammed got 100% of their goods and they worked the land and gave half to Mohammed each year. They became dhimmis like those of Khaybar.

MOHAMMED'S FINAL JIHAD

CHAPTER 23

3:53 "Our Lord! We believe in what Thou hast revealed, and we follow the Apostle; then write us down among those who bear witness."

THE PILGRIMAGE

I789 After returning from Khaybar, Mohammed sent out many raiding parties and expeditions. Seven years after Mohammed moved to Medina and one year after the treaty of Hudaybiya, Mohammed led the Muslims to the Kabah in Mecca. While there he kissed one of the stones of the Kabah and trotted around the Kabah. When he got to the corner with the Black Stone, he walked up and kissed it. He did this for three circuits of the Kabah.

I789 As Mohammed entered Mecca, the man leading his camel said this poetry:

Get out of his way, unbelievers, make way
I know Allah's truth in accepting it
We will fight you about its interpretation
As we have fought you about its revelation
We will cut off your head and remove friend from friend.

I790 After his three day stay in Mecca, the Quraysh asked him to leave as per the treaty. Mohammed asked to stay and have a wedding feast and he would invite the Quraysh. The Quraysh said no, please leave. He left.

THE RAID ON MUTA

I791-3 Mohammed sent an army of 3000 to Muta soon after his return from Mecca. Now Muta was north of Medina, near Syria. When they arrived the Muslims found a large army of the Byzantines. They argued about what to do. One of them said, "Men, you are complaining of what you came here to do. Die as martyrs. Islam does not fight with numbers or strength but with Islam. Come! We have only two prospects. Victory or martyrdom, both are fine. Let us go forward!"

I796 The Muslims were cut to ribbons. The Byzantines were professionals and superior in numbers.

I798 The Muslims who remained behind in Medina scorned the returning fighters. They threw dirt at them and said, "You are runaways. You fled from the way of Allah. You fled from jihad." Poetry was written to the effect that the men kept their distance from the Byzantine army and were afraid of death. They loved life too much and feared death.

MECCA CONQUERED

I803 At the treaty of Hudaybiya, it was agreed that the Meccans and Mohammed could make alliances between themselves and other tribes. There were two different Arab tribes, one allied with the Meccans and the other allied with Mohammed. As tribes are prone to do, there was a murder and subsequently retaliation by the other tribe. Then it was escalated by the Quraysh of Mecca when they helped out their ally. A chief came to Mohammed to tell of his losses and how it was time for Mohammed to take the cause of his ally and punish the Quraysh of Mecca.

I811 As a result of the fighting between a tribe allied with the Meccans and a tribe allied with Mohammed, he marched on Mecca with 10,000 men to punish them.

I813 The Muslims camped at a small town near Mecca. The Meccans needed to know whether Mohammed was going to enter Mecca. Many lives would be saved if the people would come out and seek protection, so they would not be killed.

I813-4 The chief of the Muslims, Abu Sufyan, came to the Muslim camp to negotiate. Abu Sufyan, the chief Meccan, spent the night in the Muslim army camp and went to Mohammed the next morning. Mohammed spoke, "Isn't it time for you to recognize that there is no god but Allah?" Abu answered, "I thought that there had been another god with Allah, he would have helped me." Mohammed replied, "Woe to you, Abu Sufyan, is it not time to recognize that I am Allah's apostle?" Abu Sufyan said, "As to that I have some doubt." He was told, "Submit and testify that there is no god but Allah and that Mohammed is his apostle before you lose your head!" So he submitted.

Abu Sufyan went ahead and announced to Mecca that Mohammed's army was coming. They were not to resist but to go into their houses, his house or the Kabah and that they would be safe.

I819 Mohammed had told his commanders only to kill those who resisted. Otherwise they were to bother no one except for those who had spoken against Mohammed. The list of those to be killed:

- One of Mohammed's secretaries, who had said that when he was recording Mohammed's Koranic revelations sometimes Mohammed let the secretary insert better speech. This caused him to lose faith and he became an apostate.
- Two singing girls who had sung satires against Mohammed.
- A Muslim tax collector who had become an apostate (left Islam).
- A man who had insulted Mohammed.

1821 Mohammed went to the Kabah and rode around it seven times. Each time he went past the Black Stone, he touched it with his stick. Then he called for the key to the Kabah and entered. There was a wooden dove carved that he picked up and broke and threw out the door. There were 360 ritual objects representing the gods of the various Arab faiths. Mohammed had them all destroyed by burning.

Mohammed announced the end of all feuds, all revenge killings, payment of blood money. Veneration of the ancestors was over.

KHALID'S DESTRUCTION OF THE NATIVE SHRINE

1840 Mohammed sent Khalid to an ancient temple near Mecca that was used by several tribes for worship. When Khalid got there, he destroyed it completely.

THE BATTLE OF HUNAIN

1840 When Mohammed took Mecca, the surrounding Arab tribes saw that if he was not opposed he would be King of Arabia. The Hawazin Arabs decided to oppose him under the leadership of Malik.

1842 Mohammed sent a spy to gather intelligence about the Arabs. When he received the information, he set about for jihad. He first borrowed armor and lances from a wealthy Meccan and then marched out with 12,000 men.

1845 When the army descended into the broad area, they found the enemy prepared and hiding, waiting to attack. The Muslim troops broke and ran. Mohammed stood in his stirrups and called out, "Where are you going? Come to me, the Apostle of Allah." Most of the men continued to retreat except his battle hardened core troops who regrouped around him. About a core of 100 lead the charge to turn the tide. They were steadfast. Mohammed looked at the carnage and said, "Now the oven is hot!"

1847 One of the Muslim women was near Mohammed and said about those who were retreating, "Kill those who flee just as you kill those who are attacking us."

9:25 *Allah has helped you in many battlefields, and on the day of Hunain, when your great numbers elated you [there were 12,000 Muslims and 4000 unbelievers], but availed you nothing [the Muslims panicked and fled], and the earth, for all its breadth, constrained you, you turned your backs in flight.*
9:26 *Then Allah sent down His tranquility on His Messenger and on the faithful, and He sent down invisible forces and He punished the unbelievers. This is the reward for those without faith. After this, Allah will turn to whom He pleases, for Allah is oft-forgiving and merciful.*

THE RAID ON TABUK

I894 Mohammed decided to raid the Byzantines. Normally he never let his men actually know where he was headed. He would announce a destination, but after they were on the way, he would announce the actual place. But this raid was far away in very hot weather, so greater preparations would need to be made. The men began to prepare, but with no enthusiasm due to the heat, it was time for harvest to begin and they remembered the last combat with the Byzantines—they lost badly.

I894 When Mohammed asked one of his best men if he wanted to go, the man replied, "Would you allow me to stay? You know how much I love women and when I see the Byzantine women, I don't know if I will be able to control myself." So Mohammed told him to stay. But the Koran had a comment:

9:45 *The only ones who will ask leave of you are those who do not believe in Allah and the Last Day, whose hearts are full of doubts, and who waver in their doubts. If they had intended to go to war, they would have prepared for war. But Allah was opposed to their marching forth and held them back. It was said, "Sit at home with those who sit." If they had taken the field with you, they would not have added to your strength but would have hurried about among you, stirring up dissension. Some of you would have listened to them. Allah knows the evildoers. They had plotted dissension before and made plots against you again until the truth arrived. Then the decree of Allah prevailed, much to their disgust.*
9:49 *Some of them say to you, "Allow me to remain at home, and do not expose me to temptation." Have they not already fallen into temptation? Hell will surround the unbelievers. If a success befalls you [Mohammed], it annoys them. If a misfortune befalls you, they say, "We took our precautions," and they turn their backs and are glad.*

I895 There was much grumbling about the heat.

9:81 *Those who were left behind were delighted at sitting behind Allah's Messenger. They hated to strive and fight with their riches and their lives for Allah's cause [jihad] and said, "Do not go out in the heat." Say: The Fire of Hell is a fiercer heat." If they would only understand. Let them laugh a little for they will weep much in payment for their deeds.*
9:83 *If Allah brings you back from the fight and they ask your permission to march out with you the next time, say, "You will never come out with me or fight an enemy with me. You were well pleased to sit at home at the first crisis, so sit at home with those who lag behind."*

I896 So Mohammed set off, but there were many Muslims who were slow to leave or they came with misgivings. After the first camp some of the Muslims left and returned to Medina. These were called hypocrites.

9:51 *Say: Nothing will happen to us except what Allah has destined for us. He is our protector. Let the faithful put their trust in Allah. Say: Can you expect for us anything other than one of the two best things—martyrdom, or victory? Allah will inflict a punishment Himself or at our hands. So wait, and we will wait with you.*
9:53 *Say: Pay your offerings willingly or unwillingly. It cannot be accepted from you because you are a wicked people. The only reasons their contributions are not accepted are because they reject Allah and His Messenger. They do not keep prayer but with sluggishness, and they do not make offerings willingly.*
9:55 *Do not let their riches or their children amaze you. Allah's plan is to punish them by means of these in this present life and for their souls to depart while they are unbelievers. They swear by Allah that they are believers when they are unbelievers, but they are people who are afraid of you [Mohammed]. If they could find a place of refuge, or caves, or a hiding place, they surely would have turned towards it running in haste.*

I902 When they got to Tabuk, the people there paid the poll tax, *jizya*. By paying the poll tax, a per person tax, they would not be attacked, killed or robbed by the Muslims. Those who paid the jizya were under the protection of Islam

I903 Mohammed sent Khalid to the fort of a Christian chief. When the chief and his brother rode out of their fort to inspect the cattle, Khalid killed the chief's brother and captured the ruler. The chief agreed to pay the poll tax to Islam. Mohammed returned to Medina.

9:95 *They will swear to you by Allah when you come back to them that you may leave them alone. So leave them alone for they are unclean. Their dwelling will be Hell in payment for their deeds. They will swear to you [Mohammed] that you will be pleased with them. But if you are pleased with them, Allah will not be pleased with those who disobey.*

9:97 *The Arabs of the desert [Bedouins] are most stout in unbelief and hypocrisy, and it is likelier that they would be unaware of the laws that Allah has sent down to His Messenger, but Allah is all knowing and wise. The Arabs of the desert look at what they spend in Allah's cause to be a tribute and wait for some change of fortune to befall them. A change for evil will be theirs. Allah hears all and knows all. Some of the desert Arabs believe in Allah and in the Last Day and deem what they give in charity as holy gifts bringing them near to Allah and to the Messenger's prayers. They do bring them nearer to Him, and soon Allah will give them His mercy. Yes, Allah is indulgent and merciful.*

The Battle of Tabuk was hard for Mohammed. The Muslims did not come out to be jihadists as they had before. But the Koran makes clear that jihad is an obligation.

9:85 *Do not let their riches or their children astonish you. Through these Allah is inclined to punish them in this world and to let their souls depart while they are still unbelievers. When a sura [chapter] was sent down saying, "Believe in Allah and strive and go to war with His Messenger," those of them who are possessed of riches demanded exemption saying, "Leave us behind that we may be with those who sit at home." They are well contented to be with those who stay behind for their hearts are sealed. They do not understand.*

9:88 *The Messenger and those who share his faith strive hard for their faith with their with purses and lives. All good things await them. These are the ones who will prosper. Allah has made ready for them Gardens beneath which the rivers flow, where they will remain forever. This is the supreme felicity.*

9:90 *Some Arabs of the desert came with excuses to avoid fighting. They who had rejected Allah and His Messenger sat at home. A painful doom will fall on those who do not believe. It will be no crime in the weak, in the sick, or in those who find no resources to contribute to Allah's cause [jihad] to stay at home provided they are sincere with Allah and His Messenger. There is no cause of blame against those who act virtuously. Allah is gracious and merciful. Nor is their blame against those who, when they came to you asking to be provided with mounts, were told, "I do not find mounts for you." They turned their backs, their eyes shedding tears of grief, because they found no means to contribute.*

9:93 *The cause for blame is only against those who ask for exemption though they are rich. They are pleased to be with those who stay behind, and Allah has set a seal upon their hearts so they do not know. They will present their excuses to you when you return to them. Say: Do not present excuses. We cannot believe you. Allah has informed us about you. Allah and His Messenger will behold your doings. You will return to the*

knower of the seen and the unseen. He will tell you the truth of what you have done.

THE PUNISHMENT OF THE THREE

1908-9 When Mohammed returned to Medina, there were many who had chosen not to go on jihad with him. But there were three who drew his attention and he ordered them shunned. No one was to go to their house or even speak to them. In a small community being publicly shunned is socially painful, and those who were being punished were hurt. After forty days, even their wives were ordered to shun their husbands.

1913 On the fiftieth day of their shunning, Mohammed announced that Allah had sent down forgiveness for the men who had slacked on their duty of jihad to Tabuk. Mohammed did not chastise them, Allah did.

> 9:117 ***Allah turned with favor to His Messenger, the Emigrants [those who left Mecca with Mohammed], and to the Helpers [the Ansars, the Muslims of Medina who supported the Meccan Muslims] who followed him in the hour of distress after the hearts of a part of them had nearly failed their duties; then He turned to them in mercy, for He was kind and merciful.***
> 9:118 ***Allah also turned in mercy to the three who were left behind. Their guilt caused them to feel that the earth, spacious as it is, constrained them. Their souls became so confined within them that they thought there was no refuge from Allah but in Him. Then He turned to them, in mercy so that they might repent. Allah is constant and merciful. Believers, fear Allah, and be with those who are truthful.***

There were men who built a mosque, but were in opposition to Mohammed. They had gone to Mohammed and asked him to come and pray there. But this was just before he had left for Tabuk and he said that he would when he returned. The Koran:

> 9:107 ***There are some who have built a mosque for mischief and for infidelity [a mosque was built by a tribe for political reasons] to cause dissent among the faithful and in preparation for him [Abu Amir] who, in time past, warred against Allah and His Messenger. They will surely swear, "Our aim was only good," but Allah bears witness that they are liars. Never set your foot in it. There is a mosque founded from its first day in piety. It is more worthy that you should stand there to pray. The men there aspire to purity, and Allah loves the purified.***
> 9:109 ***Which of the two is best? He who lays the foundation of his building on duty to Allah and the desire to please Him, or he who lays the foundation of his building on the brink of an undermined sand cliff that***

crumbles in pieces with him into the Fire of Hell? Allah does not guide the wrongdoers.
9:110 *The foundation of those who build like this [the mosque of mischief] will not cease to cause uneasiness in their hearts, until their hearts are torn to pieces. Allah is knowing and wise.*

ETERNAL JIHAD

M448 After all the victories, some Muslims said that the days of fighting were over and even began to sell their arms. But Mohammed forbid this, saying, "There shall not cease from the midst of my people a party engaged in fighting for the truth, until the Antichrist appears." Jihad was recognized as the normal state of affairs. Indeed, the Koran prepares the way for this:

9:122 *The faithful should not all go out together to fight. If a part of every troop remained behind, they could instruct themselves in their religion and warn their people when they return to them that they should guard against evil.*
9:123 *Believers, fight the unbelievers who are near you, and let them find you to be tough and hard. Know that Allah is with those who guard against evil.*

ABU BAKR LEADS THE PILGRIMAGE

I919-20 Abu Bakr led the pilgrimage from Medina to Mecca. While they were in Mecca major changes were made to the treaty of Hudaybiya, which are recorded in the Koran. The treaty is only good for four more months, then jihad will be declared if the non-Muslims don't submit to Islam.

9:1 *A declaration of immunity from Allah and His Messenger to the unbelievers with whom you have made a treaty: Travel freely in the land for four months, but know that you cannot escape Allah and that those who do not believe will be put to shame by Allah.*
9:3 *Allah and His Messenger proclaimed to the people on the day of the greater pilgrimage: "Allah and His Messenger are free from any obligations with the unbelievers. If you repent to Allah, it will be better for you, but if you turn away, then know that you cannot escape Allah. Announce a painful punishment to those who do not believe. But this does not concern those unbelievers with whom you have an agreement and who have not failed you, nor aided anyone against you. So fulfill your agreement with them to the end of its term, for Allah loves those who fear Him.*
9:5 *When the sacred months [by ancient Arab custom there were four months during which there was to be no violence] are passed, kill the unbelievers wherever you find them. Take them as captives, besiege them,*

and lie in wait for them with every kind of ambush. If they submit to Islam, observe prayer, and pay the poor tax, then let them go their way. Allah is gracious and merciful. If any one of the unbelievers seeks asylum with you, grant it that he may hear the word of Allah; then take him to a place of safety. This is because they are an ignorant people.

1922 After this time, those who practice the old native religions of Arabia will no longer be able to come to Mecca for pilgrimage.

9:17 *It is not for the unbelievers to visit or maintain the mosques of Allah while they witness against their own souls to disbelief. Their work bears no fruit; they will abide in the Fire forever. Only he who believes in Allah and the Last Day should visit the temples of Allah, observe regular prayer, and practice regular charity, and fear only Allah. These will be among the rightly guided.*

1924 The non-Muslims are unclean and must not approach the Kabah. The money that will be lost from their pilgrimages will be taken care of by Allah. Jihad will bring in the lost money.

9:28 *Oh, believers, only the unbelievers are unclean. Do not let them come near the Sacred Temple after this year of theirs. If you fear poverty from the loss of their business [breaking commercial ties with the Meccans], Allah will enrich you from His abundance if He pleases. Allah is knowing and wise.*

1924 The Koran then turns to the issue of the raid on the Byzantines at Tabuk. Muslims must answer the call to jihad. It is an obligation. If the Byzantine raid had been short and had made for easy war spoils, the Muslims would have joined readily. But instead they made excuses. A Muslim's duty is not to avoid fighting with their person and money.

9:38 *Oh, believers, what possessed you that when it was said, "March forth in Allah's cause [jihad]," you cling heavily to the earth? Do you prefer the life of this world to the next? Little is the comfort of this life compared to the one that is to come. Unless you march forth, He will punish you with a grievous penalty, and He will put another in your place. You will not harm Him at all, for Allah has power over everything.*

9:40 *If you do not assist your Messenger, it is no matter for Allah assisted him when the unbelievers drove him out, he [Mohammed] being only one of two men. When the two [Mohammed and Abu Bakr] were in the cave, the Messenger said to his companion, "Do not be distressed, for Allah is with us." Allah sent His tranquility upon him, and strengthened him with hosts you did not see. He humbled the word of those who disbelieved and exalted the word of Allah, for Allah is mighty and wise. March forth both the lightly and heavily armed, and strive hard in Allah's cause [jihad] with your substance and your persons. This is better for you if you know it.*

9:42 *Had there been a near advantage and a short journey [Mohammed marched to Tabuk against the Greeks. It was a long, hot campaign], they would certainly have followed you, but the journey was too long for them. Yet they will swear by Allah saying, "If we only could have, we would surely have gone forth with you." They would destroy their own souls. Allah knows that they are surely lying.*

9:43 *Allah forgive you, Mohammed. Why did you give them permission to stay behind before you knew those who told the truth from those who lied? Those who believe in Allah and in the Last Day do not ask for exemption from fighting with their wealth and their lives. Allah knows those who fear Him.*

1926 Those who try to avoid jihad are hypocrites. The Prophet should struggle against them. They are bound for Hell.

9:73 *Oh, Prophet, strive hard against the unbelievers and the hypocrites, and be firm with them. Hell will be their dwelling place: A wretched journey.*

1927 In the past Mohammed had prayed at funerals and gone to the graves for some of the hypocrites. But now a Muslim should not pray for a non-Muslim or stand at their grave.

9:84 *Never pray over nor stand over the grave of anyone of them who dies because they did not believe in Allah and His Messenger and died in their wickedness.*

Those who believe in Allah and the Apostle and enter jihad with their wealth and selves will prosper and enter Paradise. This is a promise from Allah.

9:111 *Allah has bought from the believers their lives and their wealth, and in return, theirs is the Garden of Paradise. They will fight on the path of Allah so they slay and are slain. It is a promise binding on Him in truth through the Law, in the Gospel, and in the Koran, and who is more faithful to His promise than Allah? Rejoice, therefore, in the pledge that you have made, for this will be the great bliss.*

1933 When Mohammed had taken Mecca and Tabuk, deputations began to come from the Arabs. The Arabs were waiting to see what would happen between the Quraysh and Mohammed. When Mohammed was victorious, the Arabs came in groups and joined with him.

110:1 *When the help of Allah and the victory arrive, and you see men entering the religion of Allah in ranks, then celebrate the praises of your Lord and pray for His forgiveness, for He is always ready to show mercy.*

1956 The kings of Himyar wrote to Mohammed that they had submitted to Islam. Mohammed wrote them back, "... I received your message and am informed of your Islam and your killing non-Muslims. Allah has guided you. ... send the one fifth of the spoils of war and tax the believers... Christians and Jews who do not convert must pay the poll tax..."

1965 Mohammed sent out tax collectors to every part of Islam to collect the tax.

MOHAMMED'S LAST YEAR

CHAPTER 24

24:51 But when Allah and His Messenger call the true believers to judge between them, their response is, "We have heard, and we obey."

THE FAREWELL PILGRIMAGE

I968 Ten years after entering Medina Mohammed made what was to be his last pilgrimage to Mecca. There he made his farewell address. He told the Muslims that usury was abolished, Allah would judge them and their works. All of the blood shed before Islam was to be left unavenged. The lunar calendar was the sacred calendar and it was not to be adjusted with respect to the solar calendar.

I969 The men have rights over their wives and the wives have rights over the men. The wives must never commit adultery nor act in a sexual manner towards others. If they do, put them in separate rooms and beat them lightly. If they refrain from these things, they have the right to food and clothing. Lay injunctions on women lightly for they are prisoners of the men and have no control over their persons.

M473 Feed and clothe your slaves well.

I969 Every Muslim is a Muslim's brother. Only take from a brother what he gives you.

I970 Mohammed led the Muslims through the rituals of the pilgrimage.

THE FINAL STATE OF CHRISTIANS AND JEWS

M453 When Mohammed first started preaching in Mecca, his religion was Arabian. Then Allah became identified with Jehovah and Jewish elements were introduced. When Mohammed moved to Medina, he argued with the Jews when they denied his status as a prophet in the Judaic line. He then annihilated the Jews and makes no more connections between Islam and the Jews. In his last statement, Jews and Christians became perpetual second class political citizens, dhimmis (pay the dhimmi tribute, jizya, and are subdued). Only those Christians and Jews who submit to Islam are protected. Islam defines Judaism and Christianity. The real Christians are those who deny the Trinity and accept Mohammed as the final prophet. The real Jews are those who accept Mohammed as the final prophet of their god, Jehovah. Both Christians and Jews must accept that the Koran is the true Scripture and that the Old Testament and New Testament are corrupt and in error. The contradictions between the Koran and the New and Old Testament are proof of the corruption of the nonbelievers.

All other Jews and Christians are false and unbelievers.

> 9:29 ***Make war on those who have received the Scriptures [Jews and Christians] but do not believe in Allah or in the Last Day. They do not forbid what Allah and His Messenger have forbidden. The Christians and Jews do not follow the religion of truth until they submit and pay the poll tax [jizya], and they are humiliated.***
> 9:30 ***The Jews say, "Ezra is the son of Allah," [this tradition is unknown in the Old Testament] and the Christians say, "The Messiah is a son of Allah." Such are the sayings in their mouths, but they resemble the saying of the unbelievers of old. Allah destroy them. How they are deluded from the truth.***
> 9:31 ***They take their rabbis and their monks and the Messiah, son of Mary, for Lords besides Allah [Both Jews and Christians of that area used the term "rabbi" for their religious leaders. Islam only applied rabbi to Allah], though they were bidden to worship one Allah only. There is no god but Allah. He is far from having the partners they associate with Him.***
> 9:32 ***They desire to put out Allah's light with their mouths, but Allah only desires to perfect His light, though the unbelievers detest it. He sent His Messenger with the guidance and a religion of the truth that He may make it victorious over every other religion, though the unbelievers will detest it.***
> 9:34 ***Oh, Believers of truth, many of the rabbis and monks devour the substance of man and hinder them from the way of Allah. To those who store up gold and silver and do not spend it on Allah's cause [jihad], give tidings of grievous torment. On that day their treasures will be heated in Hellfire and their foreheads, their sides, and their backs will be branded with them, "This is the treasure you have buried for yourselves. Now, taste your riches."***

The Christians have hidden their prophesies that Mohammed would come to fulfill the work of Christ. To believe in the divinity of Christ is to refuse to submit to Islam. Those Christians are unbelievers and infidels. Like the Jews, only those Christians who submit to Islam and become dhimmis and are ruled by the sharia (Islamic law) are actual Christians. Islam defines all religions. No religion defines itself, except Islam.

5:14 *We made a covenant with those who say, "We are Christians," but they, too, have forgotten a part of what they were taught [Islam claims that the Christians suppressed the prophecies of Jesus that Mohammed would be the final prophet] so We have stirred up animosity and hatred among them that will last until Resurrection Day. In the end, Allah will tell them what they have done.*

5:15 *Oh, people of the Scriptures, Our Messenger has come to you to clear up what you have hidden of those Scriptures and to pass over many things that are now unnecessary. Now you have a new light and a clear Book from Allah. He will use it to guide whoever seeks to follow His good pleasure to paths of peace. He will bring them out of the darkness to the light, and, by his decree, will guide them to the straight path.*

5:17 *Surely they are unbelievers who say, "Allah is the Messiah, son of Mary." Say: Who has any power against Allah if He chose to destroy the Messiah, son of Mary, his mother, and all who are on the earth together? Allah's is the sovereignty of the heavens and of the earth and of all that is between them. He creates what He will, and Allah has power over all things.*

5:72 *The unbelievers say, "Jesus is the Messiah, Son of Mary," for the Messiah said, "Oh, Children of Israel, worship Allah, my Lord and your Lord." Whoever will join other gods with Allah, He will forbid him in the Garden, and his abode will be the Fire. The wicked will have no helpers. They surely blaspheme who say, "Allah is the third of three [the Trinity]," for there is no god except one Allah, and if they do not refrain from what they say, a grievous penalty will fall on those who disbelieve. Will they not turn to Allah and ask His forgiveness? For Allah is forgiving and merciful.*

5:75 *The Messiah, Son of Mary, is but a messenger. Other messengers have passed away before him, and his mother was a saintly woman; they both ate food. See how Allah makes His signs clear to them; then see how they turn from the truth. Say: Will you worship, beside Allah, that which can neither hurt nor help you? Allah hears and knows all things.*

A SUMMARY OF MOHAMMED'S ARMED EVENTS

I973 In a nine year period Mohammed personally attended twenty-seven raids. There were thirty-eight other battles and expeditions. This is a total of sixty-five armed events, not including assassinations and executions, for an average of one armed event every seven weeks.

MOHAMMED'S DEATH

I1000 When Mohammed spoke to Aisha, his favorite wife, she complained of a headache. Mohammed said, "No, Aisha, Oh my head. Would it distress you if you were to die before me so that I might wrap you in your shroud and pray over you?" Aisha said, "I think that if you did that, that after you returned to the house you would simply spend the night with one of your other wives." But the pain became worse and he took his final illness in the house of Aisha.

I1006 Mohammed weakened and was in a great deal of pain. Later he died with his head in Aisha's lap. His final words were the perfect summation of Islam, political action based upon religion.

> B4,52,288 ***Mohammed said, "There should not be two religions no other religions besides Islam in Arabia" and that the money should be continued to be paid to influence the foreign, unbeliever ambassadors.***

T1831 Mohammed was buried beneath his bed. The bed was removed and a grave was dug where the bed had stood.

THE SHARIA

CHAPTER 25

4:170 People! The Messenger has come to you with truth from your Lord. If you believe, it will be better for you.

The Sharia is the law of Islam that is based upon the Koran, the Hadith and the Sira. It is the political aim of Islam to replace all legal codes and constitutions (which are man-made) with the Sharia, which comes from Allah.

Verses used in the Sharia:

MARRIAGE/DIVORCE/SEX

> 4:34 *Allah has made men superior to women because men spend their wealth to support them. Therefore, virtuous women are obedient, and they are to guard their unseen parts as Allah has guarded them. As for women whom you fear will rebel, admonish them first, and then send them to a separate bed, and then beat them. But if they are disobedient after that, then do nothing further; surely Allah is exalted and great!*
> 4:35 *If you fear a breach between a man and wife, then send a judge from his family, and a judge from her family. If they both want to come to a reconciliation, Allah will bring them back together. Truly Allah is all-knowing and wise!*

> 33:49 *Believers! If you marry a believing woman and divorce her before consummating the marriage, you do not have to wait out the prescribed term. Provide for her and dismiss her with honor.*

> 24:30 *Tell the men who are believers that they should look away from that which tempts them and control their lustful desires. Therefore, they will be more pure. Allah is well aware of all they do. And tell the women who are believers that they should lower their eyes and guard their purity, and they should not display their beauty and adornments except that which is normally shown. They should cover their breasts with their veils and only show their adornments to their husband, father-in-law, sons, step-sons, brothers, nephews, or their female servants, eunuch slaves, and children who are innocent and do not notice a woman's nakedness. And do not let them stamp their feet so as to reveal their hidden adornments [ankle bracelets]. Believers, all of you turn to Allah and repent so that it will go well for you.*

24:32 *And marry those among you who are single, or an honorable male or female servant. And if they are poor, then Allah will give them riches from His own bounty. Allah is bountiful and all-knowing. And for those who cannot afford to marry, let them stay pure until Allah fulfills their needs from His bounty. In regard to your slaves who wish to buy their freedom, grant it if you see there is good in them, and give them a part of the wealth that Allah has given you. Do not force your female slaves into prostitution just to gain the wealth of this world if they wish to remain pure. Yet if they are forced to do so, then truly Allah will be merciful.*

58:1 *Allah has heard the words of the woman who pleaded with you against her husband and made her complaint to Allah. [Khawlah was divorced by the old Arab custom of her husband saying, "Be to me as my mother's back."] Allah has heard both sides of the conversation, for Allah hears and sees everything.*
58:2 *Those who divorce their wives by saying, "Be to me as my mother's back," should know that they are not. The only ones who are their mothers are those who gave birth to them. Their words are certainly hateful and untrue, but surely Allah is forgiving and merciful. Those who divorce their wives in this manner, and afterwards recant their words, must free one of their slaves as a penalty before they can touch one another again. You are commanded to do this. Allah is aware of all you do. And as for those who do not have a slave to free, they must fast for two consecutive months before they can touch each other. Those who are unable to fast must feed sixty poor people. This is commanded so that you may show your faith in Allah and His Messenger. These are the limits set by Allah, and dreadful punishment awaits the unbelievers.*

65:1 *Prophet! When you or the believers divorce a woman, divorce them at the end of the prescribed legal period. Calculate carefully the number of days and fear Allah your Lord. Do not put them out of their homes or let them leave on their own unless it is proven they have committed adultery. These are the boundaries Allah has imposed, and those who overstep these boundaries wrong their own souls. You do not know if Allah will cause something to occur that will reunite the two of you.*
65:2 *When they have waited out the prescribed period, either keep them in kindness or part with them honorably. Find two honest men as witnesses from among you, and testify before Allah. This is a warning to those who believe in Allah and the Last Day. For those who fear Allah, Allah will provide a means of salvation and provide for them from sources which were never imagined. For those who put their trust in Him, Allah is All-Sufficient. Allah will surely accomplish that which He has planned. Allah has an appointed time for everything.*

65:4 If you have doubt about your wives who have ceased to menstruate, the prescribed waiting period is three months. This length of time is also prescribed for young girls [wives] who have not yet menstruated. As for women who are pregnant, they must wait until they have given birth. Allah will make His command easy for those who fear Him. This is Allah's command which He has sent down to you. Whoever fears Allah will be forgiven of his sins and He will increase his reward.
65:6 Keep your divorced wives in your home according to your means, and do not injure them so as to make life unbearable for them. If they are pregnant, keep them until they give birth. After that, if they breast-feed their children, pay them and seek mutual guidance together. But if you cannot agree, hire a wet-nurse for the child.
65:7 Let the man of wealth spend according to his means and the man who is poor according to what Allah has given him. Allah does not burden a man with more than He has given them; Allah will bring ease after difficulty.

2:221 You will not marry pagan women unless they accept the faith. A slave girl who believes is better than an idolatress, although the idolatress may please you more. Do not give your daughters away in marriage to unbelievers until they believe for a slave who is a believer is better than an idolater, though the idolater may please you more. These lure you to the Fire, but Allah calls you to Paradise and forgiveness by His will. He makes His signs clear to mankind so that they may remember.
2:222 They ask you about women's menstrual cycle. Say: It is a discomfort. Therefore, keep away from them during this time and do not come near them until they are clean again. But when they are clean, you may lie with them as Allah has commanded. Allah loves those who turn to Him and seek cleanliness.
2:223 Your women are your plowed fields: go into your fields when you like, but do some good deed beforehand and fear Allah. Keep in mind that you will meet Him. Give good news to the believers.
2:224 Do not make swearing by Allah an obstacle to doing good and guarding against evil and making peace among the people. Allah, who hears and knows all, will not punish you if you inadvertently use His name, but He will judge you for what was in your heart. Allah is forgiving and merciful.
2:226 Those who abandon their wives on oath must wait four months. If they decide to return, Allah is forgiving and merciful. If, however, they decide to divorce them, remember that Allah hears and knows all.
2:228 Divorced women must keep themselves from men for three menstrual periods. It is not lawful for them to hide what Allah has created in their wombs if they believe in Allah and the Last Day. If they are in that state, it is better for their husbands to take them back if they want

reconciliation. Women have rights similar to those of men in regard to justice, but men are a degree above them. Allah is mighty and wise.
2:229 *You may divorce your wives twice; afterwards, you must retain them with honor or release them in kindness. It is not lawful for you to take back any of the gifts you have given her unless both fear they may be unable to keep the limits set by Allah. In such a case it is not a sin for either if the wife ransoms herself. These are the limits set up by Allah, so do not exceed them, and whoever exceeds them are evil-doers.*
2:230 *If a husband divorces his wife for a third time, it is not lawful for him to take her back until she has married and divorced another husband. Then if they return to each other, it will not be a sin for either if they can keep within the limits set by Allah. Such are the limits set by Allah. He makes them clear for those who understand. But if you have divorced a woman and she has fulfilled the period of waiting, then either keep her honorably or let her leave with kindness. You must not keep her to do her evil or take advantage for if anyone does that, he harms his soul. Do not mock Allah's revelations, but remember the grace He has shown you and the Scriptures and the wisdom He has sent down as a warning. Fear Allah and know that Allah is all-knowing.*
2:232 *When you have divorced a woman and she has fulfilled the period of waiting, do not interfere with her marrying a new husband if it has been agreed between them honorably. This is commanded for everyone who has faith in Allah and the Last Day; this course of action is more virtuous and pure. Allah knows and you do not.*
2:233 *Divorced mothers should breast-feed their children for two full years if the father wishes for the child to nurse that long. They should be cared for and clothed by the father during this time. No one should pay more than they can afford. A mother should not have to suffer for her child's sake nor should the father, and these duties are the same for the father's heir. But if it is agreed upon that the child should be weaned, they should not be blamed. If you decide to have a wet-nurse for your children, there is no blame if you pay her fairly. Fear Allah and know that Allah sees everything you do.*
2:234 *As for widows, they should keep apart from men for four months and ten days after their husband's death. When they have fulfilled the waiting period, there will be no blame if they choose another and act in a decent way. Allah knows all that you do. You will not be blamed for openly proposing to widows or for holding them close to your hearts; Allah knows that you will not forget them. Do not arrange a secret meeting with them, and if you do meet, treat them honorably. You should not consummate the marriage until her waiting period is over. Know that Allah knows everything you think; therefore, beware of Him and know that Allah is forgiving and merciful.*

2:236 *You will not be blamed if you divorce your wife before you consummate the marriage or receive the dowry. Provide for her according to your means, whether rich or poor; this is a duty of the righteous. If you decide to divorce her before you consummate the marriage but after you have received the dowry, then she is entitled to half the dowry unless she or the husband agrees to relinquish it. Do not forget to show kindness to one another. Allah sees all you do.*
2:238 *Be dedicated to your prayers, especially the middle prayer [afternoon], and stand up in devotion to Allah. When you are in danger, pray while running or on horseback, and when you are safe again remember Allah for He has taught things you never knew before.*
2:240 *If you should die and leave behind a wife, you should leave her at least enough to live a year in the home; but if she leaves on her own, you are not to blame for her lawful actions. Allah is mighty and wise. Reasonable provisions must also be made for women you divorce; this is the duty of righteous men. It is in this manner that Allah makes His signs clear to you so that you will understand.*
2:243 *Remember those who fled their homes long ago in the thousands because they feared death. [The Jews fled to avoid a plague.] Allah said to them, "You will die," and then He restored them to life. Certainly Allah is generous to mankind although many do not thank Him for it.*

4:2 *Give orphans their property, and do not exchange your worthless things for their good ones or absorb their property to add it to your own for this is surely a great sin. If you fear that you will not be able to deal with orphan girls fairly, marry other women of your choice, two, or three, or four; but if you fear that you cannot treat them equally, then marry only one, or any of the slave-girls you have acquired. This will prevent you from being unjust.*
4:4 *And give the women you marry their dowries as free gifts, but if they freely give it up to you, then you are free to absorb it into your wealth. And do not entrust the feeble-minded with the land Allah has given to support them; instead, feed and clothe them with the proceeds you make from it, and speak kindly to them.*
4:6 *Test the orphans until they reach the marriageable age; then, if they are found to be of sound mind, hand their property over to them; do not deprive them by using it up wastefully before they mature. If the guardian is wealthy, he should take no part of the orphan's property, but if the guardian is poor, let him use only what is necessary. And when the property is handed over to them, call some witnesses. Allah is sufficient to account for your actions.*
4:15 *If any of your women are guilty of adultery or fornication, then bring in four of you as witnesses against them. If they admit their guilt, then shut them up in their houses until they die or until Allah makes*

some other way for them. If two of your men are guilty of an indecent act [homosexuality], punish both of them. If they ask for forgiveness and change their ways, then leave them alone, for Allah is forgiving and merciful!

4:17 *Allah will forgive those who sin unknowingly and then turn away and repent soon thereafter; Allah will show them mercy, for Allah is knowing and wise! But as for those who do evil, and then when they are about to die say, "Now I truly turn to Allah!" or those who die as unbelievers, they will not be forgiven, and a painful punishment is prepared for them.*

4:19 *Believers! It is not allowed for you to inherit the wives of your deceased family members against their will, or to prevent the wives from re-marrying in order to take away part of the dowry you have given them unless they are guilty of flagrant indecency. Treat them kindly for if you hate them, it may be that you hate that in which Allah has placed abundant goodness.*

4:20 *If you want to exchange one wife for another, do not take anything away from the dowry you have given her. Would you take it by slandering her and doing her obvious wrong? How could you take it back when you have slept with one another and entered into a firm covenant?*

4:22 *And do not marry the women your fathers have married, though in the past it was allowed, for this is an evil act, shameful and abominable. Forbidden to you for marriage are your mothers, daughters, sisters, your parents' sisters, nieces on both your brother's and sister's side, foster-mothers, foster-sisters, mothers-in-law, step-daughters in your care who were born to women you have slept with, (but if you have not slept with their mothers, it is not wrong to marry them), and your biological sons' wives. You are also forbidden to marry two sisters at the same time, with the exception of those whom you have already married [married before the Koran]. Truly Allah is forgiving and merciful! Also forbidden to you are married women unless they are your slaves. This is the command of Allah. Other than those mentioned, all other women are lawful to you to court with your wealth and with honorable intentions, not with lust. And give those you have slept with a dowry, as it is your duty. But after you have fulfilled your duty, it is not an offense to make additional agreements among you. Truly Allah is knowing and wise!*

4:25 *If any of you is not wealthy enough to marry a free, believing woman, then allow him to marry a believing slave-girl. Allah knows your faith well, and you come from one another. Marry them with their master's permission, and give them a fair dowry, given that they are chaste, honorable, and have not had lovers. If the slave you marry commits adultery after you are married, then their punishment should be half of that commanded for a free woman. This is a law for those among you who fear*

sinning, but it will be better for you if you abstain. Allah is forgiving and merciful!
4:26 *Allah wishes to make this clear to you, to guide you along the paths of those who came before you, and to turn to you in mercy. Allah is all-knowing, wise! Allah wants to turn to you in mercy, but those who follow their own desires would have you go far astray. Allah wishes to lighten your burden, for man was created weak.*

4:127 *When they ask your advice regarding women say: Allah has instructed you concerning them, and His will is laid out for you in the Scriptures concerning female orphans to whom you have not given their legal due but whom you refuse to marry. In regard to helpless children, He has commanded you to deal fairly with orphans. Allah knows all the good that you do.*
4:128 *And if a wife fears cruelty or desertion from her husband, then they are not to blame for coming to a mutual agreement between themselves, for peace is best, although people are often prone to greed. But if you do good and fear Allah, Allah knows all that you do. As hard as you try to treat all your wives equally, you cannot. Do not abandon one of them altogether, so as to leave her hanging in suspense. If you come to a mutual agreement and fear Allah, then truly Allah is forgiving and merciful. But if they separate, Allah will provide for the both of them from His abundance; Allah is vast and wise.*

LEGAL

5:38 *As to the thieves, whether men or women, cut off their hands in payment for their deeds. This is a penalty by way of warning from Allah Himself. Allah is mighty and wise. But whoever repents after his wickedness, and makes amends, Allah will turn to him, for Allah is forgiving and merciful. Do you not know that the sovereignty of the heavens and of the earth is Allah's? He punishes whom He will and forgives whom He will. Allah has power over all things.*

2:178 *Believers! Retaliation is prescribed for you in the matter of murder: the free man for the free man, a slave for a slave, a female for a female. If the brother of the slain gives a measure of forgiveness, then grant him any sensible request, and compensate him with a generous payment [blood money]. This is a merciful indulgence from your Lord. He who sins after having been pardoned will suffer a terrible fate. And there is life for you in the law of retaliation, men of understanding, so that you will protect yourselves against evil.*
2:180 *It is ordered that when you are on the verge of death that you dispense your possessions equally to parents and near relatives. This is the duty of the Allah-fearing. One who hears the will and then changes it will*

be guilty, for Allah is all-hearing and all-knowing. But if anyone fears an error or partiality on the part of the testator and brings about an agreement among the parties, then he is not to blame. Allah is forgiving and merciful.

2:220 *When they ask you about the orphans, say: To deal with them fairly is best. If you mix your affairs and theirs, then they are your brothers. Allah knows the one who does good from the one who does bad. If Allah wished, He could cause you difficulties; Allah is mighty and wise.*

2:277 *Those who have faith and do good deeds and who are committed to their prayers and give charitably, will be rewarded by their Lord, having nothing to fear or regret.*

2:278 *Believers! Fear Allah and relinquish that which is owed to you from usury if you are truly believers. If you do not, Allah and His messenger will declare war on you. If you ask forgiveness and cease your sinning, you may keep your principal. Do not wrong others, and you will not be wronged. If your debtor is in a difficult situation, give him more time to repay his debt. If you pass that payment on to charity it will be better for you, if you only knew. And fear the day when you will return to Allah. Then every soul will receive what it has earned. All will be judged fairly.*

2:282 *Believers! When you contract a loan for a certain period, write it down, or to be fair, let a scribe write it down. The scribe should not refuse to write as Allah has taught him; therefore, let the scribe record what the debtor dictates being mindful of his duty to Allah and not reducing the amount he owes. If the debtor is ignorant and unable to dictate, let his guardian do so with fairness. Call two men in to witness this, but if two men cannot be found, then call one man and two women whom you see fit to be witnesses. Therefore, if either woman makes an error, the other can correct her. Witnesses must not refuse to give testimony if they are called upon to do so; therefore, do not forget to record your debts in writing, whether they are little or much, along with the date on which they were paid. This is more fair in Allah's sight, as it ensures accuracy in proof and is the best way to avoid doubt. If, however, the transaction is one that occurs on the spot, you are not to blame if it is not recorded in writing. And have witnesses when you sell, and do not let harm come to the scribe or witnesses for it will be a sin for you if this occurs. And fear Allah and Allah will give you knowledge for He has knowledge of all things*[1].

2:283 *If you are traveling and cannot find a scribe, then make a pledge with your possessions. And if you should give an object of trust to another, let the keeper of the possession return it to the owner, and let him fear Allah, his Lord.*

---

1. The longest verse in the Koran is about contract law.

4:7 *Men will have a share in what their parents and relatives leave, and women will have a share in what their parents and relatives leave. Whether the amount is small or large, they are entitled to equal shares. But when the inheritance is divided, if other relatives, orphans, or the poor are present, give them a part of it and speak kindly to them.*
4:9 *Let those who are concerned about the welfare of their young children after their deaths be careful not to wrong the orphans. Let them fear Allah and speak fairly. Those who wrongfully absorb orphans' property will only be swallowing Fire into their stomachs, and they will endure the burning Flame!*
4:11 *It is in this manner that Allah commands you concerning your children: A male should receive a share equal to that of two females, and if there are more than two females, they should receive two-thirds of what the deceased has left. If there is only one female, she will inherit half. The father and mother of the deceased will each receive a sixth of what is left if he has a child, but if he has no children, his parents are his heirs, and his mother should receive a third. If he has brothers, his mother will only receive a sixth, after paying his inheritances and debts. You may not know whether your parents or your children are more useful, but this is Allah's law. Allah is knowing and wise!*
4:12 *Half of what your wife leaves will be yours if she has no children, but if she has children, then a fourth of what she leaves will be yours, after paying inheritances and debts. And your wives will inherit a fourth of what you leave if you have no children, but if you have children, then they will receive an eighth of what you leave, after paying inheritances and debts. And if a man or a woman does not have either parents or children, and he or she has a sibling, each of them will inherit a sixth. If there are more than two siblings, then they will have a share in a third after payment of inheritances and debts, without incurring losses to anyone. This is a commandment from Allah; Allah is knowing and gracious!*
4:13 *These are the limits set up by Allah. Those who obey Allah and His Messenger will be led into the Gardens watered by flowing rivers to live forever. This is the ultimate reward! But those who disobey Allah and His Messenger and go beyond His limits, will be led into the Fire to live forever, and it will be a humiliating torment!*
4:33 *For everyone's benefit, We have appointed heirs for parents and relatives, and as for those with whom you have entered into agreements, give them their share, for Allah witnesses all you do.*

4:92 *A believer should never kill a Muslim unless an accident occurs. Whoever kills a fellow Muslim by accident must free one of his believing slaves and pay blood-money to the victim's family unless they give it to charity. If the victim was a believer from a people at war with you, then freeing a believing slave is enough. But if the victim was from a people with whom*

you have an alliance, then his family should be paid blood-money and a believing slave must be set free. For those who cannot afford to do this, they must fast for two months straight. This is the penance commanded by Allah. Allah is all-knowing and wise!
4:93 *For those who intentionally kill another Muslim, Hell will be their punishment, where they will live forever. The wrath of Allah will be upon them, He will curse them, and they will receive terrible torture.*

4:176 *When they ask you for guidance say: Allah directs you about your distant relatives who die with neither parents nor children. If a man dies without children, but he has a sister, she will inherit half of his estate, and if she dies without children, then he will inherit half of her estate. If a woman dies without children, then her brother will be her sole heir. If a man without children has two sisters, then they will inherit two-thirds of his estate, but if he has both brothers and sisters, the brothers will receive the same amount as two sisters. Allah directs you clearly so that you will not sin; Allah knows all things.*

RELIGIOUS

2:172 *Believers, eat the good things We have given you, and give thanks to Allah if it is truly Him you worship. He has forbidden that you eat carrion [the flesh of a animal found dead], blood, and pork, also any other meat that has been sacrificed to any other besides Allah. But if one is forced by necessity and does not intend to sin, then he will be held blameless. Allah is forgiving and merciful.*

22:26 *And remember when We prepared the site of the Holy Mosque [the Kabah] for Abraham saying, "Worship none except Me, and purify My House [the Kabah] for those who walk around it and for those who stand or bow down in worship."*
22:27 *Urge the people to make the pilgrimage. They will come to you on foot and on every kind of lean and swift camel, coming from every remote mountain and valley; they will see the benefits for them, and will praise Allah's name on the appointed days over the cattle He has given to them to eat. Therefore, eat of them and feed the poor and those in need. Then let them purify themselves, fulfill their vows, and walk around the ancient House.*
22:30 *This is commanded. Those who respect Allah's sacred commands will have it better in their Lord's sight. The cattle are lawful for you to eat on pilgrimage except that which you have been told about before. So turn away from the filth of idols and avoid words of deceit.*
22:31 *Have faith in Allah alone, and do not worship any except Him. Those who worship others besides Allah are like those who have fallen from heaven and are snatched up by birds or are carried off by the wind*

to some distant land. That will be so; and those who honor Allah's signs surely show the devotion of their hearts. Your cattle are beneficial to you for a time, until they are slaughtered; then they must be sacrificed at the Ancient House [the Kabah].

22:34 *And to every people We have given a sacrificial ritual so that they may say Allah's name over the cattle He has given them to eat. Your Allah is One; surrender yourselves to Him. Bring good news to the humble, those whose hearts are filled with fear when Allah is mentioned, who demonstrate patience and perseverance in the face of obstacles, who pray regularly, and give to charity from that which We have given them.*

22:36 *And the camels have been appointed to you for sacrifice to Allah; they are very useful to you. Therefore, say Allah's name over them when you line them up for slaughter. When they are dead, eat of their meat and feed both the contented poor and the complaining beggar. We have made them subservient to you so that you might give thanks. It is neither their bodies nor their blood that reaches Allah, but it is your piety that reaches Him. Therefore, He has made them subservient to you so that you may praise Allah for guiding you. And give the good news to others who do good deeds. Truly Allah will defend those who believe; surely Allah does not love the faithless or ungrateful.*

62:9 *Believers! When you are called to prayer on Friday, the Day of Congregation, go quickly to remember Allah and leave your work. That is best for you, if you only knew! And when prayers are over, travel across the land to seek Allah's rewards, and praise Allah always so that you will prosper.*

62:11 *But no sooner do they see something to buy or some other amusement than they turn away and leave you to stand alone. [A caravan arrived when Mohammed was preaching and the Muslims ran to see the new goods] Say: What Allah has to give you is better than anything you could buy or any amusement. Allah is the best provider!*

2:148 *Every person has a goal to which they aspire; therefore, work with one another to do good deeds. Wherever you are, Allah will bring you together. Certainly Allah controls all things.*

2:149 *And from whatever place you come, turn toward the sacred Mosque, and that is indeed the truth from your Lord. Allah sees all you do. And from what ever place you come, turn toward the sacred Mosque, and wherever you are, turn towards it so that the people will have no dispute against you except the wicked among them. Do not fear them, but fear Me so that I may bestow my grace upon you and you will be guided on the right path.*

2:183 *Believers, fasting is commanded for you as it was for those before you so that you will learn to protect against evil. Fast a particular number of*

days, but if any of you are sick or on a journey you may fast the same number of days at a later time, Those who are unable to endure it may be redeemed by feeding a poor person. Whoever does good on his own will be rewarded; it is better for those of you who fast, if you only knew it.
2:185 *During the month of Ramadan, the Koran was sent down as a guide for mankind with clear signs of guidance for distinguishing right and wrong. Therefore, whoever of you is present must fast that month, and whoever is sick or on a journey will later fast the same number of days. Allah desires your comfort, not your discomfort. He wishes you to fast the entire month so that you will glorify Him for His guidance.*
2:186 *When my servants question you about Me, then surely I am near. I will answer the prayer of each who requests when he calls to Me. Let them hear My call and trust in Me so that they will be guided to the right path.*
2:187 *It is now permitted for you to lie with your spouses on the nights of fasting; you are a consolation for one another. Allah knew what you did secretly between yourselves, but He has turned to you in forgiveness. Therefore, you may now lie with one another and fulfill what Allah has ordained. Eat and drink until you are about to distinguish a white thread from a black thread in the light of the approaching dawn; then fast again until nightfall and do not touch your spouse, but instead pray at the mosque. These are the limits set by Allah, so do not come near them. It is in this way that He makes his signs clear to mankind so that they practice self-discipline.*
2:188 *Do not take one another's property by unfair means or seek to bribe the judges to take another's wealth unjustly and knowingly.*
2:189 *When they ask you about the moon's phases say: They are signs for mankind to mark the seasons and the pilgrimage. It is not righteousness if you enter your houses from the back as the pagans do. [Pilgrims of the old Arabic religions entered their houses from the back after pilgrimage.] Righteousness is found in fearing Allah. Enter your houses through the proper doors and observe your duty to Allah so that you will find success.*
2:196 *Make the pilgrimage and visit Mecca for Allah. If you are unable to go, send an offering that you have the funds for and do not shave your head until the gifts have arrived at their destination. If, however, you are sick or have an ailment of the head, you must compensate by fasting, giving to charity, or making a sacrifice. And when you are safe, if you wish to continue with the pilgrimage and visit and cannot afford an offering, then fast for three days while on the pilgrimage and seven days when you return, this should be ten days in all. This is for those who are not present in the Sacred Mosque, so be careful to keep your duty to Allah and know that He is severe in His punishment.*

2:197 *Make the pilgrimage in the months that have been appointed, and whoever plans to go on the pilgrimage then must abstain from intercourse, foul language, and hostile disputes. And whatever good you do Allah will know it. The best provision is devoutness; fear Me, those of understanding.*
2:198 *It will be no crime to seek the bounty of your Lord. [It is proper to do business during pilgrimage.] So when you come down from Mount Arafat [near Mecca] remember Allah near the sacred Monument [a ritual place in Mecca], and remember Him for His guidance when you went astray. Then pass through quickly from where the pilgrims gather and ask Allah for forgiveness; certainly Allah is forgiving and merciful. And when you have finished your holy duties, praise Allah as you praised your forefathers, but with more intense praise!*

4:29 *Believers! Do not squander your wealth among you in vain [gambling, etc.], but trade by mutual consent. Do not commit suicide. Allah is merciful to you. If you do that in aggression and injustice, you will be cast into the Fire; that is easy for Allah.*
4:31 *If you avoid the grievous sins you are forbidden, then We will cleanse you of your evil deeds and lead you into Paradise with honorable entrance. Do not covet the gifts Allah has given which have lifted up some among you. Men will be rewarded for their actions, and women will be rewarded for their actions. But ask Allah to give gifts to you of His bounty, for surely Allah knows all things.*
4:36 *Worship Allah and do not acknowledge any as His equal. Be good to your parents, your relatives, to orphans, the poor, to neighbors both new and familiar, to fellow travelers, wayfarers, and the slaves you possess. Allah does not love those who are proud and boastful, nor those who are miserly and urge others to be the same and who hide the wealth Allah has given them of His bounty. We have prepared a humiliating punishment for the unbelievers. Those who give of their wealth to charity just to be seen by others and do not believe in Allah and the Last Day choose Satan for friend. What an evil companion he has!*

5:105 *Oh, believers, guard your souls. He who strays will not hurt you when you follow the guidance. You will all return to Allah, and He will tell you what you have done.*
5:106 *Oh, believers, when death draws near to any of you, let there be witnesses between you at the time of making your will—two just men from among yourselves, or two others of a different tribe if you are traveling through the land, and the chance of death happens to you. Detain both witnesses after prayer. If you doubt them, make them both swear the following by Allah, "We will not take a bribe though it might be from a*

relative, and we will not hide the testimony of Allah, for then we would be among the wicked."
5:107 *If it is made clear that both men have been guilty of lying, let two others of those who have convicted them—the two nearest in blood—stand up in their place, and they will swear by Allah, "Our testimony is truer than the testimony of these two. We have not gone beyond the boundaries of truth, for then we would be of the unjust." This way it will be easier for men to bear a true witness, or else they would fear that another oath would be given after their oath. Be careful of your duty to Allah, for He does not guide rebellious people.*

9:36 *Twelve months is the number of months [lunar months] in a year with Allah since the day He created the heavens and the earth. Four of these months are sacred. This is the right usage. Do not be unjust to yourselves regarding them, but fight the unbelievers as they fight you altogether. Know that Allah is with those who guard against evil.*
9:37 *Postponing a sacred month is only a growth of disbelief. This leads the unbelievers to wrong. They allow it one year and forbid it another that they may make good the number of months which Allah has hallowed, and they allow that which Allah has prohibited. The evil of their deeds seems pleasing to them, but Allah does not guide the people who reject faith.*
9:60 *Charity [the poor tax] is only to be given to the poor and needy, to those who collect them, to those whose hearts are won to Islam, for ransoms, for debtors, for Allah's cause [jihad], and for the traveler. This is a law from Allah, and Allah is knowing and wise.*

5:1 *Oh, believers, fulfill your obligations. You are allowed all the four-footed animals to be taken for food with the exceptions named: game is not allowed while you are on pilgrimage. Allah ordains what He pleases.*
5:2 *Oh, believers, do not violate the rites of Allah, or the sacred month of Muharram, or the sacrificial offering, or its garlands [ornaments put upon the animals to be slaughtered in sacrifice], or those going to the Sacred House [the Kabah] seeking grace and favor from their Lord. When you are free of sacred obligations then you may hunt. Do not let the ill will that you might hold against those [the Meccans] who would keep you from the sacred mosque [the Kabah] lead you to do wrong. Rather, help one another according to goodness and piety, but do not help one another in acts of evil and malice. Fear Allah, for Allah is severe in punishment.*
5:3 *You are forbidden food that dies of itself as well as blood; swine's flesh; all that has been dedicated to any other name than that of Allah; the strangled; creatures killed by a blow, or by a fall, or by goring. You are forbidden that which has been eaten by beasts of prey, unless you make it clean by giving the death-stroke yourselves. Creatures sacrificed on*

blocks of stone are forbidden you, and to make division of the slain by consulting the divining arrows [an Arabian method of fortune telling] is impiety. Today, those who reject faith have given up on your religion. Do not fear them, but fear Me. This day I have perfected your religion for you and have completed My favors for you, and I have chosen Islam as your religion. If any is forced by hunger, without willful intentions to do wrong, Allah will be indulgent and merciful to him.
5:4 *They will ask you, Mohammed, what is lawful for them to eat. Say: All good things are lawful to you. Teach your trained hunting animals—your birds and beasts of prey—as Allah has taught you. Eat what they catch for you, and make mention of the name of Allah over it. Fear Allah, for He is swift to reckon.*
5:5 *This day, all healthful things are made lawful to you. The meats of those who have received the Scriptures [Jews] are allowed to you, as your meats are to them. It is also lawful for you to marry virtuous women who are believers and virtuous women who received the Scriptures before you did when you have given them their marriage portions and when you live with them in honor, not in fornication, and without taking them as secret lovers. Whoever denies his faith will find his work is fruitless. In the next world, he will be one of the losers.*
5:6 *Oh, believers, when you prepare for prayer, wash your faces, your hands up to the elbow, lightly rub your heads, and wash your feet to the ankles. If you are unclean, bathe your whole body, but if you are sick, on a journey, or if one of you comes from urinating or defecating or if you have touched women and you find no water, then take clean sand and rub your faces and your hands with it. Allah does not want to place a burden on you, but He desires to purify you, and He would complete His favor upon you that you may be grateful.*

5:89 *Allah will not punish you for that which is unintentional in your oaths, but He will punish you in regard to an oath taken seriously. For atonement, feed ten poor persons with such middling food as you feed your own families, or clothe them, or free a slave. If you do not have the means for this, then fast for three days. This is the atonement of your oaths when you have sworn, but keep your oaths. Thus Allah makes His signs clear to you that you may give thanks.*
5:90 *Oh, believers, surely wine and games of chance, and idols, and the divining arrows [an Arabian method of foretelling the future] are an abomination of Satan. Avoid them so that you may prosper. Only Satan would sow hatred and strife among you using wine and games of chance and turning you away from the remembrance of Allah and from prayer. Will you not, then, abstain from them? Obey Allah, and obey the Messenger, and be on your guard. If you do turn back, know that our Messenger is only bound to deliver a plain announcement.*

5:93 *There will be no blame attached to those who believe and do good works in regard to any food they have eaten in the past. Fear Allah and believe, and do the things that are right, and still fear Allah and believe, and still fear him, and do good, for Allah loves those who do good.*
5:94 *Oh, you who believe, Allah will surely make trial of you with such game as you may take with your hands, or your lances so that Allah may know who fears Him in secret. Whoever does wrong after this will suffer a grievous penalty. Oh, believers, do not kill any game while you are on pilgrimage. If any among you purposely kill game, it will be repaid in domestic animals of equal value, according to the judgment of two just persons among you, to be brought as an offering to the Kabah; or in atonement, he will feed the poor; he will pay its equivalent in fasts that he may taste the ill consequence of his deed. Allah forgives what is past, but whoever returns to it, Allah will take vengeance on him, for Allah is mighty and vengeful.*
5:96 *It is lawful for you to fish in the sea, and to eat fish for the benefit of yourselves and for those who travel, but it is unlawful for you to hunt by land while you are still on pilgrimage. Be mindful of your duty to Allah, to whom you will return.*
5:97 *Allah has appointed the Kabah, the Sacred House, to be a security for mankind, as are the sacred months, the offering, and the garlands [ornaments placed upon the sacrificial animals]. This is so you may know that Allah knows all that is in the heavens and on the earth, and that Allah has knowledge of everything. Know that Allah is severe in punishment and that Allah is forgiving and merciful.*
5:99 *The Messenger's duty is to deliver the message, and Allah knows what you bring to light and what you hide. Say: Evil and good are not equal, though the abundance of evil may please you; therefore, fear Allah, you of understanding so that you may prosper.*

CUSTOM

24:58 *Believers, let your slaves and children among you who have not yet come of age ask permission to come into your presence on three occasions: before the morning prayer, when you shed your clothes in the midday heat, and after the evening prayer. These are your three occasions for privacy. There is no blame on them if at other times when they are visiting, they come into your presence without permission. It is in this manner that Allah makes His signs clear to you, for Allah is knowing, wise. And when they have come of age [puberty], let your children ask for your permission to enter your presence, just as in the old custom. It is in this manner that Allah makes His signs clear to you, for Allah is knowing and wise.*

24:60 *As for the unmarried women past the age of childbearing, they will not be blamed it they take off their outer garments, as long as they do not show their adornments [jewelry]. It will be better for them if they do not take them off, for Allah hears and knows all.*

24:61 *It will be no offense for the blind, lame, or the sick to eat at your tables. [This verse changes an old Arab custom.] Nor will you be blamed for eating in your own houses, or the houses of your fathers, mothers, brothers, sisters, paternal or maternal uncles, paternal or maternal aunts, in the houses for which you have been given keys, and the houses of your friends. It is no offense whether you eat together or apart. And when you enter the houses, greet one another in Allah's name, a good and blessed greeting. It is in this manner that Allah makes His signs clear to you so that you may grow in understanding.*

24:27 *Believers, do not enter another's house until you have been invited [this verse changed the Arab custom of entering a house without a greeting] and have greeted them with peace. This will be better for you, and hopefully you will remember it. If there is no one in the home, do not enter it until you have been given permission. And if you are told to leave, then do so. This will make you more pure, and Allah knows all that you do. You will not be blamed for seeking shelter in an abandoned house. Allah knows what you do in the open and in secret.*

49:9 *If two parties of the believers are at war, then make peace between them. If one of them wrongs the other, fight against that party that does wrong until they come back to the commands of Allah. If they come back, make peace between them with fairness and act impartially. Allah loves those who act with justice. Only the believers are brothers, so make peace between your brothers, and fear Allah so that you may obtain mercy.*

49:11 *Oh, believers, do not let men laugh at other men who may be better than themselves, nor let women laugh at women who may be better than themselves. Do not slander one another, nor call one another offensive names. It is bad to be called wicked after having professed the faith, and whoever does not repent of this does evil.*

49:12 *Oh, believers, avoid suspicion, for some suspicions are a crime, and do neither pry nor let one of you slander another behind his back. Would any one of you like to eat the flesh of his dead brother? No, you loathe that, so loathe the other. Fear Allah, for He is oft-returning and most merciful.*

2:219 *They ask you about drinking and gambling. Say: In both of them there is great sin and profit for men, but the sin is greater than the profit. When they ask you what they should give to charity say: What you can afford. It is in this manner that Allah makes His revelations clear so that you may reflect upon them in this world and the next.*

JIHAD, CONQUEST

CHAPTER 26

8:13 This was because they opposed Allah and His messenger. Ones who oppose Allah and His messenger will be severely punished by Allah.

After Mohammed's death, Abu Bakr was elected caliph (political and religious leader) to rule over Islam. He went to war against the many Muslims who wished to leave Islam after Mohammed's death. Thousands of these apostates were killed in the Riddah wars, the war against apostasy. The rule of political Islam in Arabia was now permanent.

Umar became the next caliph and put Mohammed's final command into effect by expelling every Christian and Jew in Arabia. To this day there is no temple, church, synagogue, shrine or any house of worship except that of Islam in Arabia. Umar then launched the jihad and conquest of every neighbor of Arabia. The Islamic Empire was born and political Islam became a permanent part of world politics.

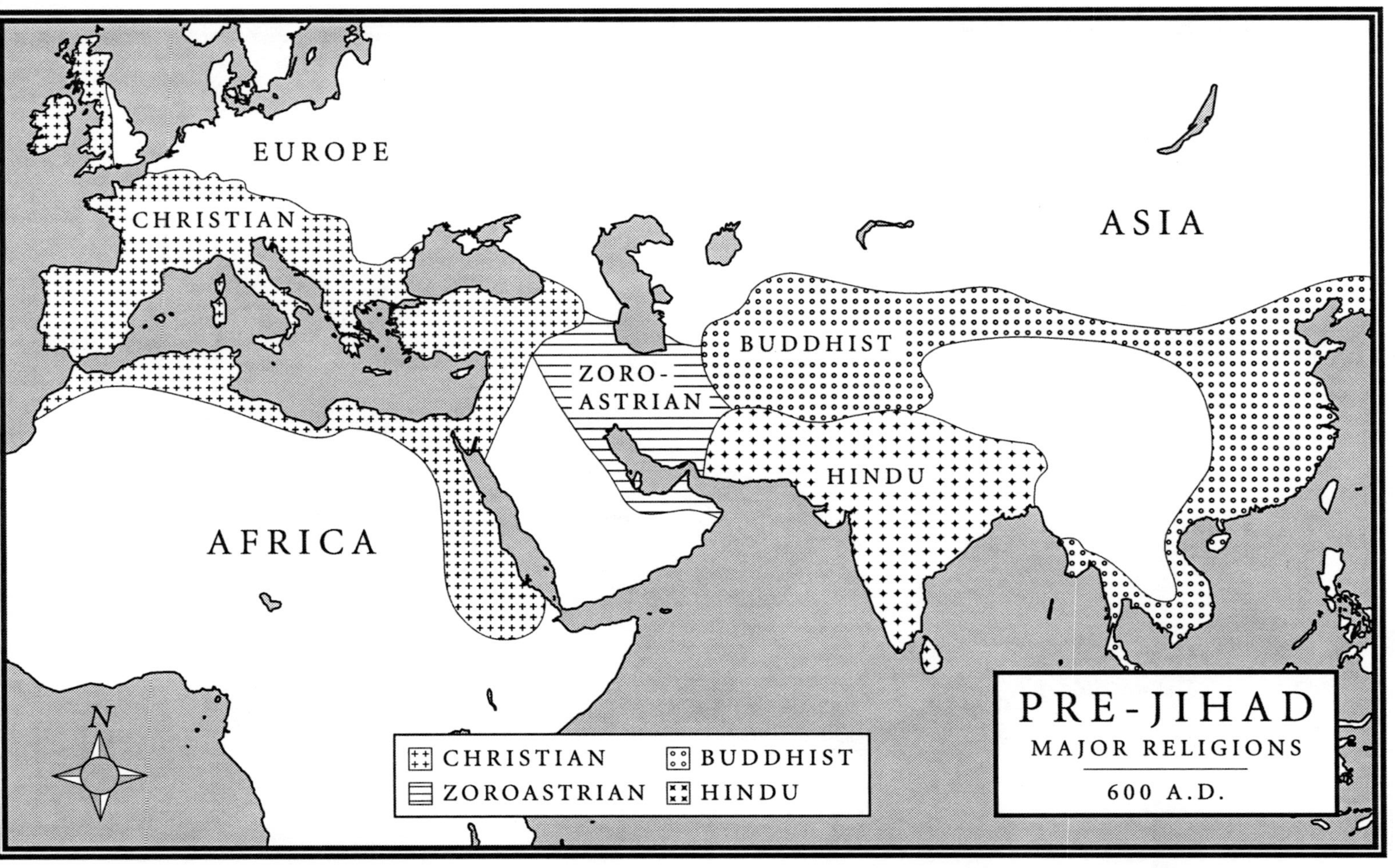
PRE-JIHAD
MAJOR RELIGIONS
600 A.D.
EUROPE
ASIA
AFRICA
CHRISTIAN
ZORO-
ASTRIAN
BUDDHIST
HINDU
N
CHRISTIAN
ZOROASTRIAN
BUDDHIST
HINDU

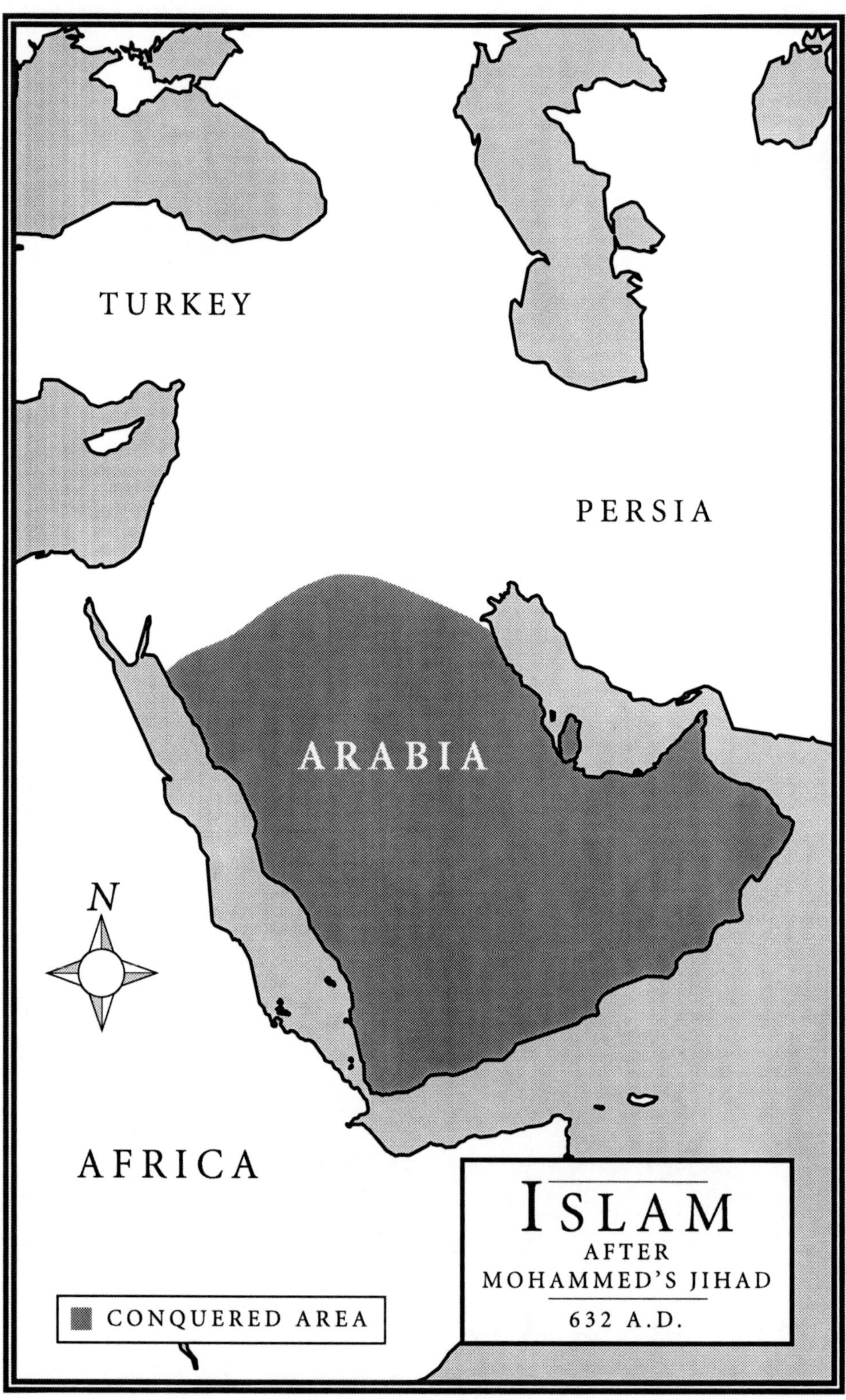
TURKEY
PERSIA
ARABIA
N
AFRICA
ISLAM
AFTER
MOHAMMED'S JIHAD
632 A.D.
CONQUERED AREA

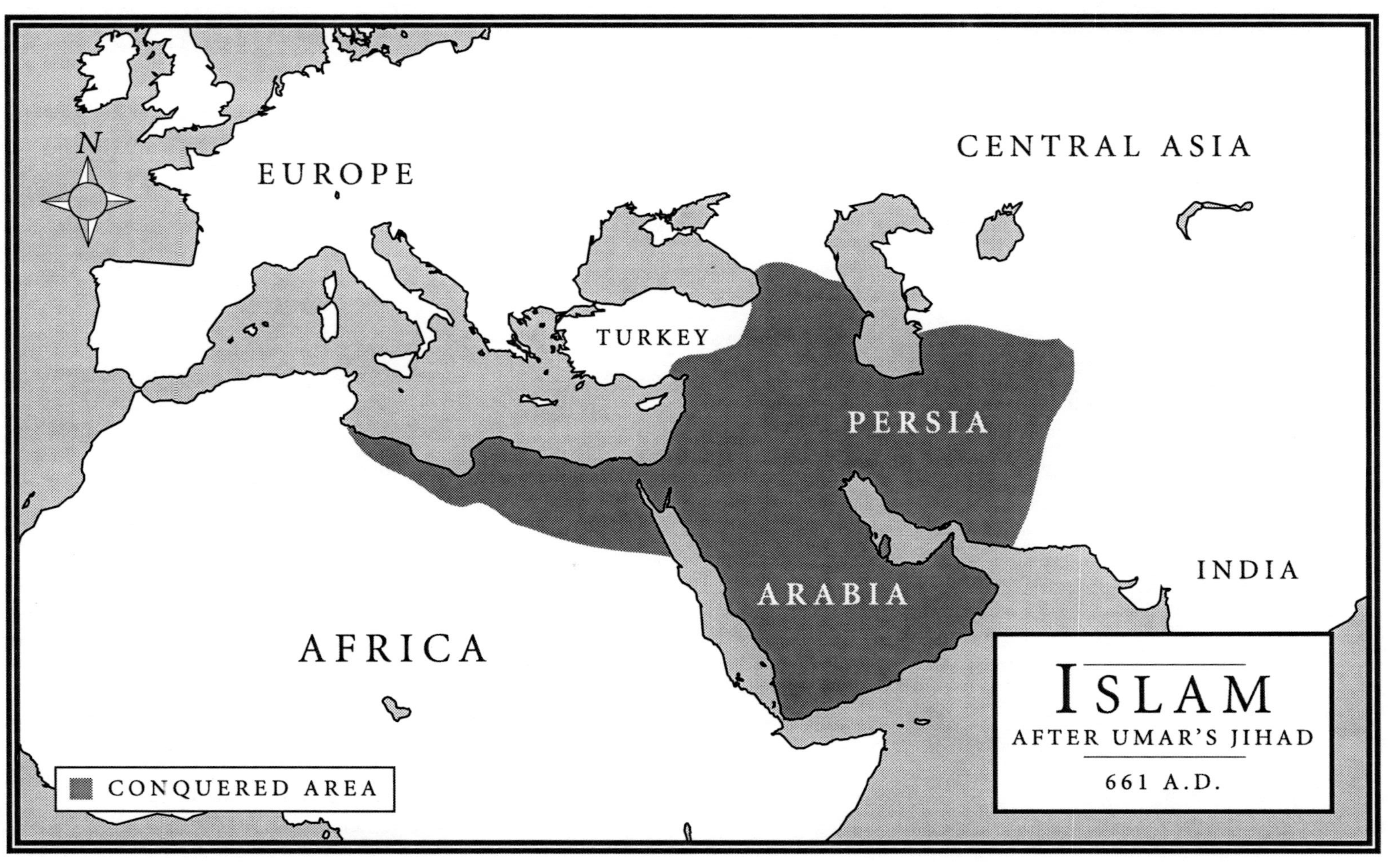
ISLAM
AFTER UMAR'S JIHAD
661 A.D.
N
EUROPE
CENTRAL ASIA
TURKEY
PERSIA
ARABIA
INDIA
AFRICA
CONQUERED AREA

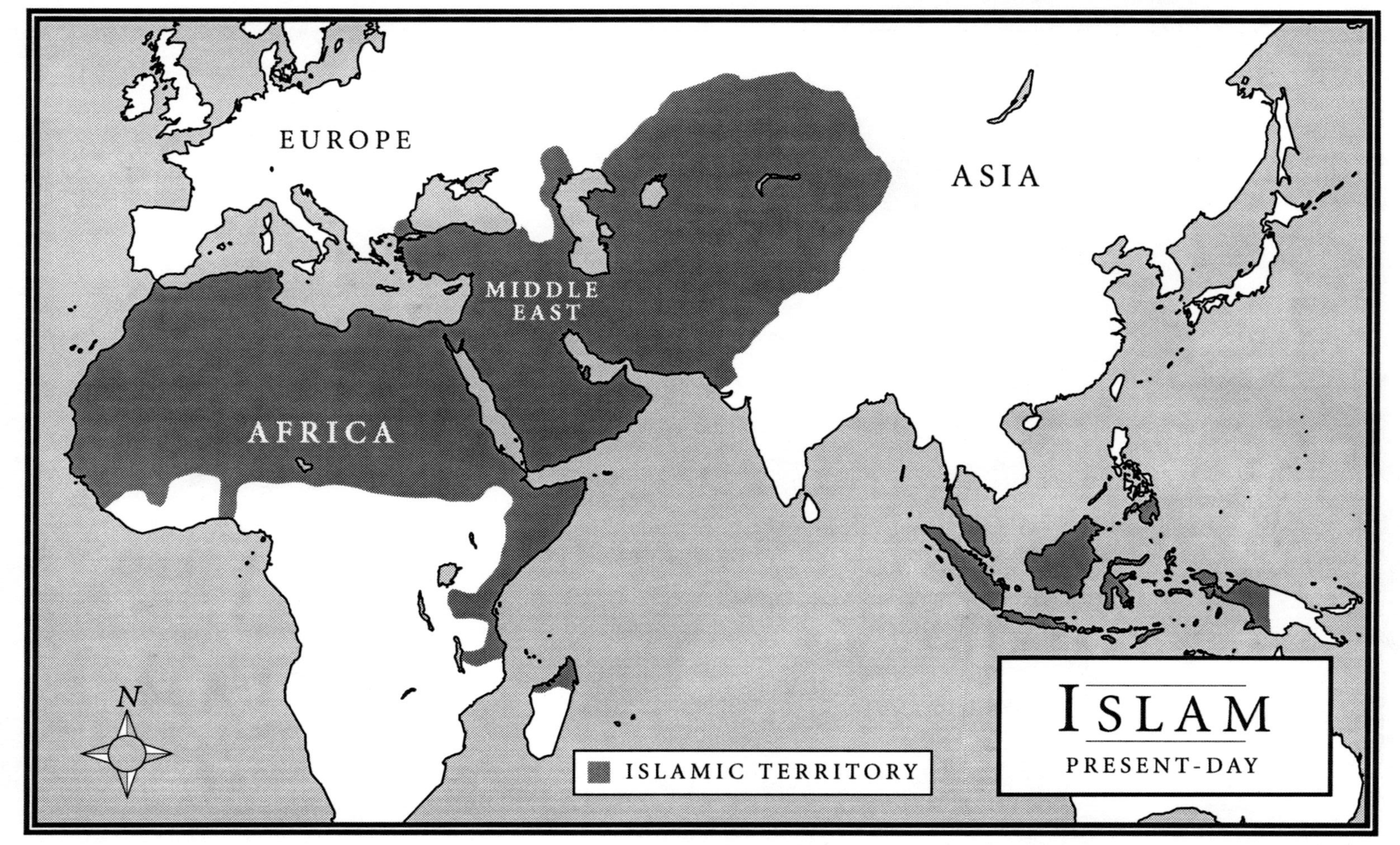
ISLAM
PRESENT-DAY
ISLAMIC TERRITORY
EUROPE
ASIA
MIDDLE
EAST
AFRICA
N

COMMENTS

CHAPTER 27

THE KORAN AND PHILOSOPHY

The Koran lays out a complete philosophic system including politics and ethics. Its metaphysics claim that the only reality is Allah and humanity is to worship Him. Human life has been pre-determined by Allah. The highest form of living is to die for Allah in jihad. Death, Paradise, and Hell are the values of Islam. The proper relationship between Allah and humanity is master/slave (Muslims are the slaves of Allah) and fear (there are over 300 references to the fear of Allah, the Merciful).

The epistemology (what is knowledge and how knowledge is acquired) of the Koran and Islam is revelation. But since Mohammed is the final prophet, the door to further knowledge is closed.

LOGIC

The Koran advances a logical system. Truth is determined by revelation. No fact or argument may refute the Koran. Logical persuasion is based upon repetition and continued assertion. Another part of the persuasion is personal attacks against those who resist Islam. The Koran advances its argument through threats against specific people and groups. If persuasion fails, then force may be used to settle the logical or political argument.

Another aspect of Koranic logic is the use of name calling and personal insults to advance the truth. The Koran, with its poetical language and repeated threats and physical violence, bases its logic on emotions. Although its intellectual truth can be contradictory, the contradictions do not need to be resolved. Understanding apparent contradictions is a key to understanding Islamic logic. In unitary logic, a contradiction shows the theory or argument is false. But in the Koran, a contradiction does not prove an argument to be false. What appears to be logical contradictions are statements of duality that offer two true choices, depending upon the circumstances. This is a dualistic logic.

How do we know that the Koran is true? Because it contains the words of Allah. How do we know that these are the words of Allah? Mohammed said they were Allah's words. How do we know that Mohammed is Allah's messenger? Mohammed reported that Allah said that Mohammed is His messenger.

DUALITY

The constant theme of Islam's perfect, eternal, and universal Koran is the division between those who believe Mohammed, and those who don't. This sacred division is dualism; nonbelievers are not fully human and fall under a separate moral code. The dualistic separation is in politics, culture and religion. This duality is carried further by two different approaches to the unbeliever in the Koran of Mecca and the Koran of Medina.

Some verses of the Koran contradict each other, but the text states a principle for resolving the contradictions. The later verse abrogates (nullifies) the earlier verse. However, since the entire Koran comes from Allah, then all verses are true, and no verse is actually false. The later, contradictory verse is merely stronger than the earlier, weaker verse. In practice, both sides of a contradiction can be true—logical duality.

ETHICS

The ethical system of the Koran is also dualistic. How a person is treated depends upon his being a believer or an unbeliever. There is one set of ethics for the believer and another set of ethics for the unbeliever. Deceit, violence and force are acceptable against the unbelievers who resist the logic of the Koran. Believers are to be treated as brothers and sisters. Good is what advances Islam. Evil is whatever resists Islam.

POLITICS

The story of the Koran culminates in the dominance of political Islam. The Koran teaches that Islam is the perfect political system and is destined to rule the entire world. The governments and constitutions of the world must all submit to political Islam. If the political systems of the unbelievers do not submit, then force, jihad, may be used. All jihad is defensive, since refusing to submit to Islam is an offense against Allah. All Muslims must support the political action of jihad. This may take several forms—fighting, proselytizing or contributing money.

The basis of the Islamic dualistic legal code, the Sharia, is found in the Koran. The Sharia treats non-Muslims, including Jews and Christians, as inferior to believers. This legal inferiority is sacred, eternal and universal.

RELIGION

Some English translations of the Koran use the word God instead of Allah. In an English speaking culture the word God is synonymous with the One-God, Jehovah/Yahweh, of the Jews and Christians. However, the meaning of both Allah and Jehovah/Yahweh is based upon their textual attributes. Allah is defined by the Koran. Jehovah/Yahweh is defined by the Old Testament. On a textual basis Jews, Muslims, and Christians do not worship the same God. As an example, red and blue are both colors, but red is not blue. Likewise, Allah and Jehovah/Yahweh are both a One-God, but they are not the same One-God. Allah is not Jehovah/Yahweh[1]. Hence, Allah is the only acceptable term for the One-God of the Koran. All humanity must face a Judgement Day. The only sure way to Paradise and to by-pass Judgement is jihad.

LOVE AND THE KORAN

While there are over 300 references in the Koran to Allah and fear, there are 49 references to love. Of these references, 39 are negative such as the 14 negative references to love of money, power, other gods and status.

Three verses command humanity to love Allah and 2 verses about how Allah loves a believer. There are 25 verses about how Allah does not love unbelievers.

This leaves 5 verses about love. Of these 5, 3 are about loving kin or a Muslim brother. One verse commands a Muslim to give for the love of Allah. This leaves only one quasi-universal verse about love: give what you love to charity and even this is contaminated by dualism since Muslim charity only goes to other Muslims.

There is not a verse about either compassion or love of an unbeliever, but there are 14 verses that teach that a Muslim is not a friend of the unbeliever. There are 99 names for Allah and not one of them is love.

TRANSLATING THE KORAN

Islam frequently claims that the Koran cannot be translated. Most of the Koran is written in a poetic style that is similar to the ancient classical

---

1. Arab Christians also use the word Allah. The word allah is derived from ***ilah***, deity or god, and ***al***, meaning the. So Allah means The-God. But the meaning of the name Allah of Arab Christians is taken from the Christian scriptures. The meaning of the name Allah of Islam comes from the Koran. The Allah of Arab Christians is not the Allah of Islam. But for Arab Christians Allah is the same as Jehovah.

texts such as the Greek ***Odyssey***. The ***Odyssey*** is an epic story that is written in poetry, which makes it possible to memorize it. The Koran is also written, for the most part, in a poetic form that is easy to memorize.

Take an English proverb: "Birds of a feather, flock together." We have the information that a flock of birds only contains one type of bird, but it is written in poetic form. Can "Birds of a feather, flock together" be translated into Arabic? No. But the meaning of "a flock of birds contains only one type of bird," can be easily translated into Arabic.

The poetry of the Koran does not translate, but the meaning of the Koran can be translated. Read many different translations of the Koran and you will find the meaning is consistent across the translations.

So, can the Koran be translated? No. Can the meaning be translated into any other language? Yes. If the meaning of a particular part of the Koran cannot be translated, then that implies that the concept is not applicable to that language. Or said another way, that part of the Koran would not be universal. But the Koran is very insistent upon the fact that it is universal. So by definition of universal, it follows that the universal meaning can be translated into all languages.

KORANIC PERSUASION

The key to understanding the Koran is Context, Chronology (the right time order of events), and Categories, CCC. Both the context and chronology come from Mohammed's life.

Some categories are obvious, such as retold tales from the Jews. But the less obvious category is ***Koranic persuasion***. The Koran is filled with violent threats against those who do not believe Mohammed and who did not believe the prophets of Allah in the past. If you highlight the violent references to the unbelievers, you will find that there are five elements that accompany the violence:

A description of the threat or violence
Who is threatened
What they did to deserve the violence
How they are wrong
Words from Allah to support his messenger, Mohammed

This entire structure is called "Koranic persuasion" and is repeated again and again. The repetition is part of the persuasion, just as repetition is necessary to all persuasion campaigns, ***e.g.*** ads and political campaigns.

The Koran of Mecca is an exact record of what took place in the intellectual and political sphere. Koranic persuasion is a recording of actual events of debate and persuasion. In many cases, there are actual quotes of

Mohammed's opponents. The Koran contains an intimate and exact view of Arabian history.

The sura (chapter) and Koranic persuasion are two of the natural organizational elements of the Koran. The element of the verse is useful but it does not allow analysis of ideas and thought. Koranic persuasion allows easy textual analysis of thought, ideas and theme. As a measure of the importance of Koranic persuasion, consider:

	Private teaching[1]	Public Teaching	Meccan–Argument	Medina
Number of times Koranic persuasion is used[2]	40	65	70	36
Percentage of text devoted to the Koranic persuasion category	70.5%	63.7%	67.2%	12.8%

This data mirrors the history of Mohammed's life. In the Meccan religious phase, the violence took the form of threats of punishment that were to occur after death in Hell. Or the mentioned violence was in ancient history, ***i.e.*** the Pharaoh being destroyed because he would not listen to Allah's prophet, Moses. In Mecca the Koranic violence referred to the far future or the distant past. However, in Medina, there is less talk about Hell, and much more physical violence against political enemies. The action of jihad replaces the rhetoric of the threat.

Approximately two thirds of the Koran of Mecca is devoted to the Koranic persuasion of "listen to Mohammed, the prophet of the only god, Allah, or you will suffer eternal torture in Hell." When Mohammed achieved political power, the religious threats became political reality. The Koranic persuasion of religion in Mecca became the political practice in Medina.

---

1. At first Mohammed only told those who were close to him about his message. Then he publicly taught Islam. The third phase in Mecca was the intense resistance of the Meccans.

2. In the second and third phases of the Meccan Koran, some of the ancient tales from Arabic lore and the Jewish literature are of the Koranic persuasion category since they have the same structure in distant time. In the second phase, 20 of the ancient tales are also Koranic persuasion. In the third phase there are 12.

Approximately 51% of the Medinan Koran text is about jihad and verbal threats directed against Jews, non-Muslims and hypocrites (half-hearted Muslims). The Koran of Medina is 10.8% anti-Jewish in nature. By comparison, only 6.8% of the text (measured by paragraphs) of Adolph Hitler's ***Mein Kamph*** is anti-Jewish.

The Meccan Koran is an historical and political document of Mohammed's campaign to convince the Arabs of the superiority of Islam. Even the repetition shows it to be history of the persuasion campaign. The Medinan Koran chronicles the exact history of the rise of Islamic political power. The Koran is both a religious text and a political/historical text. As a political/historical text, the Koran can be viewed as a biography of Mohammed.

THE METHODOLOGY OF THE SIMPLE KORAN

The ***Simple Koran*** was prepared by the CCC analytic method of:

Context—using Mohammed's life to give the circumstances and environment of the text.

Chronology—putting the verses in the original historical order[1].

Category—the method of grouping verses around the same subject. There can be discussion about which categories to use, but the Koranic persuasion method of categorization produces the simplest text.

With the analytic tools of Context, Chronology and Category, the Koran becomes a clear and simple text. The CCC analytic method most closely duplicates the historical words spoken by Mohammed.

In scientific philosophy the term, Occam's Razor, refers to the theory that the simplest theory that will explain the facts is the best theory. Using the criteria of Occam's Razor shows that Context, Chronology and Category is the best method to show the meaning of the Koran. No other method produces clarity, hence, the authors claim that CCC is the supreme method of organization of the Koran.

The classical method of presenting the Koranic text is based upon the length of the chapters. It starts with the longest sura and ends with the shortest sura. This methodology was devised by the secretary Zayd under the caliph, Umar, and there were arguments about it at the time. It is an arbitrary method of presenting the words spoken by Mohammed. It has

1. The Noldeke-Schwally order was used. Other methods of ordering differ in minor ways.

failed to produce a text that can be easily understood. Mohammed did not produce or use the classical method of presenting the Koran.

A COMMON MISCONCEPTION

Most nonbelievers think that the Koran is the basis of Islam. But Islam is founded upon the words of Allah (the Koran) and the Sunna (the words and actions of Mohammed found in the Sira and the Hadith). But the words of Allah are only about 17% of the total doctrinal texts. The words and actions of Mohammed comprise 83% of the doctrine of Islam.

FOR MORE INFORMATION

Visit:
www.cspipublishing.com

BIBLIOGRAPHY

Watt, W. Montgomery and Bell, Richard. ***Introduction to the Quran.*** Edinburgh: Edinburgh University Press, 1970.

Robinson, Neal. ***Discovering the Koran.*** London: SCM Press, 1996.

Arberry, A. J. ***The Koran Interpreted,*** NY: Touchstone, 1996.

Pickthall, Mohammed M. ***The Meaning of the Glorious Koran.*** Kuwait: Dar al-Islamiyya.

Warraq, Ibn. ***What the Koran Really Says.*** Amherst, NY: Prometheus Books, 2002.

Dawood, N. J. ***The Koran,*** London: Penguin Books, 1999.

Rodwell, J. M. ***The Koran,*** North Clarendon, VT: Tuttle Publishing, 1994.

Ali, Maulana Muhammad. ***Holy Koran.*** Columbus, Ohio: Ahmadiyyah Anjuman Ishaat Islam 1998.

Watt, W. Montgomery and M.V. McDonald. ***The History of al-Tabari, vol. VI, Muhammad at Mecca.*** New York: The State University of New York Press, 1987.

McDonald, M.V. and W. Montgomery Watt. ***The History of al-Tabari, vol. VII, The Foundation of the Community.*** New York: The State University of New York Press, 1987.

Michael Fishbone, ***The History of al-Tabari VIII The Victory of Islam.*** New York: The State University of New York Press, 1987.

Poonawala, Ismail K. ***The History of al-Tabari, vol. IX, The Last Years of the Prophet.*** New York: The State University of New York Press, 1987.

Muir, Sir William. ***Life of Mohammed.*** New York: AMS Press, 1975.

Guillaume, A. ***The Life of Muhammad,*** (Ishaq's—***Sirat Rasul Allah***). Karachi: Oxford University Press, 1967.

The Hadith of Abu Al-Bukhari, ***Sahih Bukhari***, and the Hadith of Abu Muslim, ***Sahih Muslim***, are best found on the internet. The University of Southern California is one of the best sites.

Printed in the United States
70694LV00004B/22-39

9 780978 552886